COMPETITION

DEMYSTIFIED

COMPETITION
DEMYSTIFIED

A Radically Simplified Approach
to Business Strategy

BRUCE GREENWALD AND JUDD KAHN

PORTFOLIO

PORTFOLIO
Published by the Penguin Group
Penguin Group (USA) Inc., 375 Hudson Street, New York, New York 10014, USA • Penguin
Group (Canada), 90 Eglinton Avenue East, Suite 700, Toronto, Ontario, Canada M4P 2Y3 (a
division of Pearson Penguin Canada Inc.) • Penguin Books Ltd, 80 Strand, London WC2R 0RL,
England • Penguin Ireland, 25 St. Stephen's Green, Dublin 2, Ireland (a division of Penguin
Books Ltd) • Penguin Books Australia Ltd, 250 Camberwell Road, Camberwell, Victoria 3124,
Australia (a division of Pearson Australia Group Pty Ltd) • Penguin Books India Pvt Ltd, 11
Community Centre, Panchsheel Park, New Delhi – 110 017, India • Penguin Group (NZ), Cnr
Airborne and Rosedale Roads, Albany, Auckland 1310, New Zealand (a division of Pearson New
Zealand Ltd) • Penguin Books (South Africa) (Pty) Ltd, 24 Sturdee Avenue, Rosebank,
Johannesburg 2196, South Africa

Penguin Books Ltd, Registered Offices: 80 Strand, London WC2R 0RL, England

First published in 2005 by Portfolio, a member of Penguin Group (USA) Inc.

10   9   8   7   6   5   4   3   2   1

PUBLISHER'S NOTE
This publication is designed to provide accurate and authoritative information in regard to the subject matter covered. It is sold with the understanding that the publisher is not engaged in rendering
legal, accounting or other professional services. If you require legal advice or other expert assistance, you should seek the services of a competent professional.

LIBRARY OF CONGRESS CATALOGING IN PUBLICATION DATA
Greenwald, Bruce C. N.
Competition demystified : a radically simplified approach to business strategy / Bruce Greenwald
and Judd Kahn.
    p.   cm.
Includes index.
ISBN 1-59184-057-0
1. Strategic planning.   2. Business planning.   3. Competition.   I. Kahn, Judd.   II. Title.
HD30.28.G733   2005
658.4'012—dc22   2005041948

Printed in the United States of America

To Ava, who makes many inconceivable things possible, and to Anne.

PREFACE

Anyone running a business knows that competition matters and that strategy is important. But although most experienced businesspeople recognize that these two critical elements of business are associated, few understand their essential natures or the direct relationship between them.

This book cuts through the fog that pervades many discussions of competition and strategy. Our goal is to clarify readers' understanding of strategy and to reframe their approach to it. We want executives to know how their markets work, where their competitive opportunities lie, and how to develop and protect them. To this end, we include both broad discussions of general principles and detailed case studies of actual competitive interactions. Taken together, we think they present a useful guide for people who need to make strategic decisions.

Executives often confuse strategy with planning. They think that any plan for attracting customers or increasing margins is a strategy. Any large-scale plan that requires a lot of resources or takes a long time to execute is considered strategic. Essentially, any plan that answers the question "How can we make money?" qualifies as a business strategy. As a result, too many leaders end up fighting wars they cannot win while failing to protect and exploit the advantages that are the real bases for their success.

Strategies are indeed plans for achieving and sustaining success. But they are not just any ideas for how to make a product or service and sell it profitably to customers. Rather, strategies are those plans that specifically focus on the actions and responses of competitors.

At its core, strategic thinking is about creating, protecting, and exploiting competitive advantages. On a level playing field, in a market open to all competitors on equal terms, competition will erode the returns of all players to a uniform minimum. Therefore, to earn profits above this minimum, a company must be able to do something that its competitors cannot. It must, in other words, benefit from competitive advantages. The appropriate starting point of any strategic analysis is a careful assessment of those economically advantageous aspects of a firm's market situation that cannot be replicated by its competitors or, at most, can be reproduced by only a handful of them.

The existence or absence of competitive advantages forms a kind of continental divide when it comes to strategy. On one side are the markets in which no firms benefit from significant competitive advantages. In these markets, strategy is not much of an issue. Lots of competitors have essentially equal access to customers, to technologies, and to other cost advantages. Each firm is in more or less the same competitive position. Anything that one does to improve its position can and will be immediately copied. Without any firm enjoying a competitive advantage, this process of innovation and immitation repeats itself continually. In these markets, the sensible course is not to try to outmaneuver the competitors, but rather to simply outrun them by operating as efficiently as possible.

Constant pursuit of operational efficiency is essential for companies in markets without competitive advantages. However, operational efficiency is a tactical matter, not a strategic one. It focuses internally on a company's systems, structures, people, and practices. Strategy, by definition, looks outward to the marketplace and to the actions of competitors.

On the other side of the divide are the markets where strategy is critically important. In these markets, incumbents have competitive advantages, and the race for profitability is shaped by how well companies manage the competition among their peers and how effectively they are able to fend off potential entrants. A focus on outsiders lies at the heart of business strategy. This book is a handbook on how to identify, understand, anticipate, and influence those important outsiders.

Many people have helped in the creation of our book. They include most importantly Paul Johnson, Nancy Cardwell, Barry Nalebuff, John Wright, Stephanie Land, Adrian Zackheim, Artie Williams, Paul Sonkin,

Erin Bellissimo, and colleagues at Columbia Business School and The Hummingbird Value Funds. The help and support of our families, especially Ava Seave, Anne Rogin, and Gabriel Kahn, was indispensable.

We owe a major debt to the many fearsomely intelligent and energetic students who have contributed to the development of this material through their participation in the courses from which it arose. The origins of this book lie in a second-year MBA course taught at Columbia University. The "Economics of Strategic Behavior" was first offered in 1995 with an intended enrollment of sixty students. Almost ten years later, it is now taken as an elective by over 80 percent of the students in each class. In the Executive MBA program, with more experienced students who are sponsored by their employers, upwards of two hundred out of a class of three hundred fill the single available section. The goal of this course at inception was to bring clarity of vision to the complicated field of business strategy. The course's reception suggests that this goal has been substantially achieved. Our book is an attempt to convey that clarity of vision to a wider audience for whom business strategy is a significant issue.

CONTENTS

COMPETITION

DEMYSTIFIED

CHAPTER 1

Strategy, Markets, and Competition

WHAT IS STRATEGY?

For at least the last half century, strategy has been a major focus of management concern. The Allied victory in the Second World War highlighted the necessity of grand strategy for success in warfare, and in the subsequent decades, corporate chieftains appropriated the concept for their own battlefields. Today, strategy is a primary business school discipline. Most major companies have in-house strategic planning units, and those that don't often hire teams of outside consultants to come in and guide the process.

Over the decades, definitions of strategy have changed, and the processes for developing it have undergone endless modifications and revolutions. Some companies have even abandoned formal processes altogether. Yet within all of this flux, one feature of strategy has stood out to distinguish it from other management responsibilities.

Strategy is big. Unlike tactical choices, everyone knows strategic decisions mean long-term commitments for the organization. They require large allocations of resources. Top management makes the strategic decisions. And setting strategy entails arduous research and bone-wearying meetings. Changing strategies is like changing the direction of an aircraft carrier—it doesn't happen quickly.

In World War II, the highest-level strategic decision made by the United States was whether to fight the major campaign first in Europe

TABLE 1.1

Distinctions between strategic and tactical decisions

	Strategic Decisions	Tactical (and Operational or Functional) Decisions
Management level	Top management, board of directors	Midlevel, functional, local
Resources	Corporate	Divisional, departmental
Time frame	Long term	Yearly, monthly, daily
Risk	Success or even survival	Limited
Questions	What business do we want to be in?	How do we improve delivery times?
	What critical competencies must we develop?	How big a promotional discount do we offer?
	How are we going to deal with competitors?	What is the best career path for our sales representatives?

or in the Pacific. Other strategic decisions at somewhat lower levels were the commitment to open a second front and the selection of the Normandy beaches for the invasion of Europe. On the corporate side, AT&T's two separate decisions to enter the information processing business and to spin off local telephone service were strategic choices.* Neither was successful. General Electric's policy, enunciated long before Jack Welch became CEO, that it would leave any business in which it did not have a leading market share, was a strategic principle.

Occasionally, enormous consequences flow from decisions that at the time do not look strategic. When IBM entered the personal computer business, it chose an open standards approach and made two build-or-buy decisions that probably seemed inconsequential and merely tactical. Rather than developing the operating system itself, it licensed one from a tiny company no one had heard of. It made a similar choice for the microprocessor, giving the business to another supplier. These decisions created two of the most successful business franchises of all time, Microsoft and Intel. These companies, rather than IBM, became the beneficiaries of the boom in personal computing. In retrospect, these were clearly strategic decisions with enormous conse-

---

*The Justice Department had demanded that AT&T restructure in some way, but the company itself was deeply involved in formulating the strategy by which the Regional Bell Operating Companies were spun off.

quences. If we were to look closely at the history of big outcomes, we would no doubt find that many others were not results of any strategic planning process but were either unintended by-products of some other decision or simply were results on a much larger scale than anticipated.

But big, whether measured by financial commitments or hours spent in planning, or even outcomes, is not the same thing as strategic. Although size and significance are aspects of most strategic business decisions, we propose that they are not the defining criteria. We think the dividing line between strategy and tactics lies elsewhere.

In our view, strategic decisions are those whose results depend on the actions and reactions of other economic entities. Tactical decisions are ones that can be made in isolation and hinge largely on effective implementation. Understanding this distinction is key to developing effective strategy.

Formulating effective strategy is central to business success. It is also extremely challenging. The most valuable resource in any business is management attention, especially the attention of high-level management. This attention should not be squandered on a range of unfocused or inappropriate objectives or consumed by endless discussions about the proper direction for the firm. Our goal in this book is to present a clear step-by-step process for strategic analysis, first to help a firm understand where it fits in the competitive environment and second, to guide it in its strategic choices.

STRATEGIC VS. TACTICAL ISSUES

Consider this example. Responding to the success of the Jeep in the mid 1980s, many automobile companies chose to produce a sport utility vehicle. The decision to enter the SUV market was strategic for those companies. After that, everything was tactical. Success depended on efficient performance, including the appropriate investments in plants and equipment, marketing campaigns, design and engineering time, and management attention devoted to continuous organizational improvement. That's because, given the competitive nature of this market, and the ease with which all the companies could enter, no firm needed to concern itself with the actions of its competitors. There were simply too many to worry about. Success depended on skillful implementation.

Strategic choices, in contrast to tactical ones, are outward looking. They involve two issues that every company must face.

The first issue is selecting the arena of competition, the market in which to engage. All the illustrations we've cited—the United States picking the prime theater of operations in World War II, AT&T's selection of markets to enter and to abandon, General Electric's policy of qualifying business segments in which to compete—involve this kind of choice. So did IBM's decision to outsource the operating system and the microprocessor for its PC; it opted not to compete in those markets. The choice of markets is strategic, according to our definition, because it determines the cast of external characters who will affect a company's economic future.

The second strategic issue involves the management of those external agents. In order to devise and implement effective strategy, a firm has to anticipate and, if possible, control the responses of these external agents. Both theory and experience indicate that this is no easy task. These interactions are complicated and uncertain. There are no exact prescriptions available for the managers who have to make strategic decisions or for the business scholars who have to explain why certain ones work out better than others. All the best-in-class disciplines in the world cannot predict with absolute certainty how some testosterone-crazed CEO will respond to your latest move. Yet devising strategy without taking that response into account can be a glaring mistake.

ONE SINGLE FORCE

Thanks to Michael Porter's groundbreaking work, *Competitive Strategy*, published in 1980, strategic thinking in recent years increasingly has come to recognize the importance of interactions among economic actors. By concentrating on external agents and how they behave, Porter clearly moved strategic planning in the right direction. But, for many people, identifying the many factors in Porter's complex model and figuring out how they will play off one another has proven to be frustratingly difficult. What we are proposing here is a radically simpler approach.

We agree with Porter's view that five forces—Substitutes, Suppliers, Potential Entrants, Buyers, and Competitors within the Industry—can affect the competitive environment. But, unlike Porter and many of his followers, we do not think that those forces are of equal importance. One of them is clearly much more important than the others. It is so dominant that leaders seeking to develop and pursue winning strategies should begin by ignoring the others and focus only on it. That force is *barriers to entry*—the force that underlies Porter's "Potential Entrants."

If there are barriers, then it is difficult for new firms to enter the market or for existing companies to expand, which is basically the same thing. Essentially there are only two possibilities. Either the existing firms within the market are protected by barriers to entry (or to expansion), or they are not. No other feature of the competitive landscape has as much influence on a company's success as where it stands in regard to these barriers.

If there are no barriers to entry, then many strategic concerns can be ignored. The company does not have to worry about interacting with identifiable competitors or about anticipating and influencing their behavior. There are simply too many of them to deal with.

With a universe of companies seeking profitable opportunities for investment, the returns in an unprotected industry will be driven down to levels where there is no "economic profit," that is, no returns above the costs of the invested capital. If demand conditions enable any single firm to earn unusually high returns, other companies will notice the same opportunity and flood in. Both history and theory support the truth of this proposition. As more firms enter, demand is fragmented among them. Costs per unit rise as fixed costs are spread over fewer units sold, prices fall, and the high profits that attracted the new entrants disappear.

Life in an unprotected market is a game played on a level field in which anyone can join. In these markets, often but mistakenly identified as "commodity" markets,* only the very best players will survive and prosper, and even they have to be continually on their toes. Without the

---

* Most differentiated products also compete in markets where there are no barriers to entry, so differentiation, as we will illustrate, is not sufficient to protect a firm from the ravages of a highly competitive market.

protection of barriers to entry, the only option a company has is to run itself as efficiently and effectively as possible.

Operational effectiveness might be thought of as a strategy, indeed, as the only strategy appropriate in markets without barriers to entry. However, operational effectiveness, identified by Michael Porter as doing what rivals do but doing it better, is an internal matter. According to our definition of strategy, it is tactical rather than strategic. That does not make it insignificant. Operational effectiveness can be the single most important factor in the success, or indeed in the survival, of any business. In the last chapter of this book, we describe the extent to which a determined focus on operational effectiveness may carry one firm far ahead of its competitors, even though there is nothing that distinguishes its fundamental economic position from that of its less successful rivals.

Still, the pursuit of operational effectiveness does not require consideration of all the *external* interactions that are the essence of real strategy.

BARRIERS TO ENTRY AND COMPETITIVE ADVANTAGES

The existence of barriers to entry means that incumbent firms are able to do what potential rivals cannot. Being able to do what rivals cannot is the definition of a competitive advantage. Thus, *barriers to entry* and *incumbent competitive advantages* are simply two ways of describing the same thing. *Entrant* competitive advantages, on the other hand, have no value. By definition, a successful entrant becomes the incumbent. It then is vulnerable to the next entrant, who benefits from newer technology, less expensive labor, or some other temporary competitive edge. And because there are no barriers to entry, the cycle doesn't stop. So it is only in the presence of incumbent competitive advantages that strategy, in our sense of the term, comes to the fore.

LOCAL CHAMPIONS

In an increasingly global environment, with lower trade barriers, cheaper transportation, faster flow of information, and relentless competition from both established rivals and newly liberalized economies, it might appear that competitive advantages and barriers to entry will diminish. The fate of once powerful American firms in industries like machine tools (Cincinnati), textiles (Burlington Industries, J. P. Stevens), and even automobiles (Chrysler, GM, and Ford) seems to support this position. Either profits have shrunk or companies have disappeared entirely under the onslaught of imports. But this macro view misses one essential feature of competitive advantages—that competitive advantages are almost always grounded in what are essentially "local" circumstances.

Consider the history of Wal-Mart, one of the greatest economic success stories of the late twentieth century. The retail business, especially discount retailing, is not an industry with many trade secrets or rare skills. The practices for which Wal-Mart is known, like "everyday low prices" and efficient distribution, are hardly proprietary technologies, impossible for other firms to duplicate. Yet Wal-Mart has successfully dominated many, although not all, of the markets in which it competes. The way in which it achieved this position is instructive.

Wal-Mart began as a small and regionally focused discounter in a part of the country where it had little competition. It expanded incrementally outward from this geographic base, adding new stores and distribution centers at the periphery of its existing territory. The market that it dominated and in which it first enjoyed competitive advantages was not discount retailing in the United States, but discount retailing within a clearly circumscribed region. As it pushed the boundaries of this region outward, it consolidated its position in the newly entered territory before continuing its expansion. As we shall see, when it moved too far beyond its base, its results deteriorated.

The same process of establishing local dominance and then expanding into related territories accounts for two of the other great corporate achievements of the period, although in these cases the geography in question is product market space, not physical territory.

Microsoft began by dominating one particular segment, the operating system for IBM-type personal computers. It faced some competitors at the start, including for a time IBM itself, but Microsoft was able to establish and secure competitive advantages and marginalize all the other players. It expanded successfully at the edges of this business, adding adjacent software products like word processing, spreadsheets, and other productivity tools. Even as a much larger company, with an extensive product line, the core of its profitability remains the operating system and the adjacent software.

Apple's experience stands in stark contrast. From the start, Apple took a more global approach than Microsoft. It was both a computer manufacturer and a software producer. Its Macintosh operating system anticipated the attractive features of Windows by many years—"Windows 95 = Macintosh 87," as the saying goes. Yet its comprehensive product strategy has been at best a limited and occasional success, especially when compared to Microsoft's more focused approach.

Intel's history is closer to Microsoft's. It began life as a manufacturer of memory chips in the 1970s and was profitable for a time in that market. It also designed and produced microprocessors, one of which was selected by IBM as the heart of its new PC in 1980. Intel continued in both businesses for several years, but it began to lose out on the memory chip side to companies with lower costs and fewer defects. It made the decision in 1985 to abandon that business, even though memory chips were part of its corporate DNA. By concentrating on microprocessors, Intel restored and increased its profitability and has maintained its dominance in that large market ever since.

Competitive advantages that lead to market dominance, either by a single company or by a small number of essentially equivalent firms, are much more likely to be found when the arena is local—bounded either geographically or in product space—than when it is large and scattered. That is because the sources of competitive advantage, as we will see, tend to be local and specific, not general or diffuse.

Paradoxically, in an increasingly global world, the key strategic imperative in market selection is to *think locally*. Dominance at the local level may be easier to accomplish than one might initially think. If the global economy follows the path of the more developed national economies, service industries will become increasingly important and manufacturing less significant. The distinguishing feature of most services is that they are produced and consumed locally. As a consequence, opportunities for sustained competitive advantages, properly understood, are likely to increase, not diminish. The chances of becoming the next Wal-Mart or Microsoft are infinitesimal, but the focused company that understands its markets and its particular strengths can still flourish.

WHICH COMPETITIVE ADVANTAGES?

Strategic analysis should begin with two key questions: In the market in which the firm currently competes or plans to enter, do any competitive advantages actually exist? And if they do, what kind of advantages are they?

The analysis is made easier because there are only three kinds of genuine competitive advantage:

- **Supply.** These are strictly cost advantages that allow a company to produce and deliver its products or services more cheaply than its competitors. Sometimes the lower costs stem from privileged access to crucial inputs, like aluminum ore or easily recoverable oil deposits. More frequently, cost advantages are due to proprietary technology that is protected by patents or by experience—know-how—or some combination of both.
- **Demand.** Some companies have access to market demand that their competitors cannot match. This access is not simply a matter of product differentiation or branding, since competitors may be equally able to differentiate or brand their products. These demand advantages arise because of customer captivity that is based on habit, on the costs of switching, or on the difficulties and expenses of searching for a substitute provider.
- **Economies of scale.** If costs per unit decline as volume increases, because fixed costs make up a large share of total costs, then even with the same basic technology, an incumbent firm operating at large scale will enjoy lower costs than its competitors.

Beyond these three basic sources of competitive advantage, government protection or, in financial markets, superior access to information may also be competitive advantages, but these tend to apply to relatively few and specific situations. The economic forces behind all three primary sources of competitive advantage are most likely to be present in markets that are local either geographically or in product space. Pepsi loyalists have no particular attachment to Frito-Lay salty snacks, any more than Coke drinkers prefer movies from Columbia Studios when that was owned by Coca-Cola. Nebraska Furniture Mart, the store Warren Buffett bought for Berkshire Hathaway one afternoon, is a dominant player in Omaha and its hinterland, more powerful there than Ethan Allen or other large national furniture retailers.

As we examine the workings of the different sources of competitive advantages through detailed examples, the benefits of operating in markets with limited boundaries will become apparent, as will the difficulties of establishing or sustaining dominance where the boundaries are vast. Most companies that manage to grow and still achieve a high level of profitability do it in one of three ways. They replicate their local advantages in multiple markets, like Coca-Cola. They continue to focus within their product space as that space itself becomes larger, like Intel. Or, like Wal-Mart and Microsoft, they gradually expand their activities outward from the edges of their dominant market positions.

THE PROCESS OF STRATEGIC ANALYSIS

The natural starting point for any strategic analysis is a market-by-market assessment of the existence and sources of competitive advantages.

When there are no competitive advantages present, then genuine strategic issues are of little concern. Therefore, in markets along the "Competitive Advantage: No" branch in figure 1.1, operational effectiveness—efficiency, efficiency, efficiency—is both the first priority and the last.

But for markets along the "Competitive Advantage: Yes" branch, where companies do benefit from competitive advantages, the next step is to identify the nature of the competitive advantages and then to figure out how to manage them. The alternatives are not pleasant. If the advantages dissipate, whether through poor strategy, bad execution, or simply because of the unavoidable grindings of a competitive economy, these firms will find themselves on a level economic playing field—the no-

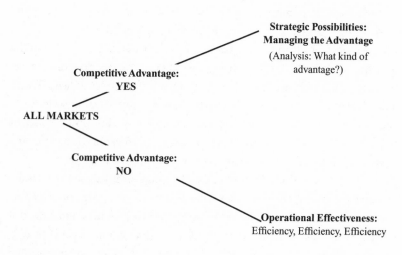

FIGURE 1.1
Strategic analysis, step one

competitive-advantage branch—where life is all work and where profits, except for the exceptionally managed companies, are average at best.

THE COMPETITIVE LANDSCAPE

MANAGING COMPETITIVE ADVANTAGES

By definition, in any market in which companies enjoy a competitive advantage, there will be a short list of legitimate competitors. At the extreme, companies such as Microsoft in the world of PC operating systems or IBM in its golden days will find themselves alone or surrounded by dwarfs. From their perspective, their competitors constitute an army of ants who can't enjoy the picnic because they are outside the barriers to entry. These firms are free to make their decisions without regard to what the ants might do in response to their initiatives. They need not spend much time anticipating specific competitive interactions.

In this situation—generally one large firm and many smaller ones—a company is either an ant or an elephant. The ants, outside the walls and looking in, operate at a competitive disadvantage. The strategy for a firm that finds itself in the ant's position is clear-cut. If it is already in the industry, it should consider getting out as painlessly as possible and returning to its owners as much of its economic resources as are salvageable. Admittedly, the list of CEOs who have followed this prescription is short. If it is considering getting into the business, the company ought to stop and look elsewhere because whatever slim chance it has for success depends entirely on the elephant competitor messing up.

And then, even if the incumbent's advantage shrinks and the barriers to entry disappear, the new firm will be just one of many entrants pursuing profit on an essentially level playing field. It should remind itself of Groucho Marx's rule not to join any club that would have him as a member. At best, economic life will be average, with normal profits; more likely, the elephant trods on it and the ant gets crushed.

For an elephant operating within the barriers, life is sweet and returns are high. But competitive advantages still have to be managed. Complacency can be fatal, as can ignoring or misunderstanding the sources of one's strength. An elephant's first priority is to sustain what it has, which requires that it recognize the sources and the limits of its competitive advantages.

A thorough understanding makes all the difference:

- It allows the firm to reinforce and protect existing advantages and to make those incremental investments that can extend them.
- It distinguishes those potential areas of growth—both geographically and in product lines—that are likely to yield high returns from tempting areas that would undermine the advantages.
- It highlights policies that extract maximum profitability from the firm's situation.
- It spots the threats that are likely to develop and identifies those competitive inroads that require strong countermeasures.

For functional departments within the firm, understanding the nature of the competitive advantages is essential for capital budgeting, for marketing, for evaluating mergers and acquisitions, and for new ventures.

In these markets of one dominant firm and an army of ants, strategic analysis for the dominant firm consists almost exclusively of understanding and managing competitive advantages. It doesn't need to confront the complexities of explicit mutual interactions among competitors. We illustrate this state in figure 1.2, which extends figure 1.1.

CONFLICTS AS GAMES: INTERACTING WITH COMPETITORS

In the remaining strategic situations, several companies enjoy roughly equivalent competitive advantages within a single market setting. The soft drink market in the United States is a prime example. Nationally, Coke and Pepsi are two elephants, with the other players considerably smaller, although in particular geographic markets, regional favorites like Dr Pepper may be legitimate competitors. Commercial aircraft manufacturing has a similar structure. Boeing and Airbus control the

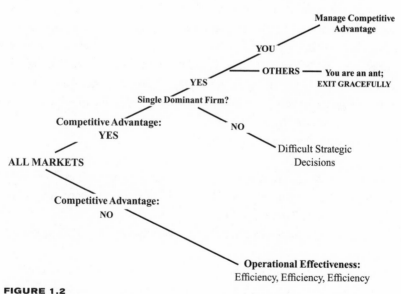

FIGURE 1.2
A single dominant firm

market for larger jets, with the smaller manufacturers like Embraer and Bombardier competing in the regional jet market. In the personal computer business, Intel and Microsoft dominate their specific niches, but they compete indirectly against one another for a share of the overall value created in the industry.

It is for companies in these markets, those that enjoy the benefits of competitive advantages but with potent competitors of similar capabilities, that strategy formulation is most intense and demanding. They face the big challenge of figuring out how to manage their competitors.

To develop an effective strategy, a company not only needs to know what its competitors are doing, but to also be able to anticipate these competitors' reactions to any move the company makes. This is the true essence of strategic planning. It embraces all of the things a company does in which a competitor's direct reactions are critical to its performance—pricing policies, new product lines, geographical expansions, capacity additions.

There are several distinct approaches that are particularly valuable in developing competitive strategies: game theory, simulation, and cooperative analysis.

Classical game theory is primarily useful because it imposes a systematic approach to collecting and organizing the mass of information about how competitors may behave. Game theory, as the *Stanford Encyclopedia of Philosophy* describes it, is "the study of the ways in which *strategic interactions* among *rational players* produce *outcomes* with respect to the *preferences* (or *utilities*) of those players, none of which might have been intended by any of them."

The salient features of a competitive situation are:

- *The players*—a restricted number of identifiable actors, generally competitors; if the list is not short and manageable, there are probably no genuine barriers to entry
- *The actions* each player can pursue—the choices that are available to them
- *The motives* that drive them—profitability is the most common in business, but other goals, like winning against competitors regardless

of the costs to oneself, may take hold and therefore need to be considered
* *The rules* that govern the game—who goes when, who knows what and when, and what penalties there are for breaking the rules

Fortunately, the fundamental dynamics of the great majority of competitive situations can be captured by two relatively simple games.

The prisoner's dilemma (PD) game has been thoroughly studied theoretically, historically, and experimentally. It describes competition that concerns price and quality. A great deal is known about how a PD game is likely to play out, and this knowledge can be brought to bear on any situation in which price/quality competition is a key to competitive interactions. We describe the PD game in chapter 7 and use it to analyze competitive interactions in chapters 9 and 10.

Another game focuses on entry/preemption behavior, by capturing the dynamics of quantity and capacity competition (unfortunately this game lacks a catchy name). Whenever a company decides to build a new plant or open a new store in a market served by a competitor, entry/preemption is the game being played. There is also a wealth of established knowledge about how this game works out. We will discuss entry/preemption in chapter 11 and illustrate its principles at play in chapters 12 and 13.

Given these available insights, a valuable approach to strategic analysis is to start by putting this received wisdom to use. First you must identify the competitive situations to which one or another of these two games can appropriately be applied. For example, if an industry's history has been dominated by a long-lived and debilitating price war, then the natural place to look for a solution is the accumulated knowledge about how to play the prisoner's dilemma game. If the industry is one in which any expansion by one firm has habitually induced its rivals to counter with their own expansions, then the entry/preemption game provides the template for strategic analysis.

In simple, straightforward interactions, it may be possible to anticipate how the game will evolve merely by listing the various courses of action and comparing the results. In practice, however, alternative possibilities multiply rapidly, and the analysis becomes intractable. In many cases, a better way to proceed is by simulation. One can assign individuals or teams to represent each competitor, provide them with appropriate choices for actions and with motives, and then play the game several times. The simulation should provide a rough sense of the dynamics of the situation, even though the outcomes are only rarely definitive.

A Cooperative Alternative

In addition to classic games and simulations, another approach to analyzing competition among the elephants is to assume that instead of battling, companies can learn how to cooperate for mutual gain and to fairly share the benefits of their jointly held competitive advantage. This type of interaction among competitors—which could also be called "bargaining"—makes all the players better off, but it requires an outlook and a disposition rarely found in this environment.

Players, nonetheless, need to think about what this ideal state of affairs would look like, even if it is not immediately practical. They need to identify joint gains and envision the best configuration of market activity. This would be the one in which costs are minimized, products and services most efficiently produced and delivered, and prices set to maximize income. In this ideal configuration, everyone in the market, including their competitors, must benefit. In other words, if this market were organized as a cartel or a monopoly, what would it look like? The players also have to decide upon a fair division of the spoils, because cooperative arrangements do not last if any participant believes it is being unfairly treated.

This analysis of the theoretically ideal market configuration has two distinct benefits. First, it identifies the possibilities that a cooperative posture might produce. Second, it helps a firm on the margin of a protected market, or a potential entrant, to set reasonable strategic goals.

For example, the relatively high-cost supplier with no captive customers should see that it cannot expect to gain any advantage through strategic alliances, competitive threats, or other means. That's because, if the market is configured efficiently, such a supplier has really no role to play. Why should other, more powerful competitors support it at the price of a reduction in overall industry performance, especially when it is they who will inevitably pay the costs? In other words, if you don't bring anything to the dance, don't expect to take anything home.

When these conditions apply, the high-cost firm's continued existence will usually hinge on irrational and noncooperative behavior from the other companies. Identifying and exploiting that behavior—making sure they don't get together—thus becomes the core of its strategy.

In practice, a high level of cooperation among firms in any market is rare. Still, contemplating cooperative possibilities reveals aspects of the strategic situation that can guide company decision making even in the absence of full-fledged cooperation. It adds a bargaining perspective as a complement to the more traditional noncooperative assumptions embodied in classical game theory and other treatments of competitive interaction.

Taken together, these three approaches—application of knowledge about specific games (prisoner's dilemma, entry/preemption), simulation, and cooperative analysis—produce a balanced and comprehensive treatment of the problems of formulating strategy in markets with a few genuine competitors, all mutually capable and conscious of one another.

This last step in the analysis is depicted in figure 1.3, which extends the previous figures to incorporate those situations in which several firms with competitive advantages share a market.

THE ROAD AHEAD

In this chapter and the two that follow, we discuss competitive advantage in general (position 1 in figure 1.3). There are only a few types of competitive advantage (demand, supply, and economies of scale) and two straightforward tests (market-share stability and high return on capital) to confirm their existence. Next, we will cover those situations in which a single firm dominates a market, using historical examples to illustrate how the different companies have identified and managed their competitive advantages, some successfully, others less so (position 2). We will then discuss competitive interactions among firms that

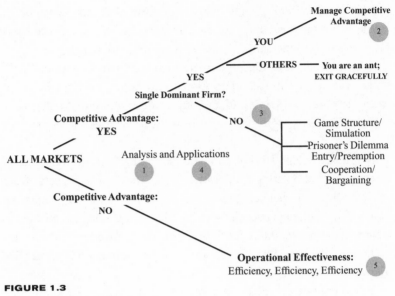

FIGURE 1.3
Architecture of the book

share a single market (position 3). For these companies, strategy can lead to continual war punctuated by the occasional cease-fire, or to long-term cooperation for mutual benefit.

In the later chapters of the book we apply the competitive advantage concepts to functional areas like valuation, mergers and acquisitions, and brand extensions (position 4). Finally, we will turn to those markets in which there are no barriers to entry or competitive advantages (position 5), to explain why some firms do much better than others even though there is no fundamental economic distinction between them. Good management matters enormously. The key to operational effectiveness is relentless focus, which requires that the enveloping fog of visionary strategic possibilities first be dissipated. This book is designed to do just that.

Like most other recent authors on strategy, we owe a debt to Michael Porter. As we mentioned earlier, Porter highlighted the importance of interactions among economic actors and identified the five forces that he feels explain the competitive world in which a company operates. He thus gave us an invaluable approach, but the complexity of his model makes it difficult to apply. It sacrifices clarity for completeness. Attending to five forces at one time is not easy, especially if none of them has any claim to priority.

We have simplified Porter's approach by concentrating first on the one force that dominates all the others: barriers to entry. Then we turn to the other forces, starting with industry competitors and direct competitive interactions where these apply and next including suppliers and customers in a bargaining context. Our purpose here is not to ignore Porter's forces but to prioritize and clarify them. Simplicity and clarity are important virtues of strategic analysis, provided we keep in mind Einstein's admonition that "Everything should be made as simple as possible, but not simpler."

CHAPTER 2

Competitive Advantages I

Supply and Demand

THE DIFFERENTIATION MYTH

According to an axiom of managerial wisdom, commodity businesses are to be avoided. Any operation in which sellers offer essentially identical products to price-sensitive customers faces an intense struggle for economic survival and must accept a lower than average level of profitability.

Strategic thinking often seems to start with this admonition: Do not allow yourself to be trapped in a commodity business. Fledgling business majors are taught that the essential first step in formulating any legitimate business plan is to differentiate your product from that of the competition. But on its own, differentiation as a strategy to escape the woes of commodity businesses has one major flaw—it doesn't work.

Differentiation may keep your product from being a generic commodity item, but it does not eliminate the intense competition and low profitability that characterize a commodity business. Although nature of the competition may change, the damage to profit persists because the problem is not lack of differentiation, but the absence of barriers to entry. Understanding the significance of barriers to entry and how they operate is the key to developing effective strategy.

There is probably no product in the world more successfully differentiated from its global competitors than a Mercedes-Benz automobile. Many newly installed heads of state seek to buttress their positions by acquiring at least one; the more grandiose opt for a fleet. Branding is a primary tactic for product differentiation, and the Mercedes-Benz star may be the most widely recognized symbol for quality in the global marketplace. Cadillac once had an equivalent position in the United States, and its name entered the vernacular as a mark of quality—"the Cadillac of burgers" (Nat Cole's commentary on a P. J. Clarke hamburger in the 1950s), "the Cadillac of bassinets" (www.epinions.com), "the Cadillac of PCs" (*BusinessWeek*, May 19, 1999). And yet, despite the recognition and the associations with quality, Mercedes-Benz and Cadillac have not been able to translate the power of their brands into exceptionally profitable businesses. In fact, their economic performance is not distinguishable from those mundane commodity businesses everyone tries so assiduously to avoid.

The process by which high returns are eroded is straightforward. In the case of automobiles, it began in the years after World War II, when Cadillac (with Lincoln in the United States) and Mercedes-Benz dominated their local markets and made exceptional profits. Those profits attracted other companies to enter these markets, seeking a share of the high returns. In the American luxury car market, the first entrants of scale were the Europeans—Mercedes, Jaguar, BMW in the 1970s—soon followed by the Japanese—Acura, Lexus, Infiniti in the 1980s.

If luxury cars had been a commodity business, the entry of new competitors would have undermined prices. But that is not what happened. Cadillacs and Lincolns continued to sell for premium prices, even after the entry of the imports. This was because the imports did not, as a rule, undercut them on price. But with a wider variety of luxury cars available, the sales and market shares of Cadillac and Lincoln began to decline. Meanwhile, the fixed costs of their differentiation strategy—product development, advertising, maintaining dealer and service networks—did not contract. As a result, the fixed cost for each auto went up, and the overall profit margin per car dropped. Cadillac and Lincoln found themselves selling fewer cars with lower profit margins. Their profitability shrank even though their products were thoroughly differentiated.

This process—in which prices remain stable, while sales fall and fixed costs per unit sold rise—differs from that which operates in a price-driven (commodity) market, but the ultimate effect on profitability is the same.

In the luxury car business, the decline did not happen all at once. When the first European brands entered the market, Cadillac and Lincoln lost some of their sales and saw their margins erode. But after this first wave, returns were still high enough to attract additional entrants. Inevitably, more competitors showed up, this time as carriage trade versions of Hondas, Toyotas, and Nissans.

The flood of entrants would only cease when lucrative profit opportunities in the luxury car market vanished. These opportunities would disappear only after entrants had fragmented the market to such an extent that high fixed costs per unit eliminated any extraordinary profit. When financial returns in this market became ordinary, the attraction ceased and entry stopped.

Given a process like this, it should be no surprise that even a brand as renowned as Mercedes-Benz has produced no better than average financial returns. By itself, product differentiation does not eliminate the corrosive impact of competition. Well-regarded brands are no better protected than commodities. High returns attract new entrants, or expansion by existing competitors, or both, in all markets. The inexorable nature of this process leads to our most important statement of strategic principle:

> If no forces interfere with the process of entry by competitors, profitability will be driven to levels at which efficient firms earn no more than a "normal" return on their invested capital. It is barriers to entry, not differentiation by itself, that creates strategic opportunities.

EFFICIENCY MATTERS

This proposition has several significant implications. The first is the connection between *efficiency* and survival in all markets where there are no barriers to entry.

In copper, steel, or bulk textiles, it is clear that if a company cannot produce at a cost at or below the price established in the market, it will fail and ultimately disappear. Since the market price of a commodity is determined in the long run by the cost levels of the most efficient producers, competitors who cannot match this level of efficiency will not survive. But essentially the same conditions also apply in markets with differentiated products.

Product differentiation is like lunch; it doesn't come for free. Companies must invest in advertising, product development, sales and service departments, purchasing specialists, distribution channels, and a host of other functions to distinguish their offerings from those of their competitors. If they cannot operate all these functions efficiently, then they will lose out to better-run rivals. The prices their products command and/or their market share will trail those of their competitors. As a consequence, the return they earn on the investments made to differentiate their products will fall below that of their more efficient competitors.

When the successful companies expand, which they inevitably do, market shares of less efficient firms decline further. Even if they can continue to charge a premium price, the returns they earn on their investments in differentiation will fall.

Ultimately, when the returns no longer justify the investment, the less efficient companies will struggle merely to stay afloat. This has been the history of many industries with differentiated products—cars, appliances, retailing, beer, airlines, office equipment, and many others. Only a few successful competitors survive, and many once-dominant firms— General Motors, Zenith, A&P, Coors, Kmart, PanAm—decline, sometimes terminally.

The need for efficiency when products are differentiated is no less crucial than when they are commodities, and it is more difficult to achieve. In a commodity business, efficient operations are largely a matter of controlling production costs. Marketing requirements are usually minimal. With differentiated products, efficiency is a matter both of production cost control and effectiveness in all the functions that underlie successful marketing.

Competition extends to dimensions beyond simple cost control. A company in a differentiated business has to manage product and packaging development, market research, a product portfolio, advertising and promotion, distribution channels, and a skilled sales force, and do it all without wasting money. Unless something interferes with the processes of competitive entry and expansion, efficient operations in all aspects of the business are key to successful performance.

The second implication of our basic proposition involves understanding the nature of a "normal" return. Investors in a business need to be compensated for the use of their capital. To be "normal," the return to capital should be equivalent to what the investor can earn elsewhere, suitably adjusted for risk. If investors can earn a 12 percent return by buying stocks in companies with average risk, then the companies have to earn 12 percent on their own average risk investments. Otherwise, investors will ultimately withdraw their capital. In practice, a management that produces a lower rate of return can hang on for many years before the process runs its course, but in the long run—and "normal" implies the average return over a period of years—the company will succumb.

BARRIERS TO ENTRY AND COMPETITIVE ADVANTAGES

Barriers to entry lie at the heart of strategy. The first task in our simplified approach to strategic thinking is to understand what barriers are and how they arise. It is essential to distinguish between the particular skills and competences that a firm may possess and genuine barriers to entry, which are characteristics of the structural economics of a particular market.

The skills and competencies of even the best-run companies are available to competitors, at least in theory. Systems can be replicated, talent hired away, managerial quality upgraded. All these are ultimately parts of the operational effectiveness of the company.

Strategy, on the other hand, is concerned with structural barriers to entry. Identifying those barriers and understanding how they operate, how they can be created, and how they must be defended is at the core of strategic formulation. If barriers to entry exist, then firms within the barriers must be able to do things that potential entrants cannot, no matter how much money they spend or how effectively they emulate the practices of the most successful companies. In other words, firms

ENTRY, EXIT, AND LONG-RUN PROFITABILITY

There is a reverse side to the entry and expansion process in industries without barriers to entry: exit and contraction. Just as extraordinary profits attract new competitors or motivate existing ones to expand, below-average profits will keep them away. If the process is sustained long enough, the less efficient firms within the industry will wither and disappear. But these two processes are not symmetrical. As any family with children knows, it is far easier to buy kittens and puppies than to drown them later. In business, the kittens and puppies are new plants, new products, new capacity of all sorts, and they are much more fun to acquire than to close down.

Because of this asymmetry, it takes longer for an industry with excess capacity and below-average returns to eliminate unnecessary assets than it does for an industry with above average returns to add new capacity. Periods of oversupply last longer than periods in which demand exceeds capacity. Though in the long run companies do need to provide investors with returns commensurate with the level of risk—to earn their cost of capital—the long run can extend beyond what anyone other than management would regard as reasonable. The problem is compounded by the longevity of new plants and products. For mature, capital-intensive businesses, these time spans are apt to be longer than for younger industries that require less in the way of plant and equipment.

Commodity businesses are generally in the mature camp, and part of their poor performance stems from their durability, even after they are no longer earning their keep. But the powerful driving force is the dynamics of entry and exit, not the distinction between commodities and differentiated products. Competitors with patient capital and an emotional commitment to the business can impair the profitability of efficient competitors for years, as the history of the airlines industry attests.

within the barriers must enjoy competitive advantages over potential entrants.

Although often treated as separate aspects of strategy, barriers to entry and competitive advantages are essentially alternative ways of describing the same thing. The only necessary qualification to this statement is that barriers to entry are identical to *incumbent* competitive advantages; whereas *entrant* competitive advantages—situations in which the latest firm to arrive in the market enjoys an edge (the benefit of the latest generation of technology, the hottest product design, no costs for maintaining legacy products or retired workers)—are of limited and transitory value.

Once an entrant actually enters a market, it becomes an incumbent. The same types of advantages it employed to gain entry and win business from existing firms—cutting-edge technology, lower labor costs, hotter fashions—now benefit the next new kid on the block. If the last firm in always has the advantage, there are, by definition, no barriers to entry and no sustainable excess returns.

Because competitive advantages belong only to the incumbents, their strategic planning must focus on maintaining and exploiting those advantages. Meanwhile, any firms bold enough to enter markets protected by barriers to entry ought to devise plans that make it less painful for incumbents to tolerate them than to eliminate them.

TYPES OF COMPETITIVE ADVANTAGES

There are really only a few types of genuine competitive advantages. Competitive advantages may be due to superior production technology and/or privileged access to resources (supply advantages). They may be due to customer preference (demand advantages), or they may be combinations of economies of scale with some level of customer preference (the interaction of supply-and-demand advantages, which we discuss in chapter 3). Measured by potency and durability, production advantages are the weakest barrier to entry; economies of scale, when combined with some customer captivity, are the strongest.

In addition, there are also advantages emanating from governmental interventions, such as licenses, tariffs and quotas, authorized monopolies, patents, direct subsidies, and various kinds of regulation. Television broadcast licenses, for example, convey powerful competitive advantages to their holders. Designation as a "Nationally Recognized Statistical Rating Organization" by the Securities and Exchange Commission helps Standard & Poor's, Moody's, and several smaller agencies maintain their dominance in the market for credit ratings, despite the steep fees they charge. Even in the most liberal economy, the state is an actor from whom some benefit more than others. Government favor aside, the other sources of competitive advantages are rooted in basic economic conditions.

SUPPLY ADVANTAGES: COMPETITIVE COSTS

One way a market incumbent obtains a competitive advantage is by having a lower cost structure that cannot be duplicated by potential rivals. The incumbent can earn attractive returns under prevailing market conditions—prices and sales levels—but potential entrants, thanks to their higher cost structures, cannot.

Such an advantage deters most sensible firms from entering the incumbent's market. If some foolishly optimistic companies make the attempt anyway, the incumbent, taking advantage of its lower cost structure, can underprice, outadvertise, outservice, or otherwise outmarket them. Ultimately, the would-be entrants fail and exit the market, leaving a discouraging lesson for any who would follow them.

Lower cost structures are due either to lower input costs or, more commonly, proprietary technology. In its most basic form, proprietary technology is a product line or a process that is protected by patents. During the term of the patent, protection is nearly absolute. Patent infringement penalties and legal fees make the potential costs to a would-be entrant impractically high, perhaps even infinite.

Historically, Xerox in copiers, Kodak and Polaroid in film, and pharmaceutical companies in a range of medicines have enjoyed these kinds of advantages for the lives of their product patents. Process patents may be equally powerful. Alcoa was able to monopolize the aluminum market for many years through patents on processes, and DuPont has a history of economic success based on both process and product patents. But patents expire, generally after seventeen years. Thus, cost advantages based on patents are only sustainable for limited periods. Compared to IBM's long-term dominance in computers, from the late 1950s to 1990, for example, or Coca-Cola's century-long history in the soda market, patent protection is relatively brief.

Outside of pharmaceuticals, patent-protected positions are relatively rare. Even within pharmaceuticals, "me-too" products—how many selective serotonin reuptake inhibitors are there on the market?—tend to undermine technological advantages. But patents are not the only source of advantages from proprietary technology.

In industries with complicated processes, learning and experience are a major source of cost reduction. The percentage of good yields in most chemical and semiconductor processes often increases dramatically over time, due to numerous small adjustments in procedures and inputs. Higher yields mean lower costs, both directly and by reducing the need for expensive interventions to maintain quality. The same adjustments can trim the amount of labor or other inputs required. Companies that are continually diligent can move down these learning curves ahead of their rivals and maintain a cost advantage for periods longer than most patents afford.

But, as with patents, there are natural limits to the sustainability of these learning-based proprietary cost advantages. Much depends on the pace of technological change. If it is swift enough, it can undermine advantages that are specific to processes that quickly become outdated. Cost advantages thus have shorter life expectancies in rapidly changing areas like semiconductors, semiconductor equipment, and biotechnology.

On the other hand, if technological change slows down as an industry matures, then rivals will eventually acquire the learned efficiencies of the leading incumbents. In the 1920s, RCA, manufacturing radios, was the premier high-tech company in the United States. But over time, the competitors caught up, and radios became no more esoteric to make than toasters. In the long run everything is a toaster, and toaster manufacturing is not known for its significant proprietary technology advantages, nor for high returns on investment.

Further, simple products and simple processes are not fertile ground for proprietary technology advantages. They are hard to patent and easy to duplicate and transfer to other firms. If a particular approach to production and/or service can be fully understood by a few employees, competitors can hire them away and learn the essentials of the processes involved.* If the technologies are simple, it is difficult for the developer to make the case for intellectual theft of proprietary property since much of the technology will look like "common sense." This limitation is particularly important in the vast and growing area of services—medical care, transaction processing, financial services, education, retailing— that account for roughly 70 percent of global economic activity. The technology in these fields tends to be either rudimentary or else it has been developed by specialist third parties. Technology that is truly proprietary must be produced within the firm. Markets in which consultants or suppliers, such as NCR in retailing, are responsible for most product or process innovations cannot be markets with substantial cost advantages based on technology, because the advantages are available to anyone willing to pay for them.

This is why the idea that information technologies will be the source of competitive advantages is misguided. Most of the innovations in information technology are created by firms like Accenture, IBM, Microsoft, SAP, Oracle, and a number of smaller and more specialized companies that make their living by disseminating innovations as widely as they can. Innovations that are common to all confer competitive advantages on none. Some firms may make better use of those innovations, but that is a matter of organizational effectiveness, not competitive advantage.

If cost advantages rooted in proprietary technology are relatively rare and short-lived, those based on lower input costs are rarer still. Labor, capital in all its various forms, raw materials, and intermediate inputs are all sold in markets that are generally competitive. Some companies have to deal with powerful unions that are able to raise labor costs. They may also face an overhang of underfunded pension and

* When Samuel Slater brought Richard Arkwright's cotton mill technology from England to Pawtucket, Rhode Island, in 1789, he carried the machine designs in his head. He was breaking English laws against the export of any technology, whether machines or the knowledge to build them.

retiree health-care liabilities. But if one company can enter the market with nonunion, low-benefit labor, others can follow, and the process of entry will eliminate any excess returns from lower labor costs.

Unionized firms may stagnate or die, yet the survivors enjoy no competitive advantages. The first company to find a lower cost of labor in a country such as China may gain a temporary benefit over rivals who are slower to move, but the benefit soon disappears as others follow.

Access to cheap capital or deep pockets is another largely illusory advantage. One lesson the Internet boom taught is how easy it can be to raise money. Companies with barely plausible business plans had virtually unlimited access to capital at rates that proved ridiculously cheap, given the risks of new and untested businesses. But that easy funding did not assure them success.

History is full of companies driven out of business by more efficient competitors—steel producers, appliance manufacturers, small-scale retailers, and nationwide chain stores. But only a small number of companies have been forced to the wall by competitors whose sole advantage was their deep pockets. In many cases, the putatively deep-pocketed firms—such as IBM, AT&T, Kodak, Japan Inc.—have chiefly hurt themselves by spending lavishly on mistaken ventures in part because they simply had the money.

An argument sometimes made, especially during the high tide of Japanese incursions into the U.S. and European manufacturing sectors, is that some companies or sectors enjoy preferred access to capital, making capital "cheap" for them. This access is often underwritten by government, as in the case of Airbus. Sometimes the "cheap" capital is based on access to funds that were raised in the past at unusually low costs. But the real cost of funds in these cases is not "cheap."

If capital markets at large offer 10 percent returns on investments, then investing capital in projects that return 2 percent is a money loser— an 8-percentage-point loser—even though the funds may have cost only 2 percent to raise. Taking advantage of "cheap" capital in this way is a stupidity, not a competitive advantage. Like all stupidities not underwritten by a government, it is unlikely to be sustainable for very long.

In the absence of government support, the notion of "cheap" capital is an economic fallacy. "Cheap" capital that is due to government support is best thought of as just another competitive advantage based on a government subsidy.

Some companies do have privileged access to raw materials (e.g., Aramco) or to advantageous geographical locations (e.g., United Airlines at Chicago's O'Hare International Airport). These advantages, though, tend to be limited both in the markets to which they apply and in the extent to which they can prevent competitive entry. Aramco can make more profit on a barrel of oil than Norway's Statoil, but so long as demand for oil is high enough, it can't keep Statoil out of the market. And United cannot extend its strong position at O'Hare to other airports.

The same is true for exceptional talent. The studio that has signed up a Julia Roberts or a Tom Cruise enjoys a competitive advantage over other studios when it comes to opening a new movie, although even stars of this magnitude are no guarantee of success. However, like other advantages based on special resources, this one is limited in several ways. First, star power is ultimately owned not by the studio but by the stars themselves. They can sign with whomever they like for the next film. Second, stars lose their appeal or their contracts expire. And there are no barriers to entry in creating the next Julia Roberts or Tom Cruise, as the armies of aspiring actors and agents attest. Third, the value of any star is limited to a particular audience and does not translate into broad market dominance.

These basic limitations apply equally to other special resources like rich mineral deposits or advantageous leases on desirable locations. With few exceptions, access to low-cost inputs is only a source of significant competitive advantage when the market is local, either geographically or in product space. Otherwise, it is not much help as a barrier to entry.

DEMAND ADVANTAGES: CUSTOMER CAPTIVITY

For an incumbent to enjoy competitive advantages on the demand side of the market, it must have access to customers that rivals cannot match. Branding, in the traditional sense of a quality image and reputation, by itself is not sufficient to establish this superior access. If an entrant has an equal opportunity to create and maintain a brand, the incumbent has no competitive advantage and no barrier impedes the process of entry.

Competitive demand advantages require that customers be captive in some degree to incumbent firms. This captivity is what gives the incumbent its preferred access. In a cigarette ad of some years ago—when there still were cigarette ads—smokers proclaimed that they "would rather fight than switch." Every company would love to have customers with this kind of loyalty.

It may not be impossible for entrants to lure loyal customers away from an incumbent. They can cut prices to the bone, or even give the product away to induce people to try it. They can tie it in to other products and otherwise make it desirable. But customer captivity still entails a competitive advantage because entrants cannot attract customers under anywhere near the same terms as the established firms.

Unless they have found a way to produce the item or deliver the service at a cost substantially below that of the incumbent, which is not likely, either the price at which they sell their offerings or the volume of sales they achieve will not be profitable for them, and therefore not sustainable. The incumbent has a competitive advantage because it can do what the challenger cannot—sell its product at a profit to its captive customers.

There are only a limited number of reasons why customers become captive to one supplier.

HABIT

Cigarette smoking is an addiction; buying a particular brand is a habit. Habit leads to customer captivity when frequent purchases of the same brand establish an allegiance that is as difficult to understand as it is to undermine. Cigarette smokers have their brands, though in a pinch they will light up a substitute; such is the pull of the addiction.

Soda drinkers are also loyal. To someone who generally asks for coffee, tea, or water, Coca-Cola and Pepsi taste pretty much alike. Yet each cola has its devotees, and they are generally firm in their commitments. Coca-Cola decided to reformulate and sweeten the drink in the 1980s, to stem the loss of young and therefore uncommitted cola lovers to Pepsi.

It made the change only after extensive taste tests among its own drinkers convinced them that the New Coke taste had more support. But when the company actually introduced New Coke and took the traditional drink off the shelves, Coca-Cola loyalists were furious. After some months of indecision, the company reversed course and reestablished Classic Coke, as it was briefly called, as the flagship brand. Coca-Cola was lucky to escape the problem it had created. As a rule, it isn't wise to antagonize captive customers.

For reasons that are not entirely evident, the same kind of attachment does not extend to beer drinkers. People who normally buy Coors or Budweiser for their homes, and order it when they eat in local restaurants, are only too eager to have a Corona or a Dos Equis in a Mexican restaurant, or a Tsingtao in a Chinese one, which may explain why Anheuser-Busch bought a stake in Tsingtao. Yet the cola drinker seldom thinks of asking for Great Wall Cola or some such brand.

Habit succeeds in holding customers captive when purchases are frequent and virtually automatic. We find this behavior in supermarkets rather than automobile dealers or computer suppliers. Most consumers enjoy shopping for a new car, and the fact that they owned a Chevrolet last time, or a BMW, doesn't mean they won't test-drive a Ford or a Lexus.

Both personal computer buyers and IT managers shop for replacement hardware on the basis of price, features, and dependability, not whether their current machines are IBMs, Dells, or HPs. They do need to think about compatibility with their existing software, but that is a legacy situation and a switching-cost issue and does not mean that they are creatures or captives of habit.

Habit is usually local in the sense that it relates to a single product, not to a company's portfolio of offerings. The habitual user of Crest toothpaste is not necessarily committed to Tide or any of the other Procter & Gamble brands.

SWITCHING COSTS

Customers are captive to their current providers when it takes substantial time, money, and effort to replace one supplier with a new one. In the computer era, software is the product most easily associated with high switching costs. The costs can become prohibitive when they involve not simply the substitution of some computer code, proprietary or commercial, but the retraining of the people in the firm who are the application users.

In addition to all the extra money and time required, any new system is likely to bump up the error rate. When the applications involved are critical to the company's operations—order entry, inventory, invoicing and shipping, patient records, or bank transactions—few want to abandon a functioning system, even for one that promises vast increases in productivity, if it holds the threat of terminating the business through systemic failure, the ultimate "killer app."

These costs are reinforced by network effects. If your computer system must work compatibly with others, then it is difficult to change to an alternative when others do not, even if the alternative is in some ways superior. The move will be costly, to ensure continued compatibility, and perhaps disastrous if the new system cannot be meshed with the existing one.

Software is not the only product or service that imposes substantial switching costs on customers and thus gives the incumbent a leg up on potential competitors. Whenever a supplier has to learn a great deal about the lives, needs, preferences, and other details of a new customer, there is a switching cost involved for the customer, who has to provide all this information, as well as a burden on the supplier to master it. This is one reason that clients don't switch lawyers lightly. Likewise, doctors who become comfortable prescribing a particular medicine may be reluctant to substitute a new drug with which they are less familiar, despite all the brochures and entreaties from the drug detail person.

Standardized products, especially if the standards are not proprietary, are one antidote to high switching costs, which is why customers like them. In its glory days, the IBM mainframe was built out of IBM components, ran an IBM operating system, used IBM-produced applications programs, and was even leased from IBM. Moving from one IBM computer to another was difficult, but switching to a new system entirely was perilous and daunting. Switching became easier as other companies offered compatible peripherals, applications programs, and financing. And the whole edifice began to collapse when new firms found ways to link desktop machines, built to open standards—thanks to IBM's design decision for its PC—into useable systems.

Changing credit cards used to require careful timing. Old card balances had to be paid off before the new credit facility became available. Then the card issuers began to offer preapproval and to encourage balance transfers. Costs of switching were reduced or eliminated, and competition in the industry intensified.

SEARCH COSTS

Customers are also tied to their existing suppliers when it is costly to locate an acceptable replacement. If the need is a new refrigerator, the search costs are minimal; information and ratings on competitive products are easily available. But for many people, finding a new doctor involves more than looking in the yellow pages or even in a health-care network directory. There is no ready source of the kind of information a prospective patient wants, and given the personal nature of the relationship, no alternative to direct experience.

High search costs are an issue when products or services are complicated, customized, and crucial. Automobile insurance is basically a standardized product, so much coverage at so much cost, with concern for the reliability of the underwriter alleviated by state regulation. Home ownership insurance, by contrast, is more detailed, and can involve the kind of coverage, the deductibles, special schedules of items included or excluded, the creditworthiness of the insurance company, its history of payment for claims, and other issues.

All these details foster an aversion to change. Only homeowners made seriously unhappy by their insurer's premium or level of service are going to take the trouble to search for a replacement, especially since the penalty for picking an inadequate insurer may be substantial. In this case, the real relationship may be with a trusted broker, not the actual underwriter, so the broker may enjoy the benefits of customer captivity because of the high switching costs.

For businesses, the more specialized and customized the product or service, the higher the search cost for a replacement. Professional services, which also may involve an intense level of personal contact, fit into this category, as do complicated manufacturing and warehousing systems. It is easier to upgrade with a current vendor or continue with a law firm even when not totally satisfied, because finding a better one is costly and risky. To avoid the danger of being locked in to a single source, many firms develop relationships with multiple suppliers, including professional service providers.

Taken together, habits, switching costs, and search costs create competitive advantages on the demand side that are more common and generally more robust than advantages stemming from the supply or cost side. But even these advantages fade over time. New customers, by definition, are unattached and available to anyone. Existing captive customers ultimately leave the scene; they move, they mature, they die. In the market for teenage consumables, existing customers inevitably become young adults, and a new, formerly preteen, generation enters the market largely uncommitted. The process is repeated throughout the life cycle, putting a natural limit on the duration of customer captivity. Even Coca-Cola, as we shall see, was vulnerable to Pepsi when the latter discovered "the Pepsi Generation." Only a very few venerable products like Heinz ketchup seem to derive any long-term benefit from some intergenerational transfer of habit.

CHAPTER 3

Competitive Advantages II

Economies of Scale and Strategy

ECONOMIES OF SCALE AND CUSTOMER CAPTIVITY

The competitive advantages we have described so far are uncomplicated. An incumbent firm may defeat entrants either because it has sustainably lower costs or, thanks to customer captivity, it enjoys higher demand than the entrants. Together, these two appear to cover fully the revenue and cost elements that determine profitability. But there is an additional potential source of competitive advantage. In fact, the truly durable competitive advantages arise from the interaction of supply-and-demand advantages, from the linkage of economies of scale with customer captivity. Once the firm understands how these operate together—sometimes in ways that are surprisingly contrary to commonly held beliefs about the attractiveness of growing markets—it can design effective strategies to reinforce them.

The competive advantage of economies of scale depend not on the absolute size of the dominant firm but on the size difference between it and its rivals, that is, on market share. If average costs per unit decline as a firm produces more, then smaller competitors will not be able to match the costs of the large firm even though they have equal access to technology and resources so long as they cannot reach the same *scale* of operation. The larger firm can be highly profitable at a price level that leaves its smaller competitors, with their higher average costs, losing money. The cost structure that underlies these economies of scale usually combines a significant level of fixed cost and a constant level of incremental variable costs. An apparel company, for example, needs the same amount of fabric and labor to make each unit and very little in the way of complicated machinery, so its level of variable to fixed costs is high. A software publisher, by contrast, has almost all fixed costs, which are the expenses of writing and checking the software code. Once the program has been finished, the costs of producing an additional unit are miniscule. So its total expenses increase very slowly, no matter the number of customers. As the scale of the enterprise grows, the fixed cost is spread over more units, the variable cost per unit stays the same, and the average cost per unit declines.

But something in addition to this cost structure is necessary for economies of scale to serve as a competitive advantage. If an entrant has equal access to customers as the incumbents have, it will be able to reach the incumbents' scale. A market in which all firms have equal access to customers and common cost structures, and in which entrants and incumbents offer similar products on similar terms, should divide more or less evenly among competitors. This holds true for differentiated markets, like kitchen appliances, as well as commodity markets. All competitors who operate effectively should achieve comparable scale and therefore comparable average cost.

For economies of scale to serve as a competitive advantage, then, they need to be coupled with some degree of incumbent customer captivity. If an efficient incumbent matches his competitors on price and other marketing features, then, thanks to the customer captivity, it will retain its dominant share of the market. Though entrants may be efficient, they will not match the incumbent's scale of operations, and their average costs will be permanently higher.

The incumbent, therefore, can lower prices to a level where it alone is profitable and increase its share of the market, or eliminate all profit from competitors who match its prices. With some degree of customer captivity, the entrants never catch up and stay permanently on the wrong side of the economies of scale differential. So the combination of even modest customer captivity with economies of scale becomes a powerful competitive advantage.

The dynamics of situations like this are worth a closer look. It seems reasonable to think that a persistent entrant will sooner or later reach an incumbent's scale of operation if it has access to the same basic technologies and resources. If the incumbent is not vigilant in defending its market position, the entrant may indeed catch up. The Japanese entry into the U.S. car market, the success of Fuji Film in taking on Kodak, and the initial significant market share captured by Bic disposable razors from Gillette in the 1980s are testimony to the vulnerability of poorly safeguarded economies of scale advantages.

Still, if an incumbent diligently defends its market share, the odds are clearly in its favor. This is why it is important that incumbents clearly understand the nature of their competitive advantages and make sure that their strategies adequately defend them. Think of Microsoft in the operating systems market, Boeing versus McDonnell-Douglas in the commercial airframe business, or Pitney-Bowes in postage equipment.

A simple example should help explain why small markets are more hospitable than large ones for attaining competitive advantages. Consider the case of an isolated town in Nebraska with a population of fifty thousand or less. A town of this size can support only one large discount store. A determined retailer who develops such a store should expect to enjoy an unchallenged monopoly. If a second store were to enter the town, neither would have enough customer traffic to be profitable. Other things being equal, the second entrant could not expect to drive out the first, so its best choice would be to stay away, leaving the monopoly intact.

At the other extreme from our Nebraska town is downtown New York City. This large market can support many essentially similar stores. The ability of even a powerful, well-financed incumbent to prevent entry by a newcomer will be limited. It cannot, in other words, establish effective barriers to entry based on economies of scale relative to its competitors. Markets of intermediate size and density, as we would expect, fall between small and large cities regarding the ability to establish and maintain barriers to entry. This general principle applies to product as well as to geographic space; the special-purpose computer in a niche market has an easier time in creating and profiting from economies of scale than the general-purpose PC competing in a much larger market.

Long before it became the global powerhouse in retailing, Wal-Mart enjoyed both high levels of profitability and a dominant market share in the south-central United States due to regional economies of scale in distribution, advertising, and store supervision. It defended its territory with an aggressive policy of "everyday low prices." Southwest Airlines, with a regional franchise in Texas and the surrounding states, was similarly profitable, as have been a lot of other strong local companies in service industries like retailing, telecommunications, housing development, banking, and health care.

DEFENDING ECONOMIES OF SCALE

The best strategy for an incumbent with economies of scale is to match the moves of an aggressive competitor, price cut for price cut, new product for new product, niche by niche. Then, customer captivity or even just customer inertia will secure the incumbent's greater market share. The entrant's average costs will be uniformly higher than the incumbent's at every stage of the struggle. While the incumbent's profits will be impaired, the entrant's will be even lower, often so much lower as to disappear altogether. The incumbent's competitive advantage survives, even under direct assault.

The combination of economies of scale coupled with better access in the future to existing customers also produces an advantage in the contest for new customers and for new technologies. Consider the competition between Intel and Advanced Micro Devices (AMD)—or any other potential entrant, like IBM or Motorola—to provide the next-generation microprocessor for Windows-compatible personal computers.

Computer manufacturers are accustomed to dealing with Intel and are comfortable with the level of quality, supply stability, and service support they have received from it. AMD may have performed nearly as well in all these areas, but with a much smaller market share and less interaction, AMD does not have the same intimate association with personal computer manufacturers. If AMD and Intel produce next-generation CPUs that are similarly advanced, at equal prices, and at roughly the same time, Intel will inevitably capture a dominant market share. All Intel need do is match AMD's offering to retain the roughly 90 percent share it currently commands. In planning its next-generation chip, Intel can afford to invest much more than AMD, knowing that its profits will be much greater, even if its CPU is no better.

A rough rule of thumb should lead Intel and AMD to invest in proportion to their current market shares. If each company invests 10 percent of current sales in R&D, Intel will outspend AMD $2.6 billion to $300 million. That enormous edge makes Intel the odds-on favorite in the race for next-generation technology. In fact, the situation is even more unequal for AMD. Should it manage to produce a better new chip, computer manufacturers would almost certainly allow Intel a significant grace period to catch up, rather than switch immediately to AMD. The history of competition between the two has seen instances both of Intel's larger investments usually paying off in superior technology and of its customer captivity allowing it time to catch up when AMD has taken a lead. Thus, economies of scale have enabled Intel to sustain its technological advantage over many generations of technology.

Economies of scale in distribution and advertising also perpetuate and amplify customer captivity across generations of consumers. Even if smaller rivals can spend the same proportion of revenue on product development, sales force, and advertising as, for example, Kellogg's, Mc-Donald's, and Coca-Cola, they can't come close to matching the giants on actual dollars deployed to attract new customers. Because of the edge it gives incumbents in both winning new generations of customers and developing new generations of technology, the combination of economies of scale and customer captivity produces the most sustainable competitive advantages.

Three features of economies of scale have major implications for the strategic decisions that incumbents must make.

First, in order to persist, competitive advantages based on economies of scale must be defended. Any market share lost to rivals narrows the leader's edge in average cost. By contrast, competitive advantages based on customer captivity or cost advantages are not affected by market share losses. Where economies of scale are important, the leader must always be on guard. If a rival introduces attractive new product features, the leader must adopt them quickly. If the rival initiates a major advertising campaign or new distribution systems, the leader has to neutralize them one way or another.

Unexploited niche markets are an open invitation to entrants looking to reach a minimally viable scale of operations. The incumbent cannot concede these niches. When the Internet became a major focus of personal computing, Microsoft had to introduce its own browser to counter Netscape and offer network alternatives to niche players like AOL. When Pepsi-Cola targeted supermarkets in the 1950s as an alternative distribution channel, Coca-Cola was too slow to respond, and Pepsi picked up market share. The American motorcycle industry did not challenge Japanese companies like Honda when they began to sell inexpensive cycles in the 1960s. That was the beginning of the end for almost all the American firms. Harley-Davidson survived, though barely and with government help, in part because the Japanese allowed it to control the heavyweight bike niche. Economies of scale need to be defended with eternal vigilance.

Second, the company has to understand that pure size is not the same thing as economies of scale, which arise when the dominant firm in a market can spread the fixed costs of being in that market across a greater number of units than its rivals. It is the share of the relevant market, rather than size per se, that creates economies of scale.

The relevant market is the area—geographic or otherwise—in which the fixed costs stay fixed. In the case of a retail company, distribution infrastructure, advertising expenditures, and store supervision expenses are largely fixed for each metropolitan area or other regional cluster. If sales are added outside the territory, fixed costs rise and economies of scale diminish. When it was still in the cellular business, AT&T's cellular operations in the Northeast and Atlantic states had larger fixed costs per dollar of revenue in that region than Verizon's, which controlled a far greater share of the territory. The fact that AT&T cellular may have been larger nationally than Verizon cellular is irrelevant.

The same conditions apply when the relevant geography is a product line rather than a physical region. Research and development costs, including the start-up costs of new production lines and product management overhead, are fixed costs associated with specific product lines.

Though IBM's total sales dwarf those of Intel, its research and development expenses are spread over a far greater range of products. In CPU development and production, which has its own particular technologies, Intel enjoys the benefits of economies of scale.

Network economies of scale are similar. Customers gain by being part of densely populated networks, but the benefits and the economies of scale extend only as far as the reach of the networks. Aetna's HMO has many more subscribers nationally than Oxford Health Plans. But because medical services are provided locally, what matters is share in a local market. In the New York metropolitan region, Oxford has more patients and more doctors enrolled than Aetna. Its 60 percent share of doctors makes it more appealing to new patients than Aetna's 20 percent share. The fact that Aetna also has 20 percent in Chicago, Los Angeles, Dallas, or even Philadelphia is irrelevant. The appropriate measure of economies of scale is comparative fixed costs within the relevant network.

There are only a few industries in which economies of scale coincide with global size. The connected markets for operating systems and CPUs is one example; Microsoft and Intel are the beneficiaries of global geographic economies of scale. The commercial airframe industry, now shared between Boeing and Airbus, is another. However, despite some other interests, each of these four companies concentrates on a single product line and hence on local product space economies of scale. General Electric, the most successful conglomerate, has always focused on its relative share within the particular markets in which it competes, not on its overall size.

Third, growth of a market is generally the enemy of competitive advantages based on economies of scale, not the friend. The strength of this advantage is directly related to the importance of fixed costs. As a market grows, fixed costs, by definition, remain constant. Variable costs, on the other hand, increase at least as fast as the market itself. The inevitable result is that fixed costs decline as a proportion of total cost.

This reduces the advantages provided by greater incumbent scale. Consider two companies, an incumbent and an entrant, competing in a market in which fixed costs are $100,000 per year. If the entrant has sales of $500,000 and the incumbent $2,500,000, then fixed costs consume 20 percent of the entrant's revenue versus 4 percent of the incumbent's, a gap of 16 percent. Now the market doubles in size, and each company doubles as well. The gap in fixed cost as a percentage of sales declines to 8 percent. At a level ten times the original, the gap drops to 1.6 percent. See table 3.1.

Moreover, growth in the market lowers the hurdle an entrant must clear in order to become viably competitive. Let us assume that the entrant can compete with the incumbent if the economies of scale advantage is no more than 2 percent against it. With fixed costs at $100,000 per year, the gap drops to that level if the entrant has sales of $5 million. So if the size of the market were $25 million, the entrant would need to capture a 20 percent share; in a market of $100 million, it would only need a 5 percent share, clearly a much lower hurdle. Even if the incumbent were the only other firm in the industry and thus had sales of $95 million, the entrant would still face less than a 2 percent competitive gap.

There are some highly visible instances of how economies of scale advantages have dwindled as markets have become international and thus massive. The global market for automobiles is so large that many competitors have reached a size, even with a small percentage of the total, at which they are no longer burdened by an economies of scale

TABLE 3.1

	Entrant	Incumbent	Incumbent's Difference
		Original market size	
Sales	$500,000	$2,500,000	$2,000,000
Fixed costs (FC)	$100,000	$100,000	–
FC as % of sales	20%	4%	16% lower
		Two times original market size	
Sales	$1,000,000	$5,000,000	$4,000,000
Fixed costs (FC)	$100,000	$100,000	–
FC as % of sales	10%	2%	8% lower
		Ten times original market size	
Sales	$5,000,000	$25,000,000	$20,000,000
Fixed costs (FC)	$100,000	$100,000	–
FC as % of sales	2%	0.4%	1.6% lower

disadvantage. For very large potential markets like Internet services and online sales, the relative importance of fixed costs are unlikely to be significant. If new entrants can capture a share sufficient to support the required infrastructure, then established companies like Amazon will find it difficult to keep them out.

Although it may seem counterintuitive, most competitive advantages based on economies of scale are found in local and niche markets, where either geographical or product spaces are limited and fixed costs remain proportionately substantial.

The postderegulation telecommunications industry is a good example of the importance of local economies of scale. The old-technology local exchange carriers, whose markets are not large enough for a second or third company to reach viable scale, have fared much better in terms of profitability than the national long-distance and cellular carriers like AT&T, MCI-WorldCom, and Sprint.

STRATEGY AND COMPETITIVE ADVANTAGE THROUGH SUPPLY OR DEMAND

Prescriptions for strategy in any particular market depend on the existence and types of competitive advantages that prevail in it.

The first and simplest case is where there are no competitive advantages in the market. There is nothing that fundamentally distinguishes an existing firm from actual and potential rivals, and the economic playing field is level. History and logic both confirm how difficult it is for a single firm to shift the basic economic structure of such a market significantly for its benefit.

A firm in an industry with no competitive advantages basically should forget visionary strategic dreams and concentrate on running itself as effectively as it can. What matters in these circumstances are efficiencies in managing costs, in product development, in marketing, in pricing to specific customer segments, in financing, and in everything else it does. If it can operate more effectively than its competitors, it will succeed.

Operational effectiveness can make one company much more profitable than its rivals even in an industry with no competitive advantages, where everyone has basically equal access to customers, resources, technology, and scale of production. In the last chapter of the book, we document for a range of industries just how large and important these differences are. Firms that are operationally effective, however, do tend to focus on a single business and on their own internal performance.

In competitive situations where a company enjoys advantages related to proprietary technologies and customer captivity, its strategy should be to both exploit and reinforce them where they can.

Exploitation can take several forms. A company with captive customers can charge more than the competition does. If the advantages stem from lower costs, it can strike a balance between underpricing competitors to increase sales and charging the same to keep the full benefit of the cost advantage. So long as the firm is either alone in the market or surrounded by a myriad of smaller and weaker competitors, it can determine the appropriate price level by trial and error. It needs to monitor its steps to see which price levels and other marketing choices provide the best return, but it does not have to worry explicitly about the reactions of particular competitors.

In fact, the process of exploitation in these cases is largely a matter of operational effectiveness. Strategies only become complicated where a small number of powerful firms enjoy competitive advantages in common. Much of the rest of this book concentrates on particular cases in which strategic interactions among the few are critical.

To reinforce its competitive advantages, a company first has to identify their sources and then to intensify the economic forces at work. If the source is cost advantages stemming from proprietary technologies, the company wants to improve them continually and to produce a successive wave of patentable innovations to preserve and extend existing advantages. The practice here is again a matter of organizational effectiveness, including making sure that investments in research and development are productive.

If the source is customer captivity, the company wants to encourage habit formation in new customers, increase switching costs, and make the search for alternatives more complicated and difficult. For expensive items, it wants to make purchases more frequent and to spread payments out over time, to ensnare the customer in an ongoing relationship that is easier to continue than to replace.

The automobile companies, facing lengthening intervals between car purchases, mastered the techniques long ago. In the late 1950s and early 1960s, they began to use highly visible annual style changes to encourage more frequent purchases. They also began accepting trade-ins and monthly payments to ease the financial burden. More recently, leasing programs have been tailored to accomplish the same thing, with customers offered new cars before the old leases have expired.

Customer loyalty programs—frequent-flier miles, affinity credit cards, and other reward plans—have the same goal, keeping captive customers in the corral. The famous Gillette strategy of selling the razor cheaply and then making money from the regular purchase of blades has been copied by other industries. Magazine subscription campaigns that offer inexpensive initial subscriptions to profit from higher-priced renewals are a variant. The common element in all these approaches is that they encourage repeated, virtually automatic and nonreflective purchases that discourage the customer from a careful consideration of alternatives.

Amplifying switching costs is usually a matter of extending and deepening the range of services offered. Microsoft has regularly added features to its basic Windows operating system, making the task of switching to other systems and mastering their intricacies more onerous. As banks move beyond simple check processing and ATM withdrawals to automatic bill payment, preestablished access to lines of credit, direct salary deposit, and other routine functions, customers become more reluctant to leave for another bank, even if it offers superior terms on some products.

The same tactic of providing more integration of multiple features raises search costs. Comparison shopping is more difficult if the alternatives are equally complicated but not exactly comparable. Few people spend their leisure time analyzing the pricing and service plans of wireless telephone companies. Also, as the importance and added value of products and services increases, so does the risk of getting a poor outcome from an alternative provider.

The same potentially poor results also raise the cost of sampling; something might go seriously wrong during the trial period. This problem extends beyond the more obvious situations like finding a new cardiologist or a residential insurance carrier. Philip Morris spent a fortune promoting the image of the Marlboro smoker. If a Marlboro Man's standing in society seems to depend on the brand of cigarette he chooses, the risk of a switch to Camels may be more than he is willing to assume. Complexity, high added value, and significance are all components of high search costs.

STRATEGY AND ECONOMIES OF SCALE

Competitive advantages based on economies of scale are in a class by themselves for two reasons.

First, as we have mentioned, they tend to be far longer lived than the two other types, and therefore more valuable. Coca-Cola is one of the most valuable brands in the world not because it is so widely recognized, but because of customer captivity and, more importantly, local economies of scale in advertising and distribution. Due to these competitive advantages, Coca-Cola has an edge in acquiring new customers. It can appeal to them (advertising) and serve them (distribution) at a much lower unit cost than can its smaller competitors. But these advantages are particular to specific geographic regions. Despite its worldwide recognition, Coca-Cola is not the dominant soft drink everywhere. In places like Korea, where a local company allied with Pepsi is currently on top, Coca-Cola is not the most valuable brand. In Venezuela, Coca-Cola suddenly displaced Pepsi only because the leading local bottler suddenly shifted allegiance.

Second, advantages based on economies of scale are vulnerable to gradual erosion and thus need to be defended vigorously. Once a competitor increases the size of its operations, it shrinks the unit cost gap between it and the leader. Each step a competitor takes toward closing the gap makes the next step easier, because its margins and therefore its resources are improving as its costs decline. At some point the entire advantage may be gone or even turn negative for the incumbent, if the entrant has become the larger firm.

These advantages can be destroyed, but they can also be created. In a market with significant fixed costs but currently served by many small competitors, an individual firm has an opportunity to acquire a dominant share. If there is also a degree of customer captivity, that dominant share will be defensible.

The best course is to establish dominance in a local market, and then expand outward from it. This is the path Sam Walton initially pursued as he established dominance in small-town Arkansas and then from that base expanded nationally. It also describes Microsoft's extension of its product space from operating systems to office applications. Even where incumbent competitors have dominant positions, lack of vigilance on their part may present openings for successful encroachment.

Wal-Mart won out over Kmart and most of its other discount store competitors by extending its economies of scale strategy into what had been the enemy's territory. Microsoft did the same to Lotus and Word-Perfect in applications software. Economies of scale, especially in local markets, are the key to creating sustainable competitive advantages.

In pursuit of these opportunities, it is important to remember that size and rapid growth of the target market are liabilities for incumbents, not assets. Big markets will support many competitors, even when there are substantial fixed costs. Markets grow rapidly because they attract many new customers, who are by definition noncaptive. They may provide a base of viable scale for new entrants.

The appropriate strategy for both incumbents and entrants is to identify niche markets, understanding that not all niches are equally attractive. An attractive niche must be characterized by customer captivity, small size relative to the level of fixed costs, and the absence of vigilant, dominant competitors. Ideally, it will also be readily extendable at the edges. The key is to "think local."

The other side of this coin is the need to defend those local markets where a firm enjoys competitive advantages by responding aggressively to all competitive initiatives however they arrive.

The incumbent can also take the first step and not wait to counter-punch. Anything it does to increase fixed costs, like advertising heavily, will present smaller competitors with the nasty alternatives of matching the expenses and hurting their margins or not matching and losing the competition for new customers. Production and product features that require capital expenditures, like building centralized facilities to provide automated processing, will also make life more difficult for smaller competitors. Accelerating product development cycles, and thereby upping the costs of research and development, is another possibility. Everything that efficiently shifts costs from variable to fixed will reinforce advantages from economies of scale.

Ill-conceived growth plans, in contrast, can do just the opposite. Grow *or* die corporate imperatives too often lead to grow *and* die results. The fates of Kmart, Kodak, RCA, Westinghouse, CBS, the original Bank of America, and AT&T, all once lustrous corporate names, are evidence of the perils of unfocused growth strategies. Instead of defending the markets in which they were dominant and profitable, they spent copiously in markets where they were newcomers battling powerful incumbents.

In contrast, companies that have stayed within their areas of fundamental competitive advantage, like Kimberly-Clark, Walgreen, Colgate-Palmolive, and Best Buy, have survived and generally flourished. Competitive advantages are invariably market-specific. They do not travel to meet the aspirations of growth-obsessed CEOs.

COMPETITIVE ADVANTAGE, STRATEGY FORMULATION, AND LOCAL OPPORTUNITIES

In the next chapter, we will provide a detailed procedure for assessing competitive advantages. The method needs to be used in the proper context. The first step in formulating strategy is to take an inventory of a firm's current and potential markets from a competitive advantage point of view.

In some markets, where there are no competitive advantages and none likely ever to emerge, the only approach is to operate efficiently. In another group of markets, where vigilant incumbents enjoy competitive advantages, potential entrants would do well to back off, and nondominant incumbents to depart. In still other markets, a firm will enjoy current competitive advantages. In these cases, its strategy should be to manage and defend them.

Finally, there will be markets in which a company can establish competitive advantages by achieving defensible economies of scale. Most of these will be local, either geographically or in product space. They are the proper focus of strategic analysis. Many companies, if they look carefully, will find possibilities for dominance in some of their markets, where they can earn above normal returns on investment. Unfortunately, these local opportunities are too often disregarded in the pursuit of ill-advised growth associated with global strategic approaches.

CHAPTER 4

Assessing Competitive Advantages

THREE STEPS

Because the concept of competitive advantage lies at the core of business strategy, it is essential to determine whether a company benefits from a competitive advantage, and if it does, to identify the sources of that advantage.

There are three basic steps to doing such an assessment:

1. Identify the competitive landscape in which the firm operates. Which markets is it really in? Who are its competitors in each one?
2. Test for the existence of competitive advantages in each market. Do incumbent firms maintain stable market shares? Are they exceptionally profitable over a substantial period?
3. Identify the likely nature of any competitive advantage that may exist. Do the incumbents have proprietary technologies or captive customers? Are there economies of scale or regulatory hurdles from which they benefit?

The first and most important step is to develop an industry map that shows the structure of competition in the relevant markets. This map will identify the market segments that make up the industry as a whole and list the leading competitors within each one. Deciding where one segment ends and another begins is not always obvious. However, if the same company names show up in adjacent market segments, then these segments can usually be treated as a single market. Mapping an industry helps a company see where it fits in the larger picture and who its competitors are, even if the segment breakdowns are not always precise.

The second step is to determine for each market segment whether it is protected by barriers to entry, or in other terms, whether some incumbent firms enjoy competitive advantages. There are two telltale signs of the existence of barriers to entry/competitive advantages:

- *Stability of market share among firms.* If companies regularly capture market share from each other, it is unlikely that any of them enjoys a position protected by competitive advantages. In contrast, if each firm can defend its share over time, then competitive advantages may be protecting their individual market positions.*

    Stability in the relative market positions of firms is a related issue. The key indicator of this is the history of the dominant firm in the segment. If the leading company has maintained its position over a period of many years, that fact strongly suggests the existence of competitive advantages. If, on the other hand, it is impossible to single out a dominant firm, or if the firm at the top changes regularly, then no single company is likely to enjoy sustainable competitive advantages.

    The history of entry and exit in a market segment provides another clue. The more movement in and out, the more turbulent the ranking of the companies that remain, and the longer the list of competitors, the less likely it is that there are barriers and competitive advantages. Where the list of names is short and stable, the chances are good that the incumbents are protected by barriers and benefit from competitive advantages.

- *Profitability of firms within the segment.* In a market without competitive advantages, entry should eliminate returns above a firm's cost of capital. If the companies in a market maintain returns on capital that

---

* It is possible that in a market protected by barriers to entry, two or three incumbents may take share from one another. But if the changes are substantial, the indication is that customer captivity is weak and that it may not be long before new entrants are breaching the barriers.

are substantially above what they have to pay to attract capital, the chances are strong that they benefit from competitive advantages/ barriers to entry. These sustainable excess returns may be restricted to a single dominant firm, or they may be shared by a limited number of companies who all enjoy competitive advantages over smaller firms and potential entrants.

There are a number of ways to measure profitability. The approaches that permit comparisons across industries calculate returns either on equity or on invested capital.

After-tax returns on invested capital averaging more than 15 to 25 percent—which would equate to 23 to 38 percent pretax return with tax rates of 35 percent—over a decade or more are clear evidence of the presence of competitive advantages. A return on capital in the range of 6–8 percent after tax generally indicates their absence.

There is one major difficulty in measuring returns on investment in any particular market. Corporations report their results for the company as a whole; they may include breakdowns for highly aggregated industry segments and for continental-sized geographic regions. But the markets where competitive advantages are likely to exist will often be local, narrowly bounded either in geography or product space. A typical company of even medium size may benefit from barriers to entry in several such markets, but stellar results there will be diluted in the financial reports by being combined with returns from other, less profitable operations. Identifying historical profitability for particular markets often requires extrapolation. The best way is to look at the reported profits of "pure play" companies, whose operations are narrowly focused within these markets. The resulting profitability calculations for focused segments are critical to any strategy for exploiting competitive advantages and minimizing the impact of competitive disadvantages.

When the analysis of market share stability and profitability are consistent with one another, the case for the existence of competitive advantage is robust. For example, Enron reported only a 6 percent return on capital for the year 2000—its most profitable year—and it needed the help of accounting manipulations to do even that. This result by itself should have cast doubt on its claim to competitive advantages in trading markets for new commodities like broadband and old ones like energy. The history of the trading operations of established Wall Street firms, in which changing relative market positions are the rule, makes the case against competitive advantage for Enron even stronger.

If market share stability and profitability indicate the existence of competitive advantages, the third step is to identify the likely source of these advantages. Do the dominant firms in this industry benefit from proprietary technologies or other cost advantages? Do they have captive customers, thanks to consumer habit formation, switching costs, or search costs? Are there significant economies of scale in the firm's operations, combined with at least some degree of customer captivity? Or, if none of these conditions seems present, do the incumbent firms profit from government intervention, such as licenses, subsidies, regulations, or some other special dispensation?

Identifying the likely source of a firm's competitive advantage serves as a check to confirm the findings from the data on market share stability and profitability. Even when market share is stable and profitability is high, a close look at the business may fail to spot any clearly identifiable cost, customer captivity, or economies of scale advantages.

The likely explanation for this discrepancy is either that the market share and profitability figures are temporary, or that they are the consequence of good management—operational effectiveness—that can be emulated by any sufficiently focused entrant. Identifying the sources of competitive advantages should help predict their likely sustainability, a necessary step for both incumbents and potential entrants when formulating their strategies.

The three-step procedure for assessing competitive advantage is depicted in figure 4.1.

THE STEPS IN PRACTICE: A LOOK AT THE FUTURE OF APPLE COMPUTER

Now let's use this procedure to look at Apple Computer. We will review its past and forecast its likely future. In its history, Apple has chosen strategies that have involved it in almost every important segment of

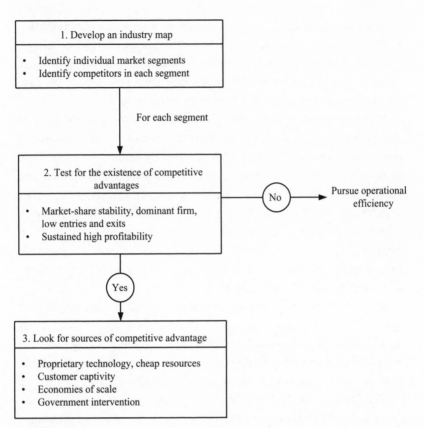

FIGURE 4.1

Assessing competitive advantage: three steps

the personal computer (PC) industry. The visionaries at Apple, first Steve Jobs, then John Sculley, then Jobs in his second tenure, have at times sought to revolutionize not simply the PC industry itself, including most of the hardware and software segments, but also the related areas of personal communications and consumer electronics.

Apple has consciously attempted to bring an inclusive vision to this collection of often unrelated segments. The hope was to reap the benefits of synergies across chip and component development, hardware design, manufacturing, software features, and even communications protocols. John Sculley, describing Apple's personal digital assistant in 1992, said of the company "we really don't invent new products, but the best ones are there already, only invisible, waiting to be discovered."

Given Apple's checkered economic history, the initial presumption has to be that its aspirations have not coincided with the economic realities of the markets in which it has competed. Since Apple has never been a particularly efficient operator, the burden has fallen almost entirely on the strategic choices it has made, its ability to benefit from competitive advantages. Apple is not alone in this position. An argument of this book is that large and diffuse, as opposed to local and specific, strategic visions are almost always misguided.

DEVELOPING AN INDUSTRY MAP: APPLE IN THE PERSONAL COMPUTER INDUSTRY

Like maps in an atlas, industry maps can be drawn at various levels of detail. Our initial effort divides the PC industry into only six segments, as shown in figure 4.2. PCs are built from components, of which the central processing unit (CPU), the chip at the heart of every personal computer, is the most important. The leading CPU manufacturers are Intel, Motorola, IBM, and AMD. Other components include keyboards, power supplies, graphic interface boards, disk storage devices, memory chips, monitors, speakers, and scores of additional parts.

Personal computer manufacturers like Dell, IBM, HP, Compaq (which merged with HP in 2002), and many others assemble these components into PC systems. They also incorporate operating system software, from companies such as Microsoft, and may add some applications software packages, such as word processors, spreadsheets, Internet browsers, financial management programs, graphics programs, security, and more. The applications programs are more frequently sold directly to users. Some of these applications programs are produced by the operating system software companies; some come from specialized providers like Adobe and Intuit.

Finally, PC owners today almost invariably connect their machines to the Internet through network service providers, like AOL, Earthlink,

FIGURE 4.2
Map of the personal computer industry (first version)

MSN, Time Warner, or the regional telephone companies that allow them to communicate with other users. Yahoo, Google, and other Internet sites are also in the network segment, broadly conceived.

An initial industry map almost invariably represents a compromise between the virtues of simplicity and tractability, on the one hand, and the requirements of comprehensiveness, on the other. Too much detail risks overwhelming the map with too many segments; too little detail risks missing important distinctions.

The appropriate amount of precision depends on the specific case, and also on what we discover in the initial analysis. The Other Components segment, for example, could be broken down into a number of separate units—printers, modems, disk drives, monitors, and so on. The Applications Software segment should ultimately also be subdivided into more niches, like database management, desktop publishing, photographic and motion picture editing, and more.

Our bias for starting simple also influences our treatment of the PC Manufacturing segment, where we have deliberately excluded game consoles, workstations, handheld computers, and other products that all compete at some level with PCs. Finer-grained divisions become necessary only if we think, after our initial foray, that Apple's future may depend significantly on the structure of competition in these particular markets. Starting with six segments allows us to keep things simple unless there is a need to make them more complex.

We next list the names of the firms that operate in each segment of the map, putting the dominant company, measured by market share, at the top (figure 4.3).

For microprocessors (CPU chips), Intel is clearly the leader, followed by AMD, IBM, and Motorola, which was Apple's primary supplier at the

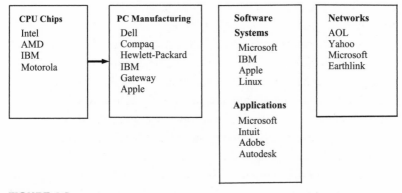

FIGURE 4.3
Map of the PC industry (with names)

introduction of the Macintosh, and later shared the business with IBM. The hardware (PC) manufacturers include Dell, HP, Compaq, IBM, Gateway, Toshiba, and of course, Apple.

Even at this early stage of the analysis, two obvious and important facts emerge. First, there is almost no overlap in names between the two segments, meaning that each has to be analyzed separately. (IBM is in both segments, but it primarily uses Intel CPUs in its own PCs.) Second, while there are only four companies in the microprocessor segment, the list of PC manufacturers is both long and incomplete, and the identity of the dominant firm is not obvious.

The Systems and Applications Software segment list is headed by Microsoft; other players are Apple, IBM (with its OS/2 system, at one time a potential competitor), and Linux, all much smaller. Two firms, IBM and Apple, are also PC manufacturers, but Microsoft makes neither chips nor PC "boxes." In cases where there is some overlap in names, the segments need to be kept distinct and treated separately so long as the dominant firms differ across segments.

Microsoft is also the dominant firm in the Applications Software segment; its office productivity suite of programs and its browser lead their categories in current sales and size of the installed base of users. Other companies with visibility, including Intuit in financial software, Adobe in graphics and typographics, Autodesk in architectural and design software, do not appear elsewhere. So there is a decision to make on whether to consolidate the segments.

It is usually preferable to begin by keeping segments distinct and then look for connections across segments. Amalgamation tends to conceal strategic issues that separate treatment may reveal. For the sake of simplicity, in this example we will use Microsoft's dominance in both system and applications software to justify combining the two segments into one software group, with the intention of revisiting the decision when we are further along in the analysis.

AOL is the dominant firm in the Networks segment. The one company whose name appears here and elsewhere is Microsoft, whose MSN has become a major competitor in the network business. But because AOL operates only in this segment, and Apple has virtually no presence, we will treat it as distinct. PC wholesaling and retailing is also a distinct segment, even though Apple does run around eighty retail outlets. Because it is not relevant to the company's competitive position, we are going to ignore it altogether.

We have also dropped the Other Components segment from this version of the map. Given the diversity of these components—printers, disk drives, memory chips, keyboards, and all the others—and the fact that each subsegment has many competitors with virtually no crossover of names, each would need to be analyzed separately. All these segments look much like the PC Manufacturing sector—a long and unstable list of competitors with no firm clearly dominant. Industries with these characteristics tend to have similar strategic implications, both in themselves and for segments upstream and downstream from them. So we can defer treatment of Other Components until we have looked closely at PC Manufacturing to see whether more detailed examination is necessary to understand Apple's strategic choices. In this case, since Apple has not tended to compete significantly in these component segments, the chances are that we will continue to ignore them.

The three segments that we cannot ignore are CPUs, Software, and PC Manufacturing. For each of these, we need to know whether competitive advantages exist, and, if they do, what they are and whether it is Apple or its competitors who benefit from them.

TESTING FOR AND IDENTIFYING COMPETITIVE
ADVANTAGES: THE CHIP SEGMENT

In the CPU industry, market share has been quite stable since the early 1980s, after the introduction of IBM's PC, around which much of the industry standardized. Intel has been the dominant supplier for two decades, through many generations of chips. Other powerful companies like IBM, NEC, and Texas Instruments have tried, over time, to gain entry but have not been particularly successful. Motorola was a major competitor in the early 1980s but since then has fallen far behind Intel. Intel's share has held fairly stable since then, hovering around 90 percent. At times, AMD has made some inroads, but Intel has always rebounded. Share stability like this is evidence of the existence of major barriers to entry and competitive advantages.

The history of Intel's profitability tells the same story. Except for a brief period in the mid 1980s, before it quit the memory chip business, Intel's average returns on capital have exceeded 30 percent after tax. The ratio of its market value to the estimated replacement cost of its net assets has continually exceeded 3 to 1; each dollar invested by Intel has created three or more dollars in shareholder value. The absence of successful entry and Intel's continued dominance in the CPU chip market is clearly a sign of a strong incumbent competitive advantage. The sources of Intel's advantage—captive customers, economies of scale, and some patent protection—are clear; we discussed them in chapters 2 and 3.

Unfortunately for Apple, it has been on the losing side in this competition. Its alliance has been with Motorola for the first generation of Macintosh CPUs, and with Motorola and IBM for the PowerPC chips. The introduction of the Macintosh, in 1984, with its graphical user interface based on a Motorola chip, secured for Apple the lead in everything graphic that might be done on a personal computer. But Intel powered ahead, and its later generation of CPUs have been capable of running Microsoft's Windows software, in most ways indistinguishable from the Macintosh interface.

Given Intel's economies of scale advantages, it has been able to outdistance Motorola in adding processing power to the CPU. Apple has been left having to play catch-up, sometimes missing an upgrade cycle. Though Motorola and Apple have won praise for the graphic and multimedia capabilities of their chip–operating system integration, the alliance has put Apple at a competitive disadvantage because each generation of CPU chips requires about $1 billion in research and development costs. Intel sells more than 100 million chips per generation, making their R&D cost per chip around $10. The Apple-Motorola-IBM alliance has sales of 10 million chips in a generation, putting their R&D cost at around $100 per chip. They are faced with the choice of severely cutting their R&D spending, which would virtually guarantee failure in the race for new technology, or shouldering the much higher cost per chip. In either case, they are playing on a field tilted against them, and will not fare well.

TESTING FOR AND IDENTIFYING COMPETITIVE ADVANTAGES: THE SOFTWARE SEGMENT

Microsoft's dominance of the software segment is even more pronounced than Intel's position in microprocessors. IBM's open architecture for the PC allowed many other companies to become manufacturers, but the operating system was standardized on Microsoft's MS-DOS. Since then, Microsoft has made the most of this privileged position, both by defending its core turf and by extending its franchise. It smothered IBM's effort to take back some of the operating system market with OS/2. It overcame Apple's initial lead in graphical user interface by developing Windows to succeed MS-DOS. It fought off potential threats to the primacy of the operating system by taking the browser market away from Netscape, and it continues to keep Linux and the open source movement a marginal factor in the desktop market, although Linux has gained more acceptance as the operating system for workstations and servers.

At the same time, Microsoft has become a leading applications provider in word processing, spreadsheet, presentation, and financial programs for the PC. Versions of the Windows operating system extend downward to personal digital assistants and mobile telephones and upward to larger server computers. It has not been able to dominate the game console business, where it is one of the three leading console manufacturers (and not yet a profitable one), or cable television systems, set-top boxes, and other markets more remote from its central strength in the desktop operating system.

In the operating systems market, its share has remained above 80 percent, often above 90 percent, for two decades. It used this dominance, and the profitability that stemmed from it, to push its way to the top of the office suite and browser businesses. Its leverage from the ownership of the operating software code insured early compatibility of applications programs, and its position as supplier of the operating system assured that PC manufacturers needed Microsoft much more than it needed any of them. Sometimes its aggressive behavior brought out the regulators, but two major antitrust cases in the United States left Microsoft atop its markets, hardly scathed by the experience. The European Union may do more damage.

It is a criminal understatement to say that Microsoft has been profitable. From its IPO in 1986 through 2000, Microsoft averaged an after-tax return on capital of 29 percent per year. In 2001 and 2002, the figure dropped to 15 percent, still high although not so stratospheric. Yet these figures, impressive as they are, do not begin to reveal the extraordinary profitability of Microsoft's core business. In 2002, the company's capital—its total debt and equity—totaled $52 billion. Since Microsoft had no debt, all of that figure represented equity.

The equity was invested in two businesses. The first business was money, cash in the bank or some close equivalent. In 2002, its average cash balance was $35 billion, on which it earned roughly $1.2 billion after tax, or around 3.5 percent. The rest of its after-tax earnings, around $6.6 billion, came from its software businesses, on an investment of $13.5 billion (debt plus equity minus cash), or a return on investment of 49 percent.* Only by blending the returns of its software operations with the returns on its mountain of cash could Microsoft report an after-tax return on capital of 15 percent. Calculated in this manner, from

---

*This actually understates the return on software, since Microsoft lost money on its game console and other noncore business.

1986 through 2000, Microsoft's software business averaged a return on capital of around 100 percent, after tax.* See table 4.1.

It is abundantly clear that Microsoft enjoys a competitive advantage. The sources of that advantage are not difficult to identify. It isn't technology. Talented computer programmers have been abundant for decades, and even though Microsoft does have copyright protection for its source code, nothing prevents other software companies from turning out comparable or superior products with their own software. Many professionals have been scornful of Microsoft's offerings for years.

The company does have captive customers, partially because much of the software they own is not compatible with other operating systems, making change expensive and time-consuming. Its economies of scale are vast, since writing standard programs is almost entirely a fixed-cost business. With its enormous customer base, Microsoft has been able to throw years of program writing into any project it thinks important and still end up spending less per unit sold than its competitors.

Finally, there is the network effect, the fact that the value of the product to the user depends on how many other people also use it. A com-

TABLE 4.1
Microsoft's returns on investment, 2002 ($ billion)

Cash at end of year	$ 38.6
Debt	$ 0
Equity	$ 52.2
Capital−cash	$ 13.6
Net income	$ 7.8
Earnings on cash	$ 1.2
Earnings on software	$ 6.6
Total return on capital	15.0%
Return on capital invested in software	48.8%

*This calculation of Microsoft's return on capital is rudimentary. We go into the mechanics of arriving at a more refined version of return on invested capital in the next section of this chapter.

petitor to Microsoft in both the operating system and applications software businesses is at a huge disadvantage, no matter the quality of its offerings.

Apple has been competing against Microsoft since IBM introduced the PC in 1981. At times it has had a superior operating system by almost any independent measure, yet it has never managed to gain much more than around 13 percent of the market, and that figure has been considerably lower since Microsoft introduced a workable version of Windows. The situation in the software segment parallels that in microprocessors, with Apple and its allies losing out to Microsoft and Intel, or "the Wintel platform," as the tight relationship between Microsoft and Intel has been called. Apple's strategy of integration has been no match for the market-specific competitive advantages that its rivals enjoy.

TESTING FOR AND IDENTIFYING COMPETITIVE ADVANTAGES: THE PC MANUFACTURING SEGMENT

The PC manufacturing segment of the industry looks nothing like the microprocessor or software segments. The dominant firm has changed over time; new companies have entered and existing ones exited; and the share of the market held by the top twenty firms has seldom exceeded 60 percent of the total. Even among the largest firms, market share changes from year to year have been substantial. Data for the years 1990–98 reveals how much market share varied from year to year, and how far the top firms in 1990 had fallen by 1998.

The basic share stability calculation is shown in table 4.2. Columns 1 and 2 are simply the share each company held in the U.S. market in 1990 and 1998. In columns 3 and 4, the combined share of the seven companies has been set to 100 percent, and each company's portion of that total has been calculated. Finally, column 5 reports the change between 1990 and 1998 in normalized shares on an absolute basis (i.e., column 4 minus column 3, leaving negative signs out). The average gain or loss for each firm over the entire period was 15 percentage points, a marked contrast with the less than 2 percentage point figures for software and CPU chips.

TABLE 4.2

Calculating market-share stability

	U.S. Market Share 1990	U.S. Market Share 1998	Normalized Market Share 1990	Normalized Market Share 1998	Absolute Change
Apple	10.9%	4.6%	29.1%	7.1%	22.1%
Compaq	4.5%	16.7%	12.0%	25.7%	13.6%
Dell	1.0%	13.2%	2.7%	20.3%	17.6%
Gateway	1.0%	8.4%	2.7%	12.9%	10.2%
HP	0.0%	7.8%	0.0%	12.0%	12.0%
IBM	16.1%	8.2%	43.0%	12.6%	30.5%
Packard Bell	3.9%	6.2%	10.4%	9.5%	0.9%
These seven companies combined	37.4%	65.1%	100.0%	100.0%	15.3%

As a first rule of thumb, if you can't count the top firms in an industry on the fingers of one hand, the chances are good that there are no barriers to entry. The rapid change in market share in table 4.2 confirms the rule. As a second rule of thumb, if over a five- to eight-year period, the average absolute share change exceeds 5 percentage points, there are no barriers to entry; if the share change is 2 percentage points or less, the barriers are formidable.

Profitability for firms in this segment has been uneven. Some of the leading companies, especially IBM and Hewlett-Packard, are so diversified that it is difficult to get a good look at how much they earn, and on how much in dedicated assets, within the PC business. Apple, Dell, Compaq, and Gateway, however, do allow a more direct view of discrete PC profitability.

Within a given industry, there are two primary approaches to gauge profitability. One uses income as a percentage of revenue, the other income as a percentage of the resources employed in the business. Net income figures are readily available, but they include items such as interest paid (or earned), taxes paid (or refunded), and extraordinary items like earnings or losses from unconsolidated investments, none of which reflect the actual operations of the business. So our preference is to look at operating income (earnings before interest and taxes, or EBIT), which omits interest, taxes, and some other extraneous charges (or additions).

We should not ignore what the companies report as extraordinary gains or charges, like the writing down of inventory or other assets, because these reflect operating business decisions even though they may accumulate unreported until some event forces an acknowledgment that something significant has occurred. To incorporate these sporadic entries in the income statement, wherever possible we take the average of "extraordinary items" for the current and four prior years, and add or subtract it from operating earnings, labeling the result "adjusted operating earnings." We divide this figure by revenue to produce the "adjusted operating margin."

For the four PC manufacturers on which we can get reasonably relevant numbers, adjusted operating margins for the ten years 1991–2000 averaged 5.8 percent (table 4.3). Net income margins were lower, largely due to taxes, although Apple had some nonoperating income that resulted in the two margin figures being the same.

Dell's operating margins, at 8 percent for the period, were the highest; Apple's, at 2.2 percent, the lowest. Among the undiversified PC makers, there is relatively little dispersion, certainly nothing like the gap between Intel and its smaller competitors. This clustering is itself a sign that there are no strong competitive advantages in the industry. Also, these operating margins are modest. For Intel, the comparable figure for this same period averages almost 32 percent. (See the appendix on methods for measuring returns.)

When we compare the four companies using different ways of measuring returns on resources, several findings stand out (table 4.4). First,

TABLE 4.3

Adjusted operating and net income margins for four PC manufacturers, 1991–2000

	Adjusted Operating Margins	Net Income Margins
Apple	2.2%	2.2%
Compaq	6.5%	3.8%
Dell	8.0%	5.5%
Gateway	6.6%	5.1%
Average	5.8%	4.1%

Dell and Gateway were much more profitable than Apple and Compaq, no matter which measure is chosen. Second, the pretax ROIC for Dell and, to a lesser extent, Gateway are suspiciously high. The explanation for these extraordinary results is that Dell's business model, mimicked by Gateway, requires very little invested capital to support large amounts of revenue and operating income. In Dell's fiscal 1998 (ending February 1, 1998), for example, the company had higher current liabilities than current assets, once surplus cash is excluded (table 4.5). Its build-to-order approach allowed it to run a very tight ship. Its revenue for the year was eight times the value of year-end receivables, fifty-three times the value of year-end inventory, and thirty-six times the value of year-end plant and equipment. Not only did Dell have negative working capital, it had more surplus cash on its balance sheet than the combined total of debt and equity. With negative invested capital, the return calculation is infinite (and only by omitting 1998 were we able to produce any figure for Dell in table 4.4).

Part of the problem is due to the shortcomings of the measurement of assets under standard accounting procedures. Much of Dell's investment is in intangibles—brand recognition, organizational capital, sales relationships, and trained personnel. None of the funds spent on developing these valuable attributes appears on a company's balance sheet, leaving invested capital understated and returns on invested capital sub-

TABLE 4.4

Return on resources measures for four
PC manufacturers, 1991–2000

	Net Income/ Assets (ROA)	Adjusted Operating Income/ Assets (ROA Adjusted)	Net Income/ Equity (ROE)	Adjusted Operating Income/ Invested Capital (ROIC)
Apple	2.6%	3.2%	0.4%	24.5%
Compaq	6.5%	10.9%	10.1%	33.6%
Dell	13.0%	18.6%	34.3%	236.9%
Gateway	15.9%	20.3%	29.3%	71.3%
Average	9.5%	13.2%	18.5%	91.6%

TABLE 4.5

Dell's invested capital, FY 1998 ($ million)

Total assets	$	4,268
Cash and securities	$	1,844
Cash at 1% of revenue	$	123
Surplus cash	$	1,721
Non-interest-bearing current liabilities	$	2,697
Invested capital	$	(150)

stantially overstated. Using returns on sales as a measure of operating efficiency, Dell and Gateway are not that different from Compaq (see table 4.3), and the difference is accounted for largely by Compaq's greater spending on research and development.

Even though the results for Apple and Compaq demonstrate decent returns on invested capital on average, there were years in which they lost money. And Gateway, whose returns for the decade look so strong, lost over a billion dollars in 2001 and $300 million in 2002. Considering all the information, both market share stability and profitability, it seems likely that the PC industry was not protected by barriers to entry during this period and that if any competitive advantages existed, they were minimal. Dell's undeniable success should be attributed to operating efficiency, both the speed with which it assembled and shipped its machines out the door and the brilliant design of a business model that made such efficient use of its assets.

It is difficult to see what the sources of competitive advantage could have been. Customer captivity is low. Both individuals and institutions upgrading their systems shop for the best current tradeoff between features and value. The only exception is among Apple's devoted users, but these have been a dwindling share of the overall market for some time. There is no proprietary technology within the manufacturing segment. Again, except for Apple, all the major manufacturers are buying their components from the same set of suppliers. Economies of scale are also hard to spot, at least historically. Fixed costs have represented a small portion of total production. Manufacturing facilities are widely dispersed, indicating no advantages to large-sized plants.

Given its leadership, Dell may benefit from being able to spread its sales and marketing operations over a larger base, and perhaps it is able to customize machines more cheaply because of its size. But these advantages are not enormous. Even as Dell increased in size, its sales per employee did not continue to grow, nor did its lead over its competitors (figure 4.4).

If any competitive advantages did exist in the past, it is certain that Apple has not been a beneficiary. If competitive advantages emerge in the future, primarily because of economies of scale combined with some customer captivity, the likely winner will be Dell, not Apple. If Dell were to stumble or even fail because of some enormous strategic miscalculation, like being left behind after a revolutionary shift in technology, the chances of Apple being the beneficiary are miniscule. The PC manufacturing segment has not been the driving force in the industry, nor the place where most of the money has been earned. Since Apple has been on the wrong side of competitive advantages in both

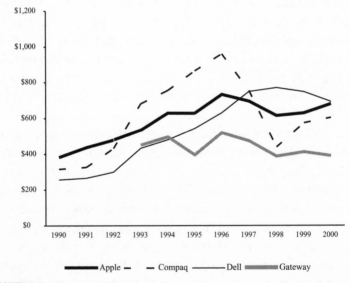

FIGURE 4.4
Sales per employee ($000)

microprocessors and software, it is not realistic to think that it will be redeemed by its role as a manufacturer of boxes.

THE BIG PICTURE FOR APPLE

If Apple does not come out on top in any of the segments that make up the personal computer industry, perhaps it can thrive by making it easy for a user to integrate some crucial parts, not only of the PC industry proper, but of other elements in the digital universe. Apple was an early—premature—entrant into what has become the personal digital assistant (PDA) market, but its Newton was a flop. The handwriting recognition software was not up to the task and became the butt of comic strip jokes. Palm put the PDA business on its feet with its easy-to-use machines in the late 1990s, and when Microsoft produced a scaled-down version of Windows that could be crammed into handhelds, a number of manufacturers came to market with pocket PCs. Neither first-mover advantage nor ease of integration with a Macintosh had been able to lift the Newton.

Apple has been more successful with its portable digital music player, the iPod, praised for its ease of use and elegant design. Apple introduced the iPod in October 2001. Over 1 million units were sold within the first two years, and Apple continued to improve the product, making it more compact and increasing its capacity to hold music. When third-party developers wrote software allowing the iPod to be synchronized with Windows-based PCs, they helped iPod sales even as they undermined the synergistic appeal of the Macintosh-iPod connection. Sparked by the success of the iPod, other companies have introduced competing products, and the final chapters in the story have yet to be written.

Arguments for the advantages of synergy are generally suspect. If a firm in one market has a competitive advantage, it may be able to expand its reach by some well-chosen move into an adjacent area. But if it does not benefit from a competitive advantage in its core business, there is nothing it does that its competitors cannot match. Putting one and one together will not produce three, no matter how many times the magic word *synergy* is invoked. If ever there were an industry, broadly considered, in which this principle applies, it is the digital universe in which Apple works, where piracy—unauthorized duplication—is a constant threat. Apple and its Macintosh have been able to delight their dedicated users with superior design and easier compatibility between different pieces of hardware and software, but synergy on this scale has not provided Apple with enough leverage to overcome the disadvantages it faces by being on the wrong side of the competitive advantages divide in both CPUs and software.

Apple operates in one field—PC manufacturing—where it is arguably on an equal footing with its competition. It has linked this business to its positions in two other industries—CPU chips and software—where it operates at a significant competitive disadvantage. Thanks to these connections, Apple is like a champion swimmer who decides to compete with a large cement block attached to each ankle. No matter how brilliant Steve Jobs is in running the company, the outcome of the race seems inevitable, and Apple does not look like the winner.

In our first pass through the PC industry, we ignored some segments that did not seem central to understanding the competitive landscape. But now a closer look may be warranted to discover whether Apple might benefit from some advantage in one of these other segments.

A CLOSER LOOK AT OTHER COMPONENTS

This segment of the PC industry, we said earlier, has had characteristics much like those of the PC Manufacturing segment: many competitors with none dominant, no discernable competitive advantages, and no benefits to integration. There may be a few exceptions to this generalization. Hewlett-Packard has dominated the printer business for both laser and inkjet printers for some years, with up to half the overall market and even more in the black-and-white laser area. But it is hard to imagine that anyone buys a Hewlett-Packard PC because they want to use the same company's laser printer. Compatibility makes the printers popular, and compatibility eliminates any benefit that owning a printer and PC from the same manufacturer might provide. The same holds true for monitors, disk drives, keyboards, and most of the other peripherals. If some peripheral manufacturers are to thrive, it will be because they have specialized in their markets, run very efficient operations, and perhaps benefited from economies of scale. The idea that Apple may create a competitive advantage by integrating itself with a particular peripheral or component seems unlikely. So this more detailed examination of the component segment does not alter our original conclusions.

A CLOSER LOOK AT APPLICATIONS SOFTWARE

Because of Microsoft's dominance of both the operating system and the office suite markets, we merged the operating systems and applications software segments together in our initial treatment. Since applications software is not confined to word processing, spreadsheets, and presentation programs, the segment is worth a second look. Personal computers are ubiquitous, and the uses to which they are put are almost uncountable. Within that broad world, there is ample room for areas of specialization, niche markets that are sizable enough to attract skilled programmers.

These markets look radically different from the individual component markets. Applications software segments are often dominated by a particular competitor—Intuit in personal and small business accounting and tax preparation, Adobe in various graphics programs, Symantec in security—whose leading market position has been stable for some years. These competitors tend to be highly profitable, with returns closer to those of Microsoft than to the hardware manufacturers. These firms enjoy a significant measure of customer captivity thanks to the time and effort that customers have made in mastering the software, which raises switching costs. Like Microsoft, even though their underlying technology is not proprietary, they benefit from major economies of scale in software development and marketing. Each of these successful niche companies appears to enjoy significant competitive advantages. But only within its niche; no firm is a dominant player in more than one vertical market.

Apple has benefited from such advantages in two applications areas. The first is graphics, broadly considered. The Macintosh has historically been the computer of choice in areas with high visual and multimedia content. In desktop publishing, photography and digital film editing, and other kinds of creative design tasks, Macintosh has maintained a strong position, even as successive Windows versions have come ever closer to matching the Macintosh's intuitive ease of use. Yet the disadvantages of being tied to an idiosyncratic operating system and its own CPU technology have gradually undermined Apple's position in these markets. In the early 1990s, analysts estimated that Apple had captured over 80 percent of the graphics and desktop publishing market. By the early 2000s, that share had fallen to roughly 50 percent.

Apple's other great strength had been in the market for educational software. The Macintosh had the lion's share of the education (K–12) market in the early 1990s, in part because of software, in part because of the effort it put into the education market, in part because of loyalty. But that share eroded because its machines were more expensive, because school districts standardized on the Windows platform, and because educators saw the benefits of educating students on the machines they were more likely to use after they left school. By 2002, the Macintosh's share of the market had fallen to under 30 percent; in 1990, it had been more than twice that. Again, competitive advantages in applications areas were undermined by the disadvantages of being outside the Microsoft-Intel platform of CPUs, operating systems, and hardware.

CONCLUSIONS

These abbreviated treatments of components and applications software are merely suggestive, not definitive. A thorough investigation of these segments would need the same detail as devoted to hardware, software, and CPU chips. We include them to drive home a point about applying strategic analysis. It is always best to begin simply and only add complexity as required. Undue complexity creates an intractable picture of the forces at work. The diagram in figure 4.5 was produced by and for John Sculley and the rest of Apple management in the early 1990s. It was intended to describe the structure of the information industry, but the result was too complicated to be useful. Apple went everywhere and nowhere. For the year ending September 2003, its sales were still down more than 40 percent from 1995 and it earned no operating income. For

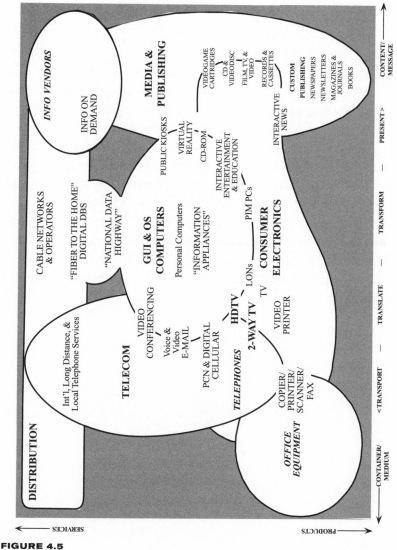

FIGURE 4.5

The Apple vision

all of Steve Jobs's brilliance and the elegance of Apple's product design, it seems consigned to always push uphill against the advantages of Microsoft and Intel. In the PC industry, Apple is going nowhere.

• • •

In the approach we recommend here, the central question is whether, in the market in which the firm operates or is considering entering, competitive advantages exist. If they are present, what are they and who has them? We have described two tests for their existence: stable market shares and a high return on investment for the dominant incumbent firms. To keep the analysis manageable, our advice is to move one step at a time. Begin with one force—potential entrants/barriers to entry—not five. Start simply and add complexity later. Whenever things become confusing, step back and simplify again. Clarity is essential for strategic analysis. Finally, "think local." Whatever historical promise existed in Apple's strategic position lay in the segment of desktop publishing and other graphic-intensive applications. It had virtually no chance in taking on the broad PC industry, and it has no chance of doing so today.

CHAPTER 5

Big Where It Counts

Wal-Mart, Coors, and Local Economies of Scale

WAL-MART: NEW WORLD CHAMPION

In four decades, the Wal-Mart juggernaut rolled out of small towns in Arkansas to become the largest retailer in the world. By any measure, it has been one of the greatest successes in business history. It is also the most compelling example of how a strategy built on a local focus can produce a company that dominates both its original market and neighboring ones into which it expands. Sam Walton and his brother Bud began to build their empire in 1945 as franchisees of the Ben Franklin variety store with a single outlet in Newport, Arkansas. Twenty years later they moved into the discount store field, convinced that rural America could support the same kind of full-line, low-priced stores that had become popular in larger cities. They were correct. When the company went public in 1970, Wal-Mart owned 30 stores, all located in small towns in Arkansas, Missouri, and Oklahoma. At the end of 1985, it had grown to 859 discount stores in twenty-two states. By the year 2000, Wal-Mart sold more merchandise than any other retailer, anywhere. It had over 3,000 stores in the United States and Puerto Rico—no state was without a Wal-Mart—and more than 1,000 stores in eight foreign countries. Its sales of $191 billion were almost twice the combined sales of Kmart, Sears, and JCPenney, other retailing giants.

Wal-Mart's arrival in a new area made existing store owners quake, as well they might. Though zoning laws and other regulations occasionally stalled the company or forced it to adjust its plans, Wal-Mart's thrust was as inexorable as the waves and as futile to resist.

The growth in sales over these thirty years was more than matched by the performance of Wal-Mart's publicly traded shares. Its market value was $36 million in 1971; it was $230 billion in early 2001.* At that level, Wal-Mart was worth fourteen times the combined market value of Sears, Kmart, and JCPenney. The reason is simple: it was more profitable and more reliable. In 2000, not a bad year for the other companies, they reported combined net income of $2.2 billion. Wal-Mart earned $5.4 billion. A year later, when Wal-Mart earned $6.3 billion, the others could muster only $394 million. See figure 5.1.

Wal-Mart managed to combine sustained growth with sustained profitability in one of the most competitive industries in the economy.

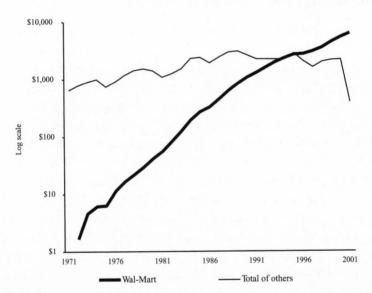

FIGURE 5.1

Net income of Wal-Mart compared with Sears, Kmart, and JCPenney ($ million)

---

* Wal-Mart, like many retailers, has a fiscal year that ends on January 31. All year-end figures here refer to the January year-end.

Each of the three other companies we have used as a benchmark was itself a leading merchant for an extended period, only to be eclipsed by Wal-Mart. When a company has been this successful in this kind of competitive environment, with no patents, government licenses, or years of productive research and development to keep would-be contenders at bay, any student of business strategy wants to identify the sources of its success.

First, we need to confirm the premise. Has Wal-Mart's record been an unalloyed triumph, or have there been blemishes that may have been overlooked? Then we can ask what Wal-Mart did that the other retailers were unable to duplicate, and we may be able to identify strategic choices that Wal-Mart might pursue to maintain and extend its superior performance. Finally, we can ask what Wal-Mart's success says about the possibilities facing other companies.

INDUSTRY ANALYSIS

An analysis of the retail industry in which Wal-Mart operates is straightforward (figure 5.2). Stores sell directly to household consumers. Upstream, Wal-Mart and its competitors are supplied by manufacturers of everything from soft drinks to washing machines, from blouses to lawn mowers. These companies range from the makers of famous national brands like Coca-Cola, to contractors who make private-label products for the retailers, to small local suppliers of nameless merchandise. Wal-Mart sells such a broad range of goods that it competes on some products with virtually every other retailer. Still, the demarcations between industries along the supply chain are distinct; the names do not carry over from one sector to another. Like most other retailers, Wal-Mart does little or no manufacturing.

The number of competitors that Wal-Mart faces within the industry suggests that the perspective we should apply, at least initially, is what we have called "army of the ants," a situation in which competitors are so numerous that none of them tries to anticipate how others will respond to its actions. As Wal-Mart grew and became an elephant among these ants, it did not need to worry about what any of the individual

FIGURE 5.2
Map of the retail industry

ants might do, but they certainly had to be nimble to avoid being squashed.

WAL-MART'S PERFORMANCE: FROM GREAT TO GOOD

We know that Wal-Mart became the giant while some former retailing heavyweights sputtered or disappeared. It must have been doing something right. But what, exactly? How did Wal-Mart grow and prosper, while the others were mediocre at best?

Before we start to answer that question, we should examine in detail Wal-Mart's performance over time. We can do that by looking at two measures of performance: operating margins and return on invested capital. Operating margins (earnings before interest and taxes, divided by net sales) are most revealing when comparing firms within the same industry, because they are likely to have similar requirements for capital. Return on invested capital (how much the company earns on the debt and equity it needs to run its business) is useful as a measure of performance between industries as well as within them. (We are using the pretax return on invested capital.) Both of these ratios are driven by operating profit and so should track one another. If they do not, it is probably a sign that there have been changes in the way the business is financed.

By comparing Wal-Mart with Kmart over the period 1971–2000, we

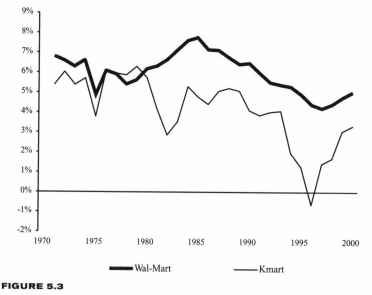

FIGURE 5.3

Wal-Mart and Kmart operating margins 1970–2000

can see that Wal-Mart was indeed the superior business (figure 5.3). Its margins exceeded Kmart's starting in 1980, when it was only about one-tenth the size of its older rival. The return on invested capital has a similar history. Wal-Mart did better than Kmart when it was still the much smaller company, and its performance was continually better from then on (fig. 5.4), with Kmart filing for Chapter 11 in January 2002.

The graph reveal a second pattern, potentially more revealing than the Wal-Mart–Kmart comparison. Wal-Mart's most profitable years, measured by return on sales and on invested capital, ended sometime in the mid 1980s. Its operating margins reached a peak of 7.8 percent in 1985 and then fell continually to a low of 4.2 percent in 1997. Return on invested capital followed suit. The years of truly high returns on investment ended in the early 1990s. After that, Wal-Mart's ROIC eroded, to stabilize in a range from 14 to 20 percent, pretax, respectable but not exceptional. Given this decline, we need to ask not only what set Wal-Mart apart from its competitors, but also what changed in its own operations

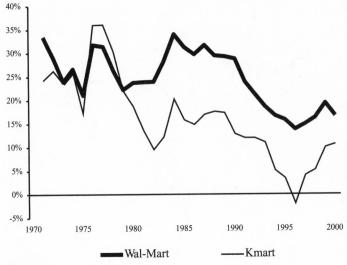

FIGURE 5.4

Wal-Mart and Kmart pretax return on invested capital,
1970–2000

that shifted it from an outstanding company to a less exceptional,
though enormous, one. We start by looking first at Wal-Mart in its
golden years around 1985, when its profitability was at a peak.

Wal-Mart in the 1980s

In these years Wal-Mart was a regional powerhouse. It ended the year
1985 operating 859 discount centers in twenty-two states. More than 80
percent of the stores were located in eleven states radiating from its
Arkansas headquarters. Wal-Mart serviced them from five warehouses;
few of the stores were more than three hundred miles from any distribution center. It used its own trucks to pick up much of the merchandise it purchased and transport the goods to the distributions centers,
from which they were dispersed on other trucks to the stores. The system was efficient. The concentration of stores allowed one truck to
serve several of them on the same trip, and to pick up new merchandise
from vendors while returning to the warehouse.

Wal-Mart's expansion in the ten years to 1985 was aided by the rapid population growth of its region, especially in the smaller towns and cities that were its choice locations. The company was sailing with the wind. But Kmart and other retailers could read demographic statistics. They were determined to share in some of the opportunities that a growing population affords. By 1985, Kmart stores were competing in more than half of Wal-Mart towns. Still, even at that date, one-third of Wal-Mart's stores had no local competition from other major discounters; they captured 10–20 percent of total retail sales in the area, an exceptional share.

In 1976 Wal-Mart had sales of $340 million. Over the prior five years it had grown at a compounded rate of 50 percent per year. In 1981, sales were $1.6 billion, and the growth rate had been 37 percent. For 1986, the comparable figures were $8.4 billion and 39 percent. This is rapid growth, and the decline in the rate after 1976 is hardly surprising, given how large the company had become and how much of its region it had penetrated.

Wal-Mart's executives, molded in the image of legendary founder Sam Walton, were men on a mission. Though they could not overcome the gravitational drag that increased mass puts on the pace of expansion, they tried to grow their firm using one old and one new strategy. The old strategy was geographical extension: spread from the center into adjacent territories, and build new distribution centers to service the stores. This move would take the company eastward into Georgia, Florida, and the Carolinas, and west and north into New Mexico, Nebraska, Iowa, and even Wisconsin.

The new strategy was diversification. Wal-Mart made a minor effort with hardware, drug, and arts and crafts stores, none of which developed into a significant part of its business. The real push came with a warehouse club format, which Wal-Mart called "Sam's Club." The concept did not originate with Wal-Mart, nor was it the only retailer to find the format attractive. A warehouse club store was—and is—very large, it had bare-bones fixtures, it stocked a limited number of items in depth, and it sold its goods for 20 percent less than supermarkets and discounters. To be profitable, the store needed to sell its merchandise very quickly, even before the bill was due. Only metropolitan areas with at least 400,000 people, of which there were around one hundred in the country, could support that kind of turnover. As early as 1985, warehouse stores began to compete with one another in these choice locations. Wal-Mart had twenty-three of them by the end of 1985, and had leased real estate to open seventeen more in 1986. Because the Sam's Club financial results were not broken out in Wal-Mart's statements, it was difficult to tell how profitable they were.

From Net Sales to Operating Income

During these years, Wal-Mart generated more income for each dollar of sales than did its competitors. To find out exactly where its advantages lay, we should compare in detail the financial results of Wal-Mart with those of other discounters. Though the entries on the income statement are the consequences, not the cause, of the differences in operations, they tell us where to look for explanations of Wal-Mart's superior performance.

Let's begin with a side-by-side look at Wal-Mart and Kmart (table 5.1). For the three years ending January 31, 1987, Wal-Mart had average operating margins of 7.4 percent; Kmart's were 4.8 percent. The difference was due entirely to much lower overhead costs. As a percentage of sales, Kmart had a lower cost of goods sold, largely because its prices were higher than Wal-Mart's. But it dissipated this advantage by spending more, per dollar of sales, on selling, general, and administrative expenses (SGA).

A report on the discount retailing industry in 1984 gives us a more precise look at the components of operating costs and helps pinpoint Wal-Mart's advantages (table 5.2). Since Wal-Mart itself was included in the industry totals, the differences between it and the other firms are understated. Still, the pattern here is similar to the comparison with Kmart. As a percentage of sales, Wal-Mart paid more to buy and receive its merchandise than did the competition, again because it offered consumers lower prices. The other retailers brought in more revenue from licensed departments. Yet Wal-Mart ended up with higher operating profits thanks to its lower costs for all the activities that make up selling, general, and administrative expenses. Compared to the others, it ran a very tight ship.

TABLE 5.1

Average operating margins, 1985–87 (percentage of sales)

	Kmart	Wal-Mart	Wal-Mart's Difference
Net sales	100.0%	100.0%	0.0%
Cost of goods sold	70.5%	74.3%	3.8% higher
SGA total	24.7%	18.3%	6.4% lower
Operating income	4.8%	7.4%	2.6% higher

What accounts for this thrift? Can we attribute it to great management and a disciplined corporate culture? Was it simply the lower costs of doing business outside of major metropolitan areas and largely in the American South? Or should we look at more structural economic factors that may be less subject to managerial control?

If the answer is management and corporate culture, then there is nothing that inhibits Wal-Mart from replicating its success anywhere, and from extending it beyond the discount center format into a number of other similar businesses. If it is the cost differentials of small-town and southern locations, then Wal-Mart should forget about moving into other parts of the country and limit its growth to filling in its historical region. If, on the other hand, the explanation lies in some structural economic factors that give Wal-Mart its competitive advantage, it ought to understand exactly what those are and design an expansion strategy that

TABLE 5.2

Industry-wide comparisons, 1984 (percentage of sales)

	Industry	Wal-Mart	Wal-Mart's Difference
Net sales	100.0%	100.0%	
License fees and other income	1.1%	0.8%	0.3% lower
Cost of goods sold	71.9%	73.7%	1.8% higher
Payroll expenses	11.2%	10.1%	1.1% lower
Advertising expenses	2.3%	1.1%	1.2% lower
Rental expenses	2.2%	1.9%	0.3% lower
Miscellaneous expenses	7.6%	5.3%	2.3% lower
SGA total	23.3%	18.4%	4.9% lower
Operating income	5.9%	8.7%	2.8% higher

targets regions and retailing formats where those advantages can be reproduced. And its competitors, current or potential, or anyone in a business with similar characteristics, should clearly do the same thing.

AN ABUNDANCE OF EXPLANATIONS

No company with a history like Wal-Mart's escapes attention. Over the years, a number of explanations have been offered to account for its success. Some are clearly mistaken, some are more plausible but don't hold up under examination, and one dominates the others. We will look at some of the most reasonable.

Explanation 1: Beat Up on the Vendors

Wal-Mart has had a reputation for using its muscle as a very big customer to wrest price concessions from its suppliers. A lower cost of goods might translate into higher profit margins. But we have already seen that Wal-Mart had a higher cost of goods sold than its competitors, so we should be skeptical about this explanation. Also, Wal-Mart's gross profit margins did not increase as it grew larger. They were at their peak, at 28.3 percent, in 1983, and fell more or less steadily to rest under 22 percent in the mid 1990s. So the bully factor does not seem to have been at work.

The amount a retailer spends on purchasing merchandise is the major part of the cost of goods sold figure, but there are other expenses that are also included (table 5.3). One is the cost of getting the goods from the vendor to the company's stores or warehouses, known as "freight in" or "inbound logistics." The fact is that Wal-Mart was more efficient in this area than its competitors; it spent 2.8 percent of sales versus an industry average of 4.1 percent. It also lost less to "shrinkage," a catch-all expression to account for items that get lost, broken, or pilfered. The industry average was 2.2 percent against 1.3 percent for Wal-Mart. When we incorporate these components into our analysis of cost of goods sold, they reveal that Wal-Mart was spending even more on merchandise, as a percentage of sales, than the industry norms.

That Wal-Mart paid more for purchases as a percentage of sales does

TABLE 5.3

Cost of goods sold comparison (percentage of sales)

	Industry	Wal-Mart	Wal-Mart's difference
Cost of goods sold	71.9%	73.7%	1.8% higher
Inbound logistics	4.1%	2.8%	1.3% lower
Shrinkage	2.2%	1.3%	0.9% lower
Purchases	65.6%	69.6%	4.0% higher

not entirely invalidate the argument that Wal-Mart used its bargaining power to extract lower prices from its suppliers. But if it indeed had the power to extract concessions, it passed those savings and more on to its own customers. Given the variety of pricing in different markets, it is impossible to offer a solid figure on how much less, overall, Wal-Mart charged relative to the other discount chains. When it went head-to-head with Kmart or Target, its prices may have been 1–2 percent lower. When the stores were spaced at least five miles away, the differences were larger, around 8–10 percent. With two-thirds of Wal-Mart's stores in competitive markets, an overall pricing difference of around 4–5 percent seems reasonable. That figure happens to be very close to our estimate of how much more Wal-Mart paid for its purchases, as a percentage of sales. If we make the realistic assumption that Wal-Mart paid the same, per item, as its major competitors, then its pricing strategy accounts for its higher cost of goods sold figure. So lower prices from suppliers were not a source of greater profit margins. Also, the fact that its costs of good sold went up even as Wal-Mart doubled in size every few years, and that early in this process, Kmart and other stores should have had much more clout with suppliers, undermines this argument.

Finally, it is not plausible to argue that Wal-Mart could muscle Coca-Cola or Procter & Gamble into giving better pricing to it than other retailers. Imagine the soda buyer threatening to drop Coca-Cola unless Wal-Mart got a larger discount than its competitors. When Coke turns him down, how much leverage does he have left with Pepsi? With smaller, more regionally based suppliers, Wal-Mart probably did have bargaining power, and might have squeezed concessions from these vendors. But so could Kmart and the others. The "bargaining with the suppliers" explanation for Wal-Mart's superior profitability doesn't stand up.

Explanation 2: Small-Town Monopolist

Did Wal-Mart owe its success to the fact that in many of its locations, it was the only store in town? Did it make these customers pay higher prices and boost its earnings with these monopoly proceeds? To address this question, we ought to look at the company's pricing strategy and see how it differed from that of its competitors.

From its beginning as a discount retailer, Wal-Mart prided itself on its low prices. All its discount stores proclaimed its slogan, "We Sell for Less." And so it did, especially in towns where it competed directly against Kmart, Target, and other discounters. A 1984 survey found that in the Dallas–Fort Worth market, where the stores were separated by five miles or so, Wal-Mart's prices were 10 percent less than Kmart's, and 7–8 percent lower than Target's. In a St. Louis suburb, the difference with an adjacent Kmart was 1.3 percent. But in those towns where it had the field to itself, Wal-Mart was less generous with its customers. It charged 6 percent more in Franklin, Tennessee, than it did in Nashville, where a Kmart offered shoppers an alternative. Kmart's differential between the towns in which it competed and those it had to itself was even greater, around 9 percent. But while Kmart and the other discounters operating in Wal-Mart country had around 12 percent of their stores in single-store towns, Wal-Mart had 33 percent. See table 5.4.

If we put all these differences together, it becomes clear Wal-Mart did milk some income out of the higher prices it charged in its monopolized towns. The overall differences with Kmart added around 0.9 percent to Wal-Mart's operating margin advantage. This was around one-third of its total operating margin advantage of 2.8 percent (see table 5.2). It is part of the explanation, but far from the whole. Moreover, as we noted earlier, Wal-Mart's average prices were 4–5 percent below those of its competitors. The extra 1 percent margin Wal-Mart extracted from one-store towns accounts for only a fraction of this gap. On balance, the one-store-town advantages were more than offset by Wal-Mart's "everyday

TABLE 5.4

Benefits of monopoly

	Kmart	Wal-Mart	Wal-Mart's Difference
Extra margin company charged in single-store towns	9.0%	6.0%	
Percentage of company's stores in single-store towns	12.0%	33.0%	
Total margin increase from single-store towns	1.1%	2.0%	0.9% higher

low price" policy. They do not explain Wal-Mart's overall superiority in performance.

Explanation 3: Better Management, Better Systems

Wal-Mart has had a well-deserved reputation for excellent management. It was an early adopter of technologies like bar-code scanning, a major productivity tool. Using scanners reduced the lines at checkout counters while helping to control inventory and automate the reordering process. The heavy capital investment of $500,000 per store did not stop Wal-Mart from moving quickly to install these machines in new stores and fitting them into existing ones. Investments like this had helped to lower the cost of labor, both salary and wages, from 11.5 percent in the late 1970s to 10.1 percent in 1985.

But electronic scanning was an industry-wide technology. Kmart moved almost as rapidly to introduce scanners, and also planned to have them throughout its stores by 1989. Target and the other discounters used the machines. So whatever benefits Wal-Mart achieved from its investments here did not account for its advantages over its competitors. The same was true of other sophisticated systems it introduced, like software to plan the merchandise mix in each store or machinery to automate warehouse operations. Wal-Mart was a purchaser of these technologies, not a developer of them. Anything it bought, its rivals could buy as well. Its progressive stance may have given it some short-term leads over the others, but they may have benefited by hiring the same consultants to do the installations, who now had Wal-Mart's experience, including the inevitable mistakes, on which to draw.

In the area of human resources management, Wal-Mart did have a claim to superiority. Its executives spent much of their time in the stores. They solicited the opinions of employees—called associates, to reflect the "we're all on the same team" philosophy of the company—on what goods to carry and how to display them. It had incentive programs that rewarded store managers for exceeding profit targets, and it lowered the rate of pilferage and shoplifting by sharing any reductions with the employees. The employees responded by endorsing Wal-Mart as a good place to work, despite salaries that were modest, even by the standards of the industry. Part of Wal-Mart's lower payroll expenses was probably attributable to these good human resource practices.

So while it is unwise to ignore the importance of better management in accounting for Wal-Mart's success, we should not make too much of it. Did management deteriorate after the golden days of the mid 1980s, or did its tasks become more difficult? Why did their management techniques not work when applied to hardware, drug, and arts and crafts stores? And Sam's Club stores, although they have multiplied in number, have not produced the same stellar results as the traditional discount centers. When Wal-Mart began to report financial information by segment, in the mid 1990s, Sam's Clubs were considerably less profitable. They earned about 45 percent less per dollar of assets allocated to them than did the discount centers. And this was after fifteen years of experience with this format, time enough to work out the kinks.

Explanation 4: Things Are Cheaper in the South

Wal-Mart had lower rental (by 0.3 percent of sales) and payroll expenses (by 1.1 percent of sales) than the industry averages. Part of these advantages may have been due to its concentration in the South, and in the smaller towns and cities of that region. Real estate was cheaper to develop and property taxes were lower there. None of Wal-Mart's workers was represented by a union, also a Southern characteristic. The savings on these two items represented 1.4 percent of sales, a hefty portion of Wal-Mart's total advantage of 4.9 percent for all SGA expenses. On the other hand, prices as well as costs tended to be lower in the South.

It is impossible to refine the analysis enough to say how much was due to the southern factor. Clearly location had something to do with these differences. But so did good management, as we have seen. The problem for Wal-Mart, circa 1986, was that opportunities for expansion in this lower-cost part of the country were limited. It had already begun to move into larger towns and cities. After 1986, much of its growth was in states far removed from its southern roots. By 2001, California, Ohio, Pennsylvania, Indiana, New York, and Wisconsin accounted for six of the top eleven states measured by the number of discount stores and supercenters.

Explanation 5: The Potent Advantages of Regional Dominance

Wal-Mart did have geography working for it, the geography of market concentration. We have seen that in 1985, more than 80 percent of its stores were in Arkansas, adjacent states, or their immediate neighbors. Though much smaller than Kmart overall, it was far larger in its home territory. Kmart had its own area of concentration in the Midwest, but any benefits it might have derived from this regional strength were diluted by its lower density in other parts of the country. Wal-Mart, by contrast, was able to make the most of its strategy of concentration, which accounts for most of its superior profitability.

Wal-Mart enjoyed a competitive advantage in this period, based largely on the combination of economies of scale with some limited customer captivity. Both the economies and the captivity are regional, not national or global. For retailing, distribution, and other industries in which most of the costs of reaching the final consumers are at the local and regional levels, these are the economies and preferences that matter.

The lower costs derived from Wal-Mart's concentration strategy came primarily from three functions of the business. First, it spent less on inbound logistics, the costs of bringing goods into its warehouses and sending them on to the discount centers. We have described Wal-Mart's system of locating warehouses to supply stores within a three-hundred-mile radius and of using its own trucks to pick up merchandise from vendors who had placed their own distribution centers in the region to serve Wal-Mart. The density of Wal-Mart stores, as well as their proximity to a distribution center, reduced the distances its trucks had to travel and allowed them to carry goods on both routes, from vendors to distribution centers and from the centers to the stores. Wal-Mart's advantage in this area, over the industry average (which included Wal-Mart's results and thus reduced the difference), was 1.3 percent of sales.*

Second, Wal-Mart's advertising expenses were lower than the average, by 1.2 percent of sales, corresponding to a relative cost advantage of over 60 percent. For retailers, advertising is local. The newspaper ads, the inserts and circulars, and the television spots were all targeted at potential customers for the stores in their vicinity. If we make the reasonable assumption that Wal-Mart and the other discounters did roughly the same amount of advertising, measured by frequency of newspapers ads, television spots, and circulars, then Wal-Mart's lower costs as a percentage of sales were due to the greater density of its stores and its customer base in the markets in which it did advertise. The television station running a thirty-second spot in Nashville charges the same whether there are three Wal-Mart stores in the area or thirty. The same arithmetic holds true for newspaper ads or circulars sent to all residents in the vicinity. The media sell their services on the basis of cost per thousand people reached. For a retailer, the more relevant number is cost per customer, or potential customer, and that depends on penetration in the market. Since Wal-Mart had almost three times the level of local sales of its competitors, its advertising cost per dollar of sales would have been one-third that of the competitors. The same strategy of concentration that served Wal-Mart well by keeping down its inbound logistics costs also worked to contain advertising expenses. It got more bang for its buck because its advertising targeted its customers more effectively than did its competitors'.

The final function in which Wal-Mart had a cost advantage over competitors was managerial oversight and supervision. From the start, Sam Walton and his executives paid close and continual attention to the stores with frequent visits. By 1985, the company employed twelve area vice presidents; each had seven or eight district managers reporting to them. The vice presidents lived near company headquarters in Bentonville, Arkansas, where they attended meetings every Friday and Sat-

---

* Wal-Mart's inbound logistics were 2.8 percent of sales, while the industry average was 4.1 percent. This amounts to a relative cost advantage of over 30 percent (2.8 percent divided by 4.1 percent), compared to store and labor cost advantages of 10–15 percent.

urday to review results and plan for the next week. Every Monday morning, all the vice presidents flew into their respective territories, where they worked the next four days visiting the stores for which they were responsible. The system functioned well for Wal-Mart. It provided abundant communication between the center and the periphery. The concentrated territories meant that the managers had more time to spend in the stores rather than driving between them. The flow of information moved in both directions. Company policy ensured that the store managers and employees even further down the chain of command could make their views and ideas known to management.

The system depended on the density of Wal-Mart stores and their proximity to Bentonville. To supervise the same number of outlets, a Kmart or Target executive had to cover a territory three or four times as large. They could not visit their stores so frequently or spend as much time when they were there. They had to live in the area and needed support from a regional office. The additional expense may have consumed 2 percent of net sales, an enormous bite when operating profits were only around 6 percent. The difference between Wal-Mart and the others (found on the "Miscellaneous expenses" line of table 5.2) is about 30 percent (2.3 percent divided by 7.6 percent), again a strikingly large relative cost advantage. Wal-Mart was able to do more with less, the often stated but seldom realized goal of managers everywhere.

The superior efficiencies Wal-Mart achieved in these three functions—inbound logistics, advertising, and executive supervision—taken together, gave the company an operating margin advantage of 4–5 percent of net sales. Wal-Mart's total advantage was only around 3 percent. Because the lower prices it charged pushed up Wal-Mart's purchases, in percentage terms, various operating savings could account for more than the entire difference in margins.

The superior efficiencies in these three functions were due to *local economies of scale*. The relevant localities are the areas in which Wal-Mart and its competitors had their stores, their warehouses, their advertising campaigns, and their managers. It made no difference that Kmart's total sales were three times those of Wal-Mart in these years (1984–85). Those were numbers national and international, and thus not relevant. They had little bearing on the physical movement of goods, on advertising designed to reach the customers who shopped in their stores, or on the supervision the company employed to manage its retail operations. For each of these, what mattered in achieving economies of scale were the number of stores and customers within the relevant boundaries. Measured in this way, Wal-Mart was bigger than its competitors. It had more stores and customers in its region than they did, without doubt, and it had a higher density of stores and customers in its region than its competitors had in theirs. So even when it was still relatively small, high geographic concentration meant high profitability for Wal-Mart.

RETAILING, CUSTOMERS, AND ECONOMIES OF SCALE

In our discussion of the competitive advantage of economies of scale, we noted that two conditions have to hold in order for a company to reap benefits from these economies. First, the fixed costs it incurs must account for a large share of total costs, with the measure of "large" related to the size of the market in which the company operates. These fixed costs can be capital investments like plant, equipment, or information technology. They can be operating expenses like advertising or managerial supervision. As these fixed costs are spread over more sales, average costs continue to decline. The company selling the most is ahead of the game.

But if the market is sufficiently big, the share of fixed costs in each unit can become so small that the average costs stop declining. Then other companies, although their sales do not equal those of the largest firm, can come close to matching its average cost, and the advantage dissipates. Clearly, economies of scale persist only so long as the decline in fixed costs for the last unit sold is still significant. In bigger total markets, there are fewer relative economies of scale. In this sense, growth may be the enemy of profitability.

Second, the competitive advantage of economies of scale has to be combined with some customer captivity in order to keep competitors at bay. Kmart could have duplicated Wal-Mart's retailing infrastructure—its stores, distribution centers, and management—within Wal-Mart's home territory, but it would not have achieved the same economies of scale unless it attracted an equivalent number of customers. That required taking customers away from Wal-Mart. Not an easy task, provided that Wal-Mart had not undermined its customers' loyalty with shoddy service, high prices, or other bad practices. Otherwise, customers had no reason to switch to Kmart, everything else being equal. If Kmart tried to compete on price by cutting its margins to the bone, or even into the bone, Wal-Mart would match the reductions. Given the larger share of customers with which it started, its costs would be lower and its pain more manageable. More advertising, in-store promotions, 0 percent interest charges on its own credit cards—any competitive move Kmart might devise, Wal-Mart could match, and at lower cost. Unless it decided on a scorched-earth strategy of winning market share no matter what damage it might inflict on itself, in the hope that Wal-Mart would blink and cede customers before Kmart was permanently crippled, there was nothing Kmart could do that would make it the equal of Wal-Mart within the region.

WHAT DID HAPPEN?

What happened is clear. Wal-Mart continued to grow after 1985 until it became the largest retailer on earth, the company feared and admired by firms around the world. But it also became considerably less profitable, measured by return on invested capital or the operating margins it earned on its revenue. The only explanation we find convincing to account for the shrinking returns is that, as it expanded across the country and overseas, it was unable to replicate the most significant competitive advantage it enjoyed in these early years: local economies of scale combined with enough customer loyalty to make it difficult for competitors to cut into this base.

When it moved into California and the rest of the Pacific Coast, it had to compete directly with Target, another successful discounter with an established presence in the area. In the Midwest, Kmart was strong. In the Northeast, Caldor had a number of stores, and although it ultimately disappeared, that was a consequence of its own expansion strategy. At best, Wal-Mart had to compete on a level playing field when it moved beyond its home region; at worst, it was the player against whom the field was slanted.

From the start, Wal-Mart has had excellent management, certainly better than Kmart, Sears, and JCPenney, other giants during this era, and better by far than Caldor, Ames, E. J. Korvette, W.T. Grant, Bradlees, and other one-time successes that have vanished. The executives adopted and implemented new technology; they spent much of their time in the stores, listening to employees and customers; they kept overhead costs low; they rarely needed to take "special charges" on their income statements, which are a sign of prior mistakes growing too large to ignore. But management of this quality, sustained over four decades, could not keep margins or return on capital at the levels they reached during the mid 1980s. They did not earn exceptional returns on Sam's Clubs, the least geographically concentrated of the wholesale club chains, or the other diversification efforts. By the late 1990s, Wal-Mart's margins and return on capital were no better than those of Target, another successful discount merchant with one strong region of its own.

The pattern of Wal-Mart's returns both over time and across market segments tends to confirm this story. As Wal-Mart began its aggressive national expansion in the mid 1980s, returns on sales and on capital declined steadily. By the mid 1990s, when Wal-Mart was a national institution, but with less regional concentration than it had had in its golden days, returns bottomed out at around 15 percent on invested capital. Then, as Wal-Mart added density by filling in the gaps, returns began to recover. The exception to this pattern was the international division, where Wal-Mart was widely dispersed across many countries. As we would expect, international returns on sales and capital appear to have been only about one-half to one-third those of the core U.S. supercenter business.

What might Wal-Mart have done in 1985 to maintain the high level of profitability and still grow its business? Probably not much. At the time, product line diversifications held little promise, although Wal-Mart has since been successful in adding groceries. As to geographic expansion, it would have had a difficult task finding a territory that had the same important features as its Arkansas-centered stronghold. The small-town and rural demography were not directly significant; Wal-Mart and Target drew customers in metropolitan areas. What did matter was the absence of established competitors. These companies had overlooked Arkansas and the region because they did not think it could support large discount stores. They did not overlook the West Coast, the Southeast, or New England, making those regions less hospitable for Wal-Mart. If it had wanted to replicate its early experience, Wal-Mart might have targeted a foreign country that was in the process of economic development but that had not yet attracted much attention from established retailers. Perhaps Brazil in the 1980s, or South Korea, would have fit the bill, provided there were not insurmountable obstacles designed to protect local interests. But in the absence of the right virgin territory, Wal-Mart seemed consigned to a "growth at a price" strategy, the price in this case being the lower returns it earned from its new investments. We should not exaggerate the decline. Wal-Mart's return on investment has remained competitive. If it did not create enormous value for its investors, at least it did not destroy wealth by operating at a competitive disadvantage.

THE STRATEGIC DIMENSION AND LOCAL DOMINANCE

A summary look at the special qualities of Wal-Mart during its most profitable period allows us to compare the significance of the different attributes that made for success (table 5.5).

There are several lessons to draw from this review:

1. *Efficiency always matters.* Good management kept payroll costs and shrinkage substantially below the industry averages.
2. *Competitive advantages, in this case local economies of scale coupled with customer captivity, matter more.* Good management could not make Sam's Clubs a runaway success, nor could it prevent the deterioration of Wal-Mart's profitability after 1985, nor assure success in international markets.
3. *Competitive advantages can enhance good management.* In this case, Wal-Mart utilized its advantage of local economies of scale by passing on a portion of its savings to its customers and by running a very tight

TABLE 5.5

Summary of Wal-Mart's cost advantages
(as a percentage of sales)

Attribute	Income Statement Entry	Industry Average	Wal-Mart	Wal-Mart's Difference
Lower prices with embedded local monopolies	Purchase costs	65.6%	69.6%	4.0% higher
Better management	Payroll costs, shrinkage	13.4%	11.4%	2.0% lower
Local economies of scale with customer preference	Distribution, advertising, other management	14.0%	9.2%	4.8% lower
Total advantage				2.8% lower

ship. It made efficient use of management's time, the scarcest of all company resources. Good management was welded to a good strategy.

4. *Competitive advantages need to be defended.* Wal-Mart's low-price approach was an intrinsic part of the local economies of scale strategy, and not a separate policy choice. Other discounters like Kmart, Caldor, and Korvette all had profitable periods during which they took advantage of their local economies of scale. But in their drive to expand beyond their home turf, itself an ill-chosen strategy, they let competitors move uncontested into their local areas and lost on two fronts.

The significance of the Wal-Mart example is due to more than its size and prominence. What appears to have been true for Wal-Mart—that the crucial competitive advantage lies in local economies of scale— applies to retail industries in general. Supermarket profitability tracks closely with local market share. Successful chains like Kroger tend to be geographically concentrated. In drugstores, Walgreen's—the Wal-Mart of that industry—has had a highly focused geographic strategy, and its returns appear to have fallen when it has relaxed that discipline. In home furnishings, even single-store operations, like Nebraska Furniture Mart, that dominate local areas are economic standouts.

The importance of geographic concentration applies beyond pure retail into services, at least to the extent that they are locally supplied. Regional banks tend to be more profitable than national ones. HMOs like Oxford Health, with strong regional positions, outperform larger competitors with customers and providers dispersed nationally. In telecommunications, locally focused competitors in both landline and wireless, like Verizon, Bell South, and Cingular, have outperformed national competitors with more dispersed customer bases like AT&T, Sprint, MCI, and Nextel. If services are the wave of the future in economic evolution, then firms would do well to make geographical dominance a key component of their strategy.

COORS GOES NATIONAL

In 1975, the year in which it became a public company, the Adolph Coors Company of Golden, Colorado, was near the top of its game. It earned almost $60 million on sales of $520 million, a margin in excess of 11 percent. By comparison, that was more than twice the net income margin of Anheuser-Busch (AB), which earned $85 million on sales of $1.65 billion. Unlike AB, which served a national market from ten breweries spread across the country, Coors operated one enormous brewery from which it sold its beer in Colorado and ten neighboring states. But the beer industry was evolving, and Coors decided to change with the times. Motivated in part by a ruling from the Federal Trade Commission, which charged it with restricting distribution, Coors began a geographical expansion that brought it into forty-four states by 1985. That strategy was not a success.

Coors did many things differently from the other large brewing companies. It ran a more integrated enterprise than its competitors. It made its own cans, grew its own grain, used water from its own sources, and generated electricity from its own coal. Its labor force was not unionized, and it put heavy emphasis on operating control and efficiency at its single, mammoth brewery. The beer that it canned and bottled was unpasteurized, intended to give it a fresher, draftlike quality taste. Some of these features contributed to a mystique that enticed celebrities like Paul Newman and Henry Kissinger to drink Coors despite the extra effort they needed, as easterners, to get their hands on the beer. What marketing director would not pray for endorsements like this?

Coors was different; that much seems certain. But did these differences make Coors better, not as a drink but as a business? And if they worked when Coors was a regional brewer in 1975, would they continue to provide Coors with advantages as it moved into a national market?

From the vantage point of 1985, the answer to the second question is clear. Coors's sales more than doubled during the period; its earnings, on the other hand, did not keep pace. They were lower in 1985 than they had been in 1975, and its net income margin had fallen to around 4 percent. During this same period, AB's position relative to Coors improved dramatically. Its sales increased more than fourfold, and its net income margin expanded from 5 percent to 6 percent. And 1985 was not an aberration. Coors has never been able to recover its competitive position. In 2000, it earned $123 million on sales of $2.4 billion, a 5 percent return. AB's profits of $1.5 billion were more than 12 percent of its much larger revenue.

What went wrong? What happened to Coors's operating efficiencies, its labor cost advantages? What about its mystique and its marketing expertise? Did they disappear as the company expanded, or had they been less significant contributors to its profits than everyone, including the company, had assumed? And did Coors have an alternative? Could it have maintained its high level of profitability by keeping its regional concentration, or would the forces of consolidation that rolled through the beer industry have reduced it to a small and inconsequential player, if it survived at all?

THE TASTE FOR BEER

In the forty years between 1945 and 1985, total beer consumption in the United States rose from 77 to 183 million barrels, a rate of slightly more than 3 percent per year. Population growth at around 2.5 annually percent accounts for most of the increase. This modest rate suggests an intense competitive environment for brewers, not quite a constant-sum situation but close enough to make one player's gain someone else's loss.

The organization of the brewing industry changed dramatically in the forty years from 1945 to 1985, with consolidation the dominant feature. In 1950, the top four companies as a group had around 20 percent of the market. In 1985, they controlled around 70 percent. Most of the other movements were related to consolidation:

- *Home consumption.* At the end of World War II, kegs accounted for more than one-third of all beer sales. By 1985, that figure had fallen to 13 percent of the total. Bottled beer and especially beer in cans had become much more popular. Part of this move reflected a decline in the tavern trade, as Americans left the bar stool for the domestic comfort of the den. Coincident with this change, the many local breweries that had emerged after the end of Prohibition were increasingly pushed aside by regional and national firms. It was the local beer makers who sold more of their output in kegs, without pasteurization, to bars and restaurants. As that part of the market declined, so did the fortune of the locals. Many names disappeared entirely; others were bought and sustained for a time by survivors.

- *Bigger plants.* Advances in packaging technology raised the size of an efficient integrated plant (brewing and packaging) from 100,000 barrels per year in 1950 to 5 million in 1985. The smaller brewers could not justify building plants of this size, and so lost out to their large competitors, especially AB and Miller, who built ever larger plants, and more of them. By 1985, AB had eleven breweries, each of them able to brew at least 4.5 million barrels annually.

- *More advertising.* In the struggle for share of the beer market, the brewers increased their spending on advertising. It rose from $50 million in 1945, or 2.6 percent of gross sales, to $1.2 billion in 1985, a whopping 10 percent of sales. Television, which barely existed in 1945, gave the brewers a new place to sink their advertising dollars. They took advantage of the medium and competed lustily to promote the advantage of their particular brand. The advertising had little sustainable effect in winning customers, though it was popular with viewers and with the networks. And it gave the national brewers one more advantage over the locals, in that the fixed advertising costs were spread over a larger revenue base.

- *More brands.* In 1975 Miller introduced its Lite brand, lower in alcohol and calories than its premium High Life beer. Before long all the other major breweries had their versions, and some also came out with superpremium or other variants of the flagship brand. Though the segmentation strategy did little to increase overall consumption, it did provide one more advantage to the big brewers over their small, local, and increasingly marginal competitors. The big players could afford the advertising costs of launching and maintaining the brand, and they had more powerful names to exploit.

There were only two big winners in the consolidation process, Anheuser-Busch and Miller. In 1965 Miller's share of the industry was an insignificant 3 percent. Twenty years later, with the brewer now run by the marketing geniuses at Philip Morris, it had lifted that portion to 20 percent. AB, the largest firm in 1965 with around 12 percent of the market, controlled 37 percent in 1985. The rest of the beer makers had either disappeared altogether or played musical chairs with what was left.

THE COORS DIFFERENCES

During this period of consolidation, Coors's share of the market remained stable at around 8 percent. It maintained its position despite—or perhaps because of—an approach to the business that set it apart from all the other brewers. When it went national after 1977, Coors counted on many of these differences to secure its success in the anticipated beer wars. First, Coors was vertically integrated to a staggering degree. It had its own strain of barley grown for it by farmers under contract and it processed for itself a large portion of the other grains that went into the beer. It designed an all-aluminum can, which it purchased from a captive manufacturer. In 1977, it bought its bottle supplier. It built much of its brewing and bottling equipment. Its much heralded "Rocky Mountain spring water," which, it claimed, gave its beer superior drinking properties, came from land the company controlled. It developed its own coal-field to supply its energy requirements.

This vertical integration may have been symptomatic of a frontier preference for self-reliance. It did not produce a permanent cost advantage. In 1977, Coors's production costs were $29 per barrel, compared with $36.60 for AB. By 1985, Coors cost had risen to $49.50. AB, still not integrated, spent $51.80, not a major difference. In retrospect, it is difficult to imagine that any of these functions gave Coors a competitive advantage over the other brewers. In areas like packaging equipment, cans and bottles, and energy sources, Coors probably operated at a disadvantage, its smaller size allowing others to benefit from economies of scale. Also, the attention of its managers, responsible for all these functions, was spread thin.

Second, Coors operated only one brewery, with an annual capacity that it had expanded from 7 million barrels in 1970 to 13 million in 1975 and finally to 16 million in 1985. This giant plant had the potential for scale economies, at least in theory. Yet with the efficient brewery size at around 5 million, it is unlikely that Coors reaped many economies of scale advantages from its behemoth that were not available to the other brewers. And its relative production cost figures confirm that whatever scale advantages existed in theory did not materialize. Also, beer is heavy (even when it is Lite). The cost of transportation from one location, which was not a problem when Coors was a regional firm, increased as Coors's distribution territory expanded. AB, with eleven breweries around the country, had shorter distances to travel and lower distributions costs.

Third, unlike the other major brewers, Coors did not pasteurize even the beer it canned and bottled. It claimed that by selling only "draft" beer, it provided its devotees with a fresher-tasting drink. It also saved some money on the energy needed for pasteurization, although that was balanced by the costs of keeping the beer cold and the facility sterile. Coors's nonpasteurization strategy mandated that it keep a tighter control over its beer as it passed from the brewery through the distribution channel to the consumer. Whatever the taste advantages, bottles and cans of Coors had a shorter shelf life than those of its rivals, and they had to be kept chilled, at least until they left the wholesalers' warehouses. These requirements added to its costs.

Finally, there was in the 1970s a mystique about Coors that set it apart from its competitors. Perhaps it was the Rocky Mountain water, perhaps the absence of pasteurization, perhaps the difficulty of getting the beer on the East Coast. For whatever reason, A-list people like Henry Kissinger, President Gerald Ford, and actors Paul Newman and Clint Eastwood made Coors their beer of choice and took pains (or had pains taken) to keep a supply on hand. Their preference for the beer overcame whatever aversion Newman, at least, may have had for Coors's antiunion labor practices. What makes Coors's aura all the more impressive is that there is so little to distinguish its taste from those of Budweiser, Miller High Life, or even some of the lower-priced local brands. The aura did not encourage or allow Coors to charge more. It collected $41.50 per barrel in 1977; AB took in $46. And AB was still getting slightly more in 1985.

DISTRIBUTION WIDENS, PROFITS SHRINK

By 1985, beer drinkers could buy Coors in forty-four states. Broadening its geographical reach was expensive. All the beer still came from Golden, Colorado; to keep it fresh, the company used refrigerated railcars and trucks. The longer shipping distance, from a median of eight hundred miles in 1977 to fifteen hundred in 1985, cost the brewer money that it could not pass on to consumers. It also needed a wholesaler network in its new territories. Because Coors had a much lower share of these new local markets than its established competitors, it had to settle for weaker wholesalers, the only ones who would agree to carry Coors as their leading brand. They were more of a drag than a source of strength as Coors tried to compete in new regions with AB and Miller. The brewer also had to ratchet up its marketing expenses, spending more for promotions and advertising to help it get established and also to keep up with the other companies, who were raising their marketing budgets. Unfortunately for Coors, this effort was diluted by being spread over a much larger geographical base. It was spending more to accomplish less.

Table 5.6 indicates the extent to which Coors transformed itself from a regional powerhouse to a diffused and weakened also-ran. In 1977, it controlled 8 percent of the national beer market by concentrating its forces in three regions. In two of these, it was the biggest seller. In the three Pacific Coast states, it competed more or less evenly with AB. Since Coors sold virtually no beer in Oregon or Washington, it was almost certainly the largest presence in California. Eight years later, its national market share was still 8 percent, but now it trailed AB in every region, including its home base in the mountain states. The three top regions accounted for 58 percent of its sales, down from 93 percent in 1977. Expansion meant dispersion, and dispersion was a blow to profitability. Part of the problem was slow sales growth. It sold 14 percent more beer in 1985 than in 1977. AB's sales, by contrast, were up more than 80 percent. But here again, dispersion hurt Coors. Its three biggest regions in 1977 had grown by 23 percent in these years. Coors had not even kept pace.

The price of expansion is evident in even a cursory look at Coors's income statements for 1977 and 1985. Again, the comparison with AB is telling (table 5.7). Even though its cost of goods sold declined in these years, from 70 percent to 67 percent of sales, advertising and other overhead costs increased enough to reduce Coors's operating income from 20 percent of sales to 9 percent in 1985. For AB, profitability went up. It lowered its cost of goods sold enough to move its operating income up to 15 percent. The entire difference between AB and Coors lies in advertising. AB spent almost three times as much in total, but $4 less per barrel, a significant advantage thanks to an economy of scale. It's good to be the king of beer.

Regional economies of scale in the beer business are potent. Advertising costs tend to be fixed on a regional basis. There are small discounts to the national advertiser—around 10 percent—but they do not compensate for the difference in advertising costs per barrel between a brewer with a 20 percent local market share and one with an 8 percent local share. Distribution costs also have a significant fixed regional component. Truck routes are shorter and warehouse use is more intensive for a company with a large local share. These costs, embedded in the cost of goods sold line, are especially significant for a heavy product like

TABLE 5.6

Anheuser-Busch and Coors, market share by region, 1977 and 1985 (sales by millions of barrels)

1977

	Total Sales	AB's Sales	AB's Share	% of AB's Sales	Coors's Sales	Coors's Share	% of Coors's Sales
New England	7.4	2.0	27%	5%		0%	0%
Southeast	18.2	6.4	35%	17%		0%	0%
East North Central	22.9	3.6	16%	10%		0%	0%
West North Central	12.2	2.7	22%	7%	0.9	7%	7%
West South Central	17.3	3.0	17%	8%	3.7	21%	29%
Mountain	8.4	2.2	26%	6%	3.1	37%	24%
Pacific	21.4	6.0	28%	16%	5.1	24%	40%
Nonreporting and export	53.8	10.9	20%	30%		0%	0%
Total	161.6	36.8	23%	100%	12.8	8%	100%
Top 3 regions		23.3		63%	11.9		93%

1985

	Total Sales	AB's Sales	AB's Share	% of AB's Sales	Coors's Sales	Coors's Share	% of Coors's Sales
New England	7.8	3.5	45%	5%	0.9	12%	6%
Southeast	25.5	11.4	45%	17%	1.7	7%	12%
East North Central	24.0	5.8	24%	9%	0.5	2%	3%
West North Central	13.0	4.4	34%	6%	1.1	8%	7%
West South Central	22.1	7.5	34%	11%	3.2	14%	22%
Mountain	10.7	4.4	41%	6%	2.1	20%	14%
Pacific	25.3	11.5	45%	17%	3.2	13%	22%
Nonreporting and export	58.0	19.5	34%	29%	2.0	3%	14%
Total	186.4	68.0	36%	100%	14.7	8%	100%
Top 3 regions		4.24		62%	8.5		58%

TABLE 5.7

Anheuser-Busch and Coors income statements,
1977 and 1985

	1977			
	AB		**Coors**	
Barrels sold (millions)	36.8		12.8	
Sales ($ millions)	$1,684		$ 532	
Sales/barrel	$46.01	100%	$41.56	100%
Cost of goods sold (COGS)	$1,340		$ 371	
COGS/barrel	$36.61	80%	$28.98	70%
Advertising costs	$ 73		$ 14	
Advertising costs/barrel	$ 1.99	4%	$ 1.09	3%
Other SGA	$ 102		$ 38	
SGA/barrel	$ 2.79	6%	$ 2.97	7%
Operating income	$ 169		$ 109	
Operating income/barrel	$ 4.62	10%	$ 8.52	20%

	1985			
	AB		**Coors**	
Barrels sold (millions)	68.0		14.7	
Sales ($ million)	$5,260		$1,079	
Sales/barrel	$ 77.35	100%	$73.40	100%
Cost of goods sold (COGS)	$3,524		$ 727	
COGS/barrel	$51.82	67%	$49.46	67%
Advertising costs	$ 471		$ 165	
Advertising costs/barrel	$ 6.93	9%	$11.22	15%
Other SGA	$ 491		$ 94	
SGA/barrel	$ 7.22	9%	$ 6.39	9%
Operating income	$ 774		$ 93	
Operating income/barrel	$11.38	15%	$ 6.33	9%

[Source: This data is from the Harvard Business School case cited in the reference, and applies only to the beer-making operations of these corporations, excluding their other lines of business.]

beer. Indeed, of the $200 retail cost per barrel in 1985, the beer itself accounted for $70. Distribution costs, including profits for wholesalers and retailers, were $110. And there were no secret production technologies that might have allowed one brewer to gain any measurable advantage over the competition.

In the twenty-five years starting in 1971, AB's operating margin moved up steadily, doubling over the period as it increased its leading market position (figure 5.4). For Coors, margins deteriorated from the start, falling below 5 percent in the 1990s, and only recovering somewhat after the company divested itself of extraneous assets and focused on efficiency. In hindsight, the decision to go national seems like a major error. But did Coors have an alternative, one that might have been recognized at the time?

STAYING HOME

Coors may have served itself better had it followed the most hallowed principle in military strategy, von Clausewitz's advice to concentrate your forces in the center of the line. For Coors, the center of the line was the eleven states in which it did business in 1975, plus a few others

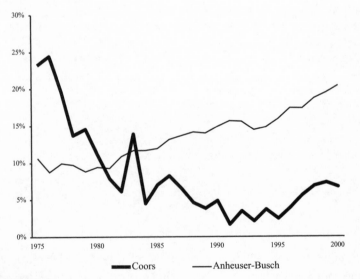

FIGURE 5.5
Operating margin, Coors and Anheuser-Busch, 1975–2000

contiguous to them, like Washington and Oregon. Had Coors been able to maintain its market share in its three regions of strength, ignoring the seductive pleas of Coors-deprived beer drinkers in the East, it would have sold more beer in 1985 than it did by spreading into forty-four states. And even if the Federal Trade Commission had pushed hard to have Coors sell its beer across the nation, the company could have satisfied the requirement formally, while charging so much for the beer to keep actual demand at a miniscule level. Its advertising expenses need not have ballooned as they did because it would not have had to spread them across the country. The freight costs would have been considerably less, and it could have maintained a network of strong wholesalers, who would have happily carried Coors exclusively, given its local popularity. Had it needed more capacity, it could have built another brewery in California, a growing market where it had a strong presence.

With a strong regional position, Coors would have been better able to defend itself against the AB juggernaut. Its beer sold in the region for less than Budweiser, and it could have met any effort by AB to win customers by lowering prices, offering other promotions, and advertising heavily. Had AB persisted, Coors could have taken some aggressive moves of its own, like contracting with some wholesalers in the Midwest to sell Coors at a deep discount. It still had the hard-to-get mystique, and a price war with Budweiser on Bud's home turf would have

TABLE 5.8

Coors in 1985 with 1977 market share

	Total	Coors %	Barrels (millions)
New England	7.8	0%	0
Southeast	25.5	0%	0
East North Central	24.0	0%	0
West North Central	13.0	7%	1.0
West South Central	22.1	21%	4.7
Mountain	10.7	37%	3.9
Pacific	25.3	24%	6.0
Nonreporting and export	58.0	0%	0
Total	186.4	8%	15.7

cost Coors much less than AB. Perhaps AB would have thought twice about building a brewery in Fort Collins, Colorado.

There is no certainty that this "think local" strategy would have succeeded. Beer drinkers are fickle, and AB's success in growing at the expense of its competitors indicates it was doing something right. Still, the approach of concentrating its efforts where it was already powerful had the promise of maintaining the company's profitability by capitalizing on its strengths, rather than dissipating them. Coors did survive, which was more than one could say for Schlitz, Blatz, and a host of regional brewers that fell by the wayside during these years. But despite the cachet, it did not prosper.

In the end, brewing beer is a business about marketing and distribution, and Coors is, in some essential ways, a Wal-Mart in disguise. Its history has been drastically different, however, for several reasons. First, because it had to lock horns with some strong national competitors, especially Anheuser-Busch, its expansion out of its regional stronghold was a more painful experience, for the family, the managers, and the shareholders. Perhaps if Kmart had been as well run as AB was, Wal-Mart's success would have been more modest. Second, Wal-Mart had a better strategy than Coors. It did not jump from Arkansas into California or the Northeast, but expanded at its periphery, where it could more readily establish the customer captivity and economies of scale that made it dominant. And it defended its base, something Coors was unable to do. Had Coors recognized the local nature of its strength, it might have done a better job sustaining its profitability.

BRICKS OR CLICKS? THE INTERNET AND COMPETITIVE ADVANTAGES

An alternative view of the future highlights the importance of the Internet. One of the articles of faith that drove the Internet mania during the last half of the 1990s was that this new medium would transform the way consumers bought books, computers, DVDs, groceries, pet supplies, drugs, banking services, fine art, and virtually everything else. Any traditional retailer that did not completely revise its business model was going to end up as roadkill on the information superhighway. The dominant merchants in this new economy would be dot-coms like Amazon, Webvan, Pets.com, Drugstore.com, and Wingspanbank.com, leaving Wal-Mart, Kroger, and Citibank in their wake.

After the mania subsided, it became obvious how excessive those predictions were about the rate at which online commerce would supplant traditional shopping. The expectation that the newly hatched, Internet-only retailers would displace their brick-and-mortar competitors also proved mistaken. The bankruptcy courts were soon littered with the remaining assets of failed B-to-C (business-to-consumer) innovators. There were some significant survivors, Amazon most prominent among them, but their path to profitability proved considerably longer than the proponents of the new economy thesis had anticipated.

The imbalance between many bankruptcies only partially offset by a few roaring successes does not mean that the Internet is insignificant as a medium of retail commerce. It takes little courage to predict that over time, more people will buy more goods and more services online, and that online transactions will encroach on old-fashioned shopping, banking, and other services. For our concerns with the economics of strategy, the question is not how big online business will become, but whether it will be profitable, and if so, for whom.

The main sources of competitive advantages are customer captivity, production advantages, and economies of scale, especially on a local level. None of them is readily compatible with Internet commerce, except in special circumstances. A customer can compare prices and services more easily on the Internet than in traditional retailers. The competition is a click away, and there are sites that list comparative prices. The open standards of the Internet make some proprietary technology inapplicable. Otherwise, the best new ideas have had a short life span before something even better has come along; think of search engines; customer service systems, like online stock trading, banking, and package shipping and customized home pages.

Finally, it is virtually impossible for any competitor to profit from economies of scale on the Internet. Internet merchants bragged about all the money they had saved by not having to building physical locations from which to sell their wares. But economies of scale entail substantial fixed costs that can then be spread over a large customer base.

With minimal required investments, the incumbent has no advantage. It takes so little to get into the game that virtually anyone can play. And there are no local boundaries to delimit the territory in which the firms operate, another element in the economies of scale equation. Also, nothing prevents traditional retailers, banks, brokers, insurance companies, newspapers, and everyone else from establishing their own Internet presence. Instead of barriers to entry, the information superhighway provided myriad on-ramps for anyone who wanted access. It has been an enormous boon to customers, but for the businesses selling to them, the destroyer of profit.*

* Every general statement has at least one or two glaring exceptions. The obvious one regarding the profitability of Internet companies is eBay. Its ability to benefit from the "network effect," a variant of economies of scale, is widely known. On the other hand, eBay has virtually no business in Japan, where the local market is dominated by Yahoo! Japan. By contrast, for all of its success as a retailer, Amazon has only reached profitability after a decade in business.

CHAPTER 6

Niche Advantages and the Dilemma of Growth

Compaq and Apple in the Personal Computer Industry

A DISRUPTIVE TECHNOLOGY

IBM introduced its personal computer in 1981. Though not the first company to move into this burgeoning industry, it was the most important. IBM's commitment to these little machines gave legitimacy to a device that had been the domain of self-taught programmers, hobbyists, and adventurous adopters of whatever new technology perched on the cutting edge. The company made several decisions at the start that defined the structure of the industry for years to come.

First, to speed development, it adopted an open architecture for the personal computer, buying off-the-shelf components from other companies and operating without patent protection. This approach meant that once the initial machines were available, anyone could produce a duplicate by buying a central processing unit (CPU), memory chips, a power supply, a motherboard, a disk drive, a chassis, an operating system, and the other elements that made up the first generation of PCs. Second, the two most important and profitable pieces, the CPU and the operating system, were proprietary to other companies. By selecting its CPU from Intel and its operating system from Microsoft, IBM created enormous wealth for the owners and many employees of these two firms. It is difficult to think of a single decision in the history of business—or anywhere else—that equals IBM's generosity in this instance.

Although it owned neither the operating system nor the microprocessor design, IBM's endorsement of MS-DOS and the Intel chip established standards in a previously anarchic environment. Writers of application software, relieved of the burden of providing multiple versions, began to offer better word processing, spreadsheet, and database programs that quickly became business essentials. With an open architecture and components readily available, IBM was soon joined by other PC manufacturers, including a number of start-up companies that saw opportunity in what they rightly predicted would be a rapidly growing industry. Most of these machines were compatible with the IBM standard.

The explosive rise of the desktop computer was as pure an instance of creative destruction as we are likely to see. It established Microsoft and Intel as two of the largest and most profitable companies on the globe. At the same time, it weakened and eventually destroyed most established manufacturers who had built mainframes and minicomputers, the ghosts of Route 128 like Digital Equipment and Prime among them. It made Silicon Valley in California and other places like Seattle and Austin into centers of computing technology. Moore's Law—Intel cofounder Gordon Moore's prediction that transistor density and hence computing power would double every year or two—became the driver of a perpetually dynamic industry. Any firm striving to flourish in this shifting universe—including at times even Microsoft and Intel—would need a talent for adaptation.

ENGINEERING A START-UP

Compaq had its origins on the back of the proverbial napkin—at most a placemat—on which Rod Canion and two other engineers from Texas Instruments outlined their business plan for venture capitalist Ben Rosen. The meeting took place in 1981, the year IBM began to ship its PC. The Canion plan was straightforward. It would produce a computer totally compatible with IBM's but better: with higher quality, superior technology, and portability (early units were the size of small sewing machines, weighed thirty-four pounds, and were soon referred to as "luggable" rather than portable). It would sell these machines through large resellers to corporate customers willing to pay a premium price for a more dependable and feature-rich computer. Rosen had been impressed with Canion and his colleagues in an earlier meeting, even though he dissuaded them from their original intent to produce hard drives for PCs. When they changed their focus, he agreed to help raise the money to get the Compaq Computer Company off the ground.

It soon took wing. In 1983, its first full year of operations, Compaq had sales of over $100 million. By 1987, five years in, its sales had grown to more than $1 billion, a milestone it reached faster than any company in history. And it was profitable, earning $137 million in 1987. All this happened in a field crowded with both new and seasoned firms that had moved to take advantage of the exploding market created by IBM's PC venture. Compaq's plan of total compatibility, high quality, and premium prices set it apart from the others.

Companies like Digital Equipment and Hewlett-Packard, rich in engineering talent and with proud heritages of building excellent minicomputers, created fine machines. But because their products were not compatible, were too expensive, and were late to the game, neither firm fared well.* Other start-ups did not match Compaq in quality and reliability. But they did have some breathing room, at first, because IBM was unable to meet the demand for the new machines, which far exceeded even its most optimistic projections. By the end of 1983, IBM had shipped over a million units, but that represented only 26 percent of the market, leaving plenty of space for some of the other firms.

With essentially no barriers to entry, there are bound to be shakeouts in an industry as dynamic as personal computers. Some of the early IBM-compatible makers like Eagle, Corona, and Leading Edge, gained an early foothold but were unable to survive once IBM caught up with its backlog and lowered its own prices. There were also shakeins. Michael Dell used his college dorm room as a just-in-time manufacturing center to sell PCs to his schoolmates. Two years later, in 1986, he produced a printed catalog and had sales of more than $150 million. Gateway 2000 copied his direct sales approach, established itself in the heartland, and designed its cartons to look like cowhides. It reached the billion-dollar sales plateau in its sixth year.

---

*HP did gain a decent share of the market after it started producing mainstream PCs. In 2002, it bought Compaq.

INDUSTRY ANALYSIS

Growth was the dominant feature of the personal computer industry. The machines became more powerful, more useful, and less expensive, a potent combination of features that put them into millions of offices and homes, both in the United States and abroad. An industry survey put sales in 1986 at $30 billion (figure 6.1). Nine years later they had increased to $159 billion, a compounded annual growth rate of 23 percent. With growth like this, there was room for many players.

The absence of barriers to entry—footloose customers, widespread access to multiple channels of distribution, simple and commonly available technologies, relatively low investment requirements, and limited economies of scale—ensured that the players arrived and competed aggressively for customers. Throughout the period, the market share of the top twenty vendors averaged around 56 percent. IBM, the early

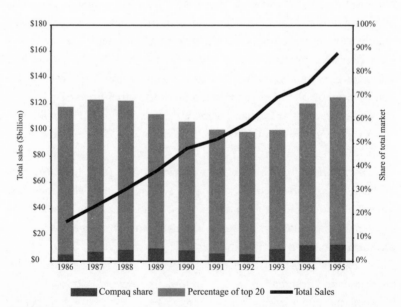

FIGURE 6.1

Total sales of the PC industry, share of top 20 PC makers, and Compaq share, 1986–95 leader, owned 24 percent of the market in 1986. By 1995, that had fallen to 8 percent, a figure matched by Compaq and Apple. The large number of manufacturers—box makers, in the jargon of the trade—and the shifting market share are strong indications that this was a highly competitive industry with ease of entry and ease of exit.

The personal computer world considered as a whole is actually composed of a group of discrete markets, with a limited overlap of players (figure 6.2). At the center are the box makers, building their machines out of components supplied mainly by other companies. The component makers are also specialists, concentrating in power supplies, memory chips, CPUs, disk drives, motherboards, keyboards, monitors, and the other pieces out of which the machines are assembled. The machines also ship with software, almost always with an operating system, and often, since the 1990s, with some core applications, like word processing and spreadsheets. Finally, there are the sales channels through which the computers reach the ultimate users. Some go to large retailers. Some go to wholesale distributors who service smaller computer stores and value-added resellers, people who combine service with delivery of machines. Dell and Gateway 2000 popularized the direct sales channel, bypassing all the intermediate steps between manufacturer and user. Their success bred emulation from Compaq, Apple, IBM, and most of the other major players, but they had to tread carefully for fear of undermining their existing channel partners.

Although the lists of players within the various market segments were subject to frequent changes—the cast of characters in figure 6.2 comes from the late 1980s—the basic structure of the industry has been remarkably stable. The only significant sector change was the emergence of network service providers like AOL in the middle to late 1990s, when the new driver of growth became the promise of the Internet and all the advantages of connectivity.

There are two important features of the structure of the PC universe that deserve comment.

First, there was only limited spillover between the box makers and the other segments. The different names of the leading competitors in each sector indicate the absence of effective joint economies. Intel

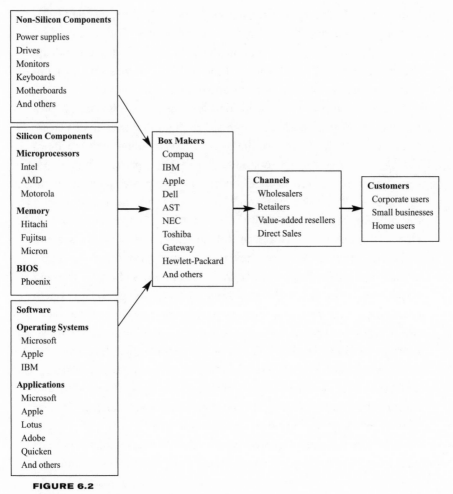

FIGURE 6.2

Map of the PC industry*

*Though this version of the PC industry map presented in chapter 4 looks different, it tells the same story.

dominates CPU production, but it neither manufactures PCs nor sells much software. With few exceptions, like keyboards and mice, Microsoft has avoided hardware manufacture. Its foray into game consoles with its Xbox system put it into competition with Sony and Nintendo, not Dell, and the jury is still out on its success in this venture. The major disk drive makers like Seagate, Maxtor, Quantum, and Iomega have seldom strayed from their niche, where intense competition has been difficult enough. Even IBM, the initial PC giant, found itself restricted to box making. It tried to separate itself from the Microsoft-using crowd by developing its own variant of MS-DOS, but the experiment with its OS-2 was unsuccessful and short-lived. IBM also made CPUs, including the PowerPC developed in partnership with Motorola and Apple. Yet its own machines had Intel inside. Compaq, which initially designed and even manufactured some of the components that other box makers bought outright did not produce chips or software.

Second, the only segments within the PC world with features suggesting that there are barriers to entry protecting incumbent firms from new entrants are operating systems and CPUs. In both there are a small number of competitors and stable market share. While the ranking of companies in the box-making segment changed frequently, Microsoft has owned the operating system business since the IBM PC was introduced. In the CPU segment, Intel has always dwarfed the other manufacturers. AMD was given a boost early on when box makers forced Intel to license its design to another chip company so that they might have a second source. AMD has occasionally been able to pressure Intel and force it to reduce prices or offer a lower-cost alternative to its top-of-the-line chip. But Intel has always been the leader, and by a wide margin.

The three basic sources of competitive advantage all help to account for the barriers to entry in these two market segments.

1. Customers prefer to stick with what they know, especially regarding software. Switching costs can be prohibitive when many users have to be taught to use unfamiliar programs. Search costs also inhibit change because the buyer has to have confidence in the reliability of the new system and the survivability of its creators.

2. Intel devotes major resources to production technology, aggressively defending patents and developing its expertise to keep yields high and defects low.

3. The most important advantage is economies of scale. Writing complicated software and designing advanced microprocessors keeps talented and expensive engineers at their terminals and benches for hundreds of thousands of work hours. On the other hand, the marginal costs of the next unit of the operating system can be as low as zero and seldom more than a few dollars, even when burned on a CD and boxed with a manual. A similar though less extreme contrast holds for the next microprocessor to come off the line.

Because they can spread their investments over millions of units, Microsoft and Intel are by far the lowest-cost producers. Microsoft has had virtually no competition in the desktop PC market. Intel has had Advanced Micro Devices as a distant second. Its research and development spending has always been larger on an absolute basis, while smaller as a percentage of sales, than AMD's. In 1988 through 1990, for example, Intel spent twice as many dollars on R&D as AMD, but only two-thirds as much per dollar of sales (twelve cents versus eighteen cents).

Network effects enhance both customer captivity and economies of scale. For programmers, computer designers, and typists in large firms, costs are reduced when users have to learn and interact only with the single software system that others are also using. The many PC manufacturers, each perpetually introducing new models, also benefit in cost, speed, and mutual compatibility by having a single chip standard on which to work. The bold innovator, seeking to separate himself from the pack, has to spend enormous sums to come up with something significantly different whose future value will be, by definition, highly speculative. All these barriers to entry have been impregnable, at least so far. It will probably take another major technological disruption to change this situation.

The contrast with the box makers could not be more extreme. There has been a long and shifting list of players throughout our prime period, with firms entering and leaving regularly. The top twenty firms accounted for rarely more than 60 percent of this market. This fluidity is an indicator of a highly competitive business, not one in which incumbents have powerful advantages.

If there were an advantage, what would be the source? Captive customers hardly seems likely. Even when the demand for more powerful microprocessors to run more complicated and graphics-intensive programs led existing users to replace older machines, the purchases were not frequent enough to be habit-forming. The standards that mattered were the operating system and the CPU, so there were no switching costs to buying a different brand. Perhaps the issue of reliability made search costs a factor, but one that was easily overcome by all the available reviews that tested and ranked machines.

A technological advantage is also unlikely. The box makers are basically assemblers, buying off-the-shelf parts and putting them together. Most of the technology is in the chips, both the microprocessors and the memory chips. There were also advances in storage systems, in battery life for portables, in screen technology, and in other components, all sparked by the industry mantra of faster, smaller, and cheaper. These were not, for the most part, the work of the box makers, who simply bought and installed them.

Finally, the box makers did not have the high-fixed-cost/low-marginal-cost structure that gives rise to economies of scale. Each computer they shipped had to have a microprocessor, an operating system, a power supply, and all the other parts that made them work. Though there may have been some volume discounts offered by their suppliers, the component cost of the last machine to come off the line was not much lower than of the first, and components accounted for most of the costs. It is rare to find economies of scale in industries with cost structures like this. Research and development costs were low. In the years when Intel was spending 12 percent of sales on R&D, Compaq spent 4.5 percent, and Dell 3.1 percent.

THE COMPAQ ADVANTAGE

As a box maker, Compaq was located squarely in one of the most competitive segments within the PC universe. In no year from 1983 through 1995 did it own as much as 9 percent of the market, nor did it ever make it to the very top of the list. And yet for most of our prime period (1986–95), it was solidly profitable. Its operating margins averaged over 13 percent, its return on invested capital over 22 percent. Compaq's approach to the business—high quality at a premium price for corporate buyers who cared more about reliability than the best bargain—worked well through several generations of machines. Measured by both growth and profitability, it outperformed IBM's PC operations.

But its history was anything but smooth. In 1984, it introduced its first line of desktop computers to complement the early portables that had been the model responsible for its early success. The machines did not sell quickly, inventory backed up, and the company had to borrow $75 million, at a costly interest rate, to pay its bills. The problem was solved with the introduction of Intel's 80386 microprocessor. The 386 was a much more powerful CPU than the 286 that had preceded it (and which Microsoft's Bill Gates referred to as "brain dead"). The demand for the 386 was strong and the supply initially limited. Compaq was among the first to market with a 386 computer, beating IBM by some months, and it had mobilized its extensive engineering resources to produce a well-functioning machine. Its only competitors in the early months of the 386 roll-out were several smaller firms that did not have Compaq's reputation for quality or the features it offered.

The next major challenge came two years later, when IBM attempted to alter the design of the PC with its PS/2, a computer that would not accept boards (holding additional memory and other features) designed for the old standard. It also introduced microchannel architecture, a faster way to move data within the machine (known as a system bus). These moves were a belated effort by IBM to regain some of the proprietary advantage it had given up when it introduced its original, easily copied, computers. Although IBM's effort did not ultimately succeed, Compaq felt that the challenge was genuine. Executives went so far as to explore a sale of the entire company to Tandy, another box maker with a strong distribution channel through its Radio Shack stores. Once again, however, Compaq's engineering muscle came to its rescue. The company added new features to its desktop line. It put together a consortium of box makers committed to a nonproprietary system bus. It also moved into the emerging laptop market, where it sold to corporations who saw the advantages of true portability and wanted the assurance provided by Compaq's reputation for quality.

A third and potentially more lethal problem emerged suddenly in the early part of 1991. After a strong year in 1990 and a good first quarter of 1991, sales of Compaq's computers started to slow. The initial information came from the retailers, who saw their inventory of Compaqs start to build. The company attributed the slowdown to the economy, which had become part of a global recession, and to the strong dollar, which made imports less expensive. Compaq responded with price cuts of up to 30 percent, but that did not help. The drop in sales continued, and operating income plummeted (see figure 6.3). The company was in trouble, and its management and directors were compelled to seek an explanation.

Ben Rosen, the venture capitalist who had helped launch the company, was still its nonexecutive chairman. He assembled a small team to

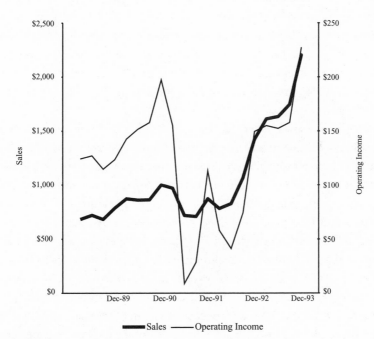

FIGURE 6.3

Compaq's sales and operating income, quarterly, 1989–93 ($ million)

investigate the situation, particularly the market into which Compaq sold its computers. They learned from Compaq's own sales force that the corporate customers were no longer willing to pay the premium for a Compaq because the quality differential had been reduced or eliminated entirely. Even more troubling, the salespeople had been giving senior management the same message for nearly a year. Unfortunately management, composed primarily of the engineers who had founded the company and grown it so successfully, had not responded. They believed that Compaq could once again design its way out of the crisis, that by introducing new features and better technology than the competition, they would win back their corporate customers whose hesitance to pay the Compaq premium was temporary. Rather than reduce their overhead to meet their competitors' price, they would maintain their technological edge and continue to produce superior machines.

The engineers, led by founder and CEO Rod Canion, had history on their side. Compaq had engineered its way through rough patches before, and until at least the middle of 1991, it was doing better than its low-cost rivals like Dell and AST. But Rosen and his allies felt that the medicine that had worked in the past was no longer the right prescription for the current difficulties. In the fall of 1991, Rosen and his group made an incognito visit to Comdex, the computer industry's premier trade show.

What they saw confirmed their belief that even Compaq's engineers would not be able to pull one more technological rabbit out of the hat. They found that many of the crucial components like keyboards, power supplies, and electronic controllers that Compaq designed or even built for itself were available from independent manufacturers for much less than it cost Compaq. Also, these components were equal to or better than those Compaq produced. Compaq's competitive edge at the top end of the market had been eliminated, and it was left with nothing to show for its higher overhead expenses. Just as Ford's plant at River Rouge, where iron ore entered at one end and finished automobiles emerged from the other end, became a victim of vertical integration as the automobile industry matured and external suppliers became more dependable and efficient, so Compaq was being hurt by doing internally too many of the steps that went into turning out a personal computer.

ECONOMIES OF SCALE IN A GROWTH INDUSTRY

Compaq's original approach to the PC industry, targeting corporate customers with higher-quality machines for which they would be willing to pay a premium, was undoubtedly a success, even though it had to work its way through several serious challenges. In the early years of the IBM-compatible business, Compaq was able to distinguish itself from its rivals and appeal to a particular segment of the overall market. It had little competition in this end of the business. Even though by 1987 or 1988 there may have been little that set a Compaq PC apart from the others, what little there was still made a difference. Compaq had the size, relative to competitors in its niche, to outspend them on engineering and assure its customers that all the components going into a Compaq machine were the best available. Within this small segment of the PC world, it had the advantage of economies of scale coupled with a small but crucial dose of customer captivity.

A few years later that advantage had disappeared for Compaq. As personal computer sales grew from $30 billion in 1986 to more than $90 billion in 1991, demand for all the components, including the high-quality ones, increased. Companies specializing in high-end power supplies, keyboards, and the other pieces were now making so many units of their single component that they could spread their engineering and manufacturing costs across a base that was comparable in size to Compaq's. And their quality improved with experience even as their prices fell, thanks to the advantages of specialization. Compaq could not keep up. The sixty engineers it employed to work on power supplies had become an expensive luxury. With 5 percent of total global sales for personal computers, it simply did not have the volume advantage over those specialized component makers, who now had 2–3 percent of the now expanded market, to benefit from economies of scale. So long as it persisted in a "do-it-ourselves" policy, it would be at a competitive disadvantage.

Rosen and his marketing-oriented supporters within the firm had to wrestle with Canion and the engineers over the strategy Compaq should take. Rosen's side won, and Canion was forced out in a bitter dispute. He was replaced by Eckhart Pfeiffer, who had been head of European operations and was chief operating officer in 1991. Pfeiffer immediately began to chop away at Compaq's cost structure. The firm followed the path of Dell, AST, and other box makers and began to buy most of its components from specialized manufacturers. By 1995, after the transition had been completed, Compaq's cost structure looked much more like Dell's than like the Compaq of 1990 (table 6.1). Its return on invested capital was lower than Dell's largely because Dell's direct model of sales allowed it to turn both receivables and inventory more frequently. Another good measure of efficiency—sales per employee—corroborated the extent of Compaq's new direction. In 1990, that figure was only slightly above $300,000. By 1995, it reached $865,000 and compared favorably with Dell, whose sales per employee were $630,000. Compaq's specialization in basic PC production, coupled with a sharp reduction in overhead, allowed it to more than double its operating income between 1990 and 1995.

Rosen's genius had been to recognize that the quality and economies of scale advantages Compaq benefited from in the 1980s were now history, and that unless Compaq changed its business plan, it was going to be struggling uphill against lower-cost but qualitatively equal competitors. He and his team decided to pursue the only strategy that makes sense in the absence of a competitive advantage; the determined pursuit of operational efficiency.

TABLE 6.1

Compaq and Dell, 1990 and 1995 ($ million, costs as a percentage of sales)

	COMPAQ				DELL	
	1990		1995		1995	
	$	%	$	%	$	%
Sales	$3,599	100%	$14,755	100%	$5,296	100%
Cost of goods sold	$2,058	57%	$11,367	77%	$4,229	80%
SGA	$ 706	20%	$ 1,353	9%	$ 639	12%
R&D	$ 186	5%	$ 511	3%	$ 51	1%
EBIT	$ 649	18%	$ 1,524	10%	$ 377	7%
ROIC		27%		21%		38%

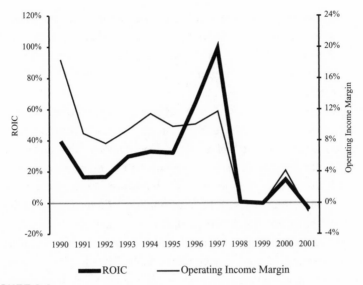

FIGURE 6.4
Compaq's return on invested capital and operating income
margin, 1990–2001

For a time, the approach was successful, as the company combined
strong sales growth with decent operating margins and high return on
invested capital (figure 6.4).*

But ingrained cultures are difficult to uproot. The engineering men-
tality and love of technology that was part of Compaq's tradition did
not disappear, even after Rod Canion left. In 1997 the company bought
Tandem Computers, a firm that specialized in producing fault-tolerant
machines designed for uninterruptible transaction processing. A year
later it bought Digital Equipment Corporation, a former engineering
star in the computing world which had fallen from grace as its minicom-
puter bastion was undermined by the personal computer revolution. At
the time of the purchase, Compaq wanted DEC for its consulting busi-

---

*The unusual spike in return on invested capital was a result of Compaq trying to emulate
Dell with a build-to-order approach to inventory. Starting in 1996, it drastically reduced its
inventory and also cut receivables while its cash rose. Since ROIC subtracts surplus cash
(cash in excess of 1 percent of sales) from the invested capital (denominator), the percentage
can change dramatically. Had we used return on equity, the year-to-year difference would
have been less.

ness, its AltaVista Internet search engine, and some in-process research. Technology acquisitions are notoriously hard to digest, and Tandem and DEC were no exceptions. Compaq lost its focus on operational efficiency, its own profitability plummeted, and in 2002, it sold itself to Hewlett-Packard.

The Compaq story is so intertwined with the history of the PC that it is easy to miss the more general significance. It lost its competitive advantage and the resulting high levels of profitability as the markets grew and allowed competitors to develop equivalent economies of scale.

This is a recurrent phenomenon. Globalization has taught this lesson in a number of industries. Take automobiles. When the United States was separated from the world automobile market, Ford and General Motors had such enormous scale, relative to the size of the domestic market, that their positions were unassailable. This dominance was especially true in the luxury car field. With globalization, due largely to the reduction of both trade barriers and transportation costs, competitors from abroad were able to expand the scale of their operations and ultimately to challenge GM and Ford within the United States. There are similar examples from other industries, like consumer appliances, machine tools, and electronic components.

For profitability, growth is a double-edged sword. It always requires additional investment, and the prospects of earning more than the cost of capital depend on the position of the firm in its industry. For companies with competitive advantages that they can maintain even as the market gets bigger, growth is an unambiguous benefit. But when markets enlarge, they often allow competitors to achieve comparable economies of scale and thereby undermine a major barrier to entry. Unprotected by barriers, companies do not produce exceptional returns.

THE APPLE VERSION

A year or so before Ben Rosen realized that Compaq needed a major recasting of its business strategy, John Sculley began to entertain similar thoughts about Apple. A marketing wiz at PepsiCo, Sculley had been recruited in 1983 to become Apple's CEO by Steve Jobs, one of the company's founders. Jobs was forced out two years later, leaving Sculley as undisputed leader of the company most emotionally identified with the PC revolution. In 1990, Apple was still one of the leaders in the business. It had more than 10 percent of the global marketplace, measured by revenue, the highest share it had ever enjoyed since IBM's PC was introduced in 1981. Its operating margins exceeded 13 percent, down from an earlier peak though still healthy by the standards of the industry. But Sculley was looking forward, and what he saw convinced him that Apple needed to take action.

The company Sculley analyzed in 1990 stood apart from the other firms in its segment of the industry. Alone among the major box makers, it used its own operating systems, both a text-based system for its Apple II line and the more exciting graphical user interface (GUI) operating system for its Macintosh line. It also manufactured or designed all of the important components and peripherals that made up a complete personal computer system. The Apple II line was targeted at the K–12 education market, where Apple had a large installed base. The Macintosh line sold into the education market, but it was also popular with home users and graphics professionals.

Macintosh machines had some important advantages when compared to their PC counterparts. They were easier to use because of the more intuitive interface. They had plug-and-play compatibility with printers and other peripherals, largely because Apple had tight control of the components and component standards. They were easier to network together than MS-DOS machines because of the operating system. They were far superior for all graphics applications, including desktop publishing and picture editing. In the still tiny but promising field of multimedia applications, where sound, images, and data would all be combined, the Macintosh was far ahead of the field. And they had devoted users, loyal to the technology and the company that had made it commercially available.

On the other hand, Sculley realized that the company and its flagship Macintosh line faced certain disadvantages that would probably outweigh its strengths. First, Macintosh machines were considerably more expensive than their PC competitors. Motorola, the sole supplier of the

Macintosh microprocessor, had missed an upgrade deadline for a more powerful version of the chip, leaving the Mac both underpowered and overpriced. Second, the Mac, despite its superior features, had never made important inroads into the corporate world other than in the graphics area. It confronted the dismal end of the chicken-and-egg dilemma. Because it owned a much smaller share of the corporate market, independent software companies did not write specialized programs for its platform. With fewer packaged applications programs available, new buyers chose PCs over Macs, pushing Mac further to the rear. Third, its strength in the educational market was probably a wasting asset. At some point, the students or their instructors were going to realize that one of the things they should be getting from computers in the classroom was proficiency on the machines and systems—overwhelmingly PCs—that they would be using after graduation.

Finally, by 1990 Microsoft had worked out enough kinks in Windows to make it workable. It released version 3.0 in that year and sold 10 million copies in the first twenty-one months. Though inferior to Macintosh OS 7.0 in almost every respect, the program's success at the box office put Apple on notice that its lead in the graphics world was under assault. Windows 3.0 was made possible in part by the faster Intel microprocessors now found in new PCs. As these continued to add muscle, the future of Windows looked bright. And the machines had the added appeal of being able to run all the legacy programs written for the MS-DOS system.

So Sculley had reason to be worried. But in the steps he took and the vision of Apple's future he articulated, he seemed to miss the larger, structural situation that Apple confronted, for which his cures and his vision were inappropriate. The most fundamental economic feature of the PC universe was that in two market segments—microprocessors and operating systems—there were powerful competitive advantages, enjoyed by Intel and Microsoft, based on economies of scale, supplemented by captive customers and some proprietary production technologies. The other segments were highly competitive. Apple earned its money in the most competitive segment, box making, where it had no competitive advantage and where its penchant for designing and manufacturing many of its own components put it at a competitive disadvantage. It spent money in writing and maintaining operating systems, where it was also at a competitive disadvantage. It depended on Motorola for its microprocessors, and Motorola operated at a competitive disadvantage to Intel, the dominant company in the segment. Microsoft also wrote some applications programs for the Macintosh, especially the spreadsheet Excel and the Word word processor, which were more popular than anything Apple produced.

A second look at our industry map, modified to focus on Apple's position in the segments in which it operated, makes clear the unfavorable position it occupied (table 6.2).

Apple operated, either by itself or in partnership with Motorola, in five market segments within the PC universe. In none of these segments did Apple possess a competitive advantage. At best, in box making, it operated on a level playing field. Some of Sculley's changes were directed at improving its position in this core business. He decided to cut costs drastically by permanently lowering the head count, by eliminating some of the perks that had made Apple's work environment so pleasurable, by moving jobs out of high-priced Silicon Valley, by cutting out some projects and activities that did not promise economic returns, and by abandoning the "not invented here" prejudice in manufacturing in favor of going to outside suppliers wherever possible.

This attack on costs allowed Apple to offer lower-priced versions of the Macintosh that were competitive with many IBM-compatible PCs. But Sculley did not take Apple out of the applications software business, nor did he alleviate the two greatest disadvantages confronting the company.

One, despite superior technology, the Macintosh operating system was a distant second to Microsoft's offerings and would likely be a millstone around the company's neck unless something changed dramatically in the industry. Two, in the race for greater processor performance, Motorola would inevitably lag behind Intel, whose larger market share would permit it to spend much more on the essential ingredient: research and development.

The argument for keeping all these distinct segments tied together was "synergy." Yet it is not immediately clear where the advantages of synergy lay, especially in the long run. Microsoft and Intel collaborated regularly and could reproduce any important joint economies that

TABLE 6.2

Segments	Dominant Players and Advantages	Stability	Profitability	*Apple's* Position?
CPUs	*Intel:* • big advantage over AMD and Motorola • price and quality are important • testing is a major cost for box makers • availability, support, familiarity • high R&D in chip design and manufacturing production give better yields, thus, large economies of scale	Yes	Yes	Far outside the barriers with Motorola.
Components and peripherals (motherboards, printers, disk drives, etc.)	No one. Apple makes many for itself.	No	No	No advantage.
Box makers	Competitive, no franchise.	No	No	Perhaps Apple could do well if it focused on efficiency and design.
Software: operating systems (OS)	*Microsoft:* • captive customers due to high switching costs • economies of scale (retool every three years as chips get more powerful) • network externalities	Yes (IBM's OS/2 was a flop)	Yes	Far outside as the second player.
Software: applications (office suites, desktop publishing, database management, CAD/CAM, vertical markets)	*Microsoft:* • extended the Windows OS into its office suite (Lotus and WordPerfect were the losers) • captive customers • economies of scale Niche players like AutoDesk in CAD/CAM	Yes for its office suite, (after introduction of Windows) and for niche leaders	Yes	No advantage for Apple's own products.

Apple might identify. Also, the evolution of the industry toward separate major players in each segment argued strongly against the existence of significant advantages from vertical integration.

Sculley's other moves were more questionable. He committed the company to introducing a series of "hit products," either new or refashioned offerings, on a very tight schedule. Some were successful, like the PowerBook, Apple's first competitive notebook computer. Some were innovative, like QuickTime, a multimedia software package that established Apple's leadership position in that field. The strategy did refresh Apple's product line, but it also required the company to maintain a large staff of programmers and product designers.

Sculley also decided that Apple needed alliances with other companies in the industry in order to capitalize on its software strengths. His first three ventures were announced in 1991. All involved IBM, formerly Apple's most important competitor in the PC world. The first was IBM's new RS6000 line of microprocessors. Apple would switch to chips built on this technology, and Motorola, also an ally, would be a second source of the new PowerPC chips. In the Taligent joint venture, the two companies would develop a new operating system to run on the old Motorola 68000 microprocessors, or Intel's line of X86 chips, or on the new PowerPC CPUs. A clever effort intended to make it easier for programmers to write applications for the system, it was also going to be enormously costly. A third venture with IBM had the goal of establishing standards for multimedia software.

An underlying rationale for these alliances was Sculley's sense that Apple was a small player on a large playing field and that by forming joint ventures with bigger allies, it could use their muscle to leverage its unique strengths. He was, he said, trying to transform the whole industry, to get some relief from the relentless margin pressure that competition was putting on the PC manufacturers. With only 10 percent of the PC market, Apple did not have the essential clout on its own. And none of these moves challenged the dominance of the Microsoft-Intel standard. IBM had not been successful in its own attempt at a competing operating system, and there was little to suggest that the Taligent venture would gain wider acceptance. It was Apple who had experience in multimedia software; what they would gain from IBM was not immediately apparent.

Sculley was a visionary. These alliances were motivated not only by his desire to restructure the personal computer industry, but also by his sense of the imminent emergence of a digital information universe. Every firm that created, published, transmitted, processed, or displayed information would be a part of this interconnected world. Long-established boundaries between telephone companies at one end and movie studios and newspapers at the other would be broken down and reorganized. This was a bold and in many ways prescient picture of the future when Sculley laid it out in 1991, a few years before the explosive growth of the World Wide Web that became the connective thread for many of these industries (see figure 4.5 on page 75 for Sculley's vision).

The question for Apple was how it might fit into this picture profitably. It might try to position itself as the indispensable center of this cosmos, the owner of a software standard essential for all multimedia processing. But here it would be directly confronted by Microsoft, with its powerful competitive advantages. If new technology should vitiate Microsoft's advantages, Apple would be just one player in a highly competitive arena in which no one was going to hand it a central position. Alternatively, Apple could try to be a leader in new products that fit into this digital universe, like a personal information manager (now called personal digital assistant) that was pocket-sized, recognized handwriting, and integrated with existing hardware. The playing field for these new products was almost certainly going to be level, without major barriers to entry. It is hard to see what competitive advantage Apple might enjoy. Finally, Apple could concentrate in one or two niches, like graphics and multimedia software, in which it might capitalize on its existing superior technology. Even here it might be confronted by the Microsoft-Intel steamroller, once better software and more powerful chips became available.

There was no easy answer to the dangers Sculley identified. None of the choices were sure successes for Apple. Each of them presented challenges, given the large number of powerful competitors, the uncertain path toward a digital information world, and Apple's existing vulnerabilities due to its position outside the mainstream of personal computing technology. Correct in recognizing the shoals toward which Apple was moving in 1990, while it was still quite profitable, Sculley could not find a course that put the company on a profitable path. He was removed in 1993, and his successor lasted only three years before he, too, was ousted.

Apple seemed to change strategies every six months. In 1994 it announced that it would license the Macintosh operating system, allowing other companies to produce clones of its machines. This program lasted three years before it was discontinued during the second tenure of Steve Jobs, who returned to the company not long after he sold his NeXT computing business to Apple for millions of shares. Jobs did manage to return Apple to profitability, centering it once again in the personal computer business, where its elegant designs and easier-to-use operating system kept it the favorite of hard-core Apple devotees. Though its sales in the year ending September 2000 were down almost 30 percent from the high of 1995, Jobs had managed to restore operating margins to the same 5 percent level they had been. Apple survived; it had hardly prospered. Its future does not look bright. See figure 6.5.

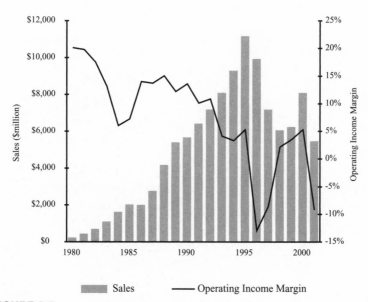

FIGURE 6.5

Apple's sales and operating income margin, 1980–2000

The contrast between Sculley's musings and Rosen's lucid prescriptions for Compaq is striking. By concentrating on operating efficiency in an environment without competitive advantages, Compaq grew larger than Apple and enjoyed some profitable years. Apple floundered (table 6.3). Even with a marketing genius of Steve Jobs's caliber, Apple's unfocused pursuit of broad but illusory competitive advantages denied it the benefits of specialization and clarity of managerial focus. As we have seen, Compaq's revival was short-lived. It could not sustain the cost discipline that returned it to profitability, and ultimately it was absorbed by Hewlett-Packard.

TABLE 6.3
Compaq and Apple, 1991 and 1997

	Compaq	Apple
Sales in $ billions, 1991	$ 3.6	$6.3
Sales in $ billions, 1997	$24.6	$7.1
Average operating margin	10.2%	1.7%

CHAPTER 7

Production Advantages Lost

Compact Discs, Data Switches, and Toasters

PHILIPS DEVELOPS THE COMPACT DISC

Philips N.V., a multinational conglomerate based in the Netherlands, has a long history in the consumer electronics business. It pioneered the audiotape cassette as an alternative to the long-playing record. In the late 1960s, some engineers in its research laboratories began to work on using lasers for digital reproduction, a technology initiated at MIT in the previous decade. Philips's first result was a video system based on optical scanning of analog, rather than digital, images engraved on discs. Though superior in reproduction quality to videotapes, the product did not gain broad acceptance, largely because this system could only play back prerecorded discs. But the engineers were impressed with the promise of laser scanning, especially when combined with digital encoding of audio and visual information. In 1979, executives in the consumer electronics division started to analyze the potential for using this technology to record music for home consumption on compact discs.

THE RECORDED MUSIC INDUSTRY IN THE UNITED STATES, CIRCA 1979

A record or tape passed through many steps between the artist in the recording studio and the customer listening to music in his home. Most market segments of the industry were highly competitive—many firms each with a small share of the market. The only exception was in the center of the music world, where a few record companies, who hired the artists and produced and marketed the records, controlled most of the business (figure 7.1).

Philips itself operated in two of these segments. It was one of many manufacturers of audio components, where it occupied no special place based on quality, design, or price. It also owned 50 percent of the record company Polygram; the German conglomerate Siemens owned the other half. One of the most assertive proponents of developing a compact disc was actually Polygram's director of marketing. Polygram was a member of the second tier of firms, behind the leaders CBS and Warner. Aside from Philips, there was little overlap between segments. Toshiba had some ties to EMI, and Sony was connected to CBS Records, but only in Japan (Sony would eventually buy CBS Records in 1988). Otherwise, each segment stood on its own. For the Philips executives, the question was—or should have been—where, within this fragmented array, they were going to make a profit from the compact disc.

THE STATE OF PLAY(BACK)

Someone wanting to buy recorded music in 1979 had essentially two choices, either long-playing vinyl records (LPs) or prerecorded tapes. Tapes came in two varieties, eight-track cartridges or cassettes. Reel-to-reel tape, which had been the original format, had disappeared as a prerecorded form, although it still was the recording technology of choice for professionals and even amateur aficionados. LPs sold over 300 million units in 1979, eight-tracks 100 million, and cassettes 83 million; they were fast catching up to the eight-track. Unlike eight-track, users could buy and record on blank cassettes, making the format more versatile even as it threatened the record companies and their contract artists with bootleg alternatives to the prerecorded originals.

The Philips executives saw the compact disc as an opportunity for the company, but only if several obstacles could be overcome. One was the issue of a standard, both for the disc itself and the disc player that would be required to make music at home. The videocassette industry, in

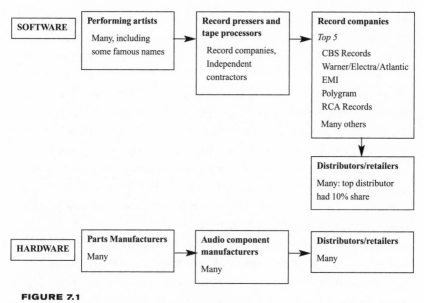

FIGURE 7.1
Map of the recorded music industry

which the Sony Betamax format competed with JVC's VHS system—and both for a while with videodiscs from RCA and Philips—was a contemporaneous example of how competing standards made it difficult for anyone to operate profitably. Also, the contest between eight-track and cassettes was still in progress with a similar consequence.

Though Philips had a head start in laser-based audio, its executives knew that Telefunken, JVC, and Sony were also working on incompatible versions of the product. Without an agreed-upon standard, the pace of adoption would be much slower. The record companies would not want to produce multiple versions of the same music, nor would the potential manufacturers of disc players be as eager to get involved without some guarantee of a large market, another mandate for a single format. So part of Philips's plan was to get a standard—its own—adopted by all the players in the industry.

The second potential obstacle was the relationship between cost and price. To be successful, the compact disc would have to be offered at a

price that would be sufficiently competitive with the alternatives to attract enough customers to make the business profitable. The disc player
would also have to be available at a price consumers would pay, even if it
cost more than the turntable it was replacing. Philips executives believed, with some support from consumer surveys, that compact discs
and players could command a premium price from at least a segment of
the market, thanks to superior sound quality and increased durability.
They were also certain that the disc players could be produced for very
little more than turntables of comparable quality once volumes had
grown large enough. The more difficult question was the cost of putting the music on a compact disc and moving it down the distribution
channel until it reached the ultimate buyer.

A third issue that was not directly addressed by Philips executives was
how, as the market for compact discs developed, Philips could distinguish itself from the legion of potential alternative disc and player suppliers. Without something setting it apart, Philips would be competing
on a level economic playing field. Profits would be driven to competitive
levels, leaving little or no room for Philips to benefit from its pioneering
development efforts. The ultimate financial success of Philips's strategy
would hinge on how well this last challenge was addressed.

DEMAND AND SUPPLY

In estimating the demand for compact discs, Philips executives focused
on buyers of jazz and classical LPs. These consumers appreciated the
added sound quality of compact discs because their preferred music had
a broader dynamic range than rock, pop, country, or other genres.
Within the U.S. market, they bought around 25 million records in 1979,
less than 10 percent of the total number of LPs sold. As a group, these
listeners had already shown a willingness to pay a 30 percent premium
for digitally remastered records, where the improvement in sound was
substantially less than between vinyl and compact disc. The executives
estimated that it would take around five years before even half of this
market made the move to compact disc. On the other hand, they knew
that some portion of the rest of the music-buying public, accounting for

over 90 percent of the total, would ultimately transition to the new technology. They figured that annual demand would exceed 18 million discs by the third year after introduction and 120 million by the seventh year. And those figures were for the United States only. If that represented half the global demand, the global pace might be double that.

Because of their relationship with Polygram, the Philips executives knew with some accuracy how much it cost to produce an LP and a cassette. They estimated that by 1982, the date at which they thought they could begin turning out discs, the variable cost structure of an LP or cassette, excluding manufacturing and packaging, would look like the figure shown in table 7.1. Costs for the CD, they believed, would be no different. The royalty paid to artists did not vary from LP to cassettes, and there was no reason to assume discs would be any different. The promotion figure of $1.33 also included a charge for profit. Distributors and retailers together marked the product up around $3.00 before it was sold to the customer. So excluding manufacturing and packaging, the cost to the consumer would be around $7.

In 1979, LP records sold for around $6.75. Assuming inflation ran at 10 percent a year through 1982 (which it did), then in three years the price might rise to around $9 per record. If customers were willing to pay a 30 percent premium for higher-quality sound, a CD might retail for between $11 and $12. With $7 committed to all costs other than manufacturing and packaging, that left at least $4 to spend making and housing the discs. If Philips could produce discs with packaging below this price, then the price-cost issue would be solved.

Hans Gout, the Polygram executive whose enthusiasm for the compact disc project was a driving force within Philips, wanted each CD dis-

TABLE 7.1

Cost estimates for unit of prerecorded music in 1982

Artists	$2.65
Promotion (including a charge for profits)	$1.33
Distribution	$3.00
Total	$6.98

tributed inside a snap-open plastic case referred to as a "jewel box." At $1.18 per box, the units were costly, considerably more than the cardboard record jacket used for LPs. Gout saw the extra expense for the jewel box as worthwhile to accentuate the quality features of the CD. Paying $1.18 for the package left $2.82 to spend on manufacturing.

In estimating what it would cost to produce a compact disc, the Philips executives did not have much experience to guide them. They knew that in the production of videodiscs, it took several years to get a line operating efficiently; yields improve as the sources of contamination are eliminated. They estimated that yields would increase and costs decline until a cumulative 50 millions units had been produced, at which point the cost per disc would stabilize at around $0.69 (table 7.2). The first firm to enter the business might profit from moving down the learning curve ahead of its tardy competitors.

These variable production costs were only one part of the manufacturing equation. The other piece was the cost of the plant and equipment necessary to inscribe the music onto the discs. The Philips engineers estimated that it would cost $25 million and take eighteen months to build the first manufacturing line with a capacity of 2 million discs per year. After that, the time would drop to one year and the equipment would improve and become less expensive. These reductions would continue for at least five years as each generation of machinery outdid its predecessor. Assuming a cost of capital of 10 percent and a 10-year depreciation schedule, the annual equipment cost per disc would

TABLE 7.2
Variable cost per CD for cumulative units produced

Cumulative Units Produced (millions)	Cost per Unit
0–5	$3.00
5–10	$2.34
10–50	$1.77
over 50	$0.69

drop from $2.50 in 1981 to $0.33 in 1986 (table 7.3). Further increases in plant size beyond the 2-million-disc capacity would not lead to significant cost-per-disc reductions.

Putting both parts of manufacturing costs together, it is clear that after three or four years, the cost of producing a disc with the latest-generation equipment would drop well below $2.80, the amount that Philips executives calculated record companies could afford to spend and still turn out a product their customers would purchase. Economies of scale in production were quite limited. For example, a fourth-generation machine would represent capital investment of $3.73 per unit of disc capacity, or a capital cost per disc of roughly $0.75. If cumulative disc output by year four had reached 50 million units, then the variable costs per disc would be another $0.69, bringing the total cost of a disc to $1.44. From the cost side, the compact disc project looked feasible.

LEARNING CURVE OR SLIPPERY SLOPE?

The picture must have looked rosy for Philips. It solved the standards problem by collaborating with Sony, combining the best features of each. It was Sony that insisted on a disc twelve centimeters in diameter, large enough to hold seventy-five minutes of music—enough for Beethoven's Ninth Symphony—a decision classical music lovers have applauded ever since. Although JVC continued for a time with its own

TABLE 7.3
Equipment cost per CD

Equipment cost per disc		Annual equipment cost per disc at 20% (COC and 10-year depreciation)
1982	$12.50	$2.50
1983	$8.35	$1.67
1984	$5.58	$1.12
1985	$3.73	$0.75
1986	$2.39	$0.48
1987	$1.67	$0.33

format, there was sufficient agreement on the Philips-Sony standard to begin production in 1982. The first music to appear on CD was Billy Joel's *52nd Street*. The Ninth Symphony followed shortly. By the end of the year, more than one hundred titles were available.

The question remained, where was Philips going to make its money? Polygram and CBS/Sony were the first record companies to adopt the new medium; they were partners with Philips and Sony in the development effort. The other record companies quickly followed suit. But none paid a royalty to Philips for its technology. Quite the opposite. Philips and Sony had to persuade them to take up the new product; they were not about to reduce their returns for the favor. No patents protected the technology. It had been developed at MIT in the 1950s. And the large record companies were the only players in the whole industry who were concentrated enough to wield some bargaining power. Philips was not in a position to coerce them.

Perhaps it could prosper as a manufacturer of compact discs. As the first mover into the field, might Philips have been able to take advantage of its earlier start down the learning curve, producing the discs at a much lower variable cost than companies just beginning to learn the intricacies of achieving high yields by keeping contamination to a minimum? Maybe the first mover could achieve a learning-curve advantage sufficient to stay permanently ahead of any competitor. There were a few problems with this plan. Although experience did help in raising yields and lowering variable costs, it was offset by the disadvantage of being the first to invest in a production line. Here, costs were lower for the latecomer, who did not have to pay the penalty for taking the lead.

The balance between these two forces would depend on how rapidly the market for CDs developed. Consider the situation of an entrant producing discs using a third-generation (year three) technology. Its capital costs per disc would be $1.12, or $1.38 less than Philips's first-generation cost of $2.50. (See table 7.3.) If Philips's cumulative volume of output over the first two years amounted to 10 million discs, its variable cost at $1.77 per unit (see table 7.2) would be $1.33 below that of the new entrant ($3.00 in table 7.2). The gains and losses from being the first mover would basically offset one another. If it used third-generation equipment, Philips would be level on capital costs and enjoy the full $1.33

advantage on variable costs. On balance, then, Philips could expect to benefit from an initial learning-curve advantage over new entrants. However, as an entrant gained experience and moved down the learning curve, this advantage would start to shrink and would disappear entirely once the entrant had produced a cumulative volume of 50 million discs. Because it was using later-generation equipment, its capital costs would be lower than Philips's.

If the CD market exploded to 200 million or more units per year, then at least some new entrants could rapidly reach a cumulative output of 50 million. It is unlikely that Philips would benefit from customer captivity, since its important customers were the large, sophisticated, and powerful major record companies. Thus, Philips's cost advantage would last for less than two years. Paradoxically, the only condition that might sustain Philips's learning curve advantage would be a slowly growing CD market, so that it would take years before competitors could reach the 50 million cumulative milestone and complete their passage down the learning curve.

From this perspective, the problem with the market for discs was not that it would be too small; it would be too large. Even if it had a head start, Philips was not going to sustain an advantage based on being the first mover for more than a few years. Unless it achieved some measure of customer captivity, there was no reason to think that Philips could keep current customers from taking their business elsewhere. And since plants could be efficiently operated at a scale of only 2 million discs per year, economies of scale in production would not be a deterrent to entry. Without captive customers, durable production advantages, or relative economies of scale, Philips would benefit from no competitive advantages as a producer of compact discs.

The situation was, or should have been, no more encouraging to Philips as a maker of audio components. Philips and Sony were the first to market with CD players, but it took very little time for every other firm in the industry to have a unit available. Since all the players used the same technology, they could only differentiate themselves by design, secondary features, and price. These attributes are rarely a recipe for profitable investment, especially for a company like Philips, which prided itself on its research and technology and paid the price in overhead costs.

With the wisdom of hindsight, it is easy to chide Philips for its compact disc strategy. However, its dream of profiting from being the first mover in a rapidly developing market is one that has been shared by a number of manufacturing firms. Most have done no better than Philips. Its experience indicates why.

Being a first mover is very much a double-edged sword. On the one hand, learning curve effects benefit a first mover as its variable costs decline with cumulative production volume. On the other hand, vintage effects—the fact that plants built later are more efficient than earlier ones—count against the first mover. In a large, rapidly growing market like CDs, cumulative volume growth and learning are rapid for both first movers and later entrants. A law of diminishing returns to learning shrinks any first-mover advantage, so that the adverse vintage effects come to predominate. At that point, it was certain that the successful compact disc business would attract competitors. Philips's profitability suffered. It might actually have been better off if CDs had been restricted to a niche market in which it would have had the field to itself for perhaps five to seven years. During this interim period, it might have been able to earn above average returns, maybe enough to compensate it for its initial development expense.

CISCO LEARNS TO CONNECT

Philips's effort to be a pioneer in the CD market as a manufacturer of discs and players worked out very well for consumers, but not so well for Philips and the other companies that followed it into the market. With the exception of some vinyl-addicted audiophiles, most serious music lovers have been delighted with the convenience and durability of the CD, and the system has replaced the long-playing record as their medium of choice. Though its permanence will be challenged by digital formats and file-sharing (piracy), the CD has clearly earned a place in the history of technology, entertainment, and computer storage media.

In many ways, the experience of Cisco in the networking business has been the mirror opposite of Philips and the CD. Cisco developed a product—the router—that could tie together disparate computing systems operating within an organization. Its initial customers were not consumers buying music, but businesses, government agencies, universities, and other institutions. Almost from the start, there were other firms in its industry; Cisco was not the only company trying to be a first mover. But Cisco was always the largest, most profitable, and fastest-growing.

Cisco managed to create competitive advantages for itself, which became stronger as its business grew. The advantage of economies of scale never became important for Philips because the CD market was large relative to the efficient plant size of 2 million discs per year. Cisco, by contrast, because of the high software content and attendant high-fixed costs for its routers, enjoyed economies of scale advantages. It managed this advantage brilliantly. Unlike Philips, Cisco earned billions of dollars from its new venture, and it made fortunes for those shareholders who got in early enough and got out before the tumultuous decline in its share price, which began in the middle of 2000.

NICHE PLAYER

Cisco grew and prospered by solving a problem. As computers and computer manufacturers proliferated in the 1970s and 1980s, disparate languages and protocols impeded the ability of systems to communicate with one another. Cisco was founded in 1984 by engineers at Stanford University who wanted to send e-mail to one another across department networks. They found, however, that although the business school and the computer science department both used machines from Hewlett-Packard, they were different models, used different protocols, and could not read each other's files. So the engineers developed the router, a specialized computer that could take the output of one system and send it on in translated form so that it could be read by other kinds of systems. (Routers actually connect networks, but that detail is not significant here.) As is often the case, solving a problem can be a path to riches, provided the problem is widely shared. It turned out that by removing the language barriers between computer systems, Cisco made networking throughout the enterprise a reality.

Cisco caught another wave that propelled it forward. The same routers that worked within the organization to tie all the separate networks together also enabled communication over the still nascent but rapidly expanding Internet, again between machines that were not inherently compatible. Cisco routers allowed companies like Boeing to tie all their systems together in what became known as an intranet, using the Internet as a transmission mechanism for company data. The impact on Boeing's work process was significant, and other companies sought Cisco out to upgrade their own networks.

A company that makes life much better for its customers gets handsomely rewarded, provided it can separate itself from competitors offering similar benefits. In Cisco's case, the rewards came in sales growth, growth in earnings, and a valuation in the stock market that outdistanced both the increase in revenue and income (figure 7.2). In 1990, Cisco had sales of $70 million. By 2000, revenue had increased to $19 billion, a compound annual rate of 66 percent. Operating income grew at 63 percent per year. The market value of its equity went from $350 million to $450 billion (figures at the end of the fiscal year, which for Cisco has been in July), a compound return in excess of 90 percent per year. For a brief period in 1999, Cisco was the largest company in the world, measured by market capitalization. Unlike Philips, it had not been undermined by competitive entrants.

Underlying the growth in sales, the high operating margins, the extraordinary return on invested capital, and the enormous increase in its market value was Cisco's dominant position in an expanding market and the competitive advantages on which this position depended. As the creator of the first router, for a while Cisco was the only player in the field. But competitors like Wellfleet and 3Com soon appeared. Cisco's market share fell from 100 percent at the beginning of 1989 to 70 percent in the first quarter of 1994. However, within two years it was back up to 80 percent.

Cisco's market had two elements missing from the CD market—substantial customer captivity and economies of scale. Routers are sophisticated pieces of equipment, a complex fusion of hardware and software. A high level of technological expertise was required to install and main-

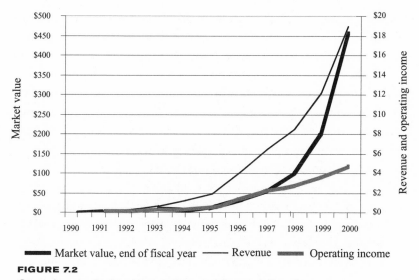

Market value, end of fiscal year ——— Revenue ▬▬ Operating income

FIGURE 7.2

Cisco's market value, sales, and operating income, 1990–2000 ($ billions)

tain the systems, an expertise not widely available except for those customers with large and skilled IT departments. The others relied on Cisco or its competitors. As they expanded their own internal networks, they naturally turned first to the vendor whose equipment they already owned, not wanting to incur the risks and costs of developing a relationship with a new supplier. This asymmetry of familiarity was abetted by another feature of routers that made it difficult for customers to switch: the routers themselves were not compatible. Cisco routers did not like to talk with their Wellfleet or 3Com cousins, so the company or agency that started with Cisco stayed with Cisco. Customers were made captive by complexity.*

Like other digital machines, the performance of routers improved rapidly. The hardware and the software got better, faster, and capable of

---

*Captivity was not simply a matter of product differentiation. Household appliances and even office equipment like PCs are differentiated by features, brand images, and perceived quality. Yet since the introduction of the original IBM PC, customers have rarely, if ever, been captive to their initial suppliers.

handling more data. Cisco's larger market share gave it a powerful economies of scale advantage over its competitors in writing the software code and designing upgraded models of the router. Having access to a stable base of customers who made up most of the market for routers, Cisco was in a position to disseminate new technologies far more efficiently than its competitors. This privileged position meant that Cisco could afford to spend more than its rivals to acquire that technology, whether through higher R&D spending or the acquisition of smaller competitors. Cisco pursued both courses aggressively. In its fiscal years 1993–96, it bought or took minority stakes in fifteen companies, and in the next quarter, October 1997, it added an additional eight. Not all of them worked out, and some were too expensive even using the inflated currency of its own shares, but Cisco was able to keep ahead of the competition by purchasing what it could not build on its own.

Thanks to its economies of scale advantages in distribution, maintenance, and R&D, whether internal or acquired, Cisco was able to extend its franchise beyond its original router competence. Sometime in the mid 1990s, local area network (LAN) switching began to challenge routers as the networking hardware of choice within the enterprise. Cisco bought its way into LAN switches and soon became the biggest supplier. In the first quarter of 1994, 3Com had 45 percent of the market, Cisco 35 percent. By the end of 1996, 3Com's share had fallen to 21 percent, and Cisco's had risen to 58 percent.

Cisco's average pretax return on invested capital during the period 1990–2000 was a giddy 142 percent (figure 7.3).* A heavy user of stock options, Cisco undoubtedly understated its costs by keeping a large share of salary expenses off the income statement. Some skeptics have suggested that if the options had been expensed, Cisco may never have been really profitable. That critique is undoubtedly exaggerated. In July 2000, Cisco had $5.5 billion in cash (up from $50 million in 1990), and investments in near cash securities of $14 billion. It had issued no debt

---

* Cisco built up a large asset on its balance sheet, which it called "Investments." This represented surplus cash invested at maturities too long to classify as a current asset. We have treated this "investment" asset as if it were cash and deducted it from Invested Capital in calculating ROIC.

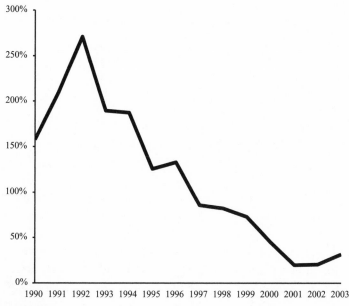

FIGURE 7.3
Cisco's pretax return on invested capital, 1990–2003

over the period, and sold less than $3 billion in net new equity. So however it might have dressed up its income statement by masking the true costs of employment, Cisco profits certainly exceeded its cost of capital throughout the 1990s.

The extent of Cisco's profitability throughout the period is apparent from figure 7.3. Even in the year ending July 2000, when the recession had already begun and the stock market experienced a severe decline from its March highs, Cisco was still flourishing. Its revenue of almost $19 billion was up 56 percent from the prior year, and its operating income of $3.2 billion had risen 13 percent as compared with 1999. Part of these gains were due to a number of acquistions. Still, there were some troubling signs. Its operating margin, at 17 percent, was down below 20 percent for the first time and was only half of what they had been in 1996. The problem lay on virtually every line of Cisco's income statement, but the main culprits were research and development.

TABLE 7.4

Cisco's increased costs as a percentage of sales, 1996–2000

Cost of sales	Total Change 1996–2000
Cost of goods sold	1.2%
Research and development	4.5%
Sales and marketing	3.1%
General and administrative	–0.6%
Amortization of goodwill and purchased intangible assets	1.5%
In-process research and development	7.3%
Total	17.0%

CHANGING CLASS

Cisco did not one day decide that it should spend more on research and development because it had all these talented engineers and wanted to keep them busy. Beneath the decline in margins lay a major change in the nature of Cisco's business. From inception, it had dominated the market for networking systems within the enterprise. Its original entry was the router, which it had invented. But as the demand for increasing scale and bandwidth grew within companies and other organizations, Cisco had been able to adapt to new technologies, like the LAN switch. By the late 1990s, the market for enterprise networking systems had become relatively mature. Most of the organizations that wanted a network already had one in place, and the advantages of upgrading the systems began to diminish. Cisco was not in a position to expand by taking business from its competitors, since it already owned the lion's share of the market. If it wanted to grow—and a company with a history of growth like Cisco's is not going to be content just maintaining its sales level—it would have to find new markets.

From where Cisco stood in the late 1990s, the natural move was to get outside the confines of corporate, university, and other user organizations and into the larger world of the telecommunications service providers. These firms included the traditional telephone companies (especially the former Bell operating companies), their recently hatched competitors (including WorldCom, Sprint, MCI, and the competitive local exchange carriers), the Internet service provider firms (AOL, Earthlink, and countless others), and other companies whose essential business it was to move voice and data across distances for their customers. They were all in the process of building up the communications infrastructure to handle an unprecedented increase in data transmission that was anticipated by virtually everyone. The demand of this "carrier class" of companies for networking equipment was going to be enormous, dwarfing the needs of the enterprises that Cisco served so profitably.

Cisco took its technological expertise, its marketing talents, and its enormous hoard of cash into the world of carrier-class customers. It ran into rough going very quickly because the differences between the enterprise market and the service provider arena were much greater than Cisco had anticipated. First, there were entrenched and sophisticated competitors. Lucent, Northern Telecom, and others had been providing switching equipment to telephone companies for decades. They were large, experienced, and had established relationships with their customers. Although they did need to move their product offerings to data transmission and packet switching from their traditional analog switched equipment, they gave every indication that they were up to the task. In addition to the usual suspects, Cisco also had to face firms younger than itself, eager to exploit their own technological prowess, and backed by IPO money from an enthusiastic investing public. As a new entrant into this market, Cisco was without the critical competitive advantages it enjoyed in the enterprise market. It had no captive customers; so far as established customer relationships were concerned, it was the outsider looking in. Without this kind of customer base, Cisco had no economies of scale in distribution or service support. Because Cisco was working on new products for new customers, it had no economies of scale advantages in research and development either.

Under these circumstances, the best Cisco could expect was to operate on a level playing field. The established telecommunications providers were big, powerful, wealthy, and technologically sophisticated. Cisco would not be able to re-create the relationships it had with many of its enterprise customers, where it was the expert and they were only too happy to have a supplier take the technology burden off their shoulders. The new companies in the telecom world, the fiber-optic carriers and Internet service providers, were large and technologically sophisticated even though they were neither profitable nor established. Like the major record companies in the CD market, these customers were unlikely to allow themselves to be captive to any single supplier. Even if they had, Cisco would not have benefited, since it was the existing telecommunications equipment firms, like Lucent, Nortel, Siemens, and Erickson, not Cisco the entrant, who had the relationships with the carriers.

Cisco entered the carrier-class business the old-fashioned way: it bought its way in. It was aggressive on pricing and generous on financing. It gave its carrier class customers easy credit terms to pay for their equipment. Cisco was rolling in cash and seemed able to afford the financing costs. But like many large, well-financed companies willing to use their balance sheets to overcome initial competitive disadvantages, Cisco's experience was not a happy one. Kodak's entry into copiers, AT&T's move into data-processing services and computers, Xerox's pursuit of office automation, IBM's attempts to unseat Microsoft in software and Xerox in copiers are all examples of highly regarded, deep-pocketed companies failing in markets that they decided to enter despite obvious competitive disadvantages. As Cisco learned, deep pockets are seldom a competitive advantage.

The speed and brutality with which this message was conveyed to Cisco were amplified by historical circumstances. In what seems obvious after the fact but was overlooked by almost everyone at the time, Cisco's carrier customers as a group were adding too much capacity. Not only were they seduced by an unduly optimistic forecast in the growth of demand—Internet use was projected to double every three months—but they ignored all the other people in the business who were also building an infrastructure to supply this anticipated demand. The great stock bubble of the late 1990s and the collapse of 2000–2002 were led up and led down by telecommunications and associated businesses. When some of the nascent ISP and telecommunications firms went bust, Cisco was left holding large and unsecured debt. More troubling still, some brand-new pieces of Cisco equipment found their way, via liquidations of bankrupt firms and the eBay auction platform, into the gray market. Cisco had to compete against its own products for what limited business remained in the carrier sector. Its strong balance sheet, which had allowed it to be so generous with credit, had come back to haunt it.

How bad did things get? Cisco's worst year was 2001, when it reported an operating loss of $2 billion, before taxes. Some of that stemmed from a restructuring charge of slightly more than $1 billion. For a company accustomed to making as much money as Cisco, with enormous margins on sales, assets, and invested capital, reporting a loss like that was a blow, even if Cisco had plenty of company in 2001, a dismal year for technology firms. Cisco's results were an amalgam of its old business, network equipment to enterprises, and its new venture into equipment for carriers. The true extent of its losses on the carrier side of the business, much greater than the total of $2 billion it reported, were masked by its continued profitability in the enterprise market.

MAKING A COMEBACK

Before the steep decline in its share price and the corresponding drop in earnings, Cisco's management had won top marks from Wall Street analysts and other industry observers for its ability to handle profitable growth and maintain its dominant position in an expanding industry. Now John Chambers and his team had to shift gears and manage during an economic and industry downturn. It took them several quarters to make the adjustment, but they were able to turn things around. Recognizing that the decline in revenue was more than just a minor cyclical incident, they moved to cut expenses and restore operating margins. They pulled Cisco back from the parts of the carrier-level networking equipment business in which it operated at a competitive disadvantage, where in order to make its original dent Cisco had had to buy its way in. Cisco did retain much of the router business. Even though Juniper Networks made some inroads here and became a legitimate competitor, Cisco continued to hold over half the market.* Its cost of goods sold began to shrink as the unprofitable parts of its carrier business were eliminated. (See figure 7.4.)

---

*Juniper's position was a difficult one. If it succeeded in entering against Cisco, that would indicate that barriers to entry in the enterprise routing market were diminishing. Thus, other Junipers were likely to follow. The alternative possibility was that Cisco's competitive advantages were fundamentally unimpaired, in which case Juniper's ultimate success in this market would be modest, at best.

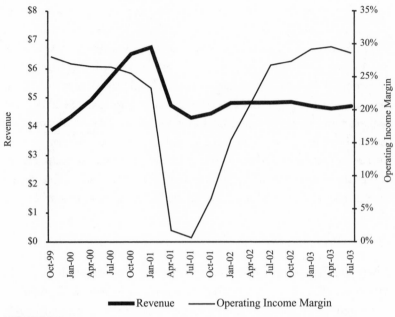

FIGURE 7.4

Cisco's quarterly revenue and operating income margin,
October 1999 through July 2003

Management also cut into overhead expenses. These had ballooned
as a portion of revenue when sales declined, starting in the April 2001
quarter. It took almost a year to bring these costs down below 45 percent of revenue, and another six quarters to get them down near 40 percent, which was still higher than they had been in the heady days before
sales dropped. Including one-time charges, Cisco's operating margins
fell from 17 percent in 2000 to a loss in 2001 but recovered up to 26 percent in 2003. This was Cisco's best year since 1999, and though it might
never return to the glory days of the mid 1990s, its management had
proved that it could operate in rough waters more successfully than
AT&T, Kodak, or Xerox.

TOASTERS?

Almost everybody makes toasters, even Philips (though not Cisco). There are more than fifty brands of toasters available in the United States. The models vary from simple and intentionally retro in design to futuristic, feature-laden, and whimsical. At a minimum, all are supposed to take a slice of bread and brown it without burning. Since most of the toasters come from companies with extensive small appliance lines, and a few from diversified giants like Philips and GE, the financial statements do not reveal how profitable toasters are to their manufacturers. But with no barriers to entry here, it is unreasonable to assume that any manufacturer is earning an exceptional return on its toaster assets. Though they differ from one another in functional and design features, one toaster is pretty much like another. If there were a sudden spurt in demand for one style or one functional element—toasters that sing when the bread is ready—then it would not be long before every manufacturer was offering a crooning toaster.

How different is a complicated and expensive piece of network equipment—a router, smart hub, or LAN switch—from a toaster? Initially very different, but ultimately, not so different at all. The success of Cisco in its original business attracted new entrants, most of whom could not put a dent in Cisco's performance during the first fifteen years of operations. Cisco's customers could not operate its equipment effectively without extensive technical and maintenance support. They were not sophisticated enough to mix and match communications equipment the way families do with household appliances. Also, the need to develop successive new generations of software and hardware makes fixed costs a permanently large part of total costs, and thus a source of economies of scale. (In contrast, in CD manufacturing, plant and equipment were a once-and-for-all expense. Economies of scale topped out at a two-million-disc-per-year plant.) All these factors created competitive advantages for Cisco, and put up barriers to entry in its enterprise-class business.

But it seems clear that these advantages diminish over time. Equipment becomes more reliable and easier to use. Support and service costs decline. Compatibility across company product lines increases as equipment functions become standardized. Research and development costs decline as product lines mature. Customers become more confident in their use of equipment and more willing to try new, lower-cost suppliers. Some of these changes have already affected Cisco. Newer companies, especially Juniper Networks, have started to take small chunks out of Cisco's business by offering even more cutting-edge technology, and older, established companies like Lucent, Alcatel, and Nortel, despite myriad problems, did not disappear.

Though Cisco recovered nicely from the telecom bust of 2001, it did not return to its glory days of the mid 1990s, when its rate of growth and enormous returns on investment propelled it briefly to the top of the market capitalization ranks. If the experience of other industries is indicative, the trends identified above will ultimately eliminate Cisco's competitive advantages entirely. No matter how complex and unique a product seems at the start, in the long run they are all toasters.

In the CD market, Philips never had the kind of honeymoon that Cisco enjoyed. It never established customer captivity; its customers were large and sophisticated, and its product did not require significant support. It also never benefited from economies of scale. Distribution and service support for raw, unrecorded CDs accounted for a tiny share of the costs, and while the original development costs may have been high, continuing R&D expenditures were negligible. Learning curve—related cost advantages, Philips's only remaining hope of competitive advantage, were undermined by the rapid-growth CD market, which allowed its competitors also to move quickly down the experience curve. Philips confronted a toaster world almost immediately.

In both these instances, the standard measures of market attractiveness are not what mattered for success. Neither huge size nor rapid growth were critical characteristics for strategy formulation. Nor were core competences the issue. Both Philips and Cisco brought high levels of relevant technical capabilities to the CD and network equipment markets, and only one of them succeeded, for a time, in producing exceptional returns.

What matters in a market are defensible competitive advantages, which size and growth may actually undermine. Size without competitive advantages was of no use to Cisco in the market for carrier-class equipment. Rapid growth in the CD market actually undercut the possibility of competitive advantages for Philips. Nor is differentiation a competitive advantage. Toasters are highly differentiated, but there are no barriers to entry and no competitive advantages in the toaster market. When products come to take on these characteristics of toasters, as most of them do over time, exceptional returns disappear.

CHAPTER 8

Games Companies Play

A Structured Approach to Competitive Strategy

PART I: THE PRISONER'S DILEMMA GAME

Our discussion so far has centered on competitive advantages: what they are; how to decide whether any firms in an industry enjoy them; how to exploit them.

For markets where there are no competitive advantages, the only strategy is a relentless focus on operational efficiency. The personal computer industry after 1990 and Philips's foray into the compact disc market are examples of companies that took this path, or should have.

Businesses like Wal-Mart in retailing and Coors in brewing did enjoy competitive advantages in their local markets. Their strategic challenge was to sustain and, if possible, to extend them. As we have seen, Wal-Mart was more successful than Coors at doing this. (These single dominant firms are at location 2 in figure 8.1.)

We turn now to more interesting and difficult situations, those in which a few firms enjoy competitive advantages within the same industry or market. Though one may be bigger than the others, the size and power distinctions are not great enough to make even the largest of them immune from assault by its competitors. These conditions are likely found in local service industries, like banking, retailing, and health-care systems, in consumer product markets, and often in entertainment and the media—the major TV networks, movie studios, and record companies. These circumstances are thorny to analyze and challenging to manage effectively. Strategic success depends on the deft handling of conscious mutual interactions among firms, which can encompass both competition and tacit cooperation. (These situations are at location 3 in Figure 8.1. The Cooperating/Bargaining elements will be treated in a later chapter.)

An examination of the rivalry between retailers Home Depot and Lowe's can reveal the range of issues that are involved when a small number of competitors interact with one another. The dimensions of that rivalry include decisions about individual pricing at the store level, particularly when a Home Depot and a Lowe's are near one another, about product line extensions, about store locations, about supplier relationships, and about levels of advertising. For every issue, the outcome of any action by Lowe's depends upon how Home Depot chooses to respond, and vice versa.

To see how complicated the strategy is for making these decisions, consider an ostensibly simple case. If Lowe's opens a store in a market that Home Depot has previously had to itself, an aggressive price response by Home Depot will have serious consequences for the new

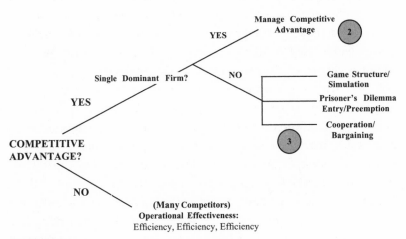

FIGURE 8.1

Competitive interactions within the competitive universe

store's profitability. Home Depot could decide to carry its response further by opening stores in markets where Lowe's has been unchallenged. Lowe's initial foray into Home Depot's territory would turn out to have been a very unfortunate move. But the countermeasures could themselves be costly for Home Depot, especially if Lowe's decides to retaliate in kind with lower prices and more store openings. Anticipating these responses from Lowe's might temper Home Depot's behavior.

Yet Home Depot might calculate that any restraint on its part would only encourage Lowe's in its penetration of Home Depot's markets, leading to price and location wars everywhere, which would be painful for both companies. Indeed, Home Depot, by adopting a truly fierce competitive stance, might even succeed in deterring Lowe's original expansion and never actually need to lower prices and open stores whose principal purpose is retaliation.

On its part, Lowe's might consider an entirely different set of strategies, avoiding a direct confrontation with Home Depot and limiting competition by having each chain concentrate in nonoverlapping market areas. By not engaging in a price war and by avoiding duplicative store overhead costs in a number of markets, both companies might walk away with significantly richer profit margins.

But, to look at the interactions one more time, what if Home Depot were to interpret Lowe's restraint as weakness? Might it take restraint as an invitation to be more aggressive and to move into all of the markets Lowe's had to itself? If that were the case, then Lowe's strategy of restraint might prove to have been an unmitigated disaster.

This situation is frustrating in its complexity. Lowe's must worry about what Home Depot is likely to do, which depends, in turn, on how Home Depot interprets Lowe's actions. This interpretation depends on how Lowe's reacts to Home Depot's behavior, the signals that Lowe's sends, and Home Depot's own readings of the business imperatives, which are influenced by Home Depot's culture. Moreover, all of these same factors apply identically to Lowe's readings of the signals Home Depot sends and on Lowe's culture. There is the danger here of infinite regress, mirrors reflecting mirrors ad infinitum. To bust out of this trap requires a clear focus and some useful simplifying assumptions.

PRICE COMPETITION AND THE PRISONER'S DILEMMA

Fortunately, the essential dynamics of most competitive interactions revolve around one of two issues: price or quantity. Of these, price competition is the most common form of interaction among a small number of competitors. There is a familiar dynamic to most of these situations, which we can get a sense of from this simplified, schematic case.

Assume that the offerings of these competing firms are basically equivalent. Then, so long as they charge the same for their product, the competitors divide the market equally. If they all charge a high price, relative to their costs, then they all earn high profits. If they all charge a low price, they still divide the market, but now each of them earns less. However, if one firm decides to charge a low price while others charge more, we can assume that the firm with the low price captures a disproportionately large share of the market. If the additional volume more than compensates for the smaller profit per unit due to the lower price, then the firm that dropped its price will see its total profits increase. At the same time, the firms that continue to charge a high price should see their volume drop so much that their profits will be less than if they also charged the low price. The essence of price competition among a restricted number of companies is that although there are large joint benefits to cooperation in setting high prices, there are strong individual incentives for firms to undermine this cooperation by offering lower prices and taking business away from the other competitors.

Competitive situations—games—of this sort take the name *prisoner's dilemma* because they imitate the choices faced by two or more accused felons who participate in a criminal activity, are caught, and are then interrogated separately. If they all cooperate with one another and refuse to confess, there is a strong probability that they will beat the charge, and they can expect a light sentence. But each of them can negotiate a deal with the police for even less jail time if he confesses and testifies against his confederates. The worst case is for an accused to maintain his innocence but have one of his confederates confess. Given these alternatives, there is a powerful temptation to abandon the group interest and confess. The incentive is both positive (get less jail time by confessing) and defensive (you had better confess because your friends can hang you out to dry if they confess and you don't). So it is no wonder that maintaining the cooperative position is difficult, both for accused felons and for competitive firms. The usual outcome is what is referred to in game theory as a "noncooperative equilibrium."

FORMAL DESCRIPTIONS OF
COMPETITIVE INTERACTIONS

Two models are widely used for formal presentations of the information relevant to describing competitive interactions. The first, known as the "normal" form in the language of game theory, is to present the information in a matrix. The second, called the "extensive" form, lays out the elements of the competitive interaction within a tree structure (this model is described in chapter 11). Although a prisoner's dilemma game can be modeled using the extensive form, it is more appropriate to use the matrix form. In price competition, the sequence of moves is not significant. The situation does not evolve over time in a way that requires long-range planning or a long-lived commitment of assets. Changing prices can be done at any time by competitors in any sequence. The matrix form of a game presents a picture that is appropriate to these kinds of simultaneous, repeatable changes.

Because of its two-dimensional design, a single matrix can only represent two competitors, one on the horizontal side, one on the vertical. The interaction between Lowe's and Home Depot is depicted in figure 8.2. In this example, Lowe's occupies the top side (horizontal dimension) of the matrix, Home Depot the left side (vertical dimension). Across the top is information about possible courses of action for Lowe's; in this example, the information is the price levels Lowe's may charge for a typical shopping basket of products. If the relevant price choices are $115 and $105 per basket, then each column in figure 8.2 represents a possible price for Lowe's.

Home Depot's corresponding choices are displayed on the left-hand side of the matrix (assuming that it is limited to the same two alternative prices as Lowe's, $115 and $105), with each row representing Home Depot's pricing decisions.

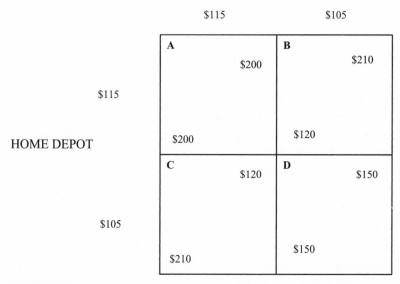

FIGURE 8.2
The matrix (or normal) form of the prisoner's dilemma

Each box in the matrix corresponds to one particular outcome of the actions; it is an intersection of a decision by Lowe's and one by Home Depot. Since these are pricing decisions, the outcomes are the levels of income (in this case, gross profit) for each company when certain prices are chosen. If both companies decide to price the goods in a typical shopping basket at $115, then the outcome in box A is that each earns $200 in gross profit per ten customers in the market. (The outcome for the player at the top, in this case Lowe's, is customarily located in the upper right-hand corner of the box; that for the player on the side, in the lower left-hand corner.) The other boxes represent outcomes from the other possible combinations of pricing decisions.

The outcomes themselves depend on the economics of this business. We are assuming that the cost of goods sold for the basket is $75. If both charge $115, they realize a gross profit of $40 per basket. If they divide the customers equally, then for every ten customers in the market, each firm captures five of them and earns $200 in gross profit. But if one firm charges $105 and the other $115, the firm with the lower price wins 70 percent of the customers, leaving only 30 percent for its competitor. If Lowe's price is $105 and Home Depot's is $115, as in box B, then Lowe's sells seven baskets to these ten customers and earns $30 gross profit on each basket, for a total of $210. Home Depot, with 30 percent of the market, earns $120 in gross profit ($40 per basket times three customers). In box C, the pricing and profitability are reversed, with Home Depot coming off best. If both firms charge $105, then each has a gross profit of $30 per basket, sells to five customers, and earns a gross profit of $150, as in box D.

The four boxes of the matrix represent the economic consequences of each of these combined pricing decisions. But profit may not be the only thing that concerns management. They may, as an example, care more about the absolute level of sales. Or they may focus on relative performance, either market share or profits, because beating Home Depot may be a deeply ingrained part of Lowe's culture (or vice versa). It is naïve to think that the bottom line is everybody's primary concern. The outcomes in the matrix should be adjusted, wherever possible, to account for these other motivations. It would be easier if all the actors were economically rational and never deviated from a focus on profitability. In fact they are not, and the payoffs really need to be calculated to reflect the motivations driving the people making the decisions. Ultimately, it is the culture of Home Depot that determines the values of different outcomes for Home Depot, the culture of Lowe's that determines the values of outcomes for Lowe's.

As we said, the matrix form is helpful for presenting a static picture of the consequences of choices. It is less helpful in depicting the sequence in which those choices are made. When choices are made virtually simultaneously—one-shot situations—the matrix is a useful model. It is also good for representing situations that repeat themselves: Home Depot lowers prices in round one and Lowe's responds; Lowe's lowers prices in round two and Home Depot responds; and so on.

After a few rounds of playing the prisoner's dilemma, intelligent competitors should be able to anticipate how the rival will react, and adjust their actions accordingly. The matrix is useful because it focuses on the consequences of choices, and allows the competitors to compare the outcomes.

The dynamic of this situation is clear. Although there are substantial benefits to cooperation—everyone charges a high price—there are also powerful incentives for individual competitors to deviate from this cooperation by reducing prices, gaining additional volume, and increasing their profits. This incentive is offensive—the deviating firm benefits from its lower price if the other companies continue to cooperate and maintain a high price. It is also defensive—if other firms are going to lower their prices, then each firm needs to protect itself by matching or even anticipating the lower price. The benefits of cooperation are constantly being undermined by the temptations to deviate and take market share. The equilibrium outcome of this game, in theory and often in practice, is a breakdown of cooperation and an industry mired in low prices. And once this low-priced equilibrium is reached, it is hard to escape from it. Any individual firm that tries to raise prices will lose so much of its business to low-priced competitors that its pioneering efforts lead to lower, not higher, profits.

REACHING EQUILIBRIUMS

The matrix form is ideal for examining *equilibriums*—outcomes that are stable because no competitor has an obvious incentive to change its action. These equilibriums depend on two conditions:

- *Stability of expectations.* Each competitor believes that the other competitors will continue to adhere to their present choices among the possible courses of action.
- *Stability of behavior.* Given the stability of expectations, no competitor can improve its outcome by choosing an alternative course of action.

The two conditions work together; if no competitor has a motive to change its current course of action (stability of behavior), then no change will occur, confirming the stability of expectations.

This concept of the likely outcome to a competitive situation is referred to in game theory as a "Nash equilibrium," after its developer John

Nash of *A Beautiful Mind* and Nobel Prize fame. In the Lowe's–Home Depot example, imagine that the current outcome has Lowe's at $115 per basket, Home Depot at $105 per basket (box C). If Lowe's expects Home Depot to keep its price at $105, Lowe's can improve its position by lowering its price to match Home Depot. With both at $105, they split the market and Lowe's gross profit rises from $120 to $150. Clearly, with Lowe's able to improve its situation by changing its price, the original situation is not an equilibrium. If Lowe's were to remain at $115, Home Depot would have no motivation to change from $105, so its position would be stable. But why would Lowe's not lower its price? For an equilibrium to exist, all the competitors must be satisfied with the status quo.

The situation is also unstable in box B, in which it is Home Depot that is charging $115 and capturing only 30 percent of the market. The more interesting situation is in box A. Here both competitors charge $115, split the market, and earn $200 in gross profits. Their joint total of $400 is the highest of the four possibilities. But if each believes that the other will maintain a price of $115, it makes sense for it to lower its price to $105, win 70 percent of the market, and pocket $210 rather than $200. So this situation is also not an equilibrium, since our second condition—stability of behavior—is not in place. The only equilibrium outcome is in box D, where both companies charge $105 per basket and earn $150 in gross profit for ten customers in the market. It makes no sense for either of them to deviate from this position and charge $115, because their gross profit would drop from $150 to $120. Since neither has an incentive to change, the first condition—stability of expectations—is also fulfilled.

The problem for our competitors is that neither does particularly well in this position, and their joint incomes are the lowest of the four alternatives. It is possible for them to achieve higher profits, but that requires more sophisticated strategies than simply pursuing their own most profitable course without regard to the competition. We will turn to these strategies later in the book. But even with more profitable approaches available, there will always be an incentive for individual competitors to deviate from these ostensibly superior outcomes.

The matrix form for presenting competitive information provides a straightforward approach to analyzing whether the current action choices and resulting outcomes are likely to be stable. Firms in situations with a few identifiable competitors can construct a matrix, place themselves and the other players into the matrix, and see whether the current situation is an equilibrium. If the answer is no, if it is clear that any player has an incentive to change its current action choices, then the firm doing the analysis can anticipate and prepare for such change. If the change has unfavorable implications, then the company can look for ways to alter the current situation to prevent such changes. For example, in our Lowe's–Home Depot case, if Lowe's thinks that Home Depot is preparing to lower its price to gain market share (move from box A to box C), Lowe's can announce that it will match whatever price Home Depot offers. That announcement will alert Home Depot that its expectations of stability on Lowe's part are mistaken, and it should reconsider its price cut.

The current outcome may look stable but not desirable. Instead of anticipating change, the company can look to induce its competitors to alter their actions and produce a more favorable outcome. In either case, and for competitive situations in general, an important step in strategic thinking is to examine the current situation to determine the extent to which it is an equilibrium.

ADDITIONAL PULLS ON EQUILIBRIUM

Situations like this one, in which there are large joint benefits from cooperation but strong individual incentives to deviate, are the most common form of competitive interactions. Our informal impression is that 80 to 90 percent of competitive interactions fit within the scope of this model. They almost invariably arise when there is direct competition among a restricted number of firms. When prices are very low and margins are small, the benefits of capturing additional business may not be large enough to make individual price cutting a profitable strategy. At that point, cooperation on pricing will be relatively easy to achieve and self-reinforcing. But as prices and profit margins rise, the gains from adding volume by cutting prices becomes more attractive. At some point, individual competitors will not be able to resist temptation, which is why sustaining cooperation on pricing is difficult. Because these situations are so common and troublesome, handling them well—achieving and maintaining the cooperative outcome, where everybody charges the higher price—is the most important skill that interacting competitors can develop.

Competition with these characteristics can take many forms other than cutting prices. In pursuit of market share, firms can spend more on advertising, on deploying a sales force, on enhancing the product, on longer warranties, on additional special features, and on anything else that makes the product more saleable, all of which are costly deals with the customers. In each case, an individual firm is willing to cut its margins in the expectation that the additional volume it wins will more than make up the forgone profits by charging less or spending more. And in each case, the firms as a group would benefit by forgoing the aggressive move to increase volume at the expense of the others. Still, the incentives for the individual firm are real and powerful, provided the margins are large, which is why it is difficult to sustain cooperation for controlling the costs of unconstrained competitive spending.

Competition for resources often follows a similar pattern. Baseball owners as a whole benefited from mutual restraints on bidding for players, restraints embedded in the "reserve clause" that kept players from leaving teams at the end of their contracts. But with the advent of television and additional sources of revenue, the restraint began to fade. Even before the reserve clause was eliminated in 1976, the owners had competed with one another by offering large bonuses for new players. After "free agency" became the rule, the demand for players who had played out their contracts became intense and salaries exploded, doing miraculous things for the investment accounts of star players but taking a large bite out of the teams' collective profitability.

TAMING THE DILEMMA

Despite the incentives to deviate and the ease with which competitors arrive at a negative equilibrium, there are steps that can be taken to reduce the impact of the prisoner's dilemma, if not eliminate it entirely. Fortunately, competitive interactions evolve over time. So it is possible to change the environment by making adjustments that support cooperation and control noncooperative behavior. These adjustments work by making deviant behavior less rewarding and cooperation less costly.

Adjustments—changing the rules, the payoffs, the players, or any of the other key factors—fall into two categories: structural and tactical. Structural adjustments are prior arrangements that directly limit the consequences of deviant behavior. Tactical adjustments are prior commitments to respond to deviations by a single firm. Their purpose is to reduce the benefits of deviation and lead the transgressor back to cooperation.

ADJUSTING THE STRUCTURE

Given the emphasis we have put on local dominance, it should be no surprise that the most elegant structural adjustment is for competitors to arrange their businesses to stay out of each other's way by occupying separate and distinct niches in the market. These niches can be defined by geography, by field specialization, even by times of the day. A striking example of distinguishing between segments of the same market was Pan Am's scheduling decision when it entered the New York–Boston air shuttle business, where Eastern Airlines had previously operated alone. Pan Am organized its flights to depart at the bottom of the hour, thirty minutes away from Eastern's. The move discouraged Eastern from trying to win Pan Am customers by cutting its prices, since a business traveler deciding to fly on the half hour was less likely to wait the extra time, even for a lower fare (for which his or her company, not the traveler, was paying). If Eastern did drop its fares, it would lose much more revenue by giving discounts to customers who would fly with it in any case than it would capture by wooing a few from Pan Am. The subsequent history of shuttle competition has born out the wisdom of Pan Am's strategy. Even as ownership has shifted from Eastern to USAir and from Pan Am to Trump to Delta, fares have been high and stable, and the offset departure times have been maintained.

Retailers and other service providers who cluster within a geographic region and avoid major overlaps with competitors are literally staying out of each other's way. Wal-Mart's initial concentration on markets it could dominate led both to economies of scale advantages and to limiting the temptation of price wars with other retail chains that have only a small presence on Wal-Mart's turf.

Concentration on nonoverlapping product niches serves the same purpose. Sotheby's and Christie's missed an opportunity to divide up the auction art market into areas of specialization, like Greek and Roman antiquities for one and Egyptian and Middle Eastern for the other, Italian Renaissance and Northern Renaissance, and so on. Had they pursued that strategy, each would have developed expertise, contacts, and reputation in its areas and been the natural choice for a seller of art within that special field. Each would have had little to gain and much to lose by cutting prices, since their clientele would not overlap. They would not have overtly colluded on setting prices, which damaged their business and their reputations and created a literal prisoner's dilemma for some of them. (We discuss the auction houses in more detail in chapter 15.)

The first structural adjustment to make, then, to escape the prisoner's dilemma is to avoid direct product competition. The adjustment can actually increase consumer choice, as in the Pan Am decision to fly on the half hour. It also can cut duplicative overhead, as in the case of the expertise needed in the auction houses, and enhance economies of scale, as in the examples of Wal-Mart and Coors, where their advantages diminished as they moved further afield.

Customer loyalty programs, if properly designed, are a second structural adjustment to limit the consequences of competitive price reductions. For example, frequent-flier programs offer customers benefits like free flights or upgrades as they accumulate miles flown on a particular airline. Two critical aspects in the design of these programs are generally absent: first, rewards must be tied to cumulative, not merely current, purchases so that they build customer loyalty over time; second, the rate at which rewards accumulate should increase with increasing volume. This last point is important, because if each mile flown earns the same unit of reward, the program is simply a general price discount. But if fliers earn rewards at an accelerating rate as they accumulate more miles, the incentive to book on their primary airline—to be loyal customers—is strengthened. They become less susceptible to the lure of discount flights on other carriers, and competing airlines are less likely to offer the lower-priced fares, since they end up reducing the charges to passengers who would have flown with them in any case. If winning customers from competitors by fare reductions becomes less attractive, the airlines as a group will be able to maintain higher prices that more than offset the cost of their frequent-flier programs.

In practice, the programs have not been effective in eliminating fare wars. Fliers built up large mile balances on several airlines, so they could be attracted by lower fares and still earn their frequent-flier miles; and the airlines hurt themselves by forming frequent-flier alliances that made travelers even more indifferent to the carrier they chose, since they might still be earning miles on a carrier where they had a large, and therefore valuable, balance. Loyalty programs only work to reduce price competition where the rewards to loyalty are substantial, and customers as a consequence concentrate their purchases. The airlines have attempted to rectify the situation by adding sunset provisions, so that unused miles expire after a set period of time, in an effort to reestablish the principle of increasing benefits to loyalty.

A third way of adjusting the structure is to limit output capacity in the market. If firms agree to restrict the amount of product that can be offered for sale, and then abide by that agreement, the benefits of price cutting by any of them will be sharply reduced or eliminated entirely. The price-cutting firm gains nothing if it cannot supply the additional customers it tries to capture by lowering its prices. Indeed, in many industries, the major problem arising from the installation of more capacity than the market can support is not the direct costs of creating and servicing the capacity. Rather, it is that with additional capacity available, a firm is tempted to lower prices in the hope that by winning more customers, it can make use of the new factories, equipment, space, time, or other assets. The price war that is likely to result undermines profitability, not only on the new business attracted, but on the preexisting business as well.

One of the most successful examples of capacity limitation has been a self-imposed code of conduct that restricted the amount of airtime that television networks could sell for commercials. Zoning laws and environmental regulations have prevented the construction of new capacity for certain kinds of activity. Industry safety standards and procedures that restrict the hours of operation or delay new construction have the same effect, as do tacit industry agreements to go slow on expansion.

For these adjustments to be successful, all the firms involved must agree to play by these rules. If some decide to deviate, they will benefit dispro-portionately at the expense of those that behave and keep their capacity limited. The cooperative situation quickly unravels, and a price war soon follows. Also, capacity limitation only works when the firms in the business are protected by barriers to entry. If newcomers can get in, no agreement by incumbents on limiting capacity can stand up. For example, restrictions on driving hours for truckers are unlikely to reduce capacity throughout the industry because any increase in shipping rates will attract new entrants like ants to a picnic.

A fourth kind of structural adjustment that also requires universal compliance by incumbents is the adoption of pricing practices that raise the cost to any firm that lowers its price. One typical arrangement is a so-called most-favored-nation (MFN) provision in industry pricing contracts. Under an MFN provision, if a firm offers a lower price or better terms to one customer, it must offer the same price or terms to all its customers. This policy keeps a company from poaching selective customers by offering lower prices, because any price reduction applies automatically to all of its customers. The costs of acquiring the new business almost invariably outweigh the gains. At the extreme, some MFN arrangements require rebates to customers who had previously paid more for an item than its current selling price. Though these arrangements appear to protect certain customers from paying more than others do for the same items, in fact all customers end up paying more because no firm is going to cut prices to gain new business. On occasion, antitrust authorities have actually enjoined the use of MFNs in an effort to maintain effective price competition among firms.

Another structural adjustment that restricts price competition is an agreement to limit purchasing and pricing decisions to a specific and narrow window in time. The television networks and other media have used preseason advertising purchase markets that operate for two to three weeks before the beginning of the annual season. During this period, advertising is implicitly sold for less than it will cost later on the spot market. By keeping the buying period short, the suppliers make it difficult for customers to play suppliers off against one another. The resulting "orderly" markets are less vulnerable to the threat of successive price reductions to which anxious media sellers might resort to fill slots if the purchasing period went on indefinitely.

Social interactions within an industry may serve as an informal but still powerful restraint on competitive behavior that undermines collective price discipline. Where there are industry norms that involve "fair" pricing among the firms, they may be strengthened by the added social stigma that attach to a deviating company. Thus, industries like ladies' undergarments, which have been characterized by remarkable discipline over many decades, tend to be industries in which the owners and managers come from similar backgrounds or geographic areas. The ability of these kinds of extra-economic connections to mitigate competition is one of the reasons why globalization of markets is often a precursor to the complete breakdown of limits on price competition, since the networks that bind owners and managers together seldom extend very far.

A final structural adjustment that restrains the degree of price and feature competition within an industry is the basic reward system, both formal and informal, within the competing firms. If a firm's bonus, promotion, and recognition systems values sales growth over profitability, then controls on price cuts that boost volume at the expense of profits are likely to be weak. Price competition within the industry is likely to be intense, and it will be impossible to maintain relatively high prices.

In an extreme version of this reward system, some firm cultures prize performance relative to competitors above other achievements. Gains in market share become more important than the growth that comes simply because the industry is expanding. Since relative performance is a zero-sum game, firms in such an industry will compete relentlessly. There is virtually no hope for a cooperative outcome to the prisoner's dilemma game of price and feature competition. Only when the culture of the firms within an industry concentrates on profits and on avoiding unnecessary risk does cooperation to the benefit of all become possible.

TACTICAL RESPONSES

Structural adjustments of the sort we have discussed are the most potent management tools for overcoming the natural tendency of prisoner's dilemma situations to leave everyone worse off than they would be if they could cooperate. They apply to direct price competition and to competition over product features, advertising, and service support, and even to competition over resources. If for some reason these structural adjustments cannot be implemented, tactical responses are a second means of escaping from the prisoner's dilemma. As complements or alternatives to structural adjustments, they can help inhibit direct competition.

Any successful tactical response in a prisoner's dilemma/price-competitive situation requires two components: an immediate—even automatic—reaction to a competitor's price reduction, and a simultaneous signal of a willingness to return jointly to higher prices. The first component makes certain that a firm that cuts prices never benefits from any reductions it has initiated. A firm under attack counters immediately and even automatically by matching the new, lower prices. This rapid response should halt customer losses to the deviant firm, which ends up suffering from the adverse consequences of lower prices without the gains from increased sales. Management of the deviant firm should realize after a round or two that lowering prices to attract customers is not a winning strategy. If management is reasonable, it will abandon the approach and return to a pricing policy that maintains higher prices for the industry. The second component, the signal of a willingness to raise prices jointly, is necessary to make sure that the firms not remain mired in the low-price environment created by the initial price cuts and the immediate and often automatic matching responses.

"Best industry price contracts" are an example of an automatic price response strategy. Such contracts provide reimbursement to customers if the price the customers pay is higher than one verifiably offered by an industry competitor. These contracts announce to customers and competitors that the firm will match any reductions a rival might make. "Meet or release" contracts are another automatic response, with the added benefit of not requiring a firm to match a rival's price if it thinks it is too low for anyone to make a profit. Advertised policies that guarantee to match or beat any price advertised by a competitor are a common form of an automatic price response.

Without tactical responses that trigger automatically, it is important for firms to be vigilant regarding competitors' prices and to be organized to respond rapidly. High-minded indifference to rivals' price-cutting behavior, and an unwillingness to step on the treadmill of lower prices, is an invitation to disaster in a prisoner's dilemma environment. The competitor benefits from its original move to lower price and the nonresponding firm suffers a loss of customers and a precipitous drop in profits. More important, if any competitor learns that aggressive price-cutting behavior works, it becomes more difficult to correct that behavior later on—an invitation to extended, profit-destroying price wars.

Selective responses are often preferable to blanket responses when a company is trying to deter noncooperative behavior. Consider the case of an established bank faced with a rival that has made an offer of below market loan rates in order to attract new customers. The target bank could respond by matching the lower rates for all its borrowers to keep them in the fold. But by being selective and matching the lower rates only for its borrowers with good credit, while letting the marginal borrowers be captured by the rival, the bank has improved the quality of its loan portfolio without antagonizing clients by having to call in loans or deny new ones. At the same time, it has passively off-loaded its suspect borrowers to its aggressive competitor, whose own loan portfolio is now more likely to experience a higher level of defaults and a reduction in profitability. Though it may take some time, this lesson to the aggressive rival is likely to curb its tendency to offer discounts in the future.

Any selective response designed to keep better customers while letting the marginal ones escape will have similar effects. An industry whose firms are equipped to meet price cutting with selective responses should enjoy greater price stability than industries where firms cannot be selective. The other side of the coin is that selectivity can be an offensive tool as well, and companies that can poach their rivals' best customers are going to do so, and thus encourage price competition.

Selectivity can take a second form. Companies responding to aggressive price behavior should pick their spots. The temptation in a price war is to attack a noncooperative rival where the rival is weakest, and weakest often means where the rival has a small market share and limited distribution. But economically, the opposite approach generally makes more sense. If a competitor cuts prices in a market where you have a dominant market share, you may be tempted to respond right there with further price cuts to teach the interloper a lesson. But this response has a "cut off your nose" quality about it. If the incumbent firm is selling 2 million units per month in the market, and the interloper is selling only 400,000, then each one-dollar reduction in price costs the incumbent $2 million per month, and the interloper $400,000. Who is being hurt more?

A better response is to pick a market where the intruder is large and the incumbent small, and to cut prices in that market. If the competitor responds, it, and not the incumbent, bears the disproportionate costs of the price war. Indeed, it may even be worthwhile to introduce—or threaten to introduce—a new product into a competitor's market solely for the purpose of letting the competitor know how painful price wars can be. What should be kept in mind is that attacking rivals is a tactic whose goal is to restore price stability and enhance industry cooperation, not an end in itself.

Like many things of value, cooperative arrangements are easier to break than to mend. The second component of a tactical adjustment in a prisoner's dilemma situation, signaling for a joint return to higher prices, is difficult to accomplish. If all managers were rational and focused on profitability, they would see the wisdom of rescinding a price decrease as soon as their competitors responded with their own lower prices. But that doesn't always happen. The path back to higher prices is made more complicated because any actions taken by the competitors need to avoid violating antitrust laws. Face-to-face meetings to argue for or negotiate a return to higher prices are clearly illegal. Using the telephone to accomplish the same ends is also unlawful, as the president of American Airlines found out when he called his counterpart at Braniff, trying to arrange for a joint price increase.

But there are approaches that are both effective and lawful. A company's management that demonstrates a public attitude stressing the welfare of the industry as a whole on all matters, not just prices, signals a willingness to cooperate that can help reestablish industry cooperation in a prisoner's dilemma environment without triggering the wrath of antitrust enforcers. Working together in activities like lobbying the government, establishing industry-wide product standards, undertaking group charitable endeavors—none of which have anything to do with setting prices—reinforces cooperative attitudes. More directly, firms can signal a willingness to raise prices by announcing actual price increases. A rapid response from competitors to go along is critical to reestablishing price discipline, just as an immediate reaction to a price reduction is necessary to discipline the aggressive price cutter. Whenever a rival demonstrates a desire to moderate price competition, it needs to be encouraged.

Like price reductions to punish aggressive behavior, price increases to promote cooperation are best carried out selectively. A price increase in a conspicuous market—Peoria, Illinois, used to be the standard—is more likely to be noticed by rivals than price increases spread randomly across the landscape. Price increases near the headquarters of a rival firm are also likely to get attention, although there is the danger that a continual reliance on them will also get the attention of the antitrust enforcers.

If a particular firm can establish a leadership position on industry matters, and if that firm has a culture that emphasizes profit over market share or sales volume, then that firm may be relied on by its competitors to resurrect industry cooperation on prices as well as the other joint concerns. Having a recognized leader with this attitude is helpful in escaping the prisoner's dilemma trap, especially after a price war and the concomitant breakdown in cooperation. Cooperation can only be reestablished if individual firms control reflexive, testosterone-induced competitive impulses. If firms have jumped into the fray without a plan for ending the conflict, the chances for a return to harmony are slim. "Never start a war you don't know how to end" is as useful a principle for companies as it is for countries.

Structural and tactical adjustments to sustain cooperation in a prisoner's dilemma are mutually reinforcing, not mutually exclusive. Having structural policies in hand may facilitate tactical responses. For example, prices that are uniform, transparent, and public are easier for firms to match than prices that vary across customers and circumstances, prices that are complicated and obscure, and price levels that are negotiated privately. When industry practice embraces uniform and publicly announced prices, it is easy for companies quickly to match a reduction put in place by any deviator looking to gain customers. The prima facie virtues of these pricing principles for both firms and customers are reinforced, for firms at least, by their effectiveness in helping to sustain industry cooperation.*

Although the discussion of responses so far has been addressed to price competition, it applies equally to competition over features, discounts, advertising, and resources. In all of these related areas, an aggressive firm decides that it can win customers by offering more, charging less, spending more to attract them, or paying more for scarce resources. In all of them, there are joint gains from cooperation but strong incentives for individual defection. Each of these initiatives is a blow to joint profitability, and each of them can be countered by the same kind of structural and tactical adjustments that work to make price competition less desirable.

And one final point to remember: understanding how the prisoner's dilemma works and the tools for coping with it can be of value to those market participants—usually customers—who actually benefit from competition and are harmed by industry cooperation. Prosecutors dealing with real prisoners know that they need to keep the prisoners isolated from one another and to bargain with them separately. Customers of companies in a cooperating industry should seek private, nontransparent price arrangements; deal with suppliers individually, offering to concentrate their business with those who defect on price or features; and cooperate with other large customers in trying to undermine industry cooperation. A knowledge of the dynamics of the prisoner's dilemma can cut both ways.

---

* These pricing structures do have some drawbacks. They may limit the revenue-harvesting benefits of price discrimination—charging more to customers who put a high value on the goods or services, like airline travelers who need tickets for tomorrow, and less to customers who put a lower value on the product, like travelers who will buy bargain fares months in advance, or take any flight available at the last minute.

CHAPTER 9

Uncivil Cola Wars

Coke and Pepsi Confront the Prisoner's Dilemma

THE PEPSI CHALLENGE

In 1974, Pepsi stood third, behind both Coca-Cola and Dr Pepper, for soda sales in Dallas, Texas. A Pepsi sales manager decided to confront Coca-Cola directly. He began offering supermarket customers a taste test, to see whether they preferred Pepsi to Coke, provided they did not know which they were drinking. (Dr Pepper was ignored.) Since Pepsi's research had previously discovered a wide preference for Pepsi—58 percent to 42 percent—in blind taste tests, he was deservedly confident that his soda would prevail. It did, and when he publicized the results, Pepsi's share of the local market increased. The gambit was so successful that the president of Pepsi USA decided to broaden it. In 1975, the challenge moved from Dallas to all the markets served by company-owned bottlers, accounting for 20 percent of the company's soda sales. In two years the company went national with the campaign, publicizing the fact that customers liked the taste of Pepsi better than Coca-Cola. It helped Pepsi extend its lead over Coke in food store sales.

The campaign was brash, effective, and more than a little humiliating for Coca-Cola, but it was only the latest in a long series of competitive attacks that Pepsi had launched at its larger, more profitable, and better established rival. The challenge did catch Coca-Cola's attention, and the Cola Wars intensified as both sides joined in fierce fighting.

This chapter will concentrate on the competition between Coca-Cola and Pepsi in the domestic soft drink business. All the forays the companies made into other industries—motion pictures, wine and spirits, snack food, television programming, equipment leasing, and even closely related products like bottled water—we are going to ignore, as the soda makers might have done as well. We are also going to pay little attention to the international operations of the firms, even though they were a large (and for Coca-Cola, the major) source of profits. The intense competition within the U.S. market—the American version of the War of the Roses—is interesting enough, especially since it took the companies, especially Coca-Cola, a long time to learn how to deal with their rivals without inflicting great damage upon themselves.

COLA DRINKS: A BRIEF HISTORY

Coca-Cola and Pepsi-Cola had similar origins. Each was created by a pharmacist in a southern city toward the end of the nineteenth century, Coca-Cola in Atlanta in 1886, Pepsi-Cola in New Bern, North Carolina, in 1893. Each started as a single drugstore counter treat, and each was good enough to expand, first to other drugstores, then through bottlers to a wider audience. Coca-Cola was immensely more successful than Pepsi during the first five or six decades. Edward Woodruff bought the company in 1919 for $25 million, a major investment for that period. Pepsi, by contrast, went into bankruptcy more than once, and often teetered on the brink. As late as 1950, when Alfred Steele became CEO of Pepsi, some employees felt he had come to liquidate the company.

But Steele did not put Pepsi out of its misery. Instead, he made it a respectable competitor of Coca-Cola, where he had been a marketing executive. He introduced larger, "family-sized" bottles, which Pepsi and its distributors sold through the newly popular supermarkets that expanded in the national suburbanization thrust following the end of World War II. In the first eight years of his tenure, Pepsi's revenues more than tripled. Steele's successor, Donald Kendall, who became CEO in 1963, continued the campaign to take market share from Coke. The company began to focus on younger drinkers, people who had not yet developed the habit of always ordering Coca-Cola. In 1975, Pepsi out-sold Coke in food stores for the first time.

For many years, Coca-Cola's primary strategy toward Pepsi had been to deny its rival's existence. Executives were forbidden from mentioning Pepsi during staff meetings, nor did they discuss it with Coca-Cola bottlers. They belatedly increased the basic Coke bottle size to twelve ounces in 1955, a move Pepsi had made twenty years earlier. And they changed their advertising slogan in 1960 from "Be Really Refreshed" to "No Wonder Coke Refreshes Best." Coca-Cola's head-in-the-sand approach was intended as some form of benign neglect—if we do nothing, maybe the problem will disappear on its own. Unfortunately for Coca-Cola, it was benign only for Pepsi, which continued to grow in the U.S. soft drink market, largely at Coca-Cola's expense. Coca-Cola needed a more effective strategy to deal with its upstart rival. The requisite first step in developing that strategy, both for the company in its actual deliberations and for its critics in retrospect, is an analysis of the industry and the competitive regime in which the company operates.

INDUSTRY ANALYSIS

On its path from flavorings and sweeteners to the thirsty consumer, a drink of soda passes through a number of corporate hands. The soda companies themselves, who manufacturer syrup and concentrate, are clearly at the center of the soft drink industry (figure 9.1). Because they have owned and operated some of the other links in the product chain, it is important to delineate precisely those elements in that chain that are properly part of this industry and those that are genuinely outside it as suppliers and customers, even if under the same corporate umbrella.

It is clear that the suppliers of raw materials are various, numerous, and not integrally related to the soda companies. Both Coca-Cola and Pepsi made some of their own cans starting in the 1960s; they were out of the packing business by 1990. On the other end of the chain, there are even more companies that sell the drinks to the consumers, whether in supermarkets, restaurants, gas stations, or baseball stadiums. They

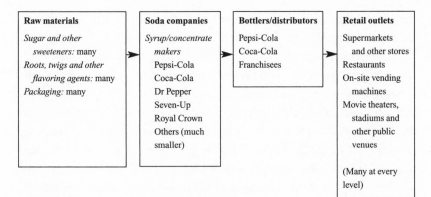

Raw materials	Soda companies	Bottlers/distributors	Retail outlets
Sugar and other sweeteners: many *Roots, twigs and other flavoring agents:* many *Packaging:* many	*Syrup/concentrate makers* Pepsi-Cola Coca-Cola Dr Pepper Seven-Up Royal Crown Others (much smaller)	Pepsi-Cola Coca-Cola Franchisees	Supermarkets and other stores Restaurants On-site vending machines Movie theaters, stadiums and other public venues (Many at every level)

FIGURE 9.1
Map of the soft drink industry

are not integrally related to the soda makers. This point might have been arguable during the period when PepsiCo owned Pizza Hut, Taco Bell, and other mass food outlets that sold soda in large quantities, but the fact that the restaurants were later spun off supports the position taken here, that the "last mile" in soda distribution is a distinct industry. Also, no beverage company ever acquired McDonald's, the dominant firm in the fast-food industry, which was successful operating as a customer of the soft drink companies, not an affiliate.

The bottlers and distributors, by contrast, are joined to the soda companies at the hip. Many of them have been owned by the companies at various times, others are franchisees. The soda companies charge them for concentrate and syrup and have raised prices at times on the promise of providing additional advertising and promotional support. Advertising has generally been split between soda companies and bottlers on a 50/50 basis, whereas two-thirds of promotional costs are borne by bottlers. Whatever the divisions, these are allied campaigns. The soda companies cannot operate successfully unless their bottlers and distributors are profitable and content. Whether company-owned or franchised, the bottlers and distributors are an integral part of the soft drink industry.

The bottling function is the part of the industry that demands the most capital investment. The high-speed lines are expensive and highly specialized; cans don't work on lines designed for bottles, nor will a twelve-ounce bottle move down a line intended for quart containers. The demand for capital has been one of the reasons why the concentrate companies have moved in and out of the bottler segment at various times, adding funds when necessary, then selling shares to the public when possible. Because Coca-Cola and Pepsi have seldom synchronized their degree of ownership involvement in the bottler segment, their financial statements are often difficult to compare. The trimmed-down concentrate maker, selling flavor to the bottlers and fountains, will have a high return on sales and an extraordinarily high return on invested capital. But if we add in some company-owned bottlers, the margins shrink.

WHICH COMPETITIVE REGIME?

We have divided markets into two competitive regimes: those with barriers to entry and those without. In which one do Coca-Cola and Pepsi operate?

Both key indicators of the presence of barriers to entry and competitive advantage—stable market shares and a high return on capital—are present here. By the time of the Pepsi Challenge, in the late 1970s, the market shares of the major players within the domestic soft drink industry had become quite stable. At the top were the two giants, Coke and Pepsi, sharing over 60 percent of the market between them. The rest of the revenue went to three other popular drinks and a host of private label, local, or other decidedly third-tier players. See table 9.1.

The shares of both Coca-Cola the drink and Coca-Cola the company did slip slightly during this period, while those of PepsiCo inched up. Though these changes were large enough to finally put Coca-Cola on notice that it had to do something about Pepsi, they are not the kind we would find in industries operating on a more level playing field, without barriers to entry. The same stability applies to the smaller brands. Seven-Up, Dr Pepper, and Royal Crown hung on to their shares of the market. They may have had fewer loyal drinkers than the two giants, but they were loyal nonetheless.

A second indicator confirms the existence of barriers. Returns to

TABLE 9.1

Market share in the soft drink business, 1977–82
(by case volume)

	1977	1978	1980	1982
Coca-Cola	26.3%	25.8%	25.3%	24.6%
Diet Coke				0.3%
Sprite	3.0%	3.0%	3.0%	2.9%
Tab	2.8%	2.9%	3.3%	4.0%
Others	4.2%	4.0%	4.3%	3.8%
Coca-Cola Company total	36.3%	35.7%	35.9%	35.6%
Pepsi-Cola	20.0%	20.4%	20.4%	20.3%
Diet Pepsi	2.4%	2.7%	3.0%	3.3%
Mountain Dew	2.2%	2.7%	3.2%	3.2%
Others	1.4%	1.2%	1.1%	1.3%
PepsiCo total	26.0%	27.0%	27.7%	28.1%
Seven-Up	7.3%	7.0%	6.3%	6.7%
Dr Pepper	5.6%	6.0%	6.0%	5.2%
Royal Crown Cola	4.6%	4.3%	4.7%	3.9%
Other companies	20.2%	20.0%	19.4%	20.5%
total non-Coke, non-Pepsi companies	37.7%	37.3%	36.4%	36.3%

Coca-Cola and PepsiCo from their soft drink businesses were exceptionally high (table 9.2).* For businesses requiring little capital investment per dollar of sales, operating margins in the 16–17 percent range translate into after-tax returns on invested capital of at least 30 percent. As this figure is roughly three times the ROIC for the average U.S. publicly traded corporation, it supports the claim that there are barriers to entry within the soft drink industry, and that Coke and Pepsi operate inside them.

But table 9.2 also reveals another important piece of information. As the contest between the two companies began to intensify in the later 1970s, the profit margin of both firms started to shrink. When Coca-

---

* Because by the mid 1970s, both Coca-Cola and PepsiCo had become conglomerates, and because both had large foreign operations, the profitability of their domestic soft drink businesses needs to be extracted from the consolidated corporate financial statements and return on capital estimated on the basis of operating figures.

TABLE 9.2
U.S. soft drink sales and operating income ($ million)

	1977	1978	1980	1982
Coca-Cola				
U.S. and Puerto Rico soft drink sales	$1,178	$1,307	$1,928	$2,281
U.S. and Pureto Rico operating income	$201	$191	$204	$250
Operating margins	17%	15%	11%	11%
PepsiCo				
U.S. soft drink sales	$876	$1,000	$1,403	$1,867
U.S. operating income	$136	$159	$177	$221
Operating margins	16%	16%	13%	12%

Cola finally picked up the gauntlet that Pepsi had been hurling for many years, it punished itself as much as its rival. We will return to this episode of corporate warfare and the players' strategies after we finish the discussion of competitive advantages in the soft drink business.

THE SOURCE OF COMPETITIVE ADVANTAGES

The existence of barriers to entry indicates that the incumbents enjoy competitive advantages that potential entrants cannot match. In the soft drink world, the sources of these advantages are easy to identify. First, on the demand side, there is the kind of customer loyalty that network executives, beer brewers, and car manufacturers only dream about. People who drink sodas drink them frequently, and they relish a consistency of experience that keeps them ordering the same brand, no matter the circumstances. A beer drinker who normally orders Budweiser will try a Kirin in a Japanese restaurant, a Tsingtao in a Chinese restaurant, or a Dos Equis when eating Mexican food. Neither Pepsi nor Coke drinkers ask for Mexican cola. And there is no upscale version of cola for devotees who become more affluent, no BMW to lease once the Ford has lost its allure.

Second, there are large economies of scale in the soda business, both at the concentrate-maker and bottler levels. Developing new products and advertising existing ones are fixed costs, unrelated to the number of cases sold. Equally important, the distribution of soda to the consumer benefits from regional scale economies. Concentrate supplied by the soda company is sent to bottlers, who add water, bubbles, and sweetener (always for Pepsi, and by the 1980s for Coke), close the containers, and send the drink on to a variety of retail outlets. As with beer, the water is heavy and thus expensive to haul over long distances. The more customers in a given region, the more economical the distribution. A bottler of Coke, selling the product to 40–50 percent of the soda drinkers in the market area, is going to have lower costs than someone peddling Dr Pepper to 5–6 percent of the drinkers.

The combination of captive customers and economies of scale creates a dominant competitive advantage, but it has not been so strong as to eliminate all the other soda firms. They can join together to use independent bottlers and distributors and make their sodas available. No one dies of thirst from not being able to find a Seven-Up. But the smaller firms do not threaten the two leviathans in the industry. They tend to get bought and sold each time an investor thinks he has discovered a way to squeeze more profit out of this variety of sugar water than the previous owner did. And these investors have a point. The second-tier brands are also protected by barriers to entry. They have loyal customers, and Dr Pepper, for one, because of its regional concentration, gains some benefits from economies of scale. The steady cash flow has made them ideal candidates for leveraged buyouts.

GUNFIGHT AT THE KO CORRAL: THE SODA MAKERS PLAY THE PRISONER'S DILEMMA

The prisoner's dilemma is like a marriage in Gomorrah. Though there are rewards for the parties to remain faithful, these are often overwhelmed by the incentive to cheat. Cheating by one member often leads to cheating by both, and the marriage dissolves under the weight of mutual distrust. In an environment like this, keeping a marriage intact demands work, attention, and the desire on both sides to cooperate in the interests of the whole.

From its inception, the Coke (ticker symbol = KO) and Pepsi marriage was a nightmare. Coke, the dominant partner, simply ignored Pepsi longer than it should have. Not until the 1970s would Coke executives even mention Pepsi in internal meetings. Pepsi, the neglected spouse, misbehaved repeatedly. In 1933, at the depth of the Depression, it effectively cut its price in half, doubling the size of the bottle to twelve ounces while keeping the price at five cents. In the 1950s, it resumed its attack. As we mentioned, Pepsi moved earlier into supplying supermarkets and it targeted those drinkers who were up for grabs: young, unattached to either brand, and with money to spend. It seduced them with pop music stars and made them into a youth phenomenon—the Pepsi Generation. It sponsored concerts and other promotions geared to this market. To drive home the point, it ridiculed Coke as the old folks' drink, something served in retirement communities and nursing homes.

For its part, Coca-Cola paid no attention to many of these moves by Pepsi, a strategy that did nothing to discourage its rival from continuing its aggressive stance. In terms of the prisoner's dilemma, Pepsi generally chose the noncooperative option, and Coca-Cola did nothing to punish it for its behavior. Table 9.3 is a chronology of initiatives and responses through 1982.

For almost all of this period, the initiative rested with Pepsi. Coca-Cola's responses were delayed, timid, and ineffective. It took twenty years for it to offer Coke in a twelve-ounce bottle; it was reluctant to compete with its own six-and-a-half-ounce skirt-shaped container, which had attained iconic status. It trailed Pepsi into the supermarkets, and it followed Pepsi's direct-store-door (DSD) delivery service. Aside from being the first to introduce a lemon-lime drink (ahead of Pepsi, that is, but certainly not Seven-Up) and a diet version of its cola (again, in front of Pepsi but not Royal Crown), Coke was playing follow the leader. As a consequence, Pepsi was able to triple its revenues in the 1950s and reduce Coca-Cola's lead in the domestic soft drink business. At the end of World War II, Coca-Cola commanded 70 percent of the market; by 1966, that had fallen to 30 percent, with Pepsi second with 20 percent.

By the late 1970s, Pepsi still trailed Coke, but it was making inroads, especially with younger drinkers and in the supermarket/food store channel. Though this success may have been cause for celebration at Pepsi headquarters, the history of conflict between the companies did

TABLE 9.3

Coke's and Pepsi's Competitive Steps, 1933–1982

YEAR	Pepsi initiates	Coca-Cola responds and initiates	Pepsi responds
1933	Lowers price of 12-oz. bottle to 5 cents; 1939: "twice as Much for a Nickel, Too" radio jingle	Coke increases size to 12 oz. in 1955	
1950	Alfred Steele becomes CEO; initiates "Beat Coke" policy	1955, Changes advertising slogan to "Be Really Refreshed"	
1950s	Introduces 24 oz bottle; focuses on sales through supermarkets		
1950–58	Increases revenue 300%		
1961		Introduces Sprite	Introduces Mountain Dew in 1964
1963		Introduces Tab	Introduces Diet Pepsi in 1964
1963	Donald Kendall becomes CEO		
1964	Launches "Pepsi Generation" campaign		
1960 and 1970s	Improves service to supermarkets through direct store door (DSD) delivery operations, better displays	Follows suit	
early 1970s	Raises price for concentrate by 20%, on par with Coke. Spends new margin on advertising and promotions	Also increases spending on ads and promotions	
1974	Begins Pepsi Challenge with blind taste tests in Dallas		
1975	Has largest share of food store sales		
1975	Extends Challenge to markets accounting for 20% of sales		
1976		CEO Austin announces that United States is not a growth area for Coca-Cola	
1977	Pepsi Challenge now nationwide	Starts price discounts in areas where Coke is strong, Pepsi weak	
1980	John Sculley, president of Pepsi USA, wants bottlers to attack Coke's stronghold in vending machines	Getting 62% of soda sales from international market [Pepsi gets 20% of its sales in these markets]	

TABLE 9.3 (continued)
Coke's and Pepsi's Competitive Steps, 1933–1982

YEAR	Pepsi initiates	Coca-Cola responds and initiates	Pepsi responds
1981		Robert Goizueta becomes CEO; announces aim to grow in U.S. market	Responds to price discounts
1982		Begins more aggressive advertising with new "Coke Is It" slogan	
1982		Begins price discounts: sells 50% of food store volume at discount	Follows suit; matches discounts
1982		Introduces Diet Coke, first use of Coke name on second brand; it becomes the largest diet drink in 1983	

not bode well for the future of this relationship. Each side seemed more interested in inflicting pain than in finding some way to achieve harmony and mutual gain. Executives in both companies were rewarded for sales growth and market share gains, even if they had to sacrifice profit to get there. A warrior culture permeated the two firms, setting the standards for attitude and behavior. These qualities are not conducive to a successful marriage. This was the environment in which Coca-Cola embarked on its long-belated response to the Pepsi Challenge.

COCA-COLA'S FIRST MOVE: A SHOT IN THE FOOT

Coca-Cola, watching its market share erode slowly and its operating margins shrink, decided to make a frontal assault on Pepsi. In 1977, it initiated a price war to gain market share. Price wars between two elephants in an industry with barriers to entry tend to flatten a lot of grass and make customers happy. They hardly ever result in a dead elephant. Still, there are better and worse ways of initiating a price contest. Coca-Cola chose the worst. Instead of lowering concentrate prices across the country, it focused on those regions where its share of the cola market was high (80 percent) and Pepsi's low (20 percent). This tactic ensured that for every dollar of revenue Pepsi gave up, Coke would surrender four dollars. In these markets, the Coke bottler was company-owned, the Pepsi bottler an independent franchisee.

In the face of this assault, Pepsi had no choice but to support the bottler with its own price cuts in concentrate or see all of its other franchisees question the company's commitment to its indispensable partners. So Pepsi rose to the Coke challenge, as Coke might have predicted had it considered carefully its own tactics. Pepsi cut prices for its concentrate and increased spending on advertising. Both companies ended up slicing into their margins. And Coca-Cola's initiative did not stop the gradual loss of market share to Pepsi.

In the normal form of the noncooperative game, the worst box for the players to find themselves in is the one in which neither cooperates (figure 9.2). Unfortunately for their joint benefit, it is also the one in which they are most likely to end up—the equilibrium—since it is the

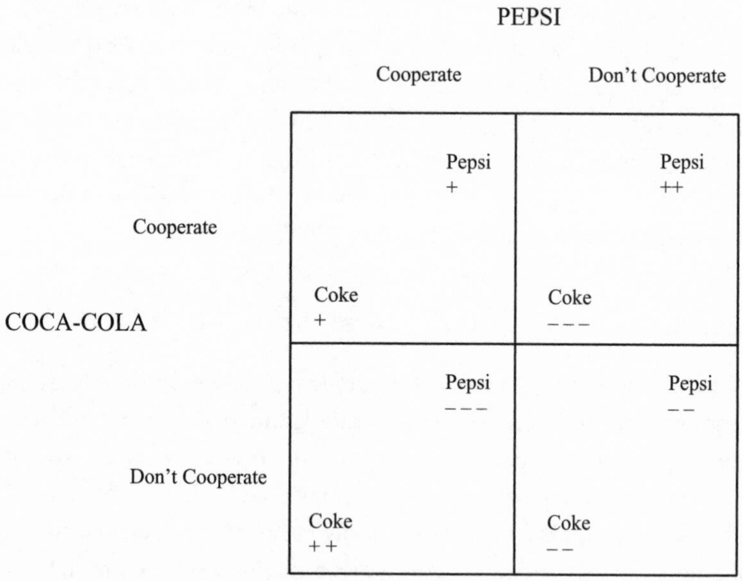

PEPSI

		Cooperate	Don't Cooperate
		Pepsi +	Pepsi ++
COCA-COLA	Cooperate		
		Coke +	Coke − − −
		Pepsi − − −	Pepsi − −
	Don't Cooperate		
		Coke + +	Coke − −

FIGURE 9.2

best choice each can make if it assumes that the other will also make that choice.

Coca-Cola's price-cutting strategy, targeted at itself more than its rival, was expensive for both firms, but more damaging to Coke.

COCA-COLA'S SECOND MOVE: BACKING INTO SUCCESS

Both companies continued to introduce new drinks during this period: diet, decaffeinated, and decaffeinated diet versions of the colas, as well as sodas with other flavorings. They were aggressive in managing and extending their shares of supermarket shelf space, capitalizing on their direct-store-door (DSD) delivery capacity. In contrast to price wars and expensive advertising, the battle for shelf space, which they fought to a draw, hurt the smaller soda brands rather than each other. Both the introduction of new beverages (development costs and advertising campaigns) and the servicing of markets with direct delivery (local scale economies) were activities that benefited from economies of scale. The proliferation of varieties and superior service allowed the two majors to shift some sales to themselves, at the expense of the smaller players.

But despite this success relative to Seven-Up, Dr Pepper, and the like, Coke was still coming out on the short end of the Pepsi Challenge. Younger consumers especially preferred the sweeter taste of Pepsi.* And sales in food stores, where customers had a choice between the two, had already tilted in Pepsi's direction. Coca-Cola was concerned that in a short time, Pepsi might legitimately claim that more people actually drank its cola, not simply that they preferred it.

By 1985, Coca-Cola had decided to confront this problem head-on. Using its Diet Coke formulation as a base, which to many consumers tasted more like Pepsi than it did Mother Coke, Coke took out the artificial sweetener and rebuilt the drink with high-fructose corn syrup. After tens of thousands of taste tests, the company introduced this sweeter formulation of its traditional drink and made the new product its flag-

---

* Warren Buffett, not only a great investor but a man who loves his sugar (and also a longtime director and large shareholder of Coca-Cola) reported that in every blind taste test in the industry, the sweeter drink always wins.

ship brand, going so far as to remove old Coke from the market. New Coke had a new can, a new slogan, and a new advertising campaign. Together with the sweeter taste, all these changes were aimed at the younger market that Pepsi had so far managed to dominate. At first the whole strategy was a disaster. New Coke may have scored higher in the Pepsi Challenge, but sales were embarrassingly low. Fortunately for Coca-Cola, an outpouring of protest from those customers committed to the original drink forced the company to reconsider its plans. Within four months, old Coca-Cola was back, first as Coca-Cola Classic, then simply as Coca-Cola, with the sweeter version now labeled New Coke.

After the fact, some analysts tried to argue that the New Coke strategy was a brilliant gambit to win more shelf space for the company, now that it had two distinct brands of the calorie- and caffeine-laden version of the drink, rather than one. This interpretation conveniently ignored the original intent, which was to abandon old Coke entirely. The company did not want to split its sales between the two and allow Pepsi to claim the top spot. But in fact the turmoil did benefit Coca-Cola. The media attention was intense, and the company realized what it had ignored when it ran the taste test—that many loyal customers had a visceral attachment to the original, a drink they identified with their youth, their country, their very identity. Pepsi did surpass the market shares of both old and new Coke, but only for a short while. By 1986, Classic Coke was back in the lead, and the combined shares of Classic, Coca-Cola (new), and Diet Coke surpassed Pepsi and its diet version, 29 percent to 23 percent (table 9.4).

The New Coke fiasco ended up providing Coca-Cola with a potential new weapon for competing in the sweeter/younger segment of the market. Now, if Coke wanted to go to war against Pepsi, it could do it on Pepsi's home turf. Sweet Coke could be used as an "attack" brand, introduced into markets where Pepsi was dominant. If New Coke were really successful, it might capture one-sixth of this market. Should Coke decide to use New Coke as a "low-priced"—warrior—brand, then Pepsi would be made to suffer. Matching the lower price, a decision Pepsi virtually had to make, would cost it six dollars in sales for every dollar it cost Coke. Meanwhile, traditional Coca-Cola could have stood aside from this fray, maintaining its status as the drink for mature cola lovers,

TABLE 9.4

Market share, 1982–86 (by case volume)

	1982	1984	1985	1986
Classic			6.1%	19.1%
Coca-Cola	24.6%	22.5%	15.0%	2.4%
Diet Coke	0.3%	5.2%	6.7%	7.3%
Sprite and Diet Sprite	3.3%	3.8%	4.3%	4.3%
Tab	4.0%	1.6%	1.1%	0.6%
Cherry Coke			1.7%	1.9%
Caffeine-free, all		1.8%	1.7%	1.7%
Others	3.4%	2.6%	2.0%	2.5%
Coca-Cola Company total	35.6%	37.5%	38.6%	39.8%
Pepsi-Cola	20.3%	19.1%	18.9%	18.6%
Diet Pepsi	3.3%	3.2%	3.9%	4.4%
Mountain Dew	3.2%	3.0%	3.0%	3.0%
Caffeine-free, all	0.4%	2.7%	2.4%	2.0%
Others	0.9%	0.7%	1.6%	2.7%
PepsiCo total	28.1%	28.7%	29.8%	30.7%
Seven-Up	6.7%	6.8%	6.0%	5.2%
Dr Pepper	5.2%	5.0%	4.9%	4.8%
Royal Crown Cola	3.9%	3.1%	3.0%	2.9%
Other companies	20.5%	18.9%	17.7%	16.6%
Total non-Coke, non-Pepsi companies	36.3%	33.8%	31.6%	29.5%

and its higher profit margins. However inadvertently, Coca-Cola had at last learned whom to punish in a price war. Now that it had this weapon, peace between the two might be possible.

WISING UP: FROM PRICE WARS TO COOPERATION

After a decade of beating each other up, and with the New Coke weapon now pointed at Pepsi, Coca-Cola and PepsiCo had fought each other to a standstill. Like our prisoners who learn to cooperate after playing the game enough times, the soda companies finally changed strategies (table 9.5). They made visible moves to signal the other side that they intended to cooperate. Coca-Cola initiated the new era with a major

TABLE 9.5

Coke's and Pepsi's competitive steps, 1984–92

YEAR	Pepsi initiates	Coca-Cola responds and initiates	Pepsi responds
1984	Begins to use 100% aspartame in diet beverages	Follows suit in some areas (cannot get enough aspartame for all)	
April 1985		Introduces "New" Coke, eliminates old Coke; enormous press coverage	Declares holiday for its employees; new ad campaign: "they blinked."
July 1985		Brings back the original as Coca-Cola Classic; by September, it is outselling new Coke 3 to 1 in food stores	
1986	Wayne Calloway becomes CEO; former promises to focus on profitability and return on equity		
1986		Buys two of its largest franchise bottlers; now owns 38% of total volume	Buys two large independent franchisees; keeps on buying until, by 1990, it owns 51% of bottler volume
1986		Sells 51% of bottler operations to public as Coca-Cola Enterprises, Inc.	Takes Pepsi Bottling Group public, selling 65% stake, in 1999
1989	Both companies raise soft drink prices 3.3% (largest increase since 1981)		
1992		Reintroduces New Coke as Coke II, available only in select markets	Increases television advertising in one Coke II market

corporate reorganization. After buying up many of the bottlers and reorganizing the bottler network, it spun off 51 percent of the company-owned bottlers to shareholders in a new entity, Coca-Cola Enterprises, and it loaded up on debt for this corporation. With so much debt to ser-

vice, Coca-Cola Enterprises had to concentrate on the tangible requirement of cash flow rather than the chimera of gaining great hunks of
market share from Pepsi. In the world of the soda giants, with only a
few players, Coca-Cola's initiative was impossible to miss and difficult
not to understand. PepsiCo responded by dropping the Pepsi Challenge,
toning down its aggressive advertising, and thus signaling that it accepted the truce. The new cooperative relationship had the desired effect where it counted most: profit margins. Operating profit margins
went up from below 10 percent for Coca-Cola to more than 20 percent.
Pepsi's gain was less dramatic but also substantial (figure 9.3).*

This harmonious and profitable state of affairs continued into the
1990s.

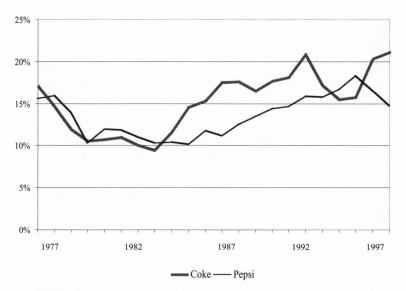

FIGURE 9.3
Operating profit margins, domestic soft drink business,
1977–98

---

* When Coca-Cola spun off the bottling company in 1986, it helped lift its soft drink margins
by separating out the lower-margin bottling operation. Pepsi did not make a similar move
until 1999, and its margins suffered by comparison.

IS CULTURE DESTINY?

Unfortunately, like bad marriages, companies have an internal dynamic that is not easily overcome, even by peace and high returns on invested capital. Wayne Calloway at PepsiCo and Robert Goizueta at Coca-Cola, aided by the statesmanlike support of board member Warren Buffett, did bring some measure of peace to the cola world. Goizueta judged his performance by two measures: return on equity and the share price. He regarded the revenue line as "the curse of all curses." During his sixteen-year leadership, the price of the company's shares appreciated by almost 30 percent per year. Calloway, who had been the president of Frito-Lay before he became the chief executive at PepsiCo, also preferred return on equity to bragging rights about market share. During his decade as CEO, the share price of Pepsi also grew dramatically, by 24 percent annually. Sadly, cancer killed both these executives while they were still young.

Their successors, Douglas Ivester at Coca-Cola and Roger Enrico at PepsiCo, were Cola Warriors, enthusiastic participants in the century-old conflict that dominated the culture of both companies. In an article in *Fortune* magazine that received much media attention, CEO-in-waiting Ivester, described as Goizueta's "pit bull," declared that Coca-Cola's policy would be to stick a hose in the mouth of its competitor, whom he saw as struggling in the pool. Enrico, a Vietnam veteran, had already published *The Other Guy Blinked: How Pepsi Won the Cola War*, a book that gloated over the New Coke episode in the ongoing struggle. The people at Coca-Cola never forgave him. Under his leadership, PepsiCo announced ambitious goals for effectively stealing share from Coke in international markets, where Coke was dominant.

Both strategies failed. Ivester did not drown Pepsi—Pepsi's market share actually increased—as he and his board of directors should have known. But he did manage to put a dent in Coca-Cola's earnings. For its part, Pepsi lost out in Venezuela, the only international market where it had a substantial share. Coca-Cola made an offer to the Pepsi bottler who had a monopoly for the country. It must have been an offer he couldn't refuse, because he switched allegiance and started to bottle and distribute Coke. One might ask what the Coca-Cola and PepsiCo boards of directors were doing while the CEOs decided to resort to the warfare strategies that had served the two companies so poorly before the truce of the late 1980s.

Ivester's tenure at Coca-Cola hardly lasted two years. He was undone by a series of problems, including several health scares in Europe and a racial discrimination lawsuit in Atlanta. His response, the board felt, was too aggressive, and he managed to damage the company's image, which was one of its most important assets. The man who wanted to drown his competitor was undone by the same uncompromising temperament. It was during his watch that Pepsi belatedly emulated Coca-Cola by spinning off its bottling business in 1999, creating what an industry journal called a "rational player." With that move, both companies raised their prices to supermarkets, which had fallen by more than 10 percent over the prior four years. Unhappily for Ivester, it was too late for him; he was gone by the end of the year.

The urge to grow, to hammer competitors and drive them out of business, or at least reduce their market share by a meaningful amount, has been a continual source of poor performance for companies that do have competitive advantages and a franchise, but are not content with it. It may be that the same aggressive personality traits that push people forward until they reach the top of the corporate ladder also move them to take on the competition, whatever the cost. It would be foolish to expect a sudden shift from warrior to corporate statesman for most of these people. Still, incentive systems that reward based on some aspect of profit, rather than for revenue or another measure of size, may focus attention on what is good for the shareholders and, by extension, other stakeholders in the company.

CHAPTER 10

Into the Henhouse

Fox Becomes a Network

FOX BROADCASTING COMPANY

In 1985, Rupert Murdoch announced that he was going to form a fourth television network in the United States. Murdoch's network would join the three incumbents that had come to dominate the industry within a decade of its inception after World War II. As part of his overall strategy, he bought six independent stations in large American cities and the Twentieth Century Fox movie studio. The News Corporation, the global media conglomerate he had built starting with one newspaper in western Australia, already owned more than one hundred newspapers and magazines in Europe, Australia, and North America, as well as television broadcasters in Europe and Australia. He saw Twentieth Century Fox as the entertainment asset at the heart of his empire, producing material he could distribute throughout all his channels.

No one ever accused Murdoch of thinking small. His plans for the News Corporation involved a major challenge. He would have to launch and keep afloat the fourth television network, something that no one had accomplished since the 1950s, until it became profitable. In reaching both that goal and his larger global vision, he expected to realize some of the supposed synergies that came from combining a production studio with a distribution system that extended far beyond the broadcast network in the United States.

THE BROADCASTING INDUSTRY

The club that Murdoch so much wanted to join had only three members: ABC, CBS, and NBC. Each of them had been successful radio networks in the 1930s, an experience that served them well as they moved into the new medium. They knew how to deal with advertisers, with local station affiliates and independents, with running news organizations, and with the entertainment component that made up a large part of the product they delivered to consumers. A fourth network, started by the engineer Allen DuMont, whose background was in the set manufacturing part of the business, lasted into the 1950s but then disappeared. Other efforts by entertainment companies like Paramount Pictures to establish themselves in the network broadcast game did not last very long.

As it evolved in the three decades after the end of WWII, the network broadcasting business was only one segment of the complete industry that brought news, sports, entertainment, and advertising—which paid for the rest—into the American home (figure 10.1).

In the development of first radio and then television, the United States differed from virtually all other countries in that the government licensed, but did not own or directly control, the airways. The ultimate revenue stream of the entire industry came from advertisers, who bought time in which to air commercials. During the golden years of radio and the early days of television, large sponsors actually produced some of the programs that advertised their wares, but by the early 1960s, they had ceded control to the networks. Production costs had risen, and the advertisers liked the flexibility of buying limited commercial segments on a range of shows and networks. They also bought time directly from the local stations, both independents and those connected to the networks.

The production of "content" was split among the networks, production companies, and local stations. The networks and the local stations produced national and local news, sporting events, and a range of other shows. The major entertainment pieces that filled the evening (prime time) hours—the comedies, dramas, and made-for-television movies—they bought from the studios. The movie studios already had the experi-

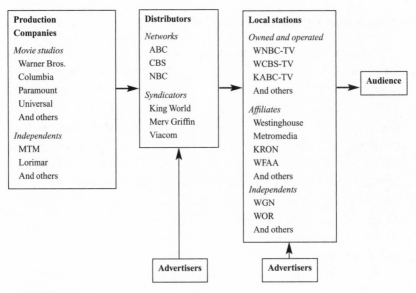

FIGURE 10.1
Map of the television industry, around 1985

ence and the infrastructure to produce this fare, and they leapt at the opportunity to grow a new revenue stream after the government ended their direct ownership of movie theaters on antitrust grounds. The glamour of the movie business, even with the "movie" confined to the small-screen world of television, attracted a number of smaller players into the production business, to compete with the established studios. There was no shortage of creative talent pitching show concepts to the networks.

The networks bought the shows they approved from the production companies, or rather, they bought enough episodes to see if the program would find an audience. If it did, they contracted for another round. The networks paid the producers between 80 and 90 percent of the producers' costs, leaving the producers to look elsewhere for full cost recovery and a profit. They found it in the syndication market. Regulations severely limited the number of prime-time shows a network might own for itself. The rest belonged to the producers, who were able to sell the rerun rights to syndicators. Syndicators put packages of shows together and resold them to local stations and even networks to run after the popularity of the shows had been established. To qualify for syndication, a show needed to last for sixty episodes, and most did not qualify. Those that did, however, provided revenue for the producers. By the 1970s, more than half the total revenue of the film studios came from its television productions: shows sold directly to the networks; syndication sales; made-for-television movies; reruns of old films.

Government regulation limited the number of local stations a network could own. Recognizing that economies of scale might make television distribution a natural monopoly, and fearful that control of major sources of news might ultimately rest in very few hands, successive administrations had allowed the companies in the business to expand but retained some upper limit. Even after the absolute number of VHF stations was raised from five to twelve, the networks were still prevented from reaching more than 25 percent of the population through their own outlets—the "owned and operated" stations. But they struck "affiliated" deals with many local stations, each of whom was committed to a single network carrying many, but not all, programs from that network. It was cheaper for the local stations to accept these popular programs than to find alternatives with the same appeal. Independent companies in the business of owning affiliates faced the same limitations on ownership as did the broadcast networks. The owned and operated and the affiliated stations were more profitable than the independents. They spent more on local programming, like news and features, and had larger audiences. The independents had to rely on reruns, old movies, local sports, and other shows with narrowly focused audiences.

The affiliated stations did not buy shows from the networks. Revenue flowed in the other direction: the networks paid the affiliates to carry their programs. For that, the networks received the fees that came from their six minutes per hour of prime-time advertisements. The affiliates had three minutes of advertising time for themselves, which they could sell to local sponsors or national advertisers or use for public service announcements. Local broadcasting, especially for the owned-and-operated and the affiliates, was the most lucrative part of the entire business. Adding the two years 1984 and 1985 together, the combined operating income of all three networks was 9 percent of their revenues. Their owned and operated stations had operating margins of 32 percent. It has been suggested that they were actually subsidizing the networks.

This vitally important connection suggests that when we look at the networks, we need to treat their owned and operated local stations, and probably even their affiliates, as part of the same segment (broadcasting per se) of the industry. But the rest—the production firms, the syndicators, and the advertisers—were clearly in separate portions of the overall industry, no more tied than a publisher is to a book merchant or a fructose grower to a beverage manufacturer.

BARRIERS TO ENTRY?

As always, we look at two features of an industry to determine whether it is protected by barriers to entry. The first is the history of market share stability. If newcomers have not been successful in establishing themselves within the industry, and if there has been little movement in the market shares of the incumbent firms, then the chances are good that barriers to entry exist. The second feature is return on capital. If the incumbent firms in the business have been earning a higher than normal return on capital, that fact supports the claim that barriers do exist. We know that prior to Fox, all those who tried to get into the broadcasting network business failed, including the DuMont Network that entered the television network business at its inception, but without the background in radio broadcasting.

The record on market share is one of exceptional stability. In the ten years between 1976 and 1986, the three networks combined had an average absolute change of 9 percentage points, which works out to 3 percentage points per network for a whole decade (table 10.1).

Calculating market share stability by treating the sum of the three networks' individual shares as if they represented 100 percent of the total audience allows us to measure movement among the three, but in this case it ignores an equally significant bit of information. As a group, the networks were losing market share at the rate of around 1 rating

TABLE 10.1

Market share changes for the three networks, 1976–86

	Rating Points		Normalized			
	1976	**1986**	**1976**	**1986**	**Change**	**Absolute**
ABC	18.7	12.8	36%	32%	−4.2%	4.2%
NBC	16.4	14.6	31%	36%	4.6%	4.6%
CBS	17.1	13.1	33%	32%	−0.4%	0.4%
Total	52.2	40.5	100%	100%		9.2%
Average over 10 years						3.1%

point per year. Some of it was going to the independent stations, some of it to the cable stations that reached 40 million homes by 1986. Even if we confirm the existence of barriers to entry protecting the incumbent networks from strong competition by start-ups, that does not mean that the networks were immune from an erosion in their audience, who found alternatives to traditional network offerings among a large number of small players.

Our other key test for the existence of barriers to entry is high return on capital. In the two years 1984 and 1985, the three networks combined had operating income of $2 billion on revenues of $15.8 billion, or 12.6 percent. These figures include both the network business and the owned and operated stations, which, as we have seen, had much higher margins. The 12–13 percent operating margins have to be seen in the context of the capital requirements for these firms. These requirements were minimal. Most ads were sold before the start of the season, limiting investments in accounts receivable. There was no inventory. During these years, distribution of the shows to the local stations was handled by AT&T, leaving only studios and broadcasting equipment as fixed assets (property, plant, and equipment). The owned and operated stations also had few capital requirements other than their own studios, broadcast antennas, and equipment. We estimate that the assets looked something like the figure in table 10.2.

We put all the assets required at about 15 percent of sales. Spontaneous liabilities (meaning accounts payable, accrued wages and taxes,

TABLE 10.2

Estimated balance sheet of networks and owned stations, 1984–85 (assets as a percentage of sales)

Cash	1%
Accounts receivable	4%
Inventory	0%
Property, plant, and equipment	10%
Total assets	15%
Spontaneous liabilities	5%
Total capital required	10%

and other non-interest-bearing obligations) finance a third of the assets.* That leaves capital requirements at around 10 percent of sales. With operating margins at 12–13 percent, the pretax return on capital amounts to 120–130 percent. Even if the investments requirements were twice our estimate, the pretax return on capital would be 60 percent or more. Given the steadiness of the revenues, the networks could easily finance their operations with half debt, half equity. The debt would provide a tax shield to keep the after-tax return on equity capital in the stratosphere.

All the signs of an industry protected by high barriers to entry are present here, in spades. Thanks to the barriers, the firms inside earned exceptional returns on capital. This is what made the industry attractive to Murdoch, as it had been to Paramount and other aspiring entrants. But it also served as a warning of how challenging it would be for a newcomer to climb the walls, get inside, and survive.

WHICH COMPETITIVE ADVANTAGES?

The only source of competitive advantages not involved in creating barriers to entry around the network business was technology. The incum-

---

*Spontaneous liabilities, which include accrued wages and other things like accounts payable and accrued expenses, are liabilities that arise from being in business. They are, in effect, loans from workers, suppliers, and others, for which the company does not have to pay interest. Spontaneous liabilities decrease the amount of capital (debt and equity) that a company needs to raise in order to pay for its assets.

bent networks had no proprietary hold on the equipment necessary to capture and send broadcast signals to the television sets that had become ubiquitous in American homes. RCA, the parent of NBC, was a manufacturer of sets, as DuMont had been, but so were a host of other companies unrelated to the broadcasters. Technology was an open field, and anyone could play.

Customer attachment was a different matter. Successful shows developed a loyal following, and they frequently lasted for years. The other networks took care not to schedule their own most popular programs at the same time. In the days before the remote channel changer (according to some historians of technology, the only rival to the ATM machine for the most humane invention in the last half of the twentieth century) a substantial portion of the viewership of one show stayed put when the hour ended and the next program began. Network executives crafted their schedules to give new programs a boost by launching them in the wake of established and popular programs. Television viewers were not completely captive customers; they could and did change channels and opt for a new program in place of an established one. Still, incumbents held an advantage over entrants, who would need to accumulate an audience over time in the face of network programming competition.

The government imposed restrictions on the broadcast industry. It rationed the scarce radio spectrum to prevent signal interference, and it used regulation to preserve the public interest in competition and free access. It limited the networks, and other nonnetwork broadcasting companies, to ownership of local stations reaching no more than 25 percent of the population. This restriction created the system of affiliated stations, associated with the networks but less tightly tied than the owned and operated ones. But most of the other government policies buttressed the barriers to entry. The Federal Communications Commission licensed local stations and assigned them the frequencies over which to broadcast. In each of the largest metropolitan areas, the FCC issued no more than seven VHF licenses. In smaller locales, even fewer VHF licenses were available. These had gone, in the 1940s, to the existing radio networks, giving them a permanent leg up in their ability to reach audiences. When cable technology emerged in the 1960s, the FCC initially constrained its geographic spread and restricted subscription services, in an effort to keep access free to viewers. Gradually, however, television audiences could tune in to more channels both through cable systems and improved UHF technology.

The government also regulated the costs that the networks paid to AT&T to transmit their programs to the stations. Originally, these charges were structured so that it cost only slightly more to send a full day's programming than it did a single hour's. This was not a pricing scheme that encouraged small broadcasters with only a few hours of programs to distribute. Things changed in the early 1980s. Competitors, including satellite operators, were allowed into the transmissions business, and the pricing structure at AT&T better reflected the number of hours carried. By 1986, government barriers to entry, once formidable, had decreased substantially.

However, economies of scale were the most powerful competitive advantage that kept the networks protected from eager new entrants, and these were not changing. Network broadcasting is largely a fixed-cost business:

- Programming costs are fixed. Networks contract for new shows before they or the producers know the size of the audience they will reach. It is true that some crucially popular shows, and especially their star performers, can demand more money for renewals. Sometimes the networks pay, sometimes they pass. In the main, however, programming costs do not rise proportionately with the size of the audience.
- Network distributions costs are fixed. AT&T did not charge more to transmit popular shows from the networks to the local stations. A new network trying to establish itself would initially be at a severe cost-per-viewer disadvantage in paying this bill.
- Local distribution costs are fixed. For broadcast signals of equivalent range, it costs no more to reach 50 percent of the potential viewers than to reach 5 percent. Even newspapers do not have an economy of scale advantage as clear-cut as broadcasters do.
- Local production costs, like news programs, are somewhat fixed. Popular newscasters get paid more than less popular ones, it seems clear, but not in proportion to the size of their audience. Studio fix-

tures don't vary with the size of the audience, nor do the cameras and other equipment that send out the signals.

- Advertising costs are fixed. The ads the networks or stations run on themselves and for themselves, and the ads they place in newspapers, magazines, or even on competing stations, do not vary with the size of their own audience. And advertising sales costs are essentially the same for all national networks regardless of viewership.

A prudent executive at that time, deciding whether to invest millions of dollars to break into the network business, must have realized how formidable was this array of competitive advantages protecting the incumbents and their profit margins. He or she would also have seen that as a group, the networks were losing market share and that some of their advantages were eroding due to changes in technology (like the remote control, the VCR, and satellite transmission) and government regulations (like easing the limitations on the reach of cable services). Even an audacious, deep-pocketed, politically savvy Australian media mogul would have been operating at a significant competitive disadvantage—never a happy strategic position. On the other hand, he may have noticed that the networks, operating behind their barriers, had worked out some rules of the game that mitigated competition despite an overall market share that was in decline. If our mogul played his cards right, he might get to take a seat at the table and prosper along with his established competitors.

COMPETITION AMONG FRIENDS

If the Coca-Cola vs. Pepsi battle was a replay of the Civil War, pitting the sons of Atlanta against aggressive Northerners in White Plains, New York, the competition between the networks was more like country club golf. All were headquartered in New York City. All had backgrounds in radio broadcasting; ABC came into existence with the forced divestiture of a portion of NBC's network in the 1940s. All moved into television at the start of the video era. Over the years, they worked out a set of tacit rules that kept competition in check and profits high. They did not undercut one another on price, either on what they would charge or what they would pay. Unlike the soda makers, they learned how to play the prisoner's dilemma for the benefit of all.

ADVERTISING ARRANGEMENTS

The networks' revenues came from selling time to sponsors. They took care never to offer this time at discount prices. First, most advertising time was prebought by the sponsors under long-term contracts. Time was available closer to the actual broadcast date in a spot market; the spot rates were higher than the contract rates. Contracting was done by all three networks during a limited time period, which restricted bargaining by ad buyers. The networks did not undercut one another on price.

Second, they restricted the supply by limiting the number of advertising minutes in prime time under the mantle of a public interest code of conduct. When the ads were sold, they came with an estimate of the size of the audience that would be reached. If actual viewers fell short of the estimate, the networks made good on the advertising contract by offering the sponsor more ad slots at no charge. This "make good" practice used up more of the precious minutes, tightening supply just at those times when, due to failure to deliver, demand might have fallen. If there were not enough buyers at an acceptable price, the networks either ran ads for their own shows or they broadcast public service announcements. They did nothing to encourage sponsors to wait until the For Sale signs were posted. The net result was that network advertising prices continued to rise steadily even as their joint market share of viewers eroded.

PURCHASING PROGRAMS

The networks approached the purchasing of programs with the same gentlemanly attitude they employed in the selling of advertising time. They did not vigorously compete with one another for new shows. Program ideas were shopped during a two-week period, so if one network expressed an interest, there was not enough time for a program's producers to see if another would outbid it. When a pilot episode had been filmed, the network retained the right to turn it down, and the studios were left to shoulder the expense. These decisions also took place within two weeks, when the networks were putting their schedules together. This time-limited competition kept the networks from bidding against one another for programs that looked like winners.

Nor did the networks try to woo established programs from one another. When a series did shift networks, like *Taxi*, which moved from ABC to NBC in 1982, it was because it had been canceled by its original network, not enticed by its new one. The cooperative stance of the networks toward programming also worked in their handling of sporting events. CBS had a long-established relationship with the National Football League. Rather than challenge it, NBC helped to start the American Football League. When the NFL and the AFL merged in the late 1960s, each network kept its relationship. Not wanting to be left out of a sport growing in popularity, but understanding how the networks played the game, ABC created *Monday Night Football* to get its share of the pie. This arrangement lasted for more than two decades.

AFFILIATING WITH THE LOCAL STATIONS

The networks did not steal one another's affiliated stations. Government regulations permitted only one affiliate per network in a given market, so there was room for all. Also, regulations made it difficult to shift a license from one local station to another, another constraint on network poaching. Still, the genteel attitude of the networks toward one another did as much as the regulatory environment to temper their competitive zeal.

ROOM FOR ONE MORE?

Rupert Murdoch had not become one of the largest global media barons by playing nice. He had gone head-to-head with competitors, unions, and governments. His announcement that he intended to challenge the existing networks had to get their attention. He already owned both the Fox studio and local stations in the large markets. He had a newspaper presence on three continents. If he decided to invade the network industry with guns blazing, he had more firepower than the networks had seen from other potential interlopers.

Still, a handicapper giving odds on a brawl between Fox and the existing networks would have had to favor the networks. They had the audiences, and they were not going to lose them quickly. Therefore, they could pay more for programs than could Fox, and they could charge more for their ads. They already had strong local affiliates in addition to their owned and operated stations. NBC, now owned by General Electric, and ABC, a division of Capital Cities Communications, had the resources to withstand a protracted conflict. CBS, in an effort to stay independent, had loaded its balance sheet with debt and was more vulnerable. Still, it had valuable assets it could sell, like the local stations it owned, and it could cut costs by consolidating operations. The lavish management style by which the networks had operated for years left them with plenty of fat to trim before they started to hit muscle or bone.

There is no doubt that a frontal assault by Murdoch, even one that ended in defeat for Fox, would have been costly for the networks. Had he competed on the price of ads, they could have matched him. But since his revenue stream was much smaller, the dollar damage to them would have been far greater. Had he bid for their programs, they could afford to pay more, but again, they had a whole schedule to defend and he was just starting out. For Fox and for the networks, abandoning the old game of carefully moderated competition for a bruising, no-holds-barred battle would have been painful.

Murdoch needed a way gain admission to the club without having to batter down the gates and undermine the value of a membership for himself and for the others. He had to let them know that his intensions were more or less harmonious with their interests. He had to make them realize that letting him enter peacefully would serve them better than a scorched-earth defense. He needed to send them signals that he knew how to play their game.

LOCAL STATIONS

Murdoch's first move was to buy six independent stations from Metromedia. He did not go after affiliates of the networks, which would have been a shot across the bow. The $1.65 billion he spent on them was considerably more than their current cash flow would justify, and he financed his purchase with debt. His plan to make them the heart of his new network would, he felt, justify the premium he had paid. To the networks, the fact that he had not tried to steal their affiliates was reassuring, as was the debt he had taken on to get into the business. His plans called for Fox Broadcasting to lose money in its early years, but with all that debt hanging over him, he was less likely to begin price wars on advertising or programming with his profitable competitors.

With the six Metromedia stations as a base, Fox went out to sign affiliates in the rest of the country. Though it did manage to contract with local stations covering more than 80 percent of the country, they were not a strong group. Most of them operated in the lower-powered UHF part of the spectrum, and they had a paltry share of the prime-time viewing audience. Fox would be starting with a small base of viewers.

ADVERTISING

Murdoch followed the lead of the established networks in subscribing to the code of conduct that put a limit on the number of advertising minutes for each half hour of prime-time broadcasting. He established his price at 20 percent below what the networks were charging per rating point. This discount was only marginally aggressive. If he were to attract advertisers to his new, unproven, and much smaller network, he had to offer them something. By pegging his prices to those of the networks, although at a discount, he signaled that he intended to cooperate, but he also let them know that they could not match him on price. If they lowered their rates, he would maintain the 20 percent discount and lower his. Since their advertising revenue would dwarf his for the foreseeable future, the pain to them would be much greater. On the other hand, if they raised rates, he would go along, albeit at his 20 percent discount. He would not be an impediment to their continued exercise of pricing power.

PROGRAMMING

Here again, Fox did not confront the networks head-on. It started with a limited schedule of original programs. The first established star Fox hired was Joan Rivers, to host a late-night talk show. Rivers had already been passed over by NBC in favor of Jay Leno to follow Johnny Carson on *The Tonight Show.* The other programs in its first years were also ones that the established networks had either rejected outright or were not likely to run. *Studs, Married with Children,* and *The Simpsons* were either too vulgar (though this may be hard to believe from the vantage point of the twenty-first century) for the other networks, or in a cartoon format, which they reserved for Saturday-morning children's shows or Disney specials.

Murdoch had made his fortune in print journalism by following the path of sensationalism in his papers. Even his broadsides were tabloids. Fox Broadcasting adopted the same approach. By going down-market, it reduced direct competition with the other networks. If this kind of programming was going to win Fox an audience, it was more likely to come from independent stations, either broadcast or cable, that were already carrying similar fare. It also targeted a teenage and youth audience that had no established viewing habits and was more easily attracted.

ROOM FOR ONLY ONE MORE

The manner in which Fox secured local stations, priced its advertising, and filled its time slots with entertainment sent strong signals to the networks that it was not going to make trouble. It did not appear checkbook in hand to steal any of their established programs or stars or woo their local affiliates. Its advertising, though offered at a discount, was still pegged to the network rates, and it did not intend to expand supply by reserving more time for ads. The message to the networks was this:

- We intend to abide by the rules of your game.
- Though you can probably crush us if you choose, it will cost you much more to fight us than to let us in. And since we have made the Fox Broadcasting System a part of our global media strategy, we are not going to go easily or quietly.
- The smart move is to let us join the club.

Considered as a prisoner's dilemma game, Fox signaled that it wanted to join the networks in the most profitable box on the board.

It was the smart move for the networks, provided they did not see Fox as the first of a number of new entrants who as a group would clearly spoil the party. Had they been faced with that challenge, they would have had no choice but to nail its hide to the barn door as a warning of what other entrants might expect. But Fox could demonstrate that it was, if not unique, at least exceptional in the field of potential networks. It had bought the six Metromedia stations, added a few others, and signed up local affiliates, which gave it national distribution. Anyone else would have to get in via cable, which would be expensive for viewers. Fox's network also was also part of a media empire that included a film studio and many newspapers and magazines. Those relationships may have looked formidable to the networks, even if they turned out to be less important than Murdoch anticipated. Putting all these features together, Fox could make the case that no one else was likely to try to enter the network business with the same prospects.

THE BUSINESS TRANSFORMED

The networks did not try to kill Fox Broadcasting when it was still in its infancy. They read Fox's signals correctly, that it would behave itself if allowed to survive. And so it did, at least for a while. But over time, the environment changed and became more competitive. Regulation was loosened to allow more cable stations to enter and expand their offerings. Subscription cable channels grew in number and appeal. Broadcast technology via satellite continued to lower the cost of distribution to local stations. The distinctions between a network and a large syndicator were breaking down, as syndicators bought first-run programming from studios and delivered it directly to independent stations on shared advertising terms. Home electronic devices like the remote control and the VCR became virtually ubiquitous, further shrinking the hold that stations had on viewers and, more important, allowing viewers to avoid watching the advertising that was footing the bill for the whole enterprise.

These developments lessened the potency of the competitive advantages that had made the network industry so profitable. The new owners of ABC, CBS, and NBC moved to cut costs by reducing staffing at the news bureaus and elsewhere, and lowering the amount they spent on programming. All of these changes had been in the works when Murdoch and Fox were moving into the business. They continued during the period while Fox was establishing itself.

The presence of Fox, combined with the decline in profitability and the change in ownership of the other networks, ultimately undermined the culture of cooperation that had held the competitive juices in check. The networks were no longer the comfortable and clubby collection of longtime associates. By 1993, Fox outbid CBS for the rights to broadcast National Football Conference games, ending a relationship of many decades' duration and sparking an extended bidding war that finally undermined the profitability of football contracts. A few years later, ABC was angling to steal David Letterman from CBS, not a trick that Leonard Goldenson would ever have tried on William Paley. It was the sort of thing in which Coke and Pepsi were expert.

WHAT ABOUT SYNERGIES?

The intended lynchpin of Murdoch's strategy had been integration, the idea that Fox Broadcasting, including the Twentieth Century Fox studio, the network, and the owned and operated stations, would have opportunities for additional profits because of their tight relationships with one another and with the other parts of the News Corporation's media holdings. As well as using Twentieth Century Fox to feed the Fox network, he planned to syndicate shows overseas. But synergies, while often invoked to justify overpaying for an asset, are difficult to realize in practice. What added benefits were to be realized by putting companies in the supply chain under the same ownership? If the industry is protected by barriers to entry, the firm is already earning superior returns on capital. If the industry is competitive, then contracting with a sister company adds nothing to either firm's earnings. In either case, it is hard to identify any gains from putting the two firms under the same ownership.

Clearly there were no barriers to entry in the production segment of the business. New players emerged all the time, thanks to the allure of the entertainment world. Companies in this business, as we should expect, had historically earned very low returns on investment. The other networks did not own any studios, in part because of regulation but more importantly because they had always found it less costly to let the studios do the creative work. In the case of Twentieth Century Fox and Fox Broadcasting, if the studio had a program that gave every indication of drawing a large audience, what would be gained from offering it to Fox Broadcasting at anything less than the going market rate? And if it had some shows that were not as promising, why should Fox pay more for them than NBC or ABC? Money might be moved from one corporate pocket to another, but the net gain to the corporation would be zero. So long as there was no shortage of supply, Fox Broadcasting gained nothing from its connection to the studio. So long as it could produce shows that other networks wanted, Twentieth Century Fox gained nothing from its connection to the broadcaster.

What about advertising time? Suppose Fox Broadcasting was unable to sell out its advertising slots. Might it not use that spare time to promote movies from Twentieth Century Fox, and do it at no cost to the studio? Perhaps, but if the time were available for nothing, the audience could not have been attractive to paying advertisers. Maybe the studio would be getting something for nothing, but it could not be very much. Free advertising on a poorly watched network could not have been the source of Murdoch's synergy strategy.

Fox's other supposed source of synergy was the ability to syndicate the studio's programs to international outlets. Here again, the issue was whether anything was to be gained by doing the syndication in a sister company of the same corporation, or going to outsiders. If international syndication was a competitive industry, there was no joint benefit in keeping syndication in-house. The syndicating arm could charge no more than could the competition, nor could it charge less and still make a profit. If international syndication was not competitive, if, that is, in certain markets, established firms were protected by barriers to entry, then the syndicating arm of Fox would be operating at a disadvantage. In this case, the studio would be better off contracting with a powerful company already in the business. Again, nothing in the corporate relationship between the studio and the syndicating arm would produce any benefit.

LEARNING FROM FOX

The history of Fox's entry into the network industry stands at the crossroads of many of the ideas in this book. The three networks enjoyed competitive advantages and barriers to entry, thanks to captive customers, government regulation, and significant economies of scale. They made a lot of their money from their ownership of local stations, which were like tollgates on the road advertisers needed to travel. The three networks had learned to play the prisoner's dilemma game and not engage in price wars, either in the amount they would pay for program content or in the rates they would charge advertisers.

These high returns, and the barriers to entry on which they depended, were one of the reasons Murdoch decided to start a competing network. He played the entry/preemption game, which we discuss at length in the next chapter, like a master. He made it clear to the incumbent networks that it would be cheaper for them to let him into the club than to try to strangle his network in the cradle. Fox succeeded in establishing itself as a fourth network where previous entrants had failed.

Despite Murdoch's brilliance and the skills of the established networks in avoiding costly price wars, the idyllic situation did not last for network television. Changes in government regulations and in technology both undermined most of the competitive advantages that had made the networks so profitable. Cable stations, VCRs, even the remote channel changer diminished customer captivity and made the networks less attractive to advertisers, which were the primary source of revenue.

The networks are still with us, Fox included, but they are not the cash-generating machines they used to be.

Finally, the Fox strategy was aimed at deriving benefits from owning businesses that boosted one another's profits. The studio would supply programming content to the network and its affiliated stations, unsold advertising time could be used to promote films from Twentieth Century Fox Studios, and the company would own a syndication operation to sell the programs overseas. Murdoch was a media baron, and if he could integrate all the components in his holdings, surely some synergies would result. But in practice, synergies also depend on barriers to entry. If the various links on the supply chain are in markets where there are no barriers, there is simply no extra profit to be extracted from a common ownership structure.

CHAPTER 11

Games Companies Play

A Structured Approach to Competitive Strategy

PART II: ENTRY/PREEMPTION GAMES

COMPETING OVER QUANTITY

After price competition, the other commonly occurring competitive situation involves the decision to enter a market or to expand in an existing market. The essential competitive actions here concern output levels and production capacities rather than prices. Competition along these dimensions is a natural complement to price competition, since prices and quantities are the two fundamental variables in market competition.

Fox's decision to enter the network arena has elements of both situations. However, the nature of quantity competition differs in several major ways from that of price competition, and the strategic imperatives involved are not identical. Understanding the dynamics of quantity competition, involving both output and capacity, therefore, is a second essential element of competitive analysis. The formal structure that captures the features of this kind of competition is known as the entry/preemption game.

The first important difference between price and capacity competition is the issue of timing. Expanding capacity requires a significant lead time and is long-lasting, in contrast to price changes, which can be quickly introduced and just as quickly rescinded. For this reason, there is often an important distinction between the players in the entry/preemption game. In the prisoner's dilemma game, all competitors have more or less equal status; anyone can be a leader or follower in changing prices. There is essentially no difference between offense and defense. In the entry/preemption game, the distinction between aggressor and defender is generally clear. In most instances, there is an established company that plays defense against entrants who are trying to get into the market and are on the attack.* Therefore, in this game, the sides have to develop distinctly different strategies if they are to succeed.

The second important difference is that in the entry/preemption game, decisions, especially mistakes, have enduring consequences. In the prisoner's dilemma game, if there are long-lived unfavorable outcomes, they are the result of persistent foolishness. At any moment, the competitors can take corrective action and make more profitable choices. But if Lowe's decides to build a store on what has been Home Depot's turf, or Monsanto adds plant capacity to increase its production of nitrate fertilizer, these facilities are in place for an extended period. When they play an entry/preemption game, competitors have to take into account these long-run consequences.

Finally, aggression plays a different role in entry/preemption games than it does in prisoner's dilemma games. In pricing competition, some firms justify extended, costly price wars with the hope that they may eventually drive their competitors out of business entirely. Historically, however, there are few instances in which well-run, long-established companies have been eliminated by a price war. Except as a reaction to the behavior of others, aggression in price competition is almost always dysfunctional. The saving grace is that the potential damage of aggressive price cutting is limited by the fact that it is readily reversible, at least in theory.

Aggression works differently in an entry/preemption game. First, given the costs of reversing direction when capacity decisions are involved, the incentives for an aggressive reaction to an entrant's initiative are reduced. Unlike for the price-cutting competitor, who can easily change course, the commitment to invest in additional capacity is not easily undone. Therefore, the justification for an aggressive response—

---

*There are instances in which several firms may be considering entering a market that is currently unoccupied by any established competitor. Each potential entrant seeks to preempt all the other competitors. These situations are relatively rare but important variants of the entry/preemption games, which we discuss later in the chapter.

that it will bring the initiator to its senses—is less robust, and the argument for accommodation becomes more compelling. The corollary is that an aggressive decision to expand capacity or output may be more effective than a tentative one, since the respondent realizes that the aggressor is not going to back off. On the other hand, the risks of aggressive behavior are heightened in the entry/preemption game. If one firm takes steps to expand output and its competitors respond in kind, the extended consequences of these capacity decisions make them hard to undo, and the mutual pain inflicted will last a long time. Because aggression is a two-edged sword in capacity decisions, a more delicate approach is required to navigate the strategic imperatives of the entry/preemption game than to manage pricing competition.

STRATEGIC APPROACHES FOR THE ENTRANT

In a typical entry/preemption situation, an established firm in a local or product market enjoys material competitive advantages over most but not all other companies. One company, also a strong player with similar advantages relative to the majority of firms with which it directly competes, considers entering the specific market in question. An example, which we discuss in detail in chapter 13, is Kodak's entry into the instant photography market, which was dominated by Polaroid. The ball is in the entrant's court; all the incumbent firm can do is prepare in a general way to resist the incursion. The outsider must decide between entering the market and staying out. Though there are a range of possible entry moves, from tentative and measured to a full-frontal assault, to keep things simple we will treat the decision as binary, a choice between either enter or don't enter. If entry occurs, the incumbent now has to decide how to respond. It may have previously adopted a fierce attitude trying to forestall any entry, but once entry has taken place—and deterrence, by definition, has failed—the world looks quite different. If it reacts aggressively to repel the entrant, the incumbent is likely to face an expensive, drawn-out conflict involving price cuts, higher advertising expenses, and extensive and costly consumer promotions. It needs to consider the two basic alternatives; either accepting the entrant, however grudgingly, or attacking it. Both alternatives have costs, and a rational decision compares them carefully.

THE TREE (OR EXTENSIVE) FORM AND ENTRY/PREEMPTION GAMES

Just as there is a natural but not obligatory fit between prisoner's dilemma (pricing) games and the matrix form of representation, so the extensive or tree form of formal presentation works well with entry/ preemption (quantity) games. Consider a potential interaction between Home Depot and Lowe's. In our example, Lowe's is well established in a particular geographic market and Home Depot is considering whether to open stores in that territory. In this case, the competitive interaction starts with Home Depot's initial decision. Conforming to our simplification decision, it can choose either to enter the market or to stay out. This option is represented in the first branches of the tree structure in figure 11.1. If Home Depot decides not to enter the market, then Lowe's has nothing to react to and the game is effectively over, at least for the moment. This event is represented by the Don't Enter branch and position D in figure 11.1.

If Home Depot decides to go ahead and open a store in this market, then Lowe's is compelled to respond. Its basic choices are to accept Home Depot's presence and not change anything about its operations, or to resist this incursion and make a competitive response. These choices are found on the upper half (Enter) of the tree, the branches Accept and Resist stemming from Lowe's decision box. If Lowe's does nothing to contest Home Depot's entrance—if it maintains its current prices, levels of advertising, and promotion; offers no special incentives to shoppers; and does not retaliate by threatening to open a store on Home Depot's turf—that may be the end of the story. We will be at position A in the figure, with the game over, or at least this inning ended.

Home Depot might take Lowe's passivity as an invitation to be more aggressive—to open stores in other Lowe's markets or try to capture much of its business in this area by aggressive pricing and promotion—so it is impossible to write a definitive *finis* in any situation that involves two

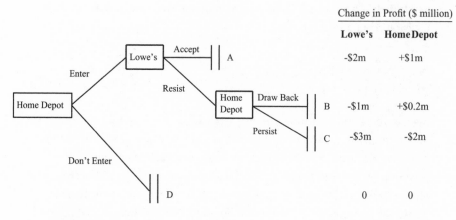

FIGURE 11.1

The tree (or extensive) form for an entry/preemption game

powerful competitors. To represent these later actions we would need to extend the Accept branch of the tree beyond our current terminus.

Lowe's, perhaps anticipating that if it rolls over and plays dead here it will only encourage Home Depot to make additional invasions, may decide to resist. It can lower its prices, up its advertising, announce future store openings in Home Depot territory, and otherwise make life uncomfortable for its rival. Now Home Depot has to decide how it wants to respond. It can persist in its aggressive strategy—lower its own prices, step up its advertising, prepare to resist any Lowe's openings in its territory—or it can decide to scale back its original ambitions and be satisfied with a lesser share of the contested market than it had intended. In either case—Home Depot persists (position C) or Home Depot draws back (position B)—a stable outcome has been reached which is likely to last for some time. The Persist choice will lead to extended economic combat between the two firms, both in this initial contested market and perhaps nationally. The Draw Back choice may produce a less aggressive outcome from both parties, each accepting the other's dominance in certain markets.

Comparing the outcomes is easier if we establish one as a base case and evaluate the others relative to that base. In this instance, the natural choice for the base case is the Don't Enter choice, to which we can assign a value of zero to each competitor, since nothing has changed. We then calculate the incremental profits or losses for Home Depot and Lowe's for each of the other three outcomes. If Home Depot enters and Lowe's accepts (position A), then Lowe's will have lower profits and Home Depot higher ones than in the Don't Enter situation. Given what we know about other markets in which the two compete directly, we estimate that Lowe's profits drop by $2 million and Home Depot's rise by $1 million.

If Lowe's decides to fight it out, then the ultimate outcome depends on how Home Depot reacts. One outcome follows the path Enter–Resist–Draw Back (position B). In this case, Lowe's losses are reduced to $1 million, and Home Depot gains only $0.2 million. Finally, if Home Depot persists by responding aggressively to Lowe's resistance (position C), the outcome is probably the worst for both. Lower prices and higher advertising and promotional expenses will cut into profitability, only partially offset by the increase in total sales in this market. That increase will also require more spending on overhead. The beneficiaries are the consumers, who get more choices and lower prices. Our assumption here is that the additional expenses will lower Lowe's profits by $3 million, Home Depot's by $2 million. As in the matrix presentation of the pricing decisions, the economic outcomes need to be adjusted to account for other motives, like concerns about sales level, relative performance, or the possible desire by Home Depot to leave no market served solely by Lowe's.

Clearly this tree structure is a better tool than the matrix for representing competitive interactions in those cases where the sequence of actions is significant and where the available choices evolve over time as the game develops. The simplicity of the matrix recommends it for situations in which timing is not important and the decisions can be repeated. One useful distinction is that the extensive form works better in situations that involve capital investment decisions, where a major commitment has to be made and the sequence of decisions does matter. The matrix form is suitable for pricing, marketing, and product feature decisions, which are more easily revocable and can be adjusted many times, depending on how the competition responds.

ASSESSING LIKELY OUTCOMES

The advantage of the extensive form (tree structure) for analysis is that it is dynamic. Steps proceed in sequence, and it is possible to think through the likely consequences of a series of actions and reactions as they progress. The process involves identifying at each future stage— each decision box—both one's own best choices and the likely responses of competitors. Putting these decisions together creates alternative paths through the tree, each ending in a particular outcome. Each outcome has a payoff, and by comparing the payoffs, it is possible to rank the various courses of action. Some can be rejected outright if the payoff is awful, like the path Enter–Resist–Persist (outcome C) in figure 11.1. Another may be provisionally embraced, like path Enter–Resist–Draw Back (outcome B), where the outcome is potentially beneficial, at least to Home Depot. Once the tree has been laid out, the analysis actually moves backward, from outcomes to prior choices.

In this case, Home Depot's final decision is whether to draw back after Lowe's has resisted, or to be aggressive and go head-to-head with all the price cuts and additional advertising costs involved. If Home Depot's executives are rational, the choice is simple—earning $0.2 million is better than losing $2 million. In the prior move, Lowe's is faced with the choice of acquiescing, which will cost it $2 million, and resisting, which will cost it either $1 million if Home Depot draws back or $3 million if Home Depot persists. Lowe's, knowing the alternatives for Home Depot, assumes it will draw back. Thus Lowe's effective choice is between resisting, leading to an ultimate loss of $1 million, or accepting, leading to a loss of $2 million. If these are the alternatives, resisting is the better decision. Home Depot's original decision on whether to enter should be made fully cognizant of how Lowe's is likely to respond at that point. In this example, discretion is clearly the appropriate course.

In a real situation, the detailed development of the tree, with its branches, to all the potential outcomes, and then the analysis of alternatives by moving backward through the tree, will be much more complicated than in this straightforward example. Rather than trying to anticipate all the possibilities from scratch, a more practical approach is to simulate the game.

The first step in a simulation is to identify the actors, their motivations, and the initial choice that sets the game in motion. Different people are assigned to the roles, and the game is played out step by step, choice by choice, until the likely paths have been developed and the outcomes evaluated. Successive trials of this sort should identify which strategies lead to better outcomes and which lead to worse. This investigation by simulation will usually be more effective in identifying the superior paths through a realistically complicated tree than an analysis that tries to anticipate all the choices through a purely mental exercise. Simulations are also the best means to incorporate historical information on real competitors, both the choices they have made in similar situations in the past, and their motivations as revealed by those choices.

Once the incumbent has made its choice, the entrant has limited flexibility. It can either retreat or advance from its initial position. In the extreme, it may decide to back out altogether. But the fixed nature of the decisions within the entry/preemption game—the fact that substantial commitments have been made and retreat is difficult—means that the outcome will be determined largely by the incumbent's reaction to entry. With so much riding on this reaction, the entrant should do whatever it can to avoid provoking an aggressive response by the incumbent. If it sees that an aggressive response is inevitable, it should stay out of the market, because a protracted struggle will almost certainly ruin any chance that its foray will be profitable. To avoid an attack by the incumbent, the newcomer wants a strategy that will make it much less costly for the incumbent to accommodate than to resist.

There are a number of ways to minimize the costs of accommodation. The first is avoiding head-to-head competition, just as in the prisoner's dilemma. If the incumbent firm focuses on upscale, sophisticated customers, then the entrant can be less threatening by targeting downscale, unsophisticated ones. It can choose a niche strategy if the incumbent has adopted a high-volume, mass-market one. It can concentrate on geographic or demographic sections within the market that have not been important to the incumbent. For example, Fox Broadcasting entered the network television market with programs the established networks would not touch, like *The Late Show Starring Joan Rivers*, *The Simpsons*, and *Married with Children*.

Second, the entrant should proceed quietly, taking one small step at a time. A brash public announcement that it plans to capture a major portion of the incumbent's business, with openly proclaimed goals for market share, is almost certainly going to trigger an aggressive reaction. The lobster dropped suddenly into a pot of boiling water struggles and tries to jump out. Lobsters eased into a pot of cold water, which is then heated gradually, remain passive, even as they become dinner.

A general nonconfrontational attitude can be reinforced with specific signals. Limitations on the entrant's capacity send a reassuring message. A single store is less threatening than five, and a new plant able to supply just 10 percent of the market is less of a concern than one able to satisfy the entire market. Idiosyncratic, restricted, and onetime sources of financing are another strong signal of limited intentions. A large and visible war chest is more likely to lead to war than to the incumbent quitting the field. Limitations in advertising reach and product lines also reduce the likelihood of a nasty reaction by the incumbent, since it can weigh the small losses it will incur by accommodation against the costliness of an aggressive response. Fox's entry strategy started with a restricted programming schedule, both a recognition of economic reality and a signal of nonaggression to the incumbent networks.

Third, to the extent that it can, the entrant should let the incumbents know that it is moving into only one market, not all the ones the incumbents dominate, and that it is unique among other potential entrants. If the existing companies see the newcomer as only the first of many, they have no choice but to resist and make an example of it, to discourage the others. Again, Fox was clever. It made sure that its challenge to the existing networks was oblique. The target audience for its programs was distinctively down-market when compared to that of its established colleagues. Fox's style would make a transition to the mainstream difficult, limiting its threat to the established firms. Also, before it entered the network business, it had put together a string of local stations that it owned or with which it had an affiliated relationship. Anyone trying to copy Fox's strategy would have difficulty replicating this move. The incumbent networks could believe that even if Fox did succeed, other newcomers were not likely to follow it into the business.

Fourth, in situations where there are a number of incumbents, as in television networks, the newcomer wants to spread the impact of its entry as widely among them as it can. Doing a little damage to a number of incumbents is less likely to provoke an aggressive response than if the entrant wounds only one of them, but that one severely. In that case, the injured incumbent would have to respond aggressively. Again, Fox's strategy was well formulated. Its first programs, late-night talk shows, put it into competition with NBC and Johnny Carson. But it followed with comedy and youth-oriented shows that competed more directly with ABC. It did not try to challenge NBC's powerful Thursday night lineup, then (1986) anchored by *The Cosby Show*.

There are a number of things an entrant can do to make it expensive for incumbents to mount an aggressive response. If the entrant makes moves that are difficult for it to reverse, it sends the signal that an incumbent is in for a long and costly fight if it tries to crush the newcomer. A venture with a large upfront investment and hefty fixed costs, especially when the firm has some flexibility as to the split between fixed and variable costs, indicates a powerful commitment by the entrant to stay in this market. By contrast, subcontracting production, sales, or some other important functions, especially when the contracts are short and carry no significant cancellation penalties, sends the opposite signal: that the entrant is cautious and has an exit strategy in hand.

When there are several incumbents, a strategy of making small inroads against each spreads the pain and makes the newcomer harder to kill, since none of the incumbents alone can deliver a mortal blow. Moreover, any incumbent firm that decides to attack the entrant runs the risk, through collateral damage, of starting a war with its existing rivals, which can be costly and protracted. For example, if either NBC, CBS, or ABC had felt the need to resist Fox's entry into the network business, and had attacked Fox by lowering its own advertising rates, that move would have shattered the cordial pricing discipline within the industry and had a destructive effect on network profitability. It is hard for an incumbent firm in these situations not to shoot itself and its established competitors in the feet, once it decides to shoot. And, if its established competitors respond in kind, the situation will become quite ugly. In Fox's case, the networks held their fire and there was no serious price competition for advertising.

Finally, an entrant may make a strong public commitment to succeeding, or at least persisting, even if its actual activity is small and focused. The purpose is to deter retaliation by established firms, but the strategy can be dangerous. The worst outcome in an entry/preemption situation is a long and protracted competitive struggle. A strong public commitment by the entrant to succeed may leave it no room for retreating, even if that becomes the rational choice. So commitments, if they do not dissuade the incumbent from resisting, may lead to competitive wars, as in the contest between Kodak and Polaroid in the instant film business.

THE INCUMBENT'S BALANCING ACT

Incumbents in an entry/preemption game have to be more careful than the entrants, since they have more to lose. Even before any specific entrant appears on the horizon, an established firm can attempt to deter entry by its general attitude and competitive posture. If it could make an irrevocable commitment to respond aggressively to all challenges, then any potential entrant with an ounce of rationality should steer clear and find some other market in which to work. In theory, this deterrent strategy, if successful, would be very inexpensive, because the incumbent would never need to make good on its threats—an assured-destruction policy without the need for destruction. In practice, however, these commitments are difficult to make and expensive to keep, even if there is only small potential for irrational entry.

An established company can assume a confrontational posture by maintaining large excess capacity to meet any additional demand created by an entrant offering lower prices. Its credibility is enhanced if its cost structure has high fixed and low variable costs, so that any additional product can be churned out at little extra expense. An advertising department and a sales organization ready to meet any competitive incursion, and a product line and geographical coverage that leaves few uncovered niches to tempt a potential entrant are all potent warnings to newcomers. Ample financial resources—the proverbial war chest—serve a similar purpose.

Corporate culture and positioning can reinforce these economic measures. A company that concentrates narrowly on one particular product, that lives or dies by its success or failure in that market, is going to be ferocious in defending itself against potential competitors. Polaroid, for example, did nothing but instant photography. At the other extreme, a diversified company with many eggs in many baskets, all of which need to be watched simultaneously by management, is less likely to go to war over any single challenge. A company with a messianic devotion to its product line, which its sees not simply as a source of profits but as a gift to humankind, is likely to be a more frightening competitor than a coolly rational economic actor for whom returns on investment are the only touchstone. The company that can convey the depth of its commitment to its business has a decent chance to keep most potential competitors at bay.

There are downsides to this strategy of preemptive ferocity. First, it is expensive to maintain excess capacity with high fixed costs, to have marketing firms on retainer to meet challenges only on the distant horizon, and to have products in many niches so as not to leave any room for an entrant. These costs have to be measured against the benefits of deterring entry, and the measurement is not simple, since no one can count all the entrants that have been successfully deterred. Second, if some entrant decides to proceed anyway and gets into a market, it may be more profitable for the incumbent firm to accommodate that entry than to respond aggressively. Protracted price and feature wars do nobody any good. Thus, an adversarial, messianic culture is a double-edged sword that at times should best be left in its sheath. An established firm should always preserve an element of rationality and avoid the extremes of a potential competitive response to entry. Once the entrant has moved in, the established firm's strategy should be to punish the newcomer as severely as possible at the lowest possible cost to itself. Just as in the prisoner's dilemma, this punishment is best delivered in the entrant's home markets. A price war hurts the leader in that market, and striking the entrant where it is strong and the incumbent only a minor factor is cheaper for the incumbent and much more costly for the entrant. This kind of reciprocity of home market invasion is an important weapon in any established firm's arsenal, and the earlier it is used, the more effective it is. If Lowe's discovers Home Depot scouting real estate locations in Lowe's core territories, it should immediately and visibly respond in kind, sending its real estate staff onto Home Depot turf, contacting real-estate brokers to make sure the story gets out. The implied threat has the additional advantage of being cheap to deliver.

STRATEGIES REGARDING UNOCCUPIED TERRITORY

A particular variant of the entry/preemption game needs to be approached with special care. There are territories in either geographic or product space that are unoccupied. They are potential sites for an entry/preemption game, but without the roles assigned to incumbent or entrant. Several equally powerful competitors may seek to claim that territory. The traditional wisdom says that the first competitor to get its stake in the ground, making an irrevocable commitment to occupying that market in force, should effectively preempt and deter its rational, but slower-moving, competitors. But in practice, the other firms considering entry are not usually put off by the early action of someone else whom they see as having only the insignificant advantage of a small lead in time.

For example, if Home Depot announces that it is going to build a store in territory previously unoccupied by it or Lowe's, Lowe's is as likely to infer that Home Depot has private information about the desirability of this market as that Home Depot is merely trying to preempt any move Lowe's may make there. If Lowe's decides not to enter, and Home Depot does, and its store becomes notably successful, the Lowe's managers are going to face sterner questioning than they would if they had followed Home Depot into the market and both stores were marginally profitable. Indeed, the history of attempts to enter virgin territory preemptively has not been a happy one for either the first mover or its slightly later competitors. In general, the watchword in the entry/preemption situation is discretion over valor, and that advice is especially true in the case of unoccupied territories, which often turn out to be lawless frontiers.

GENERAL PRINCIPLES FOR ANALYZING
COMPETITIVE INTERACTIONS

In our analysis of direct competitive interactions, we have focused on just two forms of competition: prisoner's dilemma games, which are contests over pricing, and entry/preemption games, which are contests over capacity. This restricted approach is justified primarily because these two basic games encompass the overwhelming majority of strategic situations that companies confront when interacting with a small number of equally powerful competitors. So in cases of mutual competitive interactions, an efficient first step in formulating strategy is to look for features of these two games in the situation at hand. If either is present, then it pays to exploit the wealth of existing wisdom about how these games are best played.

Most realistic competitive interactions cannot be "solved," in any formal sense, to yield an explicit best strategy. The use of just two specific games to organize information and anticipate actions is an acknowledgment of how imprecise the discipline is. Where these two models fail to capture the essence of a competitive situation, thinking in these terms alone will have limited value. Fortunately, there are other ways to handle strategic analysis. One important alternative is the adoption of a cooperative perspective, which we will discuss in chapter 14. But before addressing cooperation, there are some general principles to keep in mind no matter what kind of game is being played.

The first is to organize the relevant information systematically: who are the competitors, what ranges of actions are available to them, what are their motivations, and what are the likely sequence in which decisions will be made. It is essential to identify specifically those agents whose actions can affect a company's own profitability, whether they are current competitors, as in the prisoner's dilemma game, or potential competitors, as in entry/preemption, or some other more complex relationship. Companies that ignore this imperative often find themselves confronting an unpleasant strategic surprise.

For each agent, the analysis should reveal:

- *The range of actions that the agent has available.* If a competitor does something completely unanticipated, there has obviously been a failure of analysis.
- *The consequences for the company of the possible combinations of actions by all the relevant competitive actors.* What do the outcomes and payoffs look like for all the parties?
- How the various agents value these consequences, or, in other words, what motivates each agent?

It also helps to identify any constraints on the sequence of actions that agents are likely to take and the information firms have when they make their choices among actions. Enough information must be collected and assimilated so that scenarios can be laid out and considered, as illustrated in bare-bones form by the Lowe's–Home Depot example.

There are two possible ways to employ this information. One is to lay it out systematically in either a tree form (figure 11.1) or a matrix form (figure 11.2) and to try to reason through to a "solution" to the game. For simple situations, this approach may be fruitful. With situations of realistic complexity, reason alone will seldom unambiguously identify a precise best course of action. Still, general directions for how to proceed may emerge. For example, let us revisit the prisoner's dilemma example of Lowe's and Home Depot competing over prices and calculate the sum of the payoffs to all the players for each outcome. That is, how much did Lowe's and Home Depot profit together—including non-monetary values—in each of the four outcome boxes? If the sums, which are the joint outcomes, vary across the boxes, as they do here, then there is some scope for the firms to cooperate in order to reach the highest joint outcome (table 11.1). In this case, the biggest joint payoff comes when each firm charges $115 and they divide the market equally; the smallest comes when each charges $105. All firms benefit if they restrict the competition to choices among the high-payoff outcomes. In this case and many like it, it may make sense for competitors to cooperate at some level.

Similar calculations are possible for the entry/preemption game (table 11.2). In this instance, the best joint result is that Home Depot not get involved in the first place. Should it decide to enter, then the best

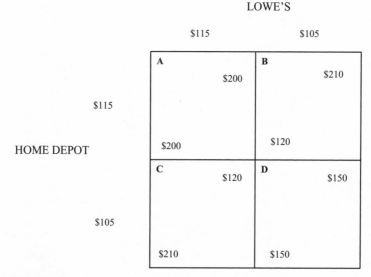

FIGURE 11.2

The matrix (or normal) form of the prisoner's dilemma

joint solution, although not the best for Home Depot, is with an entry that does not lead to full-throttle competition and a price war. Again, because of the variation in the total industry (joint) payoff, there is room for cooperation.

In contrast, if the joint payoffs are the same for all the outcomes, then there is no space for cooperation because the competitors have nothing to gain from it. In these cases, competition should and will be unrelenting. These competitive situations are conventionally described as "zero-sum" games (although "constant-sum" is more accurate). Any gain that one competitor makes can only be at the expense of its rivals. These games tend to arise when the people making the decisions care primarily about relative performance—about market share rather than revenues, profits compared to the competition rather than absolute profits, winning rather than doing well. In the extreme, where winning or losing vis-à-vis the other firm is the only thing that matters, the existence of only one winner for each outcome produces a constant-sum payoff structure and remorseless competition. When the corporate culture

TABLE 11.1

Individual and joint payoffs in the prisoner's dilemma game

	Lowe's		Home Depot		Joint
Box	Price	Payoff	Price	Payoff	Payoff
A	$115	$200	$115	$200	$400
B	$105	$210	$115	$120	$330
C	$115	$120	$105	$210	$330
D	$105	$150	$105	$150	$300

TABLE 11.2

Individual and joint payoffs in the entry/preemption game

	Change in Profit ($ million)			
		Lowe's	Home Depot	Joint
HD Enters–Lowe's Accepts		$ (2)	$ 1	$ (1)
–Lowe's Resists– HD Draws Back		$ (1)	$ 0.2	$ (0.8)
HD Persists		$ (3)	$ (2)	$ (5)
HD Does Not Enter	$0	$ 0	$ 0	$ 0

stresses relative performance, that bodes ill for profits, returns to shareholders, and employee well-being. Unfortunately, this generalization is one of the few that can be made with any confidence on the basis of "reasoning" alone.

A second approach that often works well in practice is to simulate—to "war game"—the competitive interactions between the contending parties. For simulation, the information should include a detailed description of all competitive agents, their potential actions, the returns they would realize under various industry outcomes, and their motives. These competitor profiles form the basis for the people playing the assigned roles and making the decisions within the simulation. Simulations are more effective when they are played repeatedly to produce alternative outcomes, which can then be compared against historical experience. If a company in several lines of business, for example, always drops its prices as soon as any competitor enters one of its markets, that is a good indication of how it will act in the future.

Another benefit of simulation is that, while it can handle more complexity than rational analysis, there does come a point when the number of competitor profiles becomes unmanageably large. And at that point (more than a half dozen competitors is a good rule of thumb) the simulation process also tends to be become diffuse and unwieldy. This is a fairly certain sign that there are no effective competitive advantages in the market in question, in which case analysis of direct competitive interactions is superfluous.

For most direct competitive interactions, it is best to bring multiple approaches to bear. Use the prisoner's dilemma and entry/preemption analysis when they are appropriate. Do well-planned simulations, and do them repeatedly. Consider relevant historical examples. Try to adopt a cooperative or bargaining perspective (chapter 14) and see where that leads. Competitive strategic analysis is as much an art as a science, and the artist who can see the subject from multiple perspectives will do a superior job.

CHAPTER 12

Fear of Not Flying

Kiwi Enters the Airline Industry

BLACK HOLE: THE AIRLINE INDUSTRY AND RETURNS TO INVESTORS

For investors, the airline industry has been a vale of tears. In the first edition of *The Intelligent Investor*, Benjamin Graham wrote that his book might be of use as a warning to those who bought shares in the expectation that the industry would grow.

> Such an investor may for example be a buyer of air-transport stocks because he believes their future is even more brilliant than the trend the market already reflects. For this class of investor the value of our book will lie more in its warnings against the pitfalls lurking in this favorite investment approach than in any positive technique that will help him along his path.

$$\bullet \quad \bullet \quad \bullet$$

The history of the industry in the years between 1949 and 1970 bore out Graham's predictions. Revenues grew even faster than anticipated, yet "a combination of technological problems and overexpansion of capacity made for fluctuations and even disastrous profit figures."

But the allure of the industry remained powerful. Warren Buffett, Graham's preeminent student and an investor renowned for his business acumen and disarming candor, acknowledged that he, too, had been bitten by the airline bug, ignoring all that he had learned from Graham.

Temporary insanity was the only explanation he could offer for why he took a large position in USAir preferred shares in 1989. He should have known better. As he said, since the Wright brothers, ". . . despite putting in billions and billions and billions of dollars, the net return to owners from being in the entire airline industry, if you owned it all, and if you put up all this money, is less than zero."

Investors have repeatedly accommodated airlines by providing capital. Airlines have accommodated investors by providing them with a stream of new companies and established ones emerging from bankruptcy. If insanity is indeed the explanation both for entrepreneurs creating new airlines and for investors repeatedly throwing money at them, then the madness has been more than temporary. But we may not need to resort to the insanity defense. Looking at the aggregate returns of an industry since its inception can mask periods of strength and niches of profitability. Even in the dark times of 2003, confronting a recession, fears of terrorism and war, and industry overcapacity, a few airlines managed to earn money even while others were declaring bankruptcy.

So the decision by the founders of Kiwi International Airlines to start a new carrier was risky but not necessarily suicidal. If they picked their spot with care, managed not to antagonize the big, established carriers, and did all the other things essential to nurture a small business when surrounded by larger ones, they had a chance. Though there was a long list of prior entrants who ultimately crashed and burned, a few had succeeded, most notably Southwest. But the Kiwi founders had to be aware that the airline industry did not forgive mistakes in strategy or execution.

NO GOLDEN AGE: THE INDUSTRY UNDER GOVERNMENT REGULATION

Almost from the beginning, the airline industry seemed to require some assistance from the government. In the 1920s, the Kelly Airmail Act opened mail delivery contracts up to private airline companies. The steady revenue was important for them as they started to develop commercial passenger service. But since virtually anybody could get into the game, competition was fierce and the route pattern chaotic. In 1930, the postmaster general tried to rationalize the system by awarding mail con-

tracts at his discretion. Though Congress directed that competitive bidding remain in place, the postmaster guided the process to favor three
major airlines, United, TWA, and American, each of which came to
dominate one region in the cross-country market. These companies
grew by buying smaller competitors. In 1934, President Roosevelt
learned that the airmail contracts contained rich subsidies for the favored companies and tried to put an end to the practice. After a brief
and disastrous effort to have army planes and pilots carry the mail, the
system reverted to competitive bidding. This time the competition was
legitimate, and the three airlines had to bid against Delta, Continental,
and other new carriers. All tried to grow market share by aggressive bidding; all lost money for some years.

To address this problem, Congress passed the Civil Aeronautics Act
in 1938, at the tail end of the New Deal regulatory phase. It established
the Civil Aeronautics Board (CAB), with authority over route entry and
exit, fares, mergers and acquisitions, interfirm agreements, and airmail
rates. This regulatory regime established order in the industry, so much
so that from 1938 through 1978, no new trunk line was created. The
routes were distributed to provide cross-subsidies between dense, profitable long-haul flights and shorter, more lightly traveled and money-
losing routes. The carriers could not compete on price, and they were
allowed to raise fares when their own costs increased. For a while, the
trunk carriers flourished. Even though the CAB encouraged local carriers to enter the market, the four largest trunk carriers retained 70 percent of the market into the 1960s.

Despite all the protection afforded by the regulators, the industry did
not continue to prosper. The adoption of jet aircraft, begun in the later
1950s and in full throttle over the next ten years, added enormous capacity to the trunk carriers. The planes held more passengers and traveled
much faster. All the airlines were left with seats to spare, just as they had
more debt to service to finance their new planes. The first oil shock of
1973–74 raised their operating expenses, as did inflation in the labor
market. A weak economy dampened demands for seats. The situation
was so dreary that the CAB sanctioned cooperation among the carriers
to reduce capacity in major markets. Nothing helped. There were too
many seats and not enough customers. Regulation may have been part

of the problem. Intrastate carriers, not subject to CAB fare requirements, charged less per mile, sold more of their available seats, and
earned more money than did the interstate airlines.

EVERYONE INTO THE POOL:
THE END OF REGULATION

By 1978, liberals and conservatives had joined forces to push for deregulation. There was some apprehension that travelers might be gouged if
they had only one airline to choose from for a specific destination, but
economists argued that since barriers to entry were so low, a competitor
would quickly enter any market supporting excessive fares. President
Carter had appointed economist Alfred Kahn as chairman of the CAB,
and Kahn was thoroughly committed to ending the regulatory regime.
Congress passed and Carter signed the Airline Deregulation Act in October 1978. Under its provisions, the CAB would no longer regulate
fares or routes; airlines would be free to fly where they wanted and
charge what they liked. Regulation was supposed to phase out over a
several-year period, but it unraveled almost immediately. Price controls
were gone by 1980, as were restrictions that determined which carriers
could fly what routes.

   With the end of regulation, the industry became intensely competitive. The large, established trunk carriers were challenged almost immediately by regionals looking to expand outside their areas of strength
and by new entrants trying to profit by offering lower fares on a few
profitable routes. The newcomers were not burdened by the expensive
and restrictive labor contracts that had been the norm during the regulated period, when airlines were able to raise fares to cover expenses.
Their challenge left the incumbents with no choice but to compete on
price, no matter the impact on their profitability. Some of the weaker
airlines attempted to solve their high labor cost problems through
Chapter 11 bankruptcy proceedings. When they emerged, they were
not bound by existing union contracts and could rehire workers at substantially lower wages. Wages in the industry declined through the
1980s, but these savings did not help the airlines' bottom lines. Only the
customers benefited.

Of the many unanticipated changes induced by deregulation, the most far-reaching was the emergence of a hub-and-spoke route system. Under the pressure of competition, the trunk carriers realized that they could lower costs and fill more seats by funneling traffic through hub cities, where long-distance and short-haul flights converged. A single hub connected directly to 40 cities at the ends of its spokes would link 440 city pairs with no more than one stop or change of planes. The airline could concentrate its maintenance and passenger service facilities in the hub airports. It could focus its local advertising where its route structure was most dense. There were substantial regional economies of scale for the airline that dominated a hub airport, as well as the benefits of needing to fly fewer planes to service its routes.

But all the cost and revenue advantages of a hub-and-spoke system were vulnerable to intense competition from weaker carriers who, in order to fill their seats, dropped prices below what it cost to fly the passengers. When one airline dominated a hub, it made money. When two well-established airlines served a single hub city, they often managed to keep prices stable and profitable. But a third carrier, especially one trying to break into a new market, with low labor and other fixed costs, and with an aggressive management out to earn their wings, could wreak havoc on the incumbents' income statements. One economist calculated that the arrival of a low-priced entrant in a market would do as much damage to the value of an incumbent's equity as if it had to fly its planes empty for about four months.

The incumbents found themselves in a quandary. They could match the prices and lose money on every ticket sold. They could decline to match, and lose passengers. Customer captivity, even with frequent-flier programs, was low to nonexistent. Sometimes the challenger was simply too egregious, and incumbents retaliated not simply to keep their passengers but to drive the upstart out of business.

The more strategic response, developed over some years after 1978, involved the use of a complex and opportunistic fare system to manage "yield" and "load." The airlines defined "yield" as revenue divided by revenue passenger miles (the number of passenger seat miles actually sold), "load" (or "load factor") as revenue passenger miles divided by available seat miles. Using their computerized reservations systems, the airlines could offer identical seats at wildly different prices, depending on travel restrictions, time of purchase, and the remaining availability of seats. With experience and good programming, the major airlines could continuously adjust the price structure to milk as much revenue as possible from the ticket sales. Smaller and newer competitors had neither the history, the volume, nor the sophisticated information technology to compete on this front. Their business strategy encouraged a "keep it simple" approach, for example by offering all tickets on a route with no restrictions, and at the same price.

The efficiencies of the hub-and-spoke system, fortified by yield enhancement through a complex fare structure, provided some relief to the established and well-run carriers. They had at least a temporary respite from the aggressive competitors, both new and seasoned, who were willing to lower prices to fill one more seat. But neither hub-and-spoke nor the sophisticated fare structure was sufficient to transform an industry that was marginally profitable in its good years into a reliable money maker. By 1990, the three most successful large carriers were United, American, and Delta, all with strong hub systems. Some old names like Eastern and Pan American had virtually disappeared, while others like TWA held on, but barely. Yet even the leaders had just scraped by. Over the twenty-six years from 1975 through 2000, the combined returns for the three averaged slightly less than 4 percent in pretax operating income, around 7 percent in pretax return on invested capital (figure 12.1). With returns like this, the wonder is why so many people, both operators and investors, continued to be attracted to the industry.

THE INDUSTRY IN 1990

The structure of the airline industry is straightforward (figure 12.2). At the core are the carriers, both the large trunk firms and the smaller, more regional and local ones. They fly aircraft manufactured by a few airframe companies. In 1990, only three companies were producing large aircraft: Boeing, McDonnell Douglas, and Airbus. Another group, including Embraer, Bombardier, Fokker, and a few others, made smaller planes for shorter routes. Though the airlines sometimes received financing from the manufacturers, relations between airlines and manu-

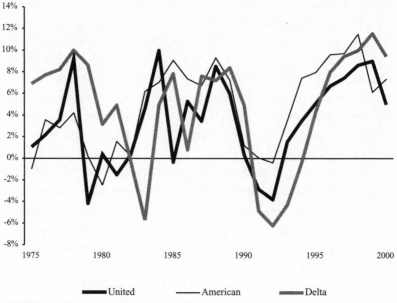

■■■United   ——American   ■■■Delta

FIGURE 12.1
Operating income margins of United, American, and Delta Airlines, 1975–2000

facturers were essentially arm's length. The arrival of Airbus as a genuine competitor in the 1980s gave the airlines some leverage in dealing with Boeing, the dominant supplier. Other essential elements for the flight, including catering, deicing, and fueling, were provided by specialized service companies. Most of the other important functions, like aircraft maintenance, baggage handling, and ticketing, the major airlines did for themselves, with the smaller carriers contracting out for some of them. Financing was provided either internally by the larger carriers, when their balance sheets were strong enough, or by third parties, either as lenders or leasers of the planes. Even start-ups like Kiwi were able to find someone who would lease them an aircraft.

Within the carrier portion of the industry, the airline companies fell into several overlapping categories. There were the large, seasoned companies like United, American, and Delta, whose routes went back far into the regulated era. These three had been the most successful of

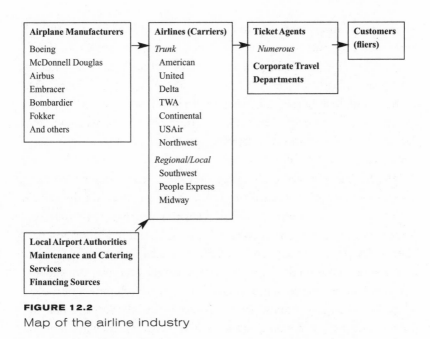

FIGURE 12.2
Map of the airline industry

the bigger airlines, even though, as we saw above, they were not consistently profitable. But within their home territories—their most significant hubs—they did earn money and maintain their market share. Other established carriers had stumbled after the end of regulation. Some, like Pan American, disappeared entirely; others, like Continental and TWA, went into bankruptcy, merged, or were bought out and reorganized. One newcomer, Southwest, had established itself as a profitable niche player, flying selected routes in Texas and the Southwest, mostly out of a hub at Love Field in Dallas. Southwest was extremely efficient. Other upstarts, like Midway, People Express, and New York Air, had had a moment or two of glory as small, focused companies, but then grew themselves into bankruptcy.

The airline companies distributed tickets through travel agents, of which there were many, through corporate travel departments who set themselves up to capture the agency discount for themselves, and directly to passengers. Some of the airlines, notably United, American, and TWA, were able to harvest some advantages through their computerized reservations systems, which they provided to ticket agents, and that were programmed to display their own flights at the top of the page. They also profited by charging other airlines a fee per ticket to qualify as "cohosts" and receive favorable placement on the screens. The systems supplied their airline owners with information on competitors' pricing and scheduling. Clearly it was better to be the owner of a popular computer reservations system than an airline needing to rent space on someone else's system.

The last player in the industry, broadly considered, was the local authorities who controlled the airports and, more importantly, the allocation of gates. In the entire production chain, gates in heavily trafficked airports were the only truly scarce resource. The local authorities, had they so chosen, could have collected for themselves whatever economic rent the competition for a limited supply would generate. But the authorities had as their main mission the economic development of the region. Their primary interest was to promote air traffic at the airport, to have strong carriers connecting their city to many others with frequent and convenient flights. So in most cases they did not try to milk the last dollar from the carriers, at the risk of reducing service.

We know that there were no substantial barriers to entry protecting the airline industry as a whole. Existing firms disappeared and new ones entered, with a pace of turnover that we do not expect to see in an industry with incumbent competitive advantages. The operating margins and returns on investment for the three leading carriers reflect intense competition among incumbents and newcomers alike. In the main, deregulation had been a bonanza for passengers, at least for those whose primary concern was price. But it had been hard on carrier profitability.

Still, within the competitive turmoil, some pockets of strength and stability persisted. As we would expect, local dominance played the critical role. United, American, Delta, Continental, and TWA all had hubs in which they were the leading carriers. Within these hubs, they maintained share stability and even profitability, as the combination of some consumer preference and local economies of scale created a competitive advantage. Travelers were more likely to make their first call to the carrier with the most flights to the most destinations and the most convenient gates; size begat traffic. And the economies of scale available to large carriers within the hubs were considerable: centralized mainte-nance; better deployment of crew, ground staff, and even airplanes; tar-geted advertising and promotion. Once a carrier dominated a hub, it could spread these essentially fixed costs over a larger passenger base. Even its frequent-flier program, designed to reward loyalty and thus keep passengers committed to one carrier, worked more effectively when that carrier was the logical choice because of its hub dominance.

KIWI TAKES OFF

The founders of Kiwi International Airlines, a grand name for a com-pany that would initiate service with a fleet comprising two used Boeing 727s, were mostly pilots who had been laid off in the turbulent years of the late 1980s. Their motivation was to put themselves and people like them back into the cockpits and cabins, working at jobs they loved. They figured that with their experience and passion, they could run their airline more intelligently and efficiently than the mismanaged car-riers whose problems had led to their unemployment. They had some-thing to prove. This kind of motivation, including a dose of revenge, does not generally make for the most realistic business plan or manage-ment strategy. But whatever its source, the approach Kiwi took to enter-ing the airline business was brilliant.

In 1990, the core of the future Kiwi team, led by former Eastern Air-lines pilot Robert Iverson, started to put together a plan to buy the New York– Boston–Washington shuttle from troubled Pan American. Within a year they had secured enough backing to make a fully funded $100 million bid. They lost out to Delta, which bought the shuttle, Pan Am's additional routes, and its other assets for $1.7 billion. Another abortive bid, this one for Midway, with different financial backing, was trumped by Northwest. But the team stayed together. Ten pilots kicked in $5,000 apiece, enough money to allow the group to continue planning. They looked into buying the Federal Aeronautics Administration certifi-cates from ailing carriers in California and Florida, but that came to naught. Then officials in the FAA and the Department of Transportation, impressed with the team's professionalism and determination, suggested that they start an airline from scratch and apply on their own for a certificate.

Financing came from forty-six pilots who each invested $50,000, from flight attendants who put in $5,000 apiece, and from some former airline executives who contributed various amounts. The company managed to raise around $7 million, hardly a fortune but enough to get off the ground. They chose Newark as their center of operations because competition there was less intense, and they became the first scheduled airline based in New Jersey. When they began flying in September 1992, they had leased two used planes to operate on three routes, Newark to Chicago, Newark to Atlanta, and Newark to Orlando. How could such a tiny, underfinanced, new enterprise hope to survive, much less flourish, in a contest with United, American, and Delta, the three most powerful airlines in the industry?

In some ways, Kiwi's position was similar to Rupert Murdoch's when he decided to challenge the network incumbents with Fox Television. The networks were already big, and they benefited from economies of scale and some customer captivity. Murdoch would clearly be operating at a disadvantage. On the other hand, the network industry was highly profitable because there were strong barriers to entry and the incumbents knew how to play the prisoner's dilemma game, to live harmoniously with one another. The airline industry had much lower barriers, confined to those carriers with strong hub dominance. In the main, the airlines did not know how to get along with one another. The history of the industry in both its regulated and deregulated phases showed how difficult it was to restrain overcapacity, and how overcapacity led, almost inevitably, to brutal price wars. With such low barriers, Kiwi did not have a problem getting into the industry. Perhaps the question was, why did it want to?

The Kiwis understood that they should not frontally antagonize the established carriers. As Iverson told *Forbes* magazine, "Our task is to stay away from their bottom lines." That meant staying small and unthreatening enough so that it would cost the airlines more to eliminate them—"to swat a fly off their backs," in Iverson's terms—than to let them live. The choice of routes was part of this strategy. The Newark-to-Chicago route would cut only minimally into United's and American's business. The Newark-to-Atlanta route would nick Delta; the flight to Orlando would take some business from Delta and Continental. By spreading the pain around, Kiwi minimized the loss to any single competitor. It also reduced its business risk by flying three routes; if any of the major carriers started a fare war to eliminate Kiwi, it would still have two routes unaffected by the competition.

Kiwi also avoided challenging the carriers directly on price. Kiwi pegged its ticket charge to the lowest restricted fare the competition was offering. It did enhance the service. Its tickets were unrestricted and required no advanced purchase. It reconfigured its planes to reduce the number of seats from 170 to 150, putting all passengers in the equivalent of business class. It served hot meals rather than snacks.

It had no substantial budget to promote itself in the public media, so it avoided another direct challenge to the incumbents. Instead, Kiwi executives went directly to its target market, the managers of smaller businesses for whom low prices and superior service made a difference. Iverson and his colleagues made the rounds of Rotary and Kiwanis Club lunches, telling the Kiwi story. Other Kiwis visited travel agents and companies, leaving literature and a good impression. This story of "the little airline that might" caught on, so that even before its first flight, it garnered more than enough press coverage to compensate for its lack of an ad budget.

Kiwi did not poach pilots, flight attendants, or other personnel from the existing airlines. A large part of its reason for being was to put these people back to work in an industry they loved and in a company they thought they could run more intelligently and profitably than the ones that had laid them off. Kiwi believed that it could earn money by having a cost structure much lower than that of the traditional carriers. It leased its planes at a bargain rate because, with so much turmoil in the industry, used planes were a glut on the market. It saved by substituting skillful public relations for expensive advertising. Its real key was supposed to be its lower labor costs. The pilots and attendants were going to earn much less than their peers at the established carriers, yet smile about it. The "can-do" attitude of its employee-owners, who would dispense with the restrictive work rules that burdened the traditional carriers, also helped. No job was beneath a pilot, attendant, or other employee. Pilots as managers could fly planes, if the need arose and a scheduled pilot called in sick. Before it began flying, the company calculated that it could break even if it filled around 50 percent of its seats. Its cost structure was planned to come in at 20 percent lower than United's per revenue passenger mile. Though this savings was substantial, Southwest's cost were some 18 percent lower still. But lower costs did not present the same kind of frontal challenge to the established airlines that well-advertised lower fares might. Kiwi did not want to arouse the slumbering giants.

WHAT THE INCUMBENTS SAW

At first, Kiwi made it easy for United, American, Delta, and Continental to ignore it. It could carry so few passengers on each of its routes that even if it filled every seat, the loss to the big carriers would be miniscule. It aimed at a segment of the market—the small business traveler—that was not a high priority with the established carriers. It did not begin a price war, even though it offered more service and convenience for the same fare. It did not steal pilots. It did not look like it had grand plans for growth; it had not raised public capital, and its employee-contribution approach to raising equity involved clear limitations on the amounts that could be accumulated. For Kiwi to become a threat rather than a pest, some of these parts of its business plan would have to change. Also, Kiwi was distinctive enough, with all those airline veterans pitching in, to make its approach difficult to replicate. Only pilots aching to get back into the cockpit would kick in their savings and pitch in to load baggage. It was unlikely that one successful Kiwi would engender a dozen more.

The Kiwi business strategy had always been aware of what the airline would look like to the established carriers. "We designed our system," Iverson told a trade journal, "to stay out of the way of the large carriers and make sure they understand we pose no threat. The seats we take away will be insignificant, so our presence in the market will have no measurable impact on their yields."

On the other hand, Kiwi did look like it might be difficult to eliminate. The pilots, flight attendants, and other airline veterans formed a
committed community. If they had not exactly pledged their lives, their
fortunes, and their sacred honor, they had come close. The $50,000 each
pilot had invested was for most a substantial sum; undoubtedly, some of
them took out second mortgages. The pilots wanted to remain pilots,
and for many of them the next best alternative was a distant second.
Should any of the established airlines decide that Kiwi had to be confronted, Kiwi had given notice that it was not going to go quickly.

Any price war with Kiwi would be protracted and costly, with most
of the cost borne by the established carriers. If United decided to confront Kiwi on the Newark-to-Chicago route, it would also challenge
American, which would have to respond. Each of them, carrying many
more passengers than Kiwi, would suffer disproportionately compared
to the small upstart. Having pegged its fares to those of the established
carriers, Kiwi had announced that it was going to meet any reduction in
price. Meanwhile, Kiwi would still be making a profit, presumably, on its
Atlanta and Orlando runs. So the fare war would not end quickly, and
the longer it lasted, the more bleeding the large airlines would do. The
real economic pain of a price war seemed more trouble than the minor
inconvenience of losing a few passengers to Kiwi.

Kiwi's entry strategy was uniformly well conceived. It made Kiwi
hard to kill without threatening the established carriers. Initially this
strategy seems to have worked well. The major airlines did not respond
aggressively during Kiwi's first three months of operations. But in early
1993, as Kiwi's success began to draw attention, Continental, which
also had a hub at Newark and thus was directly threatened, undercut
Kiwi's fares. Kiwi employees responded by accepting pay cuts to keep
the airline viable. Continental retreated and for the next year it left Kiwi
alone. Kiwi appeared to be on track for a profitable, though small-scale,
future.

KIWI GROUNDED

Unfortunately, Kiwi could not sustain its disciplined approach. In September 1992, the airline had two hundred employees, two leased planes,

and six scheduled flights per day. By September 1994, it had grown to one thousand employees, twelve planes, and forty-seven flights. Kiwi had added Tampa and West Palm Beach as destinations to its earlier roster of Newark, Chicago, Atlanta, and Orlando. It had complicated the route structure by more than doubling the direct routes connecting these cities. Nor was it through expanding. By March 1995, it had fifteen planes, operated sixty-two flights per day, and was about to add Bermuda, Myrtle Beach, Raleigh-Durham, Richmond, and Charlotte to its route structure. Kiwi's original strategy—to not get so big as to challenge the existing carriers, and to focus the business on a single hub, simple route structures, and an identifiable target market—was now history.

"Fish gotta swim," wrote Oscar Hammerstein, "and pilots gotta fly," he might have added. There were at least forty-six pilots who bought into the Kiwi mission. They were not going to be satisfied sharing six flights per day, even if each were a round-trip. They also wanted to prove that they knew better than the companies that had fired them how to operate an airline at a profit.

Also, Kiwi did not succeed in escaping the curse of other entrants. A spate of fledgling airlines—Western Pacific, ValuJet, Reno Air, Midway, Air Tran, Frontier, Vanguard, Air South, and Spirit—entered the industry at essentially the same time. The combination of cheap aircraft available for lease, a supply of laid-off former airline pilots, and the continuing labor-related problems of the major airlines proved fatally attractive to others beyond Kiwi. The influx of so many new carriers forced the existing airlines to respond. By the spring of 1994, price competition by the majors was back in force. Continental and United even started low-priced versions of themselves, Continental Lite and Shuttle by United. Kiwi found itself with too much company for a stealth strategy to succeed, even as it abandoned that strategy.

Increased size and a wider route structure could not, of course, provide Kiwi with economies of scale comparable to those enjoyed by the major airlines. Nor could they compete with the established carriers on customer preference. More frequent flights, more useful frequent-flier programs, and a perceived higher level of safety—an advantage abetted by the ValuJet crash in the spring of 1996—all favored the big carriers.

Meanwhile, Kiwi's larger and more complex route structure led to higher costs without substantially enhancing its appeal to customers.

Growth also undermined Kiwi's anticipated operating efficiency. In 1994, CEO Robert Iverson looked back on Kiwi's promising start and rhetorically asked, "How did this miracle happen?" His answer was that Kiwi employees "with a selfless sense of mission see solutions not visible through the traditional clouds of adversarial corporate storminess." With something at stake, the employees were "always thinking about how to make this company better." But this spirit seems not to have survived the influx of additional employees necessary for rapid expansion. The new employees did not have the same high level of commitment as the first generation. The Kiwi originals found themselves in a larger, more impersonal organization that could not be run only on enthusiasm and a willingness to pitch in.

After his tenure ended in February 1995, Iverson took a very different view of the company and its ethos. It had become difficult to get workers to do as they were told. Pilots refused to fly charter trips because they thought of Kiwi solely as a scheduled airline. Some flight attendants refused to make promotional announcements because they considered them undignified. Some employees gave free tickets to charities without management approval. Meetings lasted forever because everyone had to have a say. Behavior looked so churlish that one executive likened it to grade school. A structure of operations that had been well adapted to Kiwi's original strategy proved unsuitable in its new growth mode.

By the end of 1995, Kiwi had accumulated losses of more than $35 million. The company ran through three more chief executives in a few months after Iverson's removal. Finally Russell Thayer became CEO. He had experience in the industry. He had been president of Braniff when it filed for bankruptcy in 1982, and he had tried to fix Pan American before its demise in 1992. He was no more successful as a savior for Kiwi. The airline filed for Chapter 11 bankruptcy in October 1996 and ceased operations a short time later. Kiwi had a lot of company in its failure. Of the many new airlines that jumped into the deregulated industry, only Southwest, with a well-developed hub in Dallas and a famous operating efficiency, survived and flourished. (The jury is still out on Jet Blue and some other newcomers.) It is possible that Kiwi never had a realistic chance for success, given its initial competitive disadvantages and the toxic state of competition in the airline industry. Still, it did not help itself with its rapid abandonment of a strategy that was well designed and appeared to be working. Strategy ought to be a guide for action, not a rationalization for otherwise unrealistic business goals.

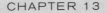

CHAPTER 13

No Instant Gratification

Kodak Takes On Polaroid

ELEPHANT AT THE GATES

George Eastman is one of the giants in the history of American industry. For most of its long life, Eastman Kodak, the company he founded, was an unblemished success story. From its inception in the 1880s as a supplier of dry photographic plates and then roll film, it came to dominate the amateur photography business both in the United States and around the world. For almost a century, Kodak had the wind at its back. Demand for home photography grew rapidly and steadily, and for much of this period, Kodak was almost unchallenged as a supplier of "the Kodak moment." From 1958 to 1967, demand in Kodak's core market grew at 13 percent after adjusting for inflation.

By the 1970s, however, the company faced an increasingly saturated market. Even its long tradition of innovation was no help in spurring increasing sales. Between 1967 and 1972, inflation-adjusted growth in its core U.S. market fell to 5.6 percent a year; between 1972 and 1977, it declined again to 3.5 percent annually. Kodak's management responded by considering expansion opportunities in what it considered adjacent markets. It settled on two: photocopiers and instant photography. Each of these markets was dominated by a well-entrenched incumbent—Xerox in copiers and Polaroid in instant photography. In neither case did Kodak develop a coherent strategy for dealing with the competitive advantages enjoyed by these firms. Both investments turned out badly,

255

especially the decision to challenge Polaroid. The Kodak versus Polaroid contest is a cautionary "how-not-to" story about market entry.

LAND'S END: THE POLAROID MISSION

Many firms have mission statements; Polaroid had a mission. Edwin Land founded the company in the 1930s to produce polarizing filters, but he seemed to have found his calling and the company's quasi-religious purpose with the development of instant photography. In a 1981 interview, Land said: "our essential concept is that the role of industry is to sense a deep human need, then bring science and technology to bear filling the need." Land wanted to satisfy the need for "connection." He proposed to help fill it with effortless and immediate photography. The level of Land's commitment was clear and total from the beginning. After introducing instant photography in 1947, Polaroid concentrated almost exclusively on this business. All of its eggs were in the instant photography basket.

Polaroid's first model, the Polaroid Land Camera, weighed five pounds, cost ninety dollars, and produced a sepia print of modest resolution in sixty seconds. The camera gave Polaroid a toehold in the amateur photography business and a monopoly on instant cameras and film. The original product sold largely because of its novelty. For the company to grow, it needed to offer more than grainy sepia prints. It spent heavily on research and development and produced a steady stream of innovations. In the years after 1947, Polaroid improved both cameras and film. It made the film speed faster, replaced sepia with black-and-white and then color prints, improved picture resolution, and changed the packaging and handling to enhance ease of use. The film development process that originally took one minute was reduced to ten seconds for black-and-white. Polaroid eliminated the waste negative material, which was messy to dispose of, and also the necessity of coating each print by hand to stabilize the image. Its cameras also improved, becoming more automatic and easier to use. A sonar device even focused the lens. By 1975, Polaroid instant photography systems were technological marvels.

Land's single-minded devotion to instant photography paid off hand-

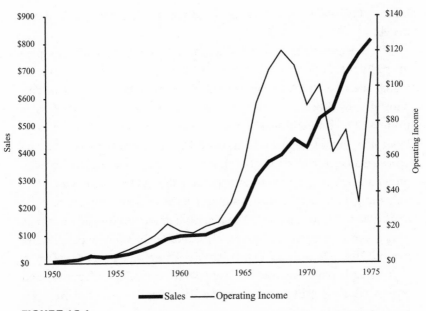

FIGURE 13.1

Polaroid's sales and operating income, 1950–75 ($ million)

somely (figure 13.1) Polaroid's sales grew from $6 million in 1950 to $98 million in 1960 and $420 million a decade later. By 1975, sales exceeded $800 million. Operating profits through the late 1960s grew even more rapidly. Subsequently, a steep run-up in research and development expenses through 1974 led to a reduced operating profit, but there was a sharp recovery in 1975.

The rapid, steady growth rate, combined with consistent profits, made Polaroid a Wall Street favorite. Throughout the period, the shares traded at hefty multiples of book value and earnings. Polaroid was a charter member of the "Nifty Fifty," an elite group of firms in the late 1960s that had become the darlings of professional money managers. These companies were considered immune to the vicissitudes of a dynamic and competitive economy. Unfortunately, Polaroid's stock price, like those of the other Nifty Fifty, declined sharply in the bear market of 1973–74. However, well-timed sales of equity, including an issue of $100 million in 1969, had solidified Polaroid's financial position. At the end of 1975, Polaroid had $180 million in cash on hand, and only $12 million in debt.

The key to Polaroid's economic position was the technology produced by the combination of Land's genius, substantial spending on research and development, and its position as the only supplier of instant photography. R&D expenses averaged more than 7 percent of sales from 1962 to 1971 and then increased sharply. Between 1962 and 1975, Polaroid spent over $600 million on R&D. This investment and the successive generation of products that Polaroid had produced were heavily protected by patents on both cameras and film. As Land later said, "The only thing that keeps us alive is our brilliance. The only thing protecting our brilliance is our patents." The patents helped the company retain its unique status in instant photography, as did the unpatented process and manufacturing know-how that Polaroid had developed over the years.

In its early days, Polaroid contracted out camera manufacturing and purchased the negative material for its films from Kodak. However, as it improved the features of its products, the technology became more complex. By 1969, Polaroid had decided largely to end the contracting out of even the nonsensitive parts of its production processes. It wanted to maintain almost complete control for reasons of quality and secrecy.

Polaroid's marketing prowess was more questionable. New product introductions tended to follow a pattern established with the first Polaroid Land Camera. The original system was expensive and relatively inconvenient. It sold slowly until the company improved product quality, lowered prices for the cameras, and gained market acceptance, first in a steady stream, later in a rush. But just at that point, Polaroid introduced a revolutionary new system whose film format was incompatible with existing cameras, and the process began all over again. The idea of blowing out camera sales by aggressive pricing and then making money on film purchased by the new captive customers never became part of Polaroid's strategy.

By the late 1960s, when Polaroid had finally achieved widespread acceptance of its first-generation cameras, the company began work on an entirely new film and camera system. In 1963, it had introduced color film as the final refinement of its original system, thereby reversing a decline in sales. But six months later it came out with an entirely new film and camera format for both color and black-and-white. The new system used film packs, more convenient than the existing rolls but requiring a new camera. This camera, the Colorpack, was priced at $100. True to the Polaroid tradition, sales initially fell short of the company's expectations. Within the year it introduced a less expensive version. By 1969, when the new system had been widely accepted, a Colorpack camera was selling at retail for $29.95.

By then, Polaroid was already contemplating its next-generation system, the SX-70, which Land considered a major step toward his goal of the ultimate in one-step photography. The SX-70 worked off a film pack that included a battery. The camera focused automatically, had a built-in flash, and offered much-improved resolution and better color. With the press of a single button, the photographer took the picture and began the film processing, which ended when a motor driven by the battery in the film pack delivered the developed photograph.

Like most Polaroid innovations, the SX-70 got off to a shaky start when it was introduced in 1972. The first camera model retailed for $180, six times the price of Polaroid's existing Colorpack camera. There were quality problems with the cameras and with the film packs, especially with the batteries. Sales trailed projections badly. It took three or four years, and the introduction of new and much less expensive SX-70 cameras, before the volume started to build. By 1976, there were only an estimated 2 million SX-70 cameras in use around the world, compared with 25 million of the simpler Colorpacks.

Polaroid's treatment of the firms that sold its cameras did little to endear it to its immediate customers. The company did not generally concern itself with the welfare of the wholesale and retail intermediaries who moved its products to the consumer. From the start it distributed the cameras and film as widely as it could, through camera shops, department and discount stores, mass merchants, drugstores, and whatever other outlets were available. It did not try to control the price of its cameras at the retail level, nor did it protect the distributors when it introduced a new model, leaving them to dispose of the old inventory. As a result, Polaroid's channel relationships were weak and often contentious.

In Edwin Land's view, it was the consumer that mattered, and here Polaroid's efforts were more successful. The company advertised heavily and its name had become synonymous with instant photography.

POLAROID'S ADVANTAGES

In 1975, a conventional assessment of Polaroid's competitive advantages in the instant photography market would have had to conclude that they were substantial. Polaroid monopolized the instant photography business until 1976; it sold all the cameras and all the film. Consumers wanting film developed on the spot had no choice but Polaroid products. In terms of market dominance and share stability, it owned the entire market and there was perfect share stability from 1947 to 1975. Polaroid also earned extraordinary returns on investment (figure 13.2). Between 1960 and 1975, its pretax return on invested capital averaged around 42 percent, unambiguously above Polaroid's cost of capital. But after peaking at 75 percent in 1966, the return began to fall. The average for 1970 through 1975 was only 20 percent.

This decline was not attributable to competition, since there was none. Rather it stemmed from Edwin Land's particular priorities and the introduction of the SX-70 generation of products. The increased research and development expense and the investment in plant and equipment associated with the development of SX-70 pushed down current returns, and as of 1975, the expected financial benefits had not yet materialized. The fact that Polaroid's returns in the 1970s were not as high as in the past reflected Land's relative lack of interest in financial performance, not any current weakness in Polaroid's competitive advantages.

These advantages had several sources. Polaroid benefited from customer captivity, proprietary technology, and economies of scale, but not in equal measure. The company did have captive customers, in the sense that once consumers owned Polaroid cameras, they had to buy Polaroid film if they wanted to take pictures. But this captivity was not especially powerful or enduring. The cost of a new camera was not an insurmountable barrier to an existing Polaroid user, provided the new model, including the film, was demonstrably better. Polaroid itself expected its existing users to upgrade when it introduced the Colorpack in 1963 and

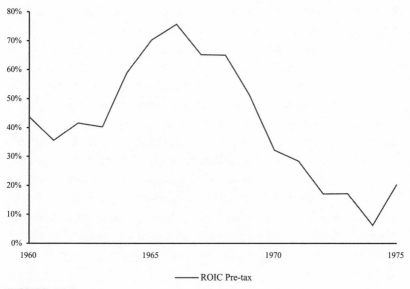

FIGURE 13.2
Polaroid's pretax return on invested capital, 1960–75

the SX-70 in 1972. The cameras were simple to operate. That was a key to their appeal, so experienced users would not have to abandon some hard-to-acquire mastery by switching.

Polaroid was better protected by the second competitive advantage, propriety technology for both its products and its processes. When the original patent for its camera design expired in 1966, it applied for additional ones to protect its advances. Also, it had accumulated a world of experience in engineering and manufacturing both cameras and instant film. Each time it came out with a new system, Polaroid itself had to spend several years fine-tuning production and eliminating problems. The SX-70 system was even more challenging than its predecessors. Given the complexity of both camera and film, it would take a great deal of money, talent, and patience for a new entrant to begin to match Polaroid's production technology, all the while being careful not to infringe on Polaroid's patents.

The third advantage, economies of scale, also protected Polaroid. Making instant cameras and instant film requires major spending for plant and equipment. The R&D investment is considerable. Polaroid laid out more than $600 million in the fourteen years between 1962 and 1975, including over $200 million in just two years to get the SX-70 system ready. Additionally, it supported a substantial advertising program. In 1975, it spent $52 million on advertising, more than 6 percent of its net sales. A new entrant, especially one with the aggressive goal of reaching half of Polaroid's sales in a year or two, would be spending more than 12 percent of its sales to match Polaroid dollar for dollar. This is hardly a formula for profitability. So economies of scale, combined with Polaroid's modest level of customer loyalty, were another substantial barrier for any new entrant to overcome. Taken together, all three competitive advantages, reinforced by fanatical dedication to instant photography, presented a daunting challenge to any potential entrant. A potential competitor might have been well advised to stay way.

OVER THE TOP: KODAK DECIDES TO HURDLE THE BARRIERS

Though Polaroid owned the instant photography market, it did face competition within the broader reaches of amateur photography. A customer could always opt for traditional film photography, where choices were abundant. Kodak was far and away the leading film producer and, at the lower end of the market, the leading camera manufacturer as well. Since George Eastman first produced his roll film and Kodak cameras in the 1880s, the company had been synonymous with ease-of-use photography for everyone. Its yellow box was among the most readily identified brand symbols anywhere photographs were taken. It dominated the photography business, not only for personal use, but also for professionals and the scientific/medical community. Until 1954, when the Justice Department forced it to separate the sale of film from the processing of that film, the company had controlled virtually the entire photographic value chain. Even when independent film processors did emerge, they bought much of the paper, chemicals, and equipment from Kodak. In 1976, twenty years after the consent decree, it still owned half the processing market when the value of the supplies is included.

Kodak was a formidable competitor, and like Polaroid, it thrived on innovation. With the largest share of the film market, it could outspend its rivals on the research and development necessary to upgrade the quality of its films, which it did relentlessly. Like Polaroid, the company had made its fortune by making picture taking simple. Its first Instamatic camera was brought to market in 1963. Within a little more than two years, Kodak had sold 10 million of them. It repeated the success ten years later when it came out with a smaller version, the Pocket Instamatic. Both cameras used film packed in cartridges designed to slip easily into place in the cameras. For the Pocket Instamatic, Kodak shrank the size of the film and its magazine so that everything could actually fit into a pocket. The company made exposure setting automatic, and it improved the flash mechanism, first into bulb cubes that could fire four times, then into permanent flash mechanisms within the camera. George Eastman would have been proud. Everything was simple, and the cameras were big sellers. The smaller film brought Kodak an even larger share of the market, and competitive processors had to buy new equipment just to keep up.

Like Polaroid, Kodak was hugely profitable. From 1950 to 1975, its pretax operating margins of 25 percent were greater than Polaroid's at 19 percent. In 1975, it had a pretax return on invested capital of 33 percent, well above both Polaroid's 20 percent and also above any reasonable estimate of its cost of capital. Sales and profits were both growing rapidly (figure 13.3). From 1950 through 1975, sales had increased from about $500 million to nearly $5 billion, or about 10 percent growth per year.* Its operating income in 1975 was nearly $1.1 billion, ten times larger than Polaroid's. Like Polaroid, Kodak was a charter member of the Nifty Fifty and was extremely well financed. At the end of 1975, it had $747 million in cash and cash equivalents, versus $126 million in debt.

Nevertheless, by the mid 1970s, there were unaccustomed pressures on Kodak's management. Annual sales growth of 10 percent was good when inflation was at 1 to 2 percent. It was less satisfactory when inflation ran to 6 percent or more. Kodak was also losing market share in some of the segments, like color print paper, that it had always domi-

---

*These figures include Kodak's chemicals business. However, sales in 1975 from film and cameras were at least $2 billion, more than two and a half times Polaroid's.

FIGURE 13.3

Kodak's sales and operating income, 1950–75 ($ million)

nated. As a result, the instant photography market, which was growing at least as fast as Kodak's core business, seemed an attractive target.

It was well known in the industry that Kodak was interested in moving onto Polaroid's turf. There was speculation in 1969 that Polaroid would allow Kodak to sell a compatible color film of Kodak's manufacture, but nothing came of that supposed agreement. So Kodak went its own way, developing a system to compete directly with Polaroid. It made no secret of the project, describing its plans in its 1973 and 1974 annual reports. The film would be litter-free, and Kodak would offer a range of cameras at widely varying prices. Since the term *instant* was already taken by the Instamatic, Kodak referred to this project as "rapid-access photography."

ELEPHANT AND TIGER

How did Kodak expect its entry strategy into the instant photography market to play out? When Walter Fallon, the Kodak executive responsible for this decision and later Kodak's CEO, looked at Polaroid, he could not have been oblivious to Polaroid's competitive advantages. Its name was synonymous with instant photography. It had decades of experience with instant cameras and film. It had economies of scale and a large base of customers already owning Polaroid cameras. And last although hardly least, it had an array of patents covering the new SX-70 technology. Admittedly, Polaroid also had weaknesses. It had poor relationships with the customers in its distribution channel, and by the end of 1975, it had not worked all the kinks out of the SX-70 system. However, on balance Fallon had to anticipate an uphill struggle.

If Polaroid were to respond aggressively to Kodak's entry, then it could be expected to match or exceed any Kodak initiative. Should Kodak try to lure customers with lower prices, Polaroid was likely to counter with even lower prices. Given its economies of scale advantage and its greater experience with technology, Polaroid's costs were likely to be significantly lower than Kodak's. If Kodak tried to offer a superior product than Polaroid, it would have to circumvent Polaroid's patents on its new features. If Kodak attempted high product quality, it would somehow have to develop an edge despite Polaroid's greater experience with the technology and the processes. If Kodak tried to beat Polaroid by spending more on advertising, Polaroid would undoubtedly respond by upping its own spending. With a greater customer base, the resulting increase in cost per customer would be greater for Kodak than for Polaroid.

It was possible, at least in theory, that Edwin Land would recognize the potential damage that aggressive competition would inflict on Polaroid. Because Polaroid would sell more cameras and much more film, given its large installed base, price cuts of any duration would hurt it more than Kodak. On the other hand, competition involving advertising or product development that incurred additional fixed costs would be more expensive for Kodak, relative to its output, than for Polaroid. Neither competitor was likely to exhaust its financial resources any time soon. The argument for restraint by Polaroid did not come down to relative strength. Given its competitive advantages, Polaroid was in the more powerful position. Rather it depended on Land embracing a cooperative posture in light of the joint financial damage that aggressive competition would impose on both firms.

Nothing in the history of Polaroid or Edwin Land suggested that he might pursue this course. Given his psychological and economic commitment to the instant photography market, he was not likely to let anyone, even an elephant of the stature of Eastman Kodak, deflect him and his company from their sacred mission. As much to the point, Polaroid had no place else to go. Kodak was involved in a number of businesses beyond photography, notably chemicals. Polaroid was a pure instant photography company. With all his eggs in this basket, Land was not going to surrender even a part of that domain without a struggle. Finally, Land had never been dedicated to bottom-line financials. The size and persistence of his investment in the SX-70 system, even before Kodak had definitively entered the instant photography market, indicated how far he was prepared to go to meet his goals of satisfying "the need for connection." Anyone looking at Polaroid should have realized that it was going to treat any new entrant as a hostile force to be contested at every turn.

Kodak, it appears, never seems to have considered a strategy of restrained entry along the lines of Fox and Kiwi. Instead of a muted approach that had at least the possibility of not provoking Polaroid, it came in with trumpets blaring. It started to hint at its entrance in its 1973 annual report. It devoted more space in 1974 and 1975. The close involvement of a senior corporate officer like Fallon reinforced the message that Kodak was not planning to settle for some minor niches within the instant photography market. From Land's perspective, Kodak "just walked deliberately into our field with a callous pretension that we didn't exist." For an entrant like Kodak challenging an incumbent who had a decidedly strong hand, this was not a constructive approach.

NO INSTANT SUCCESS

These considerations notwithstanding, Kodak told the world in February 1976 that its instant cameras and film would go on sale on May 1 in Canada and two months later in the United States. Kodak met these deadlines. It accompanied the rollout of cameras and film with a large consumer advertising campaign and a program to educate an army of retail sales personnel with the information they needed to help customers. It offered two models of cameras, the EK 4 and EK 6, to compete at different price points, and a color film that rivaled Polaroid's in quality and stability. Kodak's prices were in line with Polaroid's.

If Fallon had thought that Polaroid would surrender a significant part of its business without a fight, he was mistaken. If he thought that Kodak would be able to offer a product superior to Polaroid's, he was mistaken in that as well. When Edwin Land first got his hands on the Kodak cameras, he claimed to be "euphoric." Unlike Polaroid's SX-70 model, which folded up for convenient carrying, the EK 4 and EK 6 were bulky rigid boxes. Admittedly, Polaroid's lower-priced models were also nonfolding. But Kodak had to win over Polaroid customers, a goal requiring product superiority. Polaroid had only to hold its own, which it could achieve with product parity. Independent observers confirmed Land's initial reaction, that Kodak's cameras and film were no better than Polaroid's.

Kodak also experienced production difficulties that it should have anticipated, but did not. It could not produce film as fast as it had planned. Unable to provide the film, the company had to halt camera shipments until it could catch up. Separate difficulties in camera production delayed the introduction of some planned models. The lack of product coupled with Kodak's heavy advertising and promotion campaign worked to Polaroid's advantage. Retailers reported that customers, drawn into the stores by Kodak's efforts but frustrated by empty shelves, turned to Polaroid. People interested in instant photography were not inclined to wait to buy these cameras.

Nor was Polaroid standing still in the face of Kodak's long-awaited entry. In August 1975, the company had introduced two new SX-70 camera models, one at the high end of the line, one in the middle. In part to support these introductions, it boosted an already substantial advertising budget by $16 million for the Christmas 1975 season. Polaroid had also moved decisively to improve relationships with its distributors. Prior to Kodak's entry, its salespeople were seen by retailers as mere order takers, waiting passively for calls from customers who had no alternative choices. After Kodak arrived, the salespeople changed their approach. They began calling on stores more frequently, providing faster delivery, improved service, and higher levels of cooperative advertising.

At the same time, Polaroid tried to quash the Kodak threat in the courts. It brought suit in the United States, Canada, and the United Kingdom, claiming that Kodak had violated a number of its patents on cameras. It asked for injunctive relief to take Kodak out of the instant business in a hurry. An early ruling in its favor in the UK was overturned at the appeals level. The cases continued on. Though Polaroid no longer had the prospect of a quick victory that would eliminate Kodak from the field, Kodak was forced to defend itself on another front, and it labored with the possibility that Polaroid might ultimately win a large monetary judgment and an order forcing Kodak to abandon instant photography.

Kodak's initial sales results appear to have been disappointing, despite management's claim that the dealer orders exceeded projections. By the end of 1976, Kodak announced shipments of 1.1 million instant cameras. Unfortunately, many of these cameras remained on dealer shelves. In its 1976 annual report, Kodak could only state that "the majority were in the hands of picture-takers at year end." As a result, Kodak was forced to continue its aggressive holiday season advertising campaign into January and February, normally a quiet period for sales. By the end of its first year in the instant photography business, Kodak appears to have sold between 600,000 and 700,000 cameras to consumers. During the same period, Polaroid had camera sales of 4 million. Nevertheless, Fallon seemed to believe that he could iron out the production problems and step up to meet what its market research indicated was a powerful demand.

In the next few years, Kodak did gain on Polaroid. In 1978 it sold 5.5 million cameras, up from the 1.1 million in 1976. By then it had around 35 percent of the market, up from 15 percent. But the venture had not been profitable for Kodak. Each time it introduced a new camera model, Polaroid followed suit, especially at the low end. When Kodak offered rebates or reduced prices, Polaroid matched them, after overcoming an initial reluctance. Kodak did succeed in turning the cameras, both its own and Polaroid's, into an equivalent of Gillette's razor, sold at or below cost to spur the sale of blades, or in this case film. The price cutting, improved quality, and the attention brought to instant photography by both companies' stepped-up advertising campaigns expanded the overall market for instants. In 1975, they represented 25 percent of all still cameras sold to amateurs; in 1978, the share had increased to 45 percent. For Kodak, however, that growth was a mixed blessing. It was, after all, the dominant seller of regular cameras and film.

Unfortunately, 1978 proved to be a high-water mark both for instant cameras and for Kodak. A wave of high-quality, relatively inexpensive, and easy-to-use cameras based on the 35mm film format began to arrive from Japan. Even with processing costs included, 35mm film was cheaper than instant. When stores and kiosks offering one-hour processing began to open, the advantage of instant film was further eroded. By 1980, it seemed clear that the great growth spurt in instant photography was over. After selling more than 5 million instant cameras in 1978 and capturing close to 40 percent of the market, Kodak's fortunes declined. By 1981, its market share was down to around a third, and that translated into 3 million cameras. Things never got any better. Although Kodak's financial statements never broke out the figures for instant photography, industry analysts believed that in the company's best years in the business, it may have broken even. Between 1976 and 1983, estimates put its operating losses at more than $300 million after taxes, and this figure did not include all the money it had invested in development.

The final blows were struck in the courts. After some years of wrangling, Polaroid's patent infringement suit reached the federal bench in October 1981. It took four more years for a decision. In September 1985, Judge Rya Zobel found that Kodak had indeed infringed on seven Polaroid patents, most related to the SX-70 camera. In October, she gave Kodak until January 9, 1986, to stop making and selling both instant cameras and film. Though Kodak appealed all the way to the Supreme Court, it had no success in getting the ruling overturned. In January 1986, it announced that it was leaving the business and would lay off eight hundred full-time and many more part-time workers. Though Kodak had claimed in court that it would be seriously damaged if forced out of the instant business, it is hard to see how, since that project had never earned any money for Kodak, and had been a major sinkhole of management attention.

When the wheels of justice ground to a final decision, in 1990, Kodak had to pay Polaroid almost $900 million in damages. The award was the largest in the history of patent infringement suits, although it was much less than the $5.7 billion Polaroid felt it deserved for all the trouble Kodak had caused it. The award was also less than the $2.5 billion analysts had estimated. Still, it gave Polaroid its best payday ever, and it added $675 million in after-tax income in 1991. For Kodak, it was the last affront in what had been a disastrous mistake.

Patent protection proved to be the one competitive advantage that pushed Kodak out of the instant photography business. That the push came nine years after Kodak originally entered the industry only testifies to the company's wealth, technical talent, and determination, not to the quality of its strategic planning. The inescapable facts are that Kodak had only lost money in instant photography, it had never taken leadership from Polaroid, and it was surrendering market share even as the market itself was shrinking. From the perspective of October 1985, when Judge Zobel ordered Kodak to get out of town, it was already obvious that Kodak had made a big mistake.

But it ought to have been sufficiently clear in 1972 or thereabouts that Kodak would have a difficult time making a profit in instant photography. Polaroid enjoyed all the competitive advantages—the customers, the proprietary technology, and the economies of scale. It was clearly determined to fight to the death. Kodak was large and powerful enough to make an inroad, at great cost to itself and to Polaroid. But it was soon obvious that anything it did—promotions, lower prices, new models, technical advances, expensive advertising—Polaroid would match and generally exceed. The net result of Kodak's entry was to turn an industry that had been decently profitable for a single company into one that was a money loser for one competitor and less rewarding for the other.

AFTERMATH

Instant photography was not Kodak's only unfortunate initiative in the 1970s. At the same time it was going head-to-head with Polaroid, it took on Xerox in the copier market. Management's rationale was that it had both the technology to make copiers and a sales force already in place to market them. Its existing microfilm equipment business was starting to decline and Kodak thought it had the infrastructure in place to sell and service copiers. It began with high-end models. The cheapest Ektaprint sold for $45,000, but it planned to offer less expensive, "convenience" copiers once it had its foot in the door. Because the machines would need servicing, the rollout was confined at first to fifty major cities. "The day we deliver," the Kodak marketing head said, "we have two servicemen already in place."

Kodak's experience in the copier business paralleled its history in instant photography, except for the cease-and-desist injunction and the $873 million penalty. By the time it chose to enter, another company was already established as the dominant firm. Kodak invested heavily, in time, money, and talent, to build an acceptable product and gain entry. Its Ektaprint copiers were better than the comparable Xerox models when they were introduced in 1975. But Xerox caught up and surpassed Kodak, which had spent nine years developing the original Ektaprint and another seven before it came out with an improved machine. As in instant photography, Kodak had an early burst of success, captured a respectable piece of the market, and then started to lose ground as the incumbent responded. Kodak hung around longer in the copier business, turning to Canon to manufacture lower-volume machines and using software to incorporate its copiers into desktop publishing and prepress systems. Still, whatever it tried, Kodak always seemed to be playing catch-up. Xerox introduced a high-volume digital machine in 1990. Kodak only began working on one in 1994. Having sold its copier sales and servicing business to Danka in 1996, it continued as a manufacturer for three more years before finally selling that operation to the German company Heidelberger Druckmaschinen, the premier manufacturer of printing presses.

While management attention and resources were being consumed by these unproductive ventures, Kodak failed to protect its core business, giving up ground to Fuji and other entrants. In the 1970s, it let Fuji gain entrance into the paper business with a lower price strategy, and was slow in responding with its own price cuts. Fuji also made inroads into Kodak's basic film business. Kodak's return on capital declined from roughly 40 percent in the 1970s to under 10 percent in the early 1990s (figure 13.4). It recovered somewhat later in the decade, but its returns remained below 20 percent. In the wake of its adventures in instant pho-

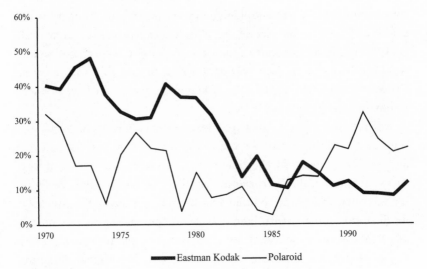

FIGURE 13.4

Eastman Kodak and Polaroid pretax return on invested capital, 1970–94

tography and copiers, Kodak ceased to be one of the leading American corporations.

Polaroid fared even worse. Profitability shrank dramatically with Kodak's entry into instant photography, recovered somewhat when Kodak left the business, and then collapsed with the advent of digital photography. Ultimately, its decline ended in bankruptcy.

Two might-have-beens are raised by this extended tale of woe. First, could Polaroid have done more to discourage Kodak from entering the instant photography business? The answer is almost certainly no.

There were more than enough obvious clues in place about how Polaroid would react to Kodak's entry, and sufficient evidence about what competition between them was likely to do to Kodak's profitability. Any reasonable reading of the situation should have convinced Kodak not to enter the business. Under these circumstances, it is not clear that there was anything else Polaroid could have done to deter Kodak.

Second, could Kodak have pursued a more Kiwilike or Foxlike strategy and entered the instant photography business successfully, if on a smaller scale? Again, the answer seems to be no. Unlike the airline and network television businesses, the instant photography market was not easily divisible. The large, upfront development costs of Kodak's entry meant that pursuing the whole market was probably the only viable strategy. On its part, given its attitude and its sense of its role in life, Polaroid would almost certainly have contested vigorously any Kodak initiative, however small. Elephants are still elephants even when they tread lightly. The only economically sensible decision for Kodak was to stay out of the market altogether.

Finally, Kodak seems to have consistently misunderstood its own competitive advantages and those of the companies it decided to challenge. It saw instant photography and photocopiers as adjacent markets into which Kodak could easily extend its expertise, its customer relations, and the value of its brand. In practice, the technology in both was different enough so that the incumbents had no problem meeting and surpassing Kodak's offerings. The existing sales force was not much help in selling copiers, and the service department proved a major cash drain. More to the point, each market had a powerful incumbent who was not going to accept Kodak's entrance without a struggle. As a result, neither market was a natural or easy extension of its existing franchise.

Meanwhile, Kodak did not aggressively defend the markets that it did dominate—photographic paper and film. It did not forcefully contest Fuji's arrival in the United States, and by the time it responded, Fuji had gained more than a foothold. Eastman Kodak was a global company that did not realize how local, as measured in market space, its advantages really were.

CHAPTER 14

Cooperation without Incarceration

Bigger Pies, Fairly Divided

THE VIEW FROM OLYMPUS

In formulating strategy, there is a natural progression of perspectives from unrestrained competition through a mix of competition and cooperation to a more purely cooperative viewpoint. We have followed that progression in this book. We began with an analysis of competitive advantages. Then we considered companies as economic agents concerned only with their own capabilities, which they seek to exploit without regard to how others might react to whatever they do. We noted that there were two situations in which this type of competition takes place.

One is in markets where the number of competitors is so large that managing mutual interactions is both impractical and of limited value to anyone acting alone. These are markets in which there are no barriers to entry. The other situation is one with an elephant surrounded by ants—Wal-Mart in its stronghold, Intel and Microsoft on the desktop. There are barriers to entry, and the companies that benefit from competitive advantages do very well, especially if they know how to exploit those advantages. But their success does not entail any measure of cooperation with their smaller rivals. What these two situations share is a model of competition among agents that is unmediated by any recognition of common interests.

When there are several firms operating within the barriers, all equipped with competitive advantages, opportunities for the exploitation of mutual benefits becomes an important issue for strategy. Elements of competition are still present, certainly, but now there is the possibility of doing better by taking the actions and reactions of others into account. We explored these situations through the lens of traditional game theory, examining effective methods of balancing competition with cooperation within the competitive situations most likely to occur—the prisoner's dilemma and entry/preemption games. We turn now to another perspective, looking at these inherently complicated situations purely as opportunities for cooperation.

Adding a viewpoint that stresses cooperation to the existing analysis of direct interactions among agents enables us to highlight things that otherwise might remain unnoticed. First, there are some interactions that are inherently dominated by the possibilities of cooperation. The first priority of software and hardware firms in the data-processing industry is to produce the best systems possible, to which they all contribute. The competition of dividing up the rewards from building those systems is a genuine but nevertheless secondary concern. Suppliers and distributors, whether of physical goods or media creations, face similar imperatives. Even producers and end-use customers, who have generally been regarded as on opposite sides of the market, almost always have mutual interests in seeing that users get the most benefit from the product involved. In these cases, the cooperative perspective is essential to formulating effective strategies.

Second, in other competitive situations, face-to-face bargaining is a common form of interaction, one that need not run afoul of antitrust laws. Relationships between unions and employers are the most obvious example. In fact, almost all interactions between large organizations that are part of the value chain, from raw material to a product in the hands or mind of the ultimate customer, involve a significant degree of face-to-face bargaining. As contemporary theories of negotiation have recognized, these exchanges are more successfully approached from a cooperative, rather than an adversarial, perspective.

Finally, even in situations that are predominantly competitive, a cooperative perspective will often yield useful strategic insights. For example, it is possible, at least in theory, to develop a model of what an industry would look like if run cooperatively with maximum efficiency as the yardstick. In this model, all the agents would behave rationally, and together their actions would produce the optimal industry outcome. Taking its cue from this analysis, a high-cost producer, finding itself frozen out entirely under this fully cooperative arrangement, must look for and exploit any less than rational behavior on the part of its more efficient competitors. Using this analysis, other firms might decide to swap business units with one another, to take advantage of their strengths and reduce their direct competitive exposure. Though this Olympian vantage point is admittedly utopian—how the world would work if everyone were reasonable, farsighted, and fair—it still has practical applications. For all these reasons, the cooperative viewpoint belongs in the portfolio of strategic perspectives.

In the organization of this book, the cooperative perspective rests on the branch where competitive advantages do exist and are shared by more than one competitor (location 3 in figure 14.1). It is a complement to the analysis utilizing classical game theory, particularly the prisoner's dilemma game discussed in chapter 8 and the entry/preemption game covered in chapter 11.

OUTCOMES FIRST

Adopting a cooperative perspective requires that we modify the focus of the analysis in important ways. Until now, we have concentrated on the capacities of firms (competitive advantage) and on their actions (competitive strategies). Outcomes—the distribution of rewards among the firms—has been treated merely as an incidental consequence of these primary forces. The cooperative perspective turns this priority on its head. The focus is on outcomes: what overall level of rewards are possible (through optimizing an industry) and how they are to be allocated among participants (through the principles of "fairness"). Tactical or strategic considerations and underlying capabilities now become secondary.

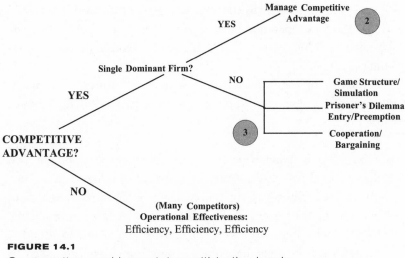

FIGURE 14.1
Cooperation and bargaining within the book

This reversal of significance rests on the assumption that in a cooperative environment, once participants have jointly decided on where they want to go, the mechanics of how to get there—which agent does what action—will be relatively straightforward. Each player will naturally "do the right thing" necessary to achieve the outcome on which everyone has agreed. Cooperation, by its very nature, precludes wasteful conflicts in which differences in capabilities might affect outcomes directly. For this reason, the capabilities of individual agents matter only to the extent that they determine the set of attainable joint rewards and the appropriate division of those rewards.

There are two important constraints that limit this set of attainable joint rewards. First, some outcomes are simply not feasible, given the economic and technological realities of the situation. In the absence of a service station infrastructure able to supply hydrogen to automobiles on demand, the fuel cell is unlikely to be widely adopted as a transportation engine, no matter how cooperative the automakers, regulators, and fuel cell development companies can be. The set of attainable joint rewards refers only to those outcomes that are actually possible. Second, the set is also constrained by the reward level that each participant could achieve should cooperation break down. Cooperation is unlikely to be sustained by voluntary participants if any of them can do better by refusing to cooperate.

In the coming pages we address the two main features of a cooperative strategy analysis—maximizing joint rewards and dividing the gains fairly.

- *Maximizing the attainable joint rewards.* This is concentrating first on the size of the pie (fully exploiting joint gains) rather than on how it is divided (getting as big a piece as possible). In the language of bargaining, this means seeking at the start to identify win-win possibilities. Only after these have been exhausted is it time to attend to the trade-offs between bargainers. There is an upper boundary to the set of feasible outcomes, that is, the best of all possible worlds currently attainable. This upper limit is defined as the line beyond which there are no joint actions that might expand the overall pie without requiring sacrifices from some of the participants. Things are as good as they are going to get, and they can't get better without somebody doing worse. Because the full exploitation of these joint gains is the essence of cooperation, we will lay out some of the most important steps firms can take to make their industry as profitable as possible.

- *Dividing the gains in rewards according to the principles of "fairness."* A stable outcome depends on fairness. If cooperation is to be sustained among a group of economic agents over any extended time, then all the participants have to feel that they are being treated fairly in the division of the rewards. Dissatisfaction, especially when buttressed by a justifiable claim of unfairness, will inevitably lead to a breakdown in cooperation. In fact, individual firms will never enter into a cooperative arrangement in the first place if they feel that the rewards they will garner within the arrangement are not commensurate with the value they contribute. We will examine carefully what constitute "fair" divisions of the pie in different cooperative situations. Companies that have a sound concept of fairness conditions should enter cooperative arrangements with a realistic sense of what they can expect to gain, not so low as to allow themselves to be exploited nor so unreasonable as to be disappointed when their unwarranted aspirations are unfulfilled.

OPTIMIZING AN INDUSTRY TO
MAXIMIZE OVERALL REWARDS

If our first goal is to make our industry as profitable as possible—to achieve the best possible joint outcomes—where do we start? We could try to expand the market for the industry's products or services, to keep other industries from encroaching on our turf, to keep down the costs of the things we need to buy as inputs, to make sure that our customers do not collude to keep their bids for our offerings artificially low. These are the kinds of moves we would make if we were simply running a single firm, only now the scale would be larger and the tactics modified to account for the fact that we are members of a group.

One thing we would certainly do is to organize the industry for maximum efficiency, to avoid wasting any resources through unnecessary duplication of effort or poor design of the processes required. Again, a single firm also wants to operate as efficiently as possible, but its task is simpler because it does not have to coordinate so many separate operating centers. To achieve the highest possible level of industry-wide efficiency, it helps to think of the industry as governed by a single intelligence capable of directing the behavior of all the constituent firms. That thought experiment should produce a model equivalent to how the industry would run if it were a coordinated monopoly.

The conventional view of a monopoly is that it is solely concerned with charging the highest appropriate price—the price that produces the greatest profit. But this is far too narrow a description of monopoly behavior. There are a number of dimensions to cooperation that are at least as important for industry performance as pricing. And pricing itself needs to be understood as part of a broader set of decisions that involve more than setting a single monopoly price for the industry. Effective cooperation has to manage:

- Pricing levels across the many subsegments that make up an entire industry
- The level and the location of the industry's production capacity
- Allocation of production to the most efficient facilities
- Cost discipline in the acquisition of resources
- Coordination of distribution and service facilities to reduce overlapping resources and keep costs down
- Organization of research and development to eliminate duplication, to disseminate innovations appropriately, and to provide incentives for continuing improvement in industry operations
- Product line management to eliminate redundancy and fully cover the relevant niche markets
- Coordination of advertising and promotion to enhance the effectiveness of industry-wide promotion while avoiding the clutter of competing and mutually neutralizing messages
- Synchronization of information systems to reduce working capital requirements and ensure that information is reliably disseminated to the relevant operating units
- Rationalization of overhead expenditures to prevent inefficient duplication and to take advantage of economies of scale possibilities
- Joint risk management to reduce financing and other related costs, many related to the fluctuations in individual firm demands that beset every industry

The list of potential areas of cooperation is both long and, in many instances, not troubled by a concern with antitrust violations. On the other hand, it is undoubtedly optimistic to think that this high level of cooperation can be established and sustained in the midst of a competitive market economy. To repeat, our purpose is to describe an extreme situation, portions of which are clearly attainable and are in actual practice.

Much can be accomplished if firms simply exercise competitive restraint in areas remote from antitrust laws. For example, firms can improve their profit margins by operating in niches where there are few direct competitors. Everyone is made better off if, instead of going head-to-head in every niche, each firm picks a territory that it has pretty much to itself. Territory can be defined by geography, product type, service specialization, or the characteristics of target customers. So long as these segments are not too closely related, the companies are unlikely to be tempted to compete with one another on price.* With each company reigning in its particular niche, the industry will have what is known as effective yield management—in which customers who are willing to pay more for an item will get the opportunity to do so, because their choice resides in a particular niche and they are not tempted to buy a lower-priced alternative in another niche, even if the two purchases look essentially equivalent to someone else.† From a cooperative perspective, price coordination is largely a matter of the effective positioning of firms across industry subsegments.

Managing the capacity of an industry involves more than simply closing plants or other facilities if the market cannot absorb all the product being turned out. It also means ensuring that the facilities that are kept open are the most cost efficient in the business. In an expanding industry, the strategy is to increase capacity of the most efficient firms and those that are most advantageously located. In a declining industry, the goal is to first shut down the highest-cost and worst-situated producers. These choices seem natural enough, what the market might itself do over time in a competitive weeding out of unprofitable operations. In a cooperative environment, the results can be accomplished more quickly and with less pain. If functions like sales and production can be separated from one another, then firms with high production costs may be able to survive as marketing and sales organizations, buying their product from the low-cost or best-situated producers. They have to specialize and excel at what they do, naturally, but there is room for them in a cooperative universe.

Efficient outsourcing, which is another way of describing this separation of functions, is a powerful means for reducing industry-wide costs

---

*If there are significant cross elasticities of demand—if buying a product in one niche increases the demand for a product in another niche—then the companies can employ price-setting tactics, as in the prisoner's dilemma game, that limit mutually destructive interference.

†The best example of effective yield management is the airlines' ability to sell virtually the same seat for different prices, depending on how far in advance the traveler books and what kind of refund or exchange rights come with the ticket. These differences reflect distinctions in customer demand that are more varied than the similarity of the product—a seat on a particular flight—would indicate.

by channeling production to the lowest-cost firms. When this shifting can be accomplished painlessly, without incurring additional expenses, then there is little else that need be done to minimize costs in the industry. If shifting production is itself costly for one reason or another, then efficient firms may license their production technologies on appropriate terms to their less economical competitors. In either case, costs have been taken out of the supply chain across the entire industry.

If production can be concentrated among a few of the most efficient firms, then competition for resources will also be constrained. In any event, for essentially generic resources, such as generally skilled labor, widely used raw materials such as energy, and financing, no single industry is likely to have a significant impact on their prices. For specialized labor with particular talents, competition within the industry may drive prices upward. But with a small number of bidders, restrained by their cooperative outlook or skilled in deploying prisoner's dilemma strategies to control aggressive tendencies, it should not be difficult to manage competition for resources, at least in theory.

In coordinating distribution and service facilities for efficiency, niches are again the key. Firms that concentrate in specific geographic or product spaces will operate more efficiently than firms that are spread thinly over large areas. Both the distribution and the service provision businesses tend to entail significant fixed costs whose level is determined by the geographic footprint of the relevant market area. These functions share the cost structure characteristic of natural monopolies—high fixed and low marginal costs with powerful economies of scale that keep a second supplier in a much inferior position.

The boundaries of the natural monopolies, in both physical and product space, extend as far as the economies of scale still operate, but no further. Once a distributor has exhausted all the territory it can serve with its existing infrastructure, for example, it is on a level playing field when it moves further afield. The same situation holds for a service provider, like an information technology maintenance organization. When it needs an entire new set of specialists to service customers with different needs or equipment, it has come to the limits of its economies of scale. But within these boundaries, a cooperative configuration in which certain firms dominate particular areas should be both efficient and stable, since these firms should enjoy competitive advantages over potential entrants, so long as they also benefit from some degree of customer captivity.

Research and development is easier to coordinate on paper than it is in practice. Theoretically, the underlying elements of efficiency are simple to define. Duplicative research activities are to be avoided, meaning that firms should not overlap one another in their research programs. Information should be widely shared, to foster benefits from the spillover value even of research that is tightly focused. Unrestrictive cross-licensing arrangements can broaden the application of research results to the product development efforts of different firms with nonoverlapping specialties. And the levels of research and development expenditures should be set to take into account both the direct benefits to the firms paying the bills and the indirect benefits to other firms in the industry. In a cooperative arrangement, there are going to be external benefits, and they should be considered when funding levels are set. Whether these expenditure levels would be higher or lower than those in a fully competitive industry is impossible to say a priori. The elimination of duplication argues for lower expenditures; wider dissemination of benefits pushes in the opposite direction.

Coordinating product lines and the advertising campaigns are the same kind of tasks in a cooperative industry as they are within an individual firm. There are trade-offs, and a balance has to be struck. On one side are the benefits of offering a full range of products and messages; on the other side are the inevitable losses through cannibalization from competing product lines and promotional campaigns. Each additional product or advertisement may take as much or more from existing business as its adds incrementally to total sales. Among firms in an industry, concentration in subsegments helps to avoid cannibalization, especially when closely related products or territories are in the hands of the same firm. For advertising and the deployment of a sales force, efforts to win business by running ads proclaiming that "our product is better than their product," or by making direct sales calls on a competitor's customers, are practices to be avoided.

Coordinating information systems, especially across firms within the same supply chain, is a growing reality that has not been a subject of antitrust enforcement. Similarly, agreement among competitors on common information standards and formats, like MP3 in digital audio or IEEE 802.11x (WiFi) in wireless communications, is widespread and uncontroversial, at least to date, from an antitrust point of view. Everyone regards the Betamax versus VHS battle in videotape, and the costs that contest imposed on firms on both sides and on customers who made the wrong choice, as something to avoid.*

Overhead efficiencies are often achieved by outsourcing to specialists. ADP, for example, has made a living in several businesses, one of them payroll processing across many industries, another back-office processing for investment companies. It has added value by achieving measurable economies of scale from handling the mass of transactions supplied to it by many firms which, had they decided to keep this function in-house, would have nowhere near the volume to match ADP's costs. In some cases, these services are provided not by pure third parties but by leading firms within the industry, like large banks that process credit card and other transactions for smaller banks. These economies are not difficult to identify in theory, nor have they been difficult to achieve in practice, even without a fully cooperative organization of functions.

Finally, there is the amorphous but crucial question of the distribution of risk. The insurance industry exists to shift some kinds of risks from individuals and firms to companies specializing in accepting risk at a price. But there are many kinds of risks that companies face, not all of them insurable by traditional methods. All industries face fluctuations in demand for their offerings. Price wars often occur when demand shrinks. They are a natural result of firms responding in their own interests, but like all price wars, they make everyone worse off, especially when there is less business to go around. Increases in capacity unwarranted by additional business create their own imbalance between supply and demand. In both cases, price and capacity coordination require competitive restraint to minimize damage and control risk.

Fluctuations in input prices, either locally or globally, have tradition-

---

*Competition over formats and standards has not disappeared. There are competing standards for the next generation of DVD players, and digital audiotape never made it into mainstream consumer technology in part because there was no agreement on a format. But most of this competition is resolved before many firms come to market with their devices.

ally been automatically smoothed out with contracts that incorporate cost sharing between suppliers and customers and across firms in the industry that are differentially affected by such changes. More recently, the same type of insurance has been provided by hedging—the use of derivative contracts to shift risk from one party to another. In a coordinated industry, arrangements of both kinds would be widespread.

From a strategic perspective, a detailed and comprehensive picture of what the industry would look like in its most effective configuration serves as a guide to the kind of cooperative arrangements that a firm ought to pursue, through explicit negotiations or other means. It also establishes goals that the company's management should set for itself. The examples we present in the following chapter reveal how far a fully cooperative approach may take an industry. But even where extensive cooperation does not seem practical, a picture of the industry from a cooperative perspective helps to define the strengths of a particular company. The roles that the company would play within a cooperative configuration, and the market positions it would occupy, highlight the specific competences that the company brings to the industry and thus the areas in which it should focus its efforts. Only after it has made these decisions is it time to turn to the question of what rewards it might reasonably expect to earn from these focused activities.

UTILIZING "FAIRNESS" PRINCIPLES TO DIVIDE THE SPOILS WHILE SUSTAINING COOPERATION

The mathematician John Nash won the Nobel Prize in Economics for, among a few other things, initiating work on the principles of "fairness" for determining the division of rewards in an industry that has achieved a stable cooperative organization (a cooperative equilibrium). Other economists have built on Nash's efforts, so that now the principles are well established. Here we will focus on three: individual rationality, symmetry, and linear invariance.

Before we turn to the principles and their practical strategic implications, it is important to understand what "fairness" means in this context. It is more than a matter of justice. For cooperation to be sustained, all of the cooperating parties need to be satisfied with the returns they receive from continuing to cooperate. If any player becomes sufficiently dissatisfied, it will inevitably abandon its cooperative behavior. Noncooperation from a single player may lead to a cascading collapse in cooperation by others.

A common example of the perils of discontent occurs in price competition. When a firm becomes unhappy with its share of the market at cooperatively maintained high prices, it will lower its own prices to gain business. Competing firms are not likely to stand by idly as their customers decamp. They protect themselves and drop their own prices. In short order, the price declines may spread throughout the industry. To keep the ball from unraveling in the first place, all the companies have to believe that they are being treated fairly in the current arrangement. This perceived fairness is essential to the stability of cooperation.

INDIVIDUAL RATIONALITY

The first condition of fairness is that no firm in a cooperative arrangement should receive less than it could obtain in a noncooperative setting. Clearly, a company that can do better by not cooperating is not going to continue to cooperate. In the language of formal game theory, this condition is referred to as "individual rationality." Unless it makes sense for each firm to cooperate, meaning that each firm does at least as well by cooperating as by refusing to cooperate, then cooperation will not be sustainable. In this sense, the original division of the spoils will not be fair.

Because of the fairness condition, it is important to consider the outcome that firms can achieve when they do not cooperate. In John Nash's term, these are "threat point" outcomes, the "threat" being noncooperation and a myopic pursuit of one's individual goals. In the language of negotiation theory, the same outcome is referred to by the acronym BATNA—the best alternative to a negotiated agreement. Whatever the name, it is the yardstick against which the firm's rewards under a cooperative arrangement are measured. In organizing a fair division of the spoils, the noncooperative outcomes for all the participants have to be taken into account.

The requirement of individual rationality has powerful implications. In many situations, it alone determines the distribution of cooperative rewards. Consider the case in which a number of firms contribute to a final end-user product in the information technology area. Some firms produce components. Other firms assemble the components into various types of equipment. Still others combine equipment, software, and service support to produce applications systems that are sold to end users. Clearly, firms at each stage in this value chain have incentives to maximize the final price of the item sold and to minimize the total costs of producing it. This is a clear instance where cooperation both is beneficial to firms and does not run afoul of antitrust laws. Despite the group interest that the firms have in securing the highest return on the item in question, the question of how this overall industry return is to be divided among participants at each stage of the production process—components, equipment, systems, and support—still needs to be settled.

The individual rationality requirement on its own may provide an answer. Let us assume that component production and equipment assembly are businesses in which there are no barriers to entry and no incumbent competitive advantages. Systems integration, on the other hand, is characterized by economies of scale in both software creation and service support, and by a sufficient degree of customer captivity to nourish the economies of scale. If the component and equipment makers existed in a world without cooperation, new entrants and internal competition would drive their economic profit to zero, meaning that they would earn a return on their invested capital equal to the cost of acquiring that capital. The threat point, or BATNA, for these companies, the point at which they would be better off without cooperating, is at this level of reward, when they earn no more than their cost of capital.

The dominant systems integrators are in a very different position. They do benefit from competitive advantages, and they earn more than their cost of capital under the noncooperating regime. Component and equipment suppliers who do not want to cooperate can be replaced readily from the sea of potential new entrants able to produce at the same cost as the original firms. As a consequence, the threat point return of the systems integrators, their BATNA, is equal to their profits under full cooperation. They collect for themselves all the benefits from cooperation. They do not have to share with the component and equipment makers, who have no better alternatives available. So it is competition within the component and equipment assembler markets that enforces cooperation from these companies without their getting any share of the excess profitability.

The principle involved here is a general one. Firms that operate without competitive advantages should not expect to earn returns above their cost of capital even when they work in a cooperative environment. All those firms that expect to prosper over the long run based on relationships they have with companies like Wal-Mart, Staples, Microsoft, Intel, and other dominant companies are almost certainly deluding themselves. They should count on earning their cost of capital and nothing more. At the same time, the Wal-Marts, Staples, Microsofts, and Intels of the world should not expect their suppliers, distributors, and other cooperators to accept returns below their cost of capital, at least over time. If the powerful companies do not let the cooperating firms earn their costs of capital, these firms will ultimately leave the business, and the supply of replacements will dry up. This is the principle of individual rationality at work on both sides of the negotiating table. As they say in country music, if you don't bring anything to the dance, you shouldn't plan to bring anything home. On the other hand, you don't have to return home with less than nothing.

The principle of individual rationality implies that the only benefits of cooperation that are subject to divvying up are those gains above the noncooperation outcomes, that is, gains that are the benefits to cooperation itself. When, among all the cooperating companies, only one firm enjoys competitive advantages over its actual and potential rivals, it will reap all the rewards. In many instances, however, more than one firm benefits from competitive advantages and has some claim on the cooperative gains. In the personal computer industry supply chain, both Microsoft and Intel enjoy significant competitive advantages. What constitutes a "fair" division of the spoils in instances like these? Fortunately, there are additional fairness conditions that govern their allocation.

SYMMETRY

Nash used the term *symmetry* to describe a second fairness condition. Under the principles of symmetry, if all the legitimate claimants to the benefits of joint cooperation, that is, all those enjoying competitive advantages and therefore not forced to cooperate by competitive pressure, look essentially the same, then they should divide the benefits of cooperation equally. Like individual rationality, the symmetry condition has to be satisfied in cases where it applies in order for cooperation to be sustained successfully over time. If, among essentially identical cooperating firms, some of them consistently appropriate a disproportionate share of the benefits of cooperation, then the firms that have been short-changed are going to be dissatisfied, and legitimately so. Firms with authentic grievances will not cooperate indefinitely. The companies that have been successful in grabbing more than their share of the spoils may do well in the short run, but over time their greed will undermine cooperation, to the detriment of everyone. Mutual recognition of the force of the symmetry condition—how it is crucial to sustaining a cooperative equilibrium—should help forestall dysfunctional wrangling over sharing the gains.

If two firms in an industry both enjoy competitive advantages, cooperation requires that both participate. Then, if the benefits of cooperation can be shared between them so that each dollar of benefit surrendered by one firm is transferred to the other one, the division of the benefits should be equal. Regardless of any differential in size, power, or other important characteristics of the firms, the benefits of cooperation—the total returns earned that exceed the sum of their individual noncooperation returns—depend equally on both firms, and both firms have equal access to them. The firms are equal in that each is essential for there to be any benefits of cooperation, and therefore, according to the symmetry condition, they ought to expect to share in them equally. If either makes a determined effort to seize more than an equal share, that move will ultimately undermine the cooperation between them, hurting them both. As in so many other areas of business strategy, a calculated restraint on aggression is essential to long-term success.

The situation that most commonly meets these symmetry criteria in practice occurs when there are competitive advantages in some links along a value chain that runs from raw material producers to end user suppliers. Firms in subsegments without competitive advantage should earn returns on investment just equal to their long-term costs of capital.

Firms enjoying exclusive competitive advantages within distinct subsegments must cooperate with one another to maximize overall profitability. They can then divide these profits seamlessly by varying the prices charged to downstream segments. Lower prices charged by an upstream monopolist that reduce its revenue and profit by $100,000 per month should add an identical amount to the revenues and profits of the downstream monopolist, given that prices to the end user and the quantity sold remain at their cooperatively determined optimal levels.

Suppose that the total economic profit from the final product offering is $10 million per month at the maximum. The mechanics of the transactions between the segments allow this amount to be divided up in any way between two or more advantaged firms supplying constituent parts of the final product. They accomplish this transfer by varying the price at which they hand off their output to downstream firms. In practice, the individual rationality condition will place constraints on how the division actually works. Suppose that if cooperation breaks down, the upstream firm will earn $2 million in economic profit, the downstream firm $4 million. The benefit of cooperation of $4 million (10 – 2 – 4) depends equally on both firms. Thus, above the threat point, they have equal access to and an equal role in the creation of this benefit. Symmetry requires that they share the $4 million equally, leaving the upstream firm with a total of $4 million in economic profit (2 + 2) and the downstream firm $6 million (4 + 2). Both firms, having an interest in sustaining mutually beneficial cooperation, should independently seek to reach such a "fair" outcome. Otherwise, either one may decide that it is being treated unfairly and might take some aggressive action which would lead to a breakdown of cooperation. The breakdown would have adverse consequences for both firms.

This principle applies in cases where there are more than two firms serving as complementary suppliers along a value chain. If these companies want cooperation to be sustained, then there has to be a mutually satisfactory division of its benefits. Microsoft and Intel have avoided explicit competition over the cooperative benefits in the PC industry, based on the principle of equality as measured by threat point returns. To date, Microsoft has reaped a larger share of total industry profits than Intel, because it has had virtually no competition whereas Intel has had AMD and other potential CPU makers at its heels. This arrangement may change should Microsoft encounter a serious threat to its dominance, perhaps from Linux. By contrast, in a case we describe in the next chapter, Nintendo's aggressive attempt to garner a disproportionate share of the video game industry's profits left other participants discontented. Their dissatisfaction created an opening for Nintendo's competitors, who moved in and undermined its position.

LINEAR INVARIANCE

The need for fairness applies to situations in which several firms, all with competitive advantages, occupy the same segment in the value chain and divide the market horizontally. In this case, the fairness principle dictates that if there are two firms in a segment, and one of them has twice the size or strength of the other, then its portion of the benefits from cooperation should be twice as large. Nash used the term *linear invariance* for this version of the fairness requirement. It works by assigning shares of a cooperatively exploited horizontal market in proportion to the cooperating firms' relative economic positions—to each his own, in other words. In the next chapter, we discuss a declining industry with chronic excess capacity. The participants managed to sustain a profitable cooperative arrangement among themselves over a long period by adhering to the linear invariance application of the fairness principle. It can serve as a model, to those many industries beset by ruinous competition, of what cooperation, coupled with a mutually acceptable "fair" division of industry returns, can achieve, as measured by industry profitability.*

---

* Nash developed a final fairness condition to cover cases of nonlinear relationships between the relative positions of cooperating firms. He called this situation "independence of irrelevant alternatives." Together with individual rationality, symmetry, and linear invariance, this condition uniquely defines a "fair" set of cooperative returns among firms in the general case. That "equilibrium" is characterized by the condition that any changes in benefit from one firm to another should lead the firm giving up some return to lose a fraction of its total benefits from cooperation equal to the gain as a fraction of its total benefit that the winning firm would receive. That is, if firm B gives up 25 percent of its benefits, firm A should be adding 25 percent to its benefits. The implications of this elegant theoretical result are unfortunately rarely apparent in practice.

PURELY HYPOTHETICAL?

The cooperative perspective is instructive even where there is no chance that the companies in a particular industry will be able to overcome their antagonisms and work out some kind of cooperative arrangement. It can identify potential areas of cooperation, even if they are limited to only one or a few of the areas we listed earlier in the chapter, like specializing research and development to avoid duplicating one another's efforts. It is also useful in highlighting a firm's genuine strengths by pointing out where it would fit if the industry were organized cooperatively. In this respect, it can help clarify realistic expectations and terms for prospective strategic alliances and relationships between suppliers and purchasers.

Finally, if a firm's own prospective position within a cooperative configuration of an industry does not look promising—at the extreme, the firm has no reason for existing if there is cooperation because, for example, it is a high-cost supplier—this information provides an important strategic insight into the company's future. Its survival will depend on the failure of the other companies in its industry to cooperative effectively with one another. If it wants to continue, it will have to improve its position before the stronger market participants learn to cooperate successfully. By recognizing the ultimate consequences for itself if others cooperate, the firm's management can get a sense of how long it has to live and how far it has to go to survive. These are essential pieces of information for formulating a useful strategy for such a disadvantaged firm. Such insights add to the overall value of a cooperative viewpoint, which is an indispensable supplement to the more standard forms of competitive analysis. In the area of competitive analysis, it is important to keep in mind the fundamental complexity of the problems at issue. Clarity depends on a picture built up carefully from a group of simplifying perspectives. A fully cooperative view of the world, however unrealistic in practice, is a perspective that contributes meaningfully to that clarity of vision.

CHAPTER 15

Cooperation

The Dos and Don'ts

Successful cooperation is neither common nor easy. The rival firms have to find a way to work in harmony to advance their joint interests, and they have to do it legally, to avoid drawing down the wrath of the agencies charged with preventing and punishing restraint of trade. The episodes presented in this chapter represent three potential outcomes of a potentially cooperative arrangement.

In the first, Nintendo allowed its drive to dominate and its sense of invulnerability blind it to the need for more jointly beneficial relationships with its suppliers and customers. As a result, they were only too happy to see competitors encroach on Nintendo's turf and cut it down to size. The second example describes the successful cooperative arrangement established by the producers of lead-based gasoline additives. They made the most of an industry condemned to a slow death by environmental regulations. Finally, the two major auction houses, Sotheby's and Christie's, decided to get together and end their practice of competing by lowering prices. Unfortunately for them, the "getting together" took the form of overt and illegal collusion, which sent one of the principals to prison and others into retirement. We suggest that they could have accomplished most of their goals without such ruinous consequences.

HOW TO BREAK A VIRTUOUS CIRCLE:
GAMES NINTENDO PLAYED

By the time Nintendo entered the market for home video games in the mid 1980s, the industry had already experienced two booms and two devastating busts in its short life. In 1982, U.S. consumers spent $3 billion on consoles and games; in 1985, the figure had dropped to $100 million. The situation was not very different in Japan until Nintendo and its little plumber Super Mario brought life and income back into the industry. Starting in Japan in 1983, and then in the United States in 1986, it sold its 8-bit game consoles into millions of homes. These consoles were Nintendo's equivalent of Gillette's razors; it made its money selling the games. In Japan, the average console owner bought twelve game cartridges; in the United States, he bought eight of them. (We say "he" advisedly, since the typical gamer was a boy between eight and fourteen years old.) By 1989, sales in North America recovered to $3 billion. And Nintendo had by far the largest share of this market, around 95 percent in Japan, 90 percent in the United States. Between consoles, games, royalties, and other sources, Nintendo's own global sales exceed $4 billion in 1992.

Nintendo succeeded largely by improving the quality of the games available. In the late 1970s, it had entered the arcade game sector with its first hit, Donkey Kong. Unlike the home console market, the coin-operated arcade business did not collapse in the next decade; revenues of $5 billion in the mid 1980s indicated that the demand for a quality game experience was still strong. The arcade machines were more powerful and much more costly than home consoles, and the arcade owners had control over which games ran on the machines. A critical problem that had plagued Atari and the other first-generation console makers was a flood of low-quality games, many of them unlicensed and even counterfeit, that swamped the market. The console makers derived no revenue from these intruders, and the poor quality of their games—at times they simply didn't work—undermined the whole industry.

Nintendo solved these problems. Its first hit for home console, Super Mario Brothers, was its own creation, as were some of the other early successes. And it improved the technology of the game console both to guard against unapproved, low-quality games and to make the systems more powerful, though not more costly, in order to produce an experience more like that of arcade games. Each game cartridge included two microchips, one to hold the game, the other a coded security chip produced by Nintendo, without which the cartridge would not play on the Nintendo console. The game chip also carried code common to all games that ran on the console. By off-loading some of the functions from the console to the cartridge, Nintendo was able to lower the console cost and make the hardware less expensive, even while it was raising the cost of game software. The console sold for $100 at retail when it was introduced in Japan in 1983; game cartridges sold for around $40.

The Nintendo approach succeeded from the very beginning. The company sold over 1 million consoles in Japan in 1983, 2 million the following year, 3 million in 1985, and almost 4 million in 1986. It had to modify the design of the console to enter the American market, making it look more like a computer and less like a toy. But after some initial hesitation on the part of retailers, the system took off and sales grew even more rapidly in the United States than in Japan. In 1989, more than 9 million customers bought the system in the United States, and they supplemented those purchases with more than 50 million game cartridges. By 1990, at least 70 percent of American households with boys aged eight to fourteen owned a video game system. More than 90 percent of them were Nintendos.

THE NINTENDO SYSTEM

The management of Nintendo understood from early on that the availability of a variety of high-quality games would be the driving force in the business. They also knew that they did not have the creative resources within their company to turn out enough games to meet the demand. With the costs of writing a single game at around $500,000, it was expensive and risky to try to produce all the games themselves, since a game, like a movie, could fail to attract an audience. They turned to licensing, allowing other companies to write games for the Nintendo system. The original licenses in Japan went to six firms, all with direct or at least relevant experience in the game world. Under the terms of the license, Nintendo was to receive a royalty of 20 percent on the wholesale price of the games. Cartridges sold at wholesale for $30; each sale produced $6 for Nintendo.

Though they had to spend a lot of money on game development and pay Nintendo a 20 percent royalty, the original six licensees got very generous terms when measured against those imposed by Nintendo on all subsequent game writers. The forty or so additional licensees that had signed up by 1988 also paid the 20 percent royalty. In addition, they had to let Nintendo do all the manufacturing, for which it charged them around $14 per unit. The initial order, for a minimum of 10,000 units, needed to be paid for in advance. When Nintendo started a similar program with outside developers in the United States, the initial order jumped to 30,000, and the cartridges were delivered at Kobe, Japan, FOB (free on board, meaning the buyer owns the goods when they leave the loading dock and must pay for the shipping), leaving it to the game writers to import and distribute them in the United States.* Nintendo itself contracted out the manufacturing of the game cartridges to Ricoh, paying roughly $4 per cartridge. The $10 margin between the $14 it charged and the money it paid Ricoh went to Nintendo. When the original six licenses expired in 1989, they were reissued with the manufacturing clause included. Some of the licensees grumbled, but they stayed with Nintendo. There was nowhere else to go.

Nintendo further controlled the game writers by limiting the number of titles they could produce in any year to five. It tested them for quality and regulated the content; it would not license games that it regarded as too violent or sexually suggestive. And as part of the license, the game writers could not offer games for other video console systems for two years. They were locked in to Nintendo. Given the overwhelming market share that Nintendo commanded, they virtually had no choice. It was write for Nintendo with the prospects of producing a few profitable hits, or write for the other consoles and live in a universe competing for the 10 percent of the market Nintendo did not own.

Nintendo was equally dominant in its relationship with game retailers.

---

* These details come from the Harvard Business School case cited in the references. The $14 charge per unit is only mentioned in the context of game writers in the United States, so the charge may have been less in Japan.

When Nintendo had initially tried to sell its game console into the U.S. market in 1985, toy retailers were unresponsive. They had been burned with the precipitous decline of the earlier-generation game machines, and may still have been trying to dispose of their unsold inventory of Atari VCS systems. Nintendo decided to change the design of the machine and distribute it through electronics retailers. Even then, it needed to sell them on consignment, charging stores only for the units they actually sold. But the system quickly became popular, and Nintendo moved from being a petitioner to a powerful vendor calling the shots.

Even retail giants like Wal-Mart, Kmart, and Toys "R" Us had to pay for their shipments virtually upon receipt, rather than using the extended terms common in the toy industry. Wal-Mart sold Nintendo systems exclusively, and all the retailers adhered to Nintendo's suggested retail pricing for systems and game cartridges. Nintendo insisted that its retailers establish prominent Nintendo game centers in their stores, and they readily complied. Because Nintendo actually shipped fewer cartridges than the retailers ordered, and fewer than the customers wanted, they could reduce allocations to any of the merchants who would not play by Nintendo's rules.

Nintendo's success and its treatment of retailers and game writers drew critics, including the head of the House Subcommittee on Antitrust, Deregulations, and Privatization. In 1989, he asked the Justice Department to investigate some of the company's practices. Two years later, Nintendo signed a consent decree with the Federal Trade Commission and some states' attorneys general agreeing to stop fixing retail prices. But its dominance among retailers and game writers was largely unaffected. There were structural reasons that explained its continuing strength.

By the late 1980s, the shape of the video game industry had stabilized in the form shown in figure 15.1. The game console producers were at the center of the industry. They designed, distributed, and promoted the machines on which the games are played. They sometimes did the manufacturing themselves, assembling them from purchased chips and other components, but just as frequently, like Nintendo, they subcontracted out manufacturing. They produced some of their own games, but these constituted a relatively small fraction of the games available.

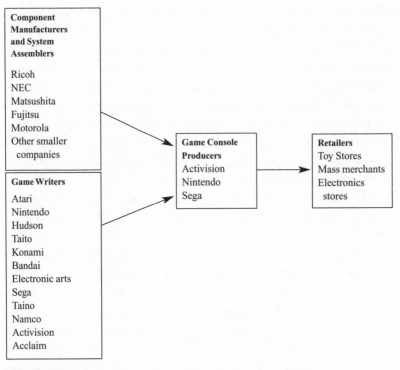

FIGURE 15.1
Map of the video game industry, late 1980s

During its rise to dominance, Nintendo faced competition in this segment from Atari, Activision, and Sega. Some early console producers like Coleco, Mattel, and Magnavox had disappeared by then, but newcomers like Sony and Microsoft entered the industry. By the early 1990s, this segment was dominated by Nintendo. Component and chip producers, who also often assemble systems for the game console companies, included well-known electronics and chip companies, as well as smaller and more obscure electronics manufacturers. This sector was highly competitive, and the console companies were just one of many groups of customers, and a relatively minor one. Games were designed and produced by a large number of creative firms, including the console producers themselves. Hudson, Electronic Arts, Taino, Komani, Bandai,

Namco, and Taino were prominent names in this sector. Finally, both consoles and game cartridges were distributed through toy stores like Toys "R" Us, mass merchants like Wal-Mart, electronics stores like Circuit City, and other specialty retailers.

Because the manufacturing sector was highly competitive and only peripherally dependent on home video games, the three key sectors were game writers, console producers, and retailers. From the later 1980s through the early and mid 1990s, Nintendo stood out as the dominant player. Looking at the industry from a cooperative perspective, the most efficient configuration was to have a single system at the center of the market. Game writers would have to bear the expense of producing only one version of each game, and they would have access to the complete universe of potential customers. Retailers would need to stock titles for only one system, and thus could offer more games with lower inventory expense than if they needed a version for each competing console. Game players would have to learn to operate only one system and would be able to play all available games on that one console.

Even the objection that a single dominant supplier would have no incentive to innovate and keep up with rapidly changing technology would not apply. The fixed research and development costs of bringing out new generations of technology would be lower with a single system supplier than with multiple suppliers developing overlapping and duplicative technologies. Successive generations of consoles with upgraded capacities could be introduced in an orderly sequence, like the innovations for the Wintel platform for PCs, instead of in haphazard fashion that rendered earlier generations of games obsolete before replacements were fully available. Finally, profits for the entire industry could be maximized with a strategy of pricing the consoles to break even and making all the profits on the sale of games.

If Nintendo had been willing to share the benefits of this organization with the game writers and the retailers, there was no inherent reason why the strategy should not have survived several generations of technology. On the other hand, if Nintendo persisted in trying to capture a disproportionate share of industry profits, then its position would survive only so long as its competitive advantages were sustainable.

WHICH COMPETITIVE ADVANTAGES?

From the time it entered the video game market with its own console system, Nintendo's success was sufficient to suggest that it did enjoy competitive advantages in the industry. It had an overwhelming and stable share of the market throughout the period, controlling 95 percent of the console business in Japan, 90 percent in the United States. The business was highly profitable. From 1984 through 1992, Nintendo averaged over 23 percent return on equity. On these two quantitative measures, Nintendo passes the incumbent competitive advantage test, at least in the period before 1992. The stock market certainly priced Nintendo as if it owned a powerful franchise. In 1991, its market capitalization of 2.4 trillion yen (over $16 billioin in 1991 exchange rate) was ten times the book value of its equity. It had a higher market value than Sony and Nissan, firms considerably larger and more established. But if someone examined the sources of these competitive advantages in 1991, it was not at all certain that they would be sustained into the future.

Captive Customers?

Its large installed base of 8-bit video game consoles gave Nintendo some degree of customer captivity, due to the switching costs a customer faced once he had bought the machine. No Nintendo owner was going to buy a game cartridge (or CD-ROM, which was becoming an alternative format) not compatible with his machine. But the strength of this customer advantage was weakened by certain inherent features of the video game business.

The customer base turned over quickly. The fourteen-year-old boys became fifteen, reduced their game-buying habits, and gave up their spot to younger kids turning eight or nine who did not already own a game console and so were not as committed to Nintendo.

The price of the console, relative to the cost of a game, was low. With the games costing $40 or more, a replacement console at $100 or $150 was no more expensive than a few games.

New technology in the form of faster chips able to process broader streams of data (16, 32, 64, and 128 bits) was becoming available, and at prices not much more than Nintendo's 8-bit warhorse. Bigger and faster microprocessors meant more realistic games. At some point, the quality differential between a fast new machine and a tired Nintendo would become large enough so that both the new younger customers, getting their first consoles as presents, and their older brothers, demanding to keep up with the youngsters, would make the switch, and all of Nintendo's arsenal of software would do it little good. Also, games get boring. The demand for new games is like Pac-Man; it eats the value of the existing collection.

Better Technology?

Nintendo was clever in putting a security chip in each of the cartridges it produced, but the chip itself was standard issue. There was nothing proprietary about its technology; it had no meaningful patents. In the drive to keep the cost of its console down, it bought commodity parts from suppliers like Ricoh. To stop a company that had found a way around its security chip from selling unlicensed games, it pressured the gaming magazines not to carry ads from the intruder. Nintendo was largely an assembler of standard parts, and it even contracted out much of the assembly. Nintendo did not owe its profitability to superior technology.

Economies of Scale?

A potential licensee needed to spend around $500,000 in creating a game. But even with the variable margin squeezed by Nintendo to $10 per copy, that fixed cost was absorbed by the first 50,000 copies sold, which represented only a tiny fraction of the total annual unit sales. With annual video game cartridge sales of 50 million units, to reach the break-even point, a particular game would have to capture only about one-tenth of 1 percent of the market. The design and production of the game consoles also exhibited few economies of scale. Research and development costs were relatively low. Manufacturing consisted of simple assembly operations, not a process in which there are likely to be any identifiable scale economies. Between 1987 and 1992, Nintendo itself averaged only about ¥14 ($100) in fixed assets for every ¥100 in sales, and this ratio did not decline significantly over time as Nintendo grew.

The Virtuous Circle

What Nintendo did have working in its favor was the virtuous circle of network externalities. Once the Nintendo system had established a substantial installed base, more outside software companies wanted to write games for it, which made the console more popular, meaning even more games, and on and on. The virtuous circle extended to retailers as well as game writers. Because retailers were reluctant to carry competing consoles and games, customers could find Nintendo products much more easily than any alternatives. And Nintendo, a great marketing organization, established displays in 10,000 outlets where customers could try out the system and the games. Having dedicated real estate within a retail store is every manufacturer's dream. Retailers, on the other hand, are generally reluctant to cede control over their primary asset: selling space. As a result, dedicated retail space is only made available to dominant manufacturers. Controlling this space reinforces their dominance, and so on.

The extraordinary penetration of Nintendo products also provided the company with the scale necessary to publish a magazine exclusively for Nintendo video game players to boost sales of its games. The magazine accepted no advertising; it rated games, previewed new releases, and offered tips on playing current games. It was priced to break even, and by 1990 it had a larger circulation, at 6 million copies per month, than any other magazine in the United States dedicated to children.

BREAKING THE CIRCLE

Despite all these benefits that reinforced its position, including the fact that the efficient configuration for this industry mandated a single console supplier, Nintendo was still vulnerable. Its virtuous circle rested on two advantages that turned out to be less solid than Nintendo assumed. One was the enormous installed based of Nintendo's console; the other was the cooperative relationship between Nintendo, the game writers, and the retailers.

The first advantage would be wiped out by each new generation of technology. As the chips advanced from 8- to 16-, 32-, 64-, 128-, and even

256-bit processors, the graphical quality and power of the new machines would render the old systems and games obsolete. Nintendo's installed base of 8-bit machines would not be attractive to either the game writers or the retailers, who sold games primarily for the new systems.

The second advantage, its relationships up- and downstream, might then tide Nintendo over until it had built up a dominant installed base of new-generation systems, but only provided that the writers and the stores felt they had mutually beneficial relationships with Nintendo. Game writers would then reserve their best next-generation games for the introduction of Nintendo systems, and stores would continue to provide Nintendo with unequaled store space. But if Nintendo had bullied these constituencies and grabbed a disproportionate share of industry profits, leaving the writers and retailers waiting for the opportunity to escape Nintendo's grip, then the opposite would happen. The best new-generation games would be retained for Nintendo's competitors, who would be welcomed by the retailers with shelf space rivaling Nintendo's.*

Nintendo did not play well with others. It did not share industry returns fairly. The terms it imposed on game writers and distributors helped to make it rich, but they did not endear it to its neighbors in the value chain. Nintendo treated the game writers particularly poorly. In the typical game cartridge, there was roughly $26 of margin between the wholesale price of $30 and the manufacturing cost of $4. Nintendo took $16, or 60 percent, for itself. The game writers, who incurred all the costs and risks of development and distribution, received $10, or less than 40 percent.

Nintendo upset the game writers in other ways. It limited them to five new titles per year. This restriction protected Nintendo from becoming too dependent on one software provider and ensured that no game writer could become successful enough to consider creating its own console system. But it frustrated the game writers, especially the most talented ones, and limited their potential returns. There was also the censoring of content that limited violence and sexuality. And Nintendo

---

* Even though Nintendo's licensees could not write for other console manufacturers for two years after signing the license, there were many ways, such as spinning off divisions or doing preliminary design work, for them to avoid the restrictions of this arrangement.

persistently shipped fewer console and game units than retailers ordered during the crucial Christmas season. This imposed shortage may have enhanced the Nintendo mystique, but it cut into the sales and profits of the game writers and retailers, who were also alienated by Nintendo's aggressive payment schedules and demands for in-store displays.

Sega brought out a 16-bit console in Japan in 1988 with better graphics and sound than the 8-bit Nintendo standard. Still, Sega initially found it difficult to induce outside developers to produce games for the system. Sega itself adapted some of the games it had created for the arcade market, but sales remained slow. The company did not back off, however. It introduced the machine in the United States in 1989, selling it for $190. Games retailed between $40 and $70. Sega targeted these games at the content niches left uncovered by Nintendo's censoring policy. Still, like Nintendo in its early days, Sega had a difficult time selling the machines. Whereas Nintendo had Wal-Mart and Toys "R" Us as its primary retailers, Sega had to rely on software stores like Babbage's.

But its fortunes changed in 1991, when a new executive decided to package both the console and its popular game Sonic the Hedgehog for $150. That did the trick. The Sega machine took off, and game writers rushed to supply product for it. Nintendo had delayed introducing its own 16-bit system, not wanting to cut into its thriving 8-bit empire. It followed Sega into the 16-bit market, but not in time to prevent the entrant from gaining enough scale so that it had no problems securing games or distribution.

Between 1992 and 1994, the two companies battled for leadership, using all the weapons in a marketer's arsenal, including deep price cuts and heavy advertising. If it were a video game, one newspaper suggested, it would be called "Marketing Kombat," an allusion to the wildly popular game Mortal Kombat. Each company claimed to be the market leader, but it didn't matter who had won the larger share. Nintendo was the clear loser. Hand-to-hand combat in the video game trenches undermined the profitability it had enjoyed when it reigned supreme in the center of the virtuous circle. Sony's entrance with a 32-bit machine in 1995 just raised the competition to a higher megahertz. In that year, there were eight or nine companies with 32-bit or better consoles vying for a piece of the action.

Nintendo's dominant position was undercut by its own decisions. It chose to milk its 8-bit franchise rather than immediately respond to Sega in the 16-bit world. Also, its policy of keeping shipments below demand inadvertently handed customers to Sega. But even before Sega's Sonic the Hedgehog showed up, Nintendo had prepared the ground for Sega and subsequent competitors. Once Sega had established its credibility, the retailers and especially the game writers rushed to its support. It was the game writers who really undermined Nintendo. Conventional wisdom in the video game industry is that the distinctiveness of the product lies in the software. To cite one particular ad, "It's in the game." By alienating the game writers, Nintendo gave "the game" to Sega and Sony.

There is no certainty that a cooperative strategy would have prevented the software firms from signing up to develop games for Sega and Sony. All we know for certain is as soon as Sega showed a little traction with its 16-bit player, they rushed to supply games for its system. The developers were delighted to have multiple console makers in the market, even though it cost more to turn out games for different platforms. They were able to negotiate better deals with the hardware companies. In fact, power had shifted from Nintendo to the developers. "In the game industry," according to a *BusinessWeek* story, "content rules. No matter how technologically advanced a console may be, it's doomed without enticing game titles." Now Sega, Sony, Nintendo, and ultimately Microsoft were the supplicants, offering the developers better terms on the costs of producing a CD (PlayStation machines used CDs rather than game cartridges) and reduced royalty charges. They also began to help with development expenses. Because of the more complex graphics now demanded, development could cost up to $10 million per game, twenty times the average when Nintendo's 8-bit standard held sway.

Nintendo went from a company with a dominant position in an industry and a high return on capital to one competitor among many with at best ordinary returns on investment, in large part because it did not play well with others. It claimed so much of the industry profit for itself that both developers and retailers were ready to support new consoler makers. To see how savvy companies can manage to do well by working together, we look next at a grubbier industry with nothing like the glamour or future of electronic games—the providers of lead-based additives for gasoline.

LEAD INTO GOLD: GETTING ALONG IN THE GASOLINE ADDITIVE BUSINESS

Consider an industry with these characteristics:

- Its product is a commodity
- There is substantial overcapacity
- Demand is guaranteed to decline rapidly
- It gets bad press and bad marks from government agencies and public interest groups

Under these circumstances, it is difficult to believe that the businesses operating within this industry would be able to make any profit and inconceivable that they would earn exceptional returns.

The managers of companies producing the lead-based additives used to boost octane ratings of gasoline (reduce knocking) were able to pull off this difficult feat because they knew how to pull together. Even after the Federal Trade Commission took exception to some of their business practices, they found ways to cooperate and share the wealth. They responded to shrinking demand by reducing their own capacity. One by one the companies left the business altogether, selling out to the remaining players or simply shutting down. By the time the last of them had exited, in the late 1990s, they had had a twenty-year history of making money in a bad business.

In 1974 there were four U.S. companies in the lead-based additive industry: Ethyl, DuPont, PPG, and Nalco. Together they produced around 1 billion pounds of these chemical compounds. The Ethyl Corporation had been in the business since 1924, originally as a joint venture between General Motors and Standard Oil of New Jersey. A patent protected it from competition until 1948, when DuPont entered the business to capture some of the market and the attractive returns Ethyl was earning. (In fact, DuPont had done production for Ethyl until the expiration of the patent allowed it to sell the additive for itself.) PPG, through its purchase of Houston Chemical Company, and Nalco were encouraged and assisted in getting into the business by Mobil and Amoco, respectively. These big refiners were major users of the additives, and they sought to spur competition and reduce their costs by sponsoring additional firms in the additive business. In every instance these hopes were disappointed. Ethyl managed to co-opt each successive entrant, limit competition, and sustain industry profitability.

Prospects for the industry changed sharply in 1973, when the Environmental Protection Agency issued regulations intended to implement parts of the Clean Air Act of 1970. The regulations were intended to phase out the use of lead-based additives over time. They relied on two tools. First, starting with model year 1975, all new cars sold in the United States had to be equipped with catalytic converters designed to reduce harmful exhaust omissions from automobiles. The converters could not operate properly with lead-based additives in the gasoline, so refiners had to produce unleaded gas for all new cars. Second, the EPA tried to deal with lead directly by reducing the amount refiners could put into their gasoline. Ethyl was able to delay the implementation of the regulation until 1976, but after that the quantity of permissible lead per gallon, and thus the total market for the additives, began a steady decline. The billion pounds of additives sold in the mid 1970s was reduced to around 200 million pounds ten years later, and to almost nothing by 1996. Part of the drop came as cars sold before 1975 grew old and left the roads; part came from the regulations on grams of lead per gallon.

Although the medical case against lead in the air was disputed for a time, the hazardous nature of the additive compounds was always clear. They were flammable and explosive, toxic in contact with the body, and dangerous to breathe. Refineries tried to keep no more than a ten-day supply on hand to minimize the dangers. The compounds required special equipment both for transportation and for storage. Still, the companies were able to ship the liquid in common carriers. The ability to use common carriers rather than company-owned and dedicated fleets fit perfectly with the commodity nature of the cargo.

THE LEAD ADDITIVE INDUSTRY

The structure of the industry that produced and bought these compounds was uncomplicated. A small number of chemical companies bought raw materials, especially lead, processed them into two different additives, tetraethyl lead (TEL) and tetramethyl lead (TML), and sold them to gasoline refiners. Nalco used a different process to make its TML, but in practice its additives were interchangeable with the others. All the producing companies were diversified, especially DuPont and PPG. Even Ethyl, the pioneer and the company with the largest market share, derived only 17 percent of its sales from these additives. Their customers were basically domestic and offshore gasoline refineries, principally those operated by large integrated oil companies. After the EPA began to limit use in the United States, the producers tried to maintain their sales by finding foreign customers. They did sell some compounds abroad, but because of high shipping costs and the hazardous nature of the material, these sales were generally from plants also located overseas. There were also non-U.S. companies in this market.

Raw materials accounted for most of the costs of production. All the producers needed to buy lead. Ethyl and DuPont made most of the rest of their inputs; PPG and Nalco relied more on outside suppliers. No doubt there were cost differences among the four companies, but not so much as to encourage any of them to take advantage of a position as low-cost producer.

It is difficult to see any significant competitive advantage that distinguished one firm in the business from another. Ever since the original Ethyl patent expired in the 1940s, none of them had proprietary technology. Their customers, especially the largest of them, bought from more than one additive producer. Contracts generally ran for one year. When they came up for renewal, the refiners encouraged the producers to compete for their business in the only way that made a difference—price.

No refiner tried to differentiate its own gasoline by claiming that its lead came from Ethyl or DuPont. So although there were established relationships between sellers and customers, and perhaps some switching costs if the formulations were different, there was nothing so powerful in the nexus between producer and refiner to indicate customer captivity. A maverick additive producer could have expanded its business at any time, simply by lowering its prices.

The organization of production into a small number of plants—never more than seven—to supply the whole industry suggests that there may have been some economies of scale. But the large plants did not drive out the small ones, indicating that scale economies were limited. And without some customer captivity, economies of scale in themselves do not create a sustained competitive advantage.

Barriers to entry are another story. An insurmountable barrier protected the four firms in the business. The EPA's regulatory announcement in 1973 posted an unmistakable Do Not Trespass sign for any firms contemplating entering the lead-based additive industry. Even if some company could have secured the necessary permits from local authorities—highly unlikely given the concerns about atmospheric lead—who would want to build a plant to produce a chemical scheduled to disappear? By putting the industry on a certain path to extinction, the EPA ensured that the existing firms would have the business to themselves, to profit as best they could during the slow path to disappearance.

COOPERATION AMONG FRIENDS

In seeking to encourage some price competition among the lead additive producers, the major oil companies had always been disappointed. New entrants to the industry quickly went native. They learned to play along with the incumbents and to frustrate their sponsors. Perhaps the regional concentration of the industry had something to do with the ease of acclimation. Except for one DuPont facility in New Jersey and another in California, all the plants were on the Gulf Coast in Texas or Louisiana, within a three-hundred-mile radius of one another and near to the refineries they supplied. The engineers running the plants came from similar backgrounds. In any case, both before and after environmental regulations signaled the ultimate end of the industry, the players had found ways of working together to keep in check what otherwise might have been brutal competition.

Most of the methods they used were checks on themselves, to make it more difficult to give customers discounts or otherwise to deviate from established prices:

- *Uniform pricing.* Prices were quoted to include both the cost of the chemicals and the cost of delivery. By including transportation in the quoted price, the suppliers prevented themselves from offering a hidden discount with a lower delivery charge.
- *Advance notice of price changes.* When one of the suppliers wanted to change—raise—the list price of the additive, the contracts called for it to give its customers thirty days' notice, during which time they could order more supply at the existing price. Until 1977, the additive manufacturers issued press releases to announce these changes, but then ceased on advice of counsel. The refiners tried to induce other suppliers not to follow the leader in raising prices, but almost always to no avail. There were thirty price increases in the five years starting in 1974, and all of them held. Ethyl and DuPont were the initiators, with PPG and Nalco following suit. The solidarity continued even after the press releases stopped. The thirty-day advance notice of price increases meant that any supplier wishing to maintain the lower price had to signal that intention thirty days before the increases by other firms went into effect. If it gave the signal, the other firms would simply rescind the announced price increases and the deviant firm's intransigence would yield no benefit, other than to the customers.
- *Most-favored-nation pricing.* Applied not to import duties but to the actual prices charged for the chemicals, this policy assured every customer that it was getting the best price available. More to the point, it put the suppliers in a self-imposed straitjacket, preventing them from offering any special discount to a particular customer on the grounds that they would have to give the same break to everyone. Ethyl and DuPont put the clause in their contracts, and Nalco followed suit on many of its own.

Rounding out these pricing tactics was another practice the four suppliers adopted: joint sourcing and producing. Simply put, an order placed with one supplier might be delivered from another supplier's

TABLE 15.1

Capacity, production, and sales of lead-based additives, 1977 (millions of pounds)

	Capacity		Production		Sales	
Ethyl	475	37%	432	48%	312	35%
DuPont	544	43%	250	28%	317	35%
PPG	113	9%	97	11%	150	17%
Nalco	137	11%	122	14%	121	13%
	1,269	100%	901	100%	900	100%

plant, depending on location, availability of chemicals, and other practical considerations, like relative productivity. The four manufacturers maintained a settlement system among themselves, netting out all the shipments made for one another and paying only the balances. Capacity, production, and sales figures for 1977 reveal the joint sourcing program in operation (table 15.1).

DuPont had the largest capacity but trailed Ethyl in production. The two had comparable sales volume. Clearly Ethyl brewed more additive than it sold, supplying some of DuPont's and also PPG's customers. Joint sourcing eliminated much of the cost differential among the suppliers, who could all take advantage of Ethyl's efficiency. Taking cost out of the equation removed whatever incentive the low-cost producer might have to gain market share at the expense of the other three firms and minimized overall industry costs. Market share of sales varied only slightly from year to year. In 1974, Ethyl controlled 33.5 percent of the market; in 1977, the number had inched up to 34.6 percent. Indeed, there was a remarkable consistency in share changes. A large company with a share of the market below 35 percent tended to increase share, whereas a comparable company with more than 35 percent of the market generally lost share. For the small competitors Nalco and PPG, this focal share was 15 percent. It appears that none of the firms labored to increase its share of the market permanently.

The stability of market share of sales coupled with joint sourcing led to an unusual rationality in capacity management. Since high-cost plants tended to operate at low capacity under joint sourcing, they were the plants most likely to be shuttered as overall demand declined. In

1980, Ethyl closed its oldest plant in Houston. DuPont followed a year later, shutting its Antioch, California, facility. PPG left the business entirely in 1982. Joint sourcing created an incentive structure that both eliminated excess capacity and closed the least-efficient plants first. The net result was a strategy to manage capacity in order to minimize overall industry costs.

ENTER THE FEDERAL TRADE COMMISSION

Eventually, the four additive companies must have been doing something wrong because they came to the attention of the FTC for alleged anticompetitive practices. In 1979 the commission charged that four of their marketing practices were in violation of Section 5 of the Federal Trade Commission Act:

- The thirty-day advance notice of list price changes
- Issuing press releases about these changes
- Selling the product on a uniform delivered price basis
- Using most-favored-nation pricing clauses in contracts

Because of these practices, the FTC contended, the four producers were able to "reduce uncertainty about competitors' prices," and thus reduce or even eliminate price competition in the lead-based additive market. Even though the practices themselves were not unlawful, by using them to maintain price uniformity and stability the producers were accused of breaking the law. The complaint said nothing about the policy of joint sourcing.

Two years later an administrative law judge upheld most of the complaint. Price signaling was out. Instead of preannouncing a price change to the industry, now the producers had thirty days after it had gone into effect to make the change public. The most-favored-nation clauses were forbidden, on the grounds they "discourage discounting and promote price uniformity." The judge said nothing about the Robinson-Patman Act, which prohibits a seller from price discrimination among buyers. The judge found that the four producers constituted an "oligopoly," and as such, were proscribed from practices that were not in themselves illegal.

It took two additional years, until 1983, for the FTC itself to reaffirm most of the judge's ruling. Even though there was no collusion to fix prices, the commission wrote, the companies had restrained competition. Ethyl and DuPont were ordered to stop:

- Announcing price changes before a time agreed upon between the company and the purchaser
- Offering a single price to include delivery regardless of destination
- Guaranteeing customers that they would receive the lowest price available to any customer

The commission did not uphold the prohibition on press conferences announcing price changes. It excluded Nalco from the ruling because Nalco was an acknowledged price follower. By 1983, PPG was no longer in the industry.

At the time of the ruling, the companies had already stopped announcing price changes beforehand. They were able to replace a single price (uniform delivered pricing) with FOB pricing (in which the buyer owns the goods when they leave the loading dock and pays directly for shipping). Under either approach, the producers could not hide discounts by subsidizing shipping costs. As to most-favored-nation pricing clauses, they might be removed from contracts but maintained in practice. What customer, after all, did not want assurance that nobody else was getting a better price?

Even when barred from using some of the specific tactics the additive makers had employed to curb their own competitive juices, they continued to be masters of the prisoner's dilemma game. By the time the FTC had issued its ruling, they had had years of experience in effective cooperation. So next to nothing changed as a consequence of the FTC's intervention. The industry continued its mandated decline and the producers continued to earn money even as they sold less of the additives. In 1981, Ethyl's additive business accounted for 17 percent of its sales and 33 percent of its profits. Since the capital employed had no substantial liquidation value, the return on capital was extraordinary.

EXIT THE PRODUCERS

If the Federal Trade Commission's ruling had no discernible effect on the effectiveness of cooperation among the lead additive producers, environmental regulations both within the United States and abroad continued to reduce demand. Suppliers responded by closing plants, investing the cash from lead-based additives into other products, and remaining focused on working for mutual benefits. Nalco left the business, but Ethyl and DuPont continued production, Ethyl at a plant in Ontario, Canada, DuPont in New Jersey. The other major international player was Associated Octel, a company based in England but with Great Lakes Chemical, headquartered in Indiana, as the majority owner. Until July 1994, DuPont supplied Ethyl with much of its product. After DuPont closed its operations, Ethyl turned to Octel, signing an agreement in 1996 which guaranteed Ethyl a dedicated portion of Octel's production to sell through Ethyl's distribution channels. Ethyl then ceased production at its Ontario plant. The two companies proclaimed that they would continue to compete with one another in the sale and marketing of lead antiknock compounds.

Octel remained in the business for one reason: it was highly profitable. In 1994, Octel earned $240 million of operating profit on sales of $520 million, a margin of almost 47 percent. All the rest of Great Lakes Chemicals earned $162 million on revenues of $1,480 million, a margin of 11 percent. Great Lakes used its profits from lead-based additives to make acquisitions, preparing for the day when the lead business would be entirely gone.

Ethyl displayed a similar disparity between earnings in lead-based additives and everything else, even though it was largely a reseller of chemicals made elsewhere. Between 1994 and 1996, the additives accounted for 23 percent of the company's total sales and 63 percent of its profits. In 1998, after its additive revenues had declined to $117 million, it still made $51 million in operating profits, a 44 percent return. The rest of the company had operating margins of 11 percent.

How energetically Ethyl and Octel competed for the small business remaining was revealed in 1998 when the FTC reentered the scene, charging that the arrangement the companies had reached violated antitrust laws. Octel and Ethyl settled with the commission by agreeing to change some features of the original contract. Under the new arrangement, Ethyl could buy more than a fixed portion of Octel's output and Octel would have to sell Ethyl all that Ethyl wanted to serve its current and new customers in the United States. Ostensibly this would increase competition between them, as would the other changes. The amount Ethyl was charged would no longer be tied to Octel's retail price. The companies would no longer disclose their prices to one another. The companies agreed to notify the commission in advance of any acquisition of assets used in the distribution of the compounds within the United States or manufacture anywhere in the world. Finally, there would also be prior notification of any proposed agreements with other competitors to sell them lead-based antiknock additives.

If it intended to protect American consumers, the FTC might have better looked elsewhere. Lead additives had virtually disappeared from the U.S. market, and they were vanishing elsewhere in the world as well. And no provisions in this ruling would do much to guarantee vigorous competition. Neither Ethyl nor Octel was going to cut prices to secure a somewhat larger share of a dying but still lucrative business. Octel, with the world as its market, continued to enjoy high margins on sales (table 15.2). After a tough year in 2000, its operating income recovered even as its revenue declined. As Ethyl and Nalco before it, Octel used its cash flow from TEL (one of the lead-based additives) to expand its specialty chemicals business. Like them, its returns from specialty chemicals did not come close to what it was making in the lead additive business.

Octel will be the last to leave. But like all the other producers that departed before it, it will make a graceful exit, at least as measured by profitability. By cooperating with one another even while complying with antitrust laws, these companies experienced a long history of turning lead into gold.

TABLE 15.2

Octel Corporation sales and operating income by segment, 2000–2002 ($ million)

	2000	2001	2002
TEL			
Sales	$ 300	$ 265	$ 257
Operating income	$ 59	$ 69	$ 118
Margins	20%	26%	46%
Specialty Chemicals			
Sales	$ 122	$ 156	$ 181
Operating income	$ 11	$ 13	$ 10
Margins	9%	8%	6%

KEEP YOUR DISTANCE: SOTHEBY'S AND CHRISTIE'S TURN COOPERATION INTO A GENUINE PRISONER'S DILEMMA

For all their heritage, prestige, and cachet, Sotheby's and Christie's, the two leading auction houses, were mediocre businesses. By 1990 they dominated the auction markets for fine art and other expensive goods in Britain and the United States. They had steadily encroached on the business of the art dealers by selling directly to collectors. Still, the volatility of the market for expensive paintings and the other luxury items that went under their hammers left the two houses vulnerable to the pain that a business with high fixed costs feels when revenue shrinks. In 1974, in the aftermath of the oil embargo and recession, the two houses both imposed a charge on buyers—the buyer's premium—where previously it was only the sellers who had paid. The auctioneers were probably trying to help recycle some of the rapidly growing wealth in the hands of oil sheikhs from the Persian Gulf, who were now in the market for trophy paintings.

The buyer's premium gave Sotheby's and Christie's a new source of revenue and may have made it easier for them to compete with one another by lowering the commission they charged to the sellers. And lower it they did. The tipsy art market of the late 1980s sobered up starting in 1990. Japanese buyers for top pictures stopped bidding—even stopped paying for works they had supposedly bought—the U.S. economy slowed, and the Gulf War made customers wary. The auction houses saw their business decline and turned to the oldest marketing ploy available: they cut prices.

To induce sellers to put their items up for auction, and to try to attract business from one another, Sotheby's and Christie's lowered their seller's commission, sometimes to zero. They also offered inexpensive advance loans on items to be auctioned during the next round of sales. They started to print elaborate catalogs, often as a vanity inducement to the sellers. They gave lavish parties. They even donated money to their sellers' favorite charities. None of these practices brought business back to where it had been in 1989, and they certainly did nothing to improve the earnings of the houses (figure 15.2).

When the going gets tough, the toffs get together. In 1992, Sotheby's changed the buyer's commission from a flat 10 percent of the sale to a sliding amount that was intended to bring in more revenue. Seven

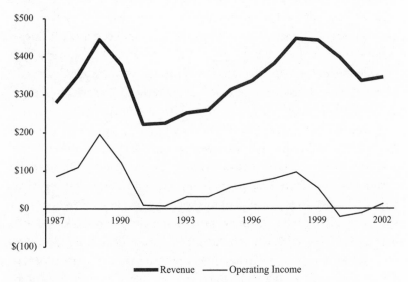

Revenue ——— Operating Income

FIGURE 15.2

Sotheby's revenue and operating income, 1987–2002 ($million)

weeks later Christie's followed suit. The timing is interesting. By accounts offered to the courts, the first actual meetings between the heads of the two houses, A. Alfred Taubman of Sotheby's and Sir Anthony Tennant of Christie's, did not take place until 1993. Taubman, the shopping mall magnate who had served as a white knight for Sotheby's in 1983, buying a controlling interest to keep it out of the hands of Marshall Cogan and Steven Swid, flew to London to meet Sir A., as he was identified in Taubman's records. According to the testimony of their respective seconds, Diana D. (Dede) Brooks of Sotheby's and Christopher Davidge of Christie's, Taubman and Tennant directed Davidge and Brooks to work out details of an agreement under which the firms would not undercut one another on the commission rate offered to sellers.

In 1995, Christie's announced that it was changing its seller's fee from a flat 10 percent to a sliding scale, ranging from 2 percent to 20 percent depending on the size of the sale. Over time, the arrangement came to include a "no poaching" clause on key staff members and an accord not to subsidize the sellers by offering below market interest rates on loan advances. The companies also shared their "grandfathered" lists with one another, clients to whom they charged reduced or even zero fees. Neither was supposed to pursue names on the other's list, nor to offer these same advantageous terms to people not on the lists. According to Brooks, Taubman wanted the houses to collude on the estimates they provided sellers as to the likely value of their art at auction, but she told him that those decisions were made by the respective professional staffs of the two auction firms, who could not be controlled.

Rumors could not be controlled either. By 1997, it was widely known that the Justice Department was investigating the auction houses for actions that violated antitrust laws. Perhaps Justice had been tipped off by customers who discovered, sometime in the mid 1990s, that the firms would no longer offer lower commission rates and wondered how such solidarity might have been maintained in the absence of collusion. Just before the end of 1999, Christopher Davidge cut a deal with the government. In exchange for no prison time for himself and other members of Christie's, he offered documents to prove the illegal behavior of Taubman, Tennant, and their accomplices.

In 2000, the Justice Department pressured Diana Brooks to give up her former boss, Alfred Taubman, in exchange for a stay-out-of-jail card. She did her part, pled guilty, and in the end, Taubman was the only person to serve time. Sentenced to a one-year term in 2001, he was released from prison after serving nine months. Each auction house paid a civil fine of $256 million, equal to around four years of Sotheby's average pretax profits in the years 1995–98. Sir Anthony Tennant always maintained his innocence, but just to make sure, he stayed in England where he was safe from extradition on an antitrust violation.

The truly striking aspect of this story is how ineffective Christie's and Sotheby's were at cooperating to sustain profitability, despite their illegal agreements. Profit margins at Sotheby's did grow between 1992 and 1996, as the art market recovered from its collapse in the early 1990s. After 1996, however, even as the art market improved, margins remained static. By 1998, with revenues at or near their precollusion 1989 peak, operating earnings at Sotheby's were only half their 1989 level. And with only a slight decline in 1999 sales, operating profits at Sotheby's fell by almost 50 percent.

Davidge, his Christie's colleagues, and Diana Brooks may not have known how to play the cooperation game without violating antitrust laws, but they did know how to play the prisoner's dilemma game, at least in the first round. The New York *Observer* commented about the prosecution, "They needed Mr. Davidge's notes and testimony to win conditional amnesty from the U.S. government, under a controversial program in which the crook who squeals first in such a conspiracy gets off scot-free." Though scot-free may not always be part of the deal, the crook who squeals first always does better; otherwise, why would he or she squeal? The more interesting question is what alternatives the two auction houses had to this illegal collusion as a way of ending a painful war over price and perks.

Christie's and Sotheby's, which together shared some 90–95 percent of the high-end auction market, should have been able to benefit from economies of scale and significant customer captivity. Smaller and newer auction houses had made no inroads into their market share for many years. Also, at least until they entered their period of intense competition, both organizations were highly profitable. The key to continued success was restraint on competition, which required primarily that they stay out of each other's way. Geographically, it was not really possible for two firms like these to divvy up territory. Each had major establishments in London and New York, as befits their British ancestry and the strength of the market in the United States. They also had satellite offices, and in some cases selling rooms, in major cities around the world. But these locations were more for acquiring material than for auctioning it. For all expensive items, buyers come to the auction in the most cosmopolitan locations. So Sotheby's and Christie's both needed a presence in New York and London. In fact, they benefited from running their auctions almost simultaneously, because more buyers were enticed to make the trip to town.

With geography an unwieldy knife with which to slice the pie, field specialization—product market niches—remained the obvious choice by which to divide the business. Instead of selling everything from Cycladic figures and ancient Sumerian pottery to paintings by Roy Lichtenstein and Keith Haring, each house could have concentrated on particular periods and types of art. They could also have selected specialties from the broad range of other objects offered for sale, like antique Persian carpets, jewelry, and clocks and barometric measuring devices from the age of Louis XIV.

The auction houses handled such a variety of goods that, in theory at least, staking out a set of nonconflicting claims to territory should have been fairly simple. Each field required overhead to support it, particularly the experts who validate claims about authenticity, research provenance, and estimate a value for the item. If Sotheby's had become the place to go for eighteenth-century French paintings and decorative arts, and Christie's had emerged as the dominant firm for color field abstraction, then sellers would have had to choose an auction house on the basis of what they were trying to sell. A further advantage of such specialization would have been a significant reduction in overall overhead costs, since substantial duplication of effort would have been eliminated.

There were two problems that would have made this type of division more difficult to accomplish in practice than on paper. First, estate sales may encompass a variety of works that don't fit neatly into any single auction house's specialization. Second, while Dutch master paintings from the seventeenth century may bring more at auction than Postimpressionist works, there are many fewer of them outside of museums. So a fair division of the playing field needed to focus on the value to the auction house of a piece of the turf, not its attractiveness on any other basis. Despite these difficulties, it may have been possible for the firms to work out an informal and tacit arrangement without colluding directly.

In 1992, before the first reported meetings of Taubman and Tennant, Sotheby's announced an increase in fees charged to buyers, and Christie's came along after a decorous delay of seven weeks. Could Sotheby's have also announced that it was deemphasizing its Egyptian and ancient Middle Eastern departments, and concentrating instead on Greek and Roman antiquities and the period to AD 1200 in Europe? Christie's might have announced, some time later, that it was going strengthen its Egyptian department and also its expertise in the early Renaissance. And, over time and more subtly than we are describing here, the two might have divided up the map of the fine art and object markets like the European imperialists carved up Africa in the nineteenth century, hopefully to better effect. The estate sale issue would have been handled naturally, leaving it up to the executors to decide among the auction houses on the basis of their respective strengths. And nothing says that the estate property could not have been sold in a series of auctions.

· · ·

The contrast between the histories of Nintendo and the auction houses, on the one hand, and the lead-based gasoline additive industry on the other clearly points up the benefits of effective cooperation among firms. Just as clearly, it underscores the perils of inexpert cooperation that crosses the legality line. A well-formulated strategy will not immediately or solely look to salvation through cooperation. But the story of the lead-based additive industry demonstrates how useful a cooperative perspective can be under the right conditions. The optimum situation is an industry where several firms coexist within well-established barriers.

CHAPTER 16

Valuation from a
Strategic Perspective

Improving Investment Decisions

STRATEGY AND VALUE

Even though investment decisions are generally strategic by anyone's definition of the term, the financial analysis employed to support these decisions generally ignores strategic issues. It is almost always built around calculations of future cash flows, both negative during the investing phase and positive during the harvesting period, created by the investment. The cash flows are then discounted by an appropriate cost of capital, and all the cash flows added together produce the net present value of the investment.

The cash flows themselves are based on estimates of future sales, profit margins, tax rates, capital investment requirements, and the cost of capital. Underlying them are another set of estimates regarding market size and growth rates, attainable market shares, gross margins, overhead expense ratios, working and fixed capital requirements, leverage (debt to equity ratios), and the costs of the components of the overall capital structure (cost of debt and cost of equity). Many of these variables, especially market share, margins, overhead expenses, and capital requirements, will depend on the intensity of future competition. But it is difficult to forecast precisely how competition will affect each of them. Moreover, competitive conditions do not influence these variables independently; the intensity of competition affects many of them simultaneously.

Given these difficulties, it is not surprising that strategic insights are rarely integrated effectively into the investment decision process. Yet omitting an examination of the competitive environment simply because it cannot be neatly incorporated into a financial model ignores crucial information and impairs the quality of the analysis. The strategic perspective developed in this book, particularly the emphasis on competitive advantages and barriers to entry, provides an alternative framework for investment planning that is in many ways superior to the net present value approach.

THE VALUE OF NET PRESENT VALUE

The core of any investment planning process is a method for ranking projects by their value to decide where capital should be directed. The method ought to include the ability to value an entire company, since the purchase of a company is itself a potential project. In theory, the correct value of a project is the value of future benefits discounted at an appropriate cost of capital, minus the value of future costs, usually discounted at the same cost of capital. The result is mathematically equal to the value of the present and future net cash flows appropriately discounted, the familiar net present value (NPV) of financial analysis. The problem is that although the method is true in theory, it is seriously flawed when put into practice.

The NPV approach has three fundamental shortcomings. First, it does not segregate reliable information from unreliable information when assessing the value of a project. A typical NPV model estimates net cash flows for several years into the future from the date at which the project is undertaken, incorporating the initial investment expenditures as negative cash flows. Five to ten years of cash flows are usually estimated explicitly. Cash flows beyond the last date are usually lumped together into something called a "terminal value." A common method for calculating the terminal value is to derive the accounting earnings from the cash flows in the last explicitly estimated year and then to multiply those earnings by a factor that represents an appropriate ratio of value to earnings (i.e., a P/E ratio). If the accounting earnings are estimated to be $12 million and the appropriate factor is a P/E ratio of 15 to 1, then the terminal value is $180 million.

How does one arrive at the appropriate factor, the proper price to earnings ratio? That depends on the characteristics of the business, whether a project or a company, at the terminal date. It is usually selected by finding publicly traded companies whose current operating characteristics resemble those forecast for the enterprise in its terminal year, and then looking at how the securities markets value their earnings, meaning the P/E at which they trade. The important characteristics for selecting a similar company are growth rates, profitability, capital intensity, and riskiness.

Despite the apparent precision, this approach is largely conjecture. Calculating the characteristics of an enterprise seven and more years in the future is a very inexact exercise. Also, precise comparisons between enterprises rarely exist, so the selection of comparison companies is subjective. Rolling dice to come up with an appropriate valuation factor seven years hence would be about as precise.

An alternative to the ratio valuation approach is to assume that the project stabilizes after the end of the terminal year. Profitability, capital intensity, risk—and hence the cost of capital—and most importantly, annual growth in sales, profits, and investment are all assumed to stay constant beyond the terminal year. By making these assumptions, it is possible to calculate a cash flow for the first postterminal year, that is, year eight if year seven is the terminal year. Then the present value of all postterminal-year cash flows can be calculated from a familiar formula, namely

$$\text{Terminal Value} = CF_{t+1} \div (R - G)$$

where CF_{t+1} is the net cash flow in the first postterminal year, R is the cost of capital beyond the terminal year, and G is the annual growth rate for the same period (table 16.1).

Since this terminal value measure consists of a cash flow figure (CF_{t+1}) multiplied by a valuation factor ($1/(R - G)$), it is actually a version of the factor-based approach (using a P/E just described. While it does have the advantage of making explicit the assumptions underlying the valuation factor, a closer look reveals just how inexact a factor-based approach can be.

TABLE 16.1

Cash flows and terminal value

Year	1	2	3	4	5	6	7 (terminal)	8 and beyond
Cash flow	explicit	explicit	explicit	explicit	explicit	explicit	explicit	year 7 plus growth
Value measure	NPV	NPV	NPV	NPV	NPV	NPV	NPV	$CF_{t+1} \div (R - G)$ (Net Present Value of this cash flow)

Suppose the projected net cash flow for year eight, the first year after the last explicit cash flow estimate, is $120 million. The projected cost of capital going forward is 10 percent, and the projected growth rate after year seven is 6 percent. Then the terminal value of the enterprise, capturing the contribution of the cash flows from year eight forward, is $3 billion ($120 million $\div$ (0.10 – 0.06)).* This is a simple calculation. But if the estimates of the cost of capital and the growth rate for these years are each off by 1 percent, which is not a large error, then the terminal value could be as high as $6 billion ($120 million $\div$ (0.09 – 0.07)) or as low as $2 billion ($120 million $\div$ (0.11 – 0.05)). This three-to-one range of plausible terminal values represents the level of uncertainty that applies to these calculations in practice.

This wide range of plausible values has unfortunate implications for the use of NPV calculations in making investment decisions. Experience indicates that, except for the simplest projects focused on cost reduction, it is the terminal values that typically account for by far the greatest portion of any project's net present value. With these terminal value calculations so imprecise, the reliability of the overall NPV calculation is seriously compromised, as are the investment decisions based on these estimates.

The problem is not the method of calculating terminal values. No better methods exist. The problem is intrinsic to the NPV approach. An NPV calculation takes reliable information, usually near-term cash flow estimates, and combines that with unreliable information, which are the

---

* To incorporate this terminal value into the full net present value calculation, it has to be discounted back to the present from the date at which it is created, in this case year eight.

estimated cash flows from a distant future that make up the terminal value. Then, after applying discount rates, it simply adds all these cash flows together. It is an axiom of engineering that combining good information with bad information does not produce information of average quality. The result is bad information, because the errors from the bad information dominate the whole calculation. A fundamental problem with the NPV approach is that it does not effectively segregate good from bad information about the value of the project.

A second practical shortcoming of the NPV approach to valuation is one to which we have already alluded. A valuation procedure is a method for moving from assumptions about the future to a calculated value of a project which unfolds over the course of that future. Ideally, it should be based on assumptions about the future that can reliably and sensibly be made today. Otherwise, the value calculation will be of little use.

For example, a sensible opinion can be formed about whether the automobile industry will still be economically viable twenty years from today. We can also form reasonable views of whether Ford or any company in the industry is likely, twenty years in the future, to enjoy significant competitive advantages over the other automobile manufacturers (not likely). For a company such as Microsoft, which does enjoy significant competitive advantages today, we can think reasonably about the chances that these advantages will survive the next twenty years, whether they will increase, decrease, or continue as is.

But it is hard to forecast exactly how fast Ford's sales will grow over the next two decades, what its profit margins will be, or how much it will be required to invest per dollar of revenue. Likewise, for a company like Microsoft, projecting sales growth and profit margins is difficult for its current products and even more difficult for the new products it will introduce over that time. Yet these are the assumptions that have to be made to arrive at a value based on NPV analysis.

It is possible to make strategic assumptions about competitive advantages with more confidence, but these are not readily incorporated into an NPV calculation. Taken together, the NPV approach's reliance on assumptions that are difficult to make and its omission of assumptions that can be made with more certainty are a second major shortcoming.

A third difficulty with the NPV approach is that it discards much information that is relevant to the calculation of the economic value of a company. There are two parts to value creation. The first is the resources that are devoted to the value creation process, the assets that the company employs. The second part is the distributable cash flows that are created by these invested resources. The NPV approach focuses exclusively on the cash flows. In a competitive environment, the two will be closely related. The assets will earn ordinary—cost of capital—returns. Therefore, knowing the resource levels will tell a good deal about likely future cash flows.

But if the resources are not used effectively, then the value of the cash flows they generate will fall short of the dollars invested. There will always be other firms that can do better with similar resources, and competition from these firms will inevitably produce losses for the inefficient user. Even firms efficient in their use of resources may not create excess value in their cash flows, so long as competition from equally efficient producers whittles away those excess returns. The crucial point is that in a competitive environment, resource requirements carry important implications about likely future cash flows, and the NPV approach takes no advantage of this information.

All these criticisms of NPV would be immaterial if there were no alternative approach to valuation that met these objections. But in fact there is such an alternative. It does segregate reliable from unreliable information; it does incorporate strategic judgments about the current and future state of competition in the industry; it does pay attention to a company's resources. Because this approach has been developed and applied by investors in marketable securities, starting with Benjamin Graham and continuing through Warren Buffett and a host of others, we will describe this alternative methodology in the context of valuing a company as a whole. Later we will show how the same basic valuation approach applies to other kinds of investment projects.

A STRATEGIC APPROACH TO VALUATION

FIRST CUT: ASSETS

The most reliable information for valuing a company is the information on its balance sheet. Both the assets and the liabilities exist in the present and can in principle be inspected at any moment, even if they are intangible. Placing a value on them generally requires no projection of future developments. For some of the balance sheet items, most obviously cash and marketable securities on the asset side and short-term debt on the liabilities side, there is no uncertainty about their worth. For other items, the valuation is more involved. Still, the process of valuing assets and liabilities, even where judgments need to be made, is informative.

The first important judgment is whether the product market in which the company operates will be economically viable going forward. In the case of Ford, the question is whether the global automotive industry is likely to exist for the foreseeable future. If the answer is no, then the value of Ford's assets is their liquidation value. Accounts receivable and inventory will have to be written down from their balance sheet levels. The discount will be small for accounts receivable, since they are largely recoverable in liquidation. For inventories, the discount will be larger, since some items may be obsolete and worth little. The value of plant, property, and equipment (PPE) for a nonviable industry will depend on whether they are specific to the industry or general purpose. Industry-specific PPE will be worth only its scrap value. General-purpose PPE, such as office buildings, will usually trade in active secondhand markets, and these market values should be realized in liquidation. Intangibles, like brands, customer relationships, and product portfolios, will have limited or no value in liquidation. The liabilities must be subtracted from the value of the assets, generally at full value, since in any liquidation short of bankruptcy, they must be fully paid off.

On the other hand, if the industry is viable, then the assets employed will have to be reproduced at some point, and they should be valued at reproduction cost. The reproduction cost of an asset is the cost of reproducing its economic function as efficiently as possible. For cash and marketable securities, there is no discrepancy between reported value and reproduction cost. For accounts receivable, the reproduction cost will actually be slightly higher than accounting book value. Receivables are essentially loans to customers generated by sales made in the normal course of business, and some of the loans will not be repaid.

The reproduction value of inventory is the cost of producing equivalent amounts of salable inventory, which may be higher or lower than the book figure, depending on whether LIFO or FIFO accounting is being used, and on the trends in production costs. For PPE, the reproduction value is the cost of producing equivalent facilities from the cheapest source, either newly created or secondhand. Calculating this figure requires substantial industry knowledge, but it does not depend on projecting future cash flows.

Finally, for a viable industry, intangibles like customer relationships, organizational development, workforce acquisition and training, and product portfolios will have positive reproduction costs.* These can be calculated by developing scenarios for producing them efficiently. For example, the cost of a product portfolio is the R&D expenditure necessary to produce from scratch and make ready for sale an equivalent set of products. There may be private market transactions, in which a sophisticated buyer purchases intangibles for cash, that can be helpful in determining the reproduction value. For example, when a record company buys an independent label with its stable of recording artists, or when a major drug company buys a start-up firm with a promising product, or when a cable company buys a local cable system with its customer contracts, a reproduction value has been put on these intangible assets.

Calculating the reproduction value of the assets of a firm in a viable business, just like establishing the liquidation value, does not require projections into the future. The necessary information is all currently available. Also, in working down the balance sheet, the estimates of value move from the most certain (cash and marketable securities) to the least certain (the intangibles). These distinctions are important; a valuation in which intangibles like brand equity are a significant part of the whole is less trustworthy than one in which cash, receivables, and general-purpose PPE represent most of the total value. Finally, assets further down the balance sheet require more industry expertise to calculate their reproduction values. But this expertise is no greater than what is necessary to make any informed investment decision in the industry in question.

The merit of incorporating strategic analysis into the valuation

---

* These are resources a competitor would need even though some of them do not show up on the balance sheet, having been treated by accounting convention as operating expenses rather than capital investments.

process becomes apparent when we look at a company in an industry without incumbent competitive advantages. Suppose, as an example, that the reproduction value of Ford's assets is $40 billion. These assets are currently generating a cash flow of $8 billion per year. At a cost of capital of 10 percent, usually a reasonable assumption, the cash flow is worth $80 billion, twice the reproduction costs of the assets. This discrepancy is an open invitation. Under these conditions, an entrant into Ford's market or, more likely, another auto company seeking to expand, can create $80 billion in value for a $40 billion investment. With no barriers to stand in its way, the entrant makes the investment and moves in. But now, with more competition, the earnings begin to decline, both for Ford and for the newcomer. If they drop to $6 billion for Ford, reducing the value of the investment to $60 billion, that is still sufficiently enticing for other firms to join. Only when the value of future earnings has been driven down to the reproduction cost of $40 billion will the process of entry cease and the profitability of the industry stabilize. In industries with no barriers to entry, competition will eventually make the reproduction value of the assets equal to the value of future earnings.

SECOND CUT: CURRENT EARNINGS POWER VALUE

After the assets and liabilities, the second most reliable piece of information for determining the value of a company is the cash flow the company can distribute over the near term. The source of this information is the current and recently reported earnings and cash flow statements. These returns represent only a small fraction of the company's value, but they can be used to answer an important question: If this level of net cash flow were to be sustained forever, neither growing nor shrinking, what would the company be worth? This figure is based on accounting information, which is relatively solid. It does call for extrapolation into an uncertain future, so it is less reliable than an asset-based valuation. But because it assumes no growth, it is less uncertain than standard NPV calculations. We will refer to this second approach to valuation as an earnings power value. As we shall see, comparing earnings power value with the reproduction costs of the assets sheds light on the competitive position of the firm in its market.

The starting point in determining the earnings power value of a company is the current net cash flow. Ideally, this number should equal reported earnings, but because of accrual accounting, there is almost always a discrepancy between them. Also, for a variety of transitory reasons, even current cash flow may differ from the sustainable average cash flow that can be extracted from a company's current operating situation. Therefore, to move from reported earnings to sustainable distributable earnings—what we are calling "earnings power"—requires a number of adjustments. None of them are particularly challenging, but they may looking daunting to people who have not spent much time reading financial statements.

First, in order to eliminate the effects of financial leverage—how much debt the company carries as a percentage of its assets—the place to begin is with operating earnings (EBIT—earnings before interest and taxes), rather than net earnings. This allows us to disregard both the interest payments a company makes and the tax benefits it gets from using debt financing.

Second, what are euphemistically called "nonrecurring items" have to be incorporated into the calculation. In an ideal world, these charges would be infrequent, equally divided between positive and negative changes, and would not affect long-term sustainable earnings. But in the practice of some companies, the charges are frequent, they are overwhelmingly negative, and they cram into single years losses that have been incurred over many prior years and may be incurred in future years. Rather than one-time, truly nonrecurring events, they are often attempts to enhance the perceived level of "normal" earnings by collecting mistaken initiatives and segregating them into what management hopes will be dismissible lumps. A sensible way to treat them when they appear regularly is to calculate their average level over a period of years, either in dollar terms or relative to sales, and to subtract this average level from the more recently reporting operating earnings before charges.

Third, after eliminating these accounting manipulations, current earnings must be adjusted to account for any cyclical variation that may cause them to be either above or below their sustainable level. There are a number of ways to make the adjustment. The simplest is to calculate the average operating margins (EBIT divided by sales) over a period of years and then apply that average margin to current sales to derive a current operating earnings level. Margins tend to fluctuate more severely over the business cycle than do sales. However, if sales are also sensitive to the cycle, they too should be adjusted to an average level.

Fourth, accounting depreciation as calculated for the financial statement may diverge widely from true economic depreciation. Economic depreciation should equal the amount that needs to be spent in the current year to return a firm's capital stock at the end of the year to where it was at the start of the year. This figure is maintenance capital expense; it omits capital expenditures for growth. It depends on current prices of plant and equipment. Accounting depreciation relies on historical costs and conventional rules based on the rates at which plant and equipment have historically had to be replaced. Since equipment prices have been declining in recent years and accounting depreciation measures usually overstate the rate at which structures wear out, accounting depreciation should generally exceed the actual expense required to maintain the capital stock (maintenance capital expense). The typical adjustment will increase reported earnings. In contrast, in the inflationary environment of the late 1970s and early 1980s, historical costs were below replacement costs, and the typical adjustment reduced reported earnings.

Fifth, special circumstances may call for further adjustments: a consolidated subsidiary may be included as a reported share of equity earning rather than actual cash flow in potential earnings; a division's management may be insensitive to pricing opportunities, leaving its current earnings below its potential because of unexploited pricing power; a money-losing operation that could be closed down may conceal the true extent of sustainable earnings in the rest of a company.

Finally, taxes charged for accounting purposes may vary widely from year to year. The pretax operating earnings adjusted as indicated here should be converted to after-tax earnings using an average sustainable tax rate. The result of all this effort should be a figure representing what a company without debt could repeatedly earn, after taxes, based on its most recently reported results. This is the *earnings power* of a company, the amount of cash that it can distribute to its owners each year without impairing the productive assets of the firm.

Earnings power is an annual flow of funds. To convert it into *earnings power value* (EPV), which is the present value of all those flows in the future, the first step is to divide earnings power by the cost of capital. The cost of capital should be calculated as the weighted average of the cost of debt capital, after tax, and the cost of equity capital. It represents what the firm has to pay to investors each year to attract the necessary investment voluntarily. The weighted average cost is the after-tax cost of debt capital times the fraction of capital raised through debt plus the after-tax cost of equity capital times the fraction raised through equity. The sustainable ratio of debt to total capital should be the lower of two figures: either the amount of debt the firm can carry on average without seriously impairing its operating performance, or the firm's historical average debt level. Because of the lower cost of debt financing due to the tax savings, the preferred figure is the first one. But if the management does not care to capture this advantage now or in the foreseeable future, then management's actual behavior is the relevant figure for calculating the average cost of capital.*

To illustrate the process, consider a company with reported after-tax current earnings of $100 million. After adjustments, this figure is raised to an after-tax earnings power of $135 million per year. The company is financed one-third by debt and two-thirds by equity. It pays 9 percent interest on its debt. The cost of its equity is 10.8 percent (that is the observed return on equity investments of comparable risk). With a tax rate of 40 percent, the weighted average cost of capital (R) is 9 percent:

$$R = (1/3 \times [9\% \times (1 - 40\%)]) + (2/3 \times 10.8\%) = 9\%$$

With a cost of capital of 9 percent, the earnings power value of the firm is $1.5 billion:

$$EPV = \$135 \text{ million} \div 0.09 = \$1.500 \text{ million}$$

---

*An average debt level above what the company can reasonably bear without impairment is unlikely to be sustainable.

This represents the value of the ongoing operations of the firm, assuming no growth or deterioration in the future.*

The EPV calculated here is that of the firm as a whole. The value of the equity is this total value less the value of the firm's outstanding debt. Using the asset approach, the comparable value of the entire firm is the value of the assets, either liquidation or reproduction value, less the non-debt liabilities, such as accounts payable and accruals. The value of the equity is this figure minus the debt liabilities. The reason for focusing on the overall firm rather than just the equity value is that the estimate for the entire firm is more reliable, especially when the firm has a high level of debt.

Because growth has been excluded from this valuation, and because it uses current cash flow, not cash flow five to ten years into the future, the EPV is far less subject to error than valuations dependent on establishing a terminal value some eight or ten years in the future. A 1 percent error in estimating the firm's cost of capital will lead to a range of EPV values from $1,700 million, if the cost of capital is 8 percent, to $1,350 million if it is 10 percent. This is much narrower than the potential range of error using the terminal value estimate which includes a rate of growth.

However, if the concern is only with the equity value of the firm, then those errors can be greatly magnified. Suppose that the error range on the EPV of the firm as a whole is plus or minus $150 million around the mean estimate of $1,500 million. This is plus or minus 10 percent, a small number as these things go. But if the firm has debt of $1,200 million, whose value is relatively certain, then the entire $150 million error applies to the value of the equity, whose base level is now $300 million ($1,500 million less $1,200 million in debt). This is an error range of plus or minus 50 percent, which makes the estimate highly uncertain.

To understand fully the effect of leverage on risk, it is best to start with the overall enterprise value and then adjust from there to see the impact on the value of the equity portion. In what follows, therefore, the asset values and EPV will refer to the enterprise as a whole.

---

*If the firm has valuable assets that are not necessary to its basic operations, and whose returns are not included in operating earnings, for example excess cash or real estate, the value of these assets should be added to the earnings power value to get the total value of the firm.

PUTTING ASSETS AND EARNINGS TOGETHER: FRANCHISE VALUE

Leaving aside the question of growth, assets and earnings powers value are two distinct ways to estimate the value of a firm. A comparison between them can result in three possible configurations: EPV exceeds asset value; they are essentially equal; asset value exceeds EPV. Each configuration has strategic implications.

If the EPV exceeds the asset value, that means that the current level of enterprise earnings power is creating value in excess of the reproduction cost of the assets. As we have seen, if there are no barriers to entry, newcomers attracted by these high returns will enter the industry and continue to enter until the opportunity for value creation has been eliminated by competition. Unless there are barriers to entry, an EPV that exceeds the reproduction cost of the assets cannot be sustained. Therefore, the only instances in which properly calculated EPVs do exceed asset values are situations in which there are barriers to entry and incumbents do enjoy identifiable and sustainable competitive advantages.

The difference between the asset value and the EPV is precisely the value of the current level of competitive advantages. We will call it the "franchise value"—the excess return earned by the firm with competitive advantages. Whether a particular franchise value is sustainable, and thus whether the EPV is the appropriate measure of total value, can be judged from the size of the franchise value relative to sales, assets, and the competitive advantages at work. Clearly, the greater the franchise value, the more powerful must be the competitive advantages that create and are necessary to sustain it.

Consider as an example a company with an asset value at reproduction cost of $1,200 million, an earnings power of $240 million after tax, sales of $1,000 million, and a cost of capital of 10 percent (table 16.2). The EPV of this firm is $2,400 million. An entrant needs to earn $120 million after tax to cover its cost of capital ($1,200 million x 10 %). The excess return that must be defended by competitive advantages, which is the franchise value, is $120 million after tax ($240 million current earnings minus $120 million competitive earnings). Since the after-tax income is 60 percent of pretax income, then the advantage comes to

TABLE 16.2

Calculating the franchise margin ($ million)

Asset value	$ 1,200
Sales	$ 1,000
Earnings power	$ 240
Cost of capital	10%
EPV (earnings power divided by cost of capital)	$ 2,400
Tax rate	40%
Competitive earnings	$ 120
Franchise earnings (earnings power minus competitive earnings)	$ 120
Pretax franchise earnings ($120 ÷ (1 – 40%))	$ 200
Franchise margin on sales ($200 ÷ $1,000)	20%

$200 million pretax ($120 million ÷ (1 – .40%)). This amounts to a pretax margin on sales of 20 percent above the competitive margin ($200 million ÷ $1,000 sales).

To justify an EPV of $2,400 million, the firm must benefit from a combination of competitive advantages in higher prices due to customer captivity and lower costs due to either proprietary technology or economies of scale equal to 20 percent of sales. The valuation decision—whether to use the value of the assets or the value of the earnings power—comes down to a strategic judgment of whether the enterprise enjoys competitive advantages of this magnitude. Being able to compare the asset value to the EPV allows us to place the focus of the valuation decision directly and simply in the strategic arena, which is where it belongs.

The second possibility stemming from the comparison of asset value to EPV is that they are approximately equal. This is what would be expected in the majority of industries where no firm enjoys significant competitive advantages. If an analysis confirms that market share is unstable, that no firms are earning extraordinary returns on capital, and that there are no identifiable sources of competitive advantage, then we have an uncontested estimate of value, based on both the resource and the income method of valuation, confirmed by strategic judgment. This figure is a much more reliable fix on the value of a firm than an NPV analysis alone.

The final possibility is that the asset value exceeds the EPV of the enterprise. Provided that both valuations have been done properly, and that, for instance, the reproduction value of the assets was not used if the liquidation value was called for, then the only possible source of this discrepancy is deficient management. The management is not producing returns commensurate with the value of the assets being put to work. In this case, the strategic approach points to the critical question for evaluating the company, namely, what can be done either to improve or to replace management. The NPV approach is not likely to raise this issue, which points to a further shortcoming of this standard method of valuation.

THIRD CUT: THE VALUE OF GROWTH

It is now time to integrate the effects of growth into this strategic valuation framework, by identifying the situations in which growth is bad, when it is neutral, and when it is good.

When Growth Is Bad

In the last situation described, the one in which the asset value is higher than the EPV, growth will make things worse. Growth is simply one way in which resources are put to work. The management is doing a poor job utilizing the resources it currently has. Suppose this management were to invest $100 million either in a new enterprise or to expand the current one. The cost of capital is 10 percent, which represents what, on average, that capital will earn elsewhere in projects of equal risk. If past performance is any guide, management will earn less than 10 percent on its investments. Without competitive advantages it will certainly not earn more. Suppose that management earns 8 percent on the $100 million, or $8 million per year. Since the capital cost is $10 million per year, paid to the new investors who put in the $100 million, the net benefits of the underlying growth to the old investors is a negative $2 million. So the first important fact about growth is that in the hands of poor management, or at a competitive disadvantage, growth destroys value. In these circumstances, the more energetic the management in pursuing growth, the more value it will destroy.

When Growth Is Neutral

In the second situation, where asset value equals EPV and strategic analysis confirms the absence of competitive advantages, growth neither creates nor destroys value. The company earns an average return, which is the cost of capital, and its return on growth will be the same. On the $100 million in new capital, it will return $10 million, all of which will go to the new investors who have provided that capital, and there will be nothing left over for the existing owners. Its operating income goes up by $10 million, but all of that goes to pay for the capital required. Growth on a level playing field, like entry into a market without competitive advantages, neither creates nor destroys value. In this case, leaving growth out of the valuation is entirely appropriate.

When Growth Is Good

Only growth in the presence of existing competitive advantages creates value. This is the first situation described above, where EPV exceeds asset value and in which there are identifiable and sustainable competitive advantages. In this case, the return on the $100 million invested will exceed the annual cost of $10 million, leaving something for the old shareholders. If the reproduction cost of the assets is the first tranche of value, and the earnings power is the second tranche, then the value of growth is the third tranche (figure 16.1). Although a full NPV analysis can be useful in "growth is good" situations, to estimate the value of the enterprise including growth, the strategic approach is even more essential. It highlights the one element that makes growth valuable, which is the existence of sustainable competitive advantages in a growing market. It also organizes the final value measure into tranches of increasing uncertainty.

In "growth is good" situations, the value of the assets may be small relative to the value including growth, but it does represent the value that will endure if the competitive advantages evaporate and the barriers to entry come down. The second tranche, the excess of earnings power value over asset value, represents the value of current competitive advantages without growth; this is the next most reliable piece. The value of the growth is the most uncertain, both because it requires pro-

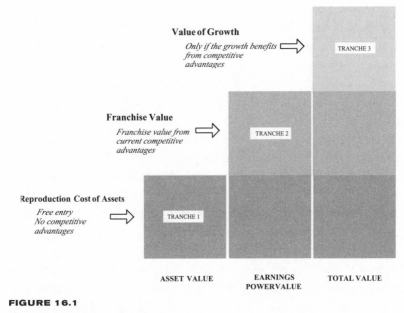

Value of Growth

Only if the growth benefits ⟹
from competitive
advantages

TRANCHE 3

Franchise Value

Franchise value from ⟹
current competitive
advantages

TRANCHE 2

Reproduction Cost of Assets

Free entry ⟹
No competitive
advantages

TRANCHE 1

ASSET VALUE   EARNINGS   TOTAL VALUE
              POWER VALUE

FIGURE 16.1
Three tranches of value

jections into the future and because it depends upon the ability to grow within a franchise, which is difficult.

The strategic approach also provides insight into the possible magnitude of that growth. Since one of the distinguishing features of an industry with barriers to entry is stable market shares for the incumbents, then the growth of the individual firm will eventually be limited to the growth of the industry. In many cases it may be easier to assess the growth rate for an industry than for a single firm. Sometimes, however, the growth rate of the industry, say for microprocessors or PC software, may be highly unpredictable. In these cases, assigning a reliable value to the incumbents like Intel and Microsoft is simply impossible.

CONCLUDING THOUGHTS ON VALUATION

The strategic approach to valuation—asset value, earnings power value, assessment of competitive advantages, and the value of growth—has been applied here to decisions to invest in a company as a whole. Such decisions pertain chiefly to financial market investments, whether by firms or individuals. This method of valuation has been developed primarily by generations of value investors, beginning with Benjamin Graham and David Dodd and continuing through people like Walter Schloss, Warren Buffett, Mario Gabelli, and Seth Klarman.* Their successful records over long periods of time is part of the argument in favor of this method. For securities investments, there is an additional dimension that these investors bring to the process. When they have identified a stock that their valuation indicates is selling for less than its actual economic value, they require a sufficient *margin of safety*, in Benjamin Graham's famous phrase, which is the size of the gap between the market price and the fundamental value. For a company in a competitive industry, that margin has to lie in the difference between the market price and the asset value. For companies that do enjoy a sustainable competitive advantage, the difference may lie between the market price and the EPV, certainly if the market price is not more than the asset value. In this situation, the value of the franchise would be the margin of safety. And for those rare companies that can grow profitably, the value of the growth might provide the margin, so long as the shares are selling for no more than the value of the current earnings power. So strategic analysis is at the core of their investment method.

FROM COMPANIES TO PROJECTS

The same method for valuation applies to investment projects on a scale smaller than entire companies. The strategic issues still dominate. The first step is to segregate the early investments, which create assets, from the subsequent income flows. The former constitute the asset value of the project; the latter are the earnings power value, including growth. Any excess of EPV over asset value must be justified by identifying sustainable competitive advantages. Optimistic growth and margin assumptions incorporated into a highly uncertain terminal value are not

---

*Warren Buffett's well-known essay "The Superinvestors of Graham and Doddsville" recounts the success of members of this informal group into the early 1980s.

dependable. If no clear competitive advantages can be identified, then no matter how rapid the growth forecast, it will not affect the value of the project. A business case analysis under these circumstances that simply assumes no further growth once a project reaches maturity will generally provide a better valuation measure for investment decisions than a fully developed but error-prone NPV.

Without competitive advantages, investments will generally return the cost of capital, meaning they will not add any value for the existing owners. This is as true for projects like expansions into new territory and the development of new product lines as it is for entire companies. The only exceptions come from superior management, which can use resources more efficiently than other firms and so squeeze out higher returns. We discuss the positive potential of great management in the last chapter. On the other hand, investments made under the protective umbrella of a well-established competitive advantage will almost always be worth doing, either to exploit opportunities or to secure the existing franchise. We discuss this issue more completely in the following chapter on corporate development.

CHAPTER 17

Corporate Development and Strategy

Mergers and Acquisitions, New Ventures, and Brand Extensions

Mergers and acquisitions, new ventures, and brand extensions—all aspects of corporate development—are unquestionably strategic business functions. By all the traditional criteria for distinguishing between strategic and tactical decisions, corporate development issues qualify as strategic. The commitments in question are large, they involve the overall direction of the enterprise, and they have long-term consequences.

The most common method for evaluating alternative courses of action in these areas is a business case analysis consisting of detailed projections of future distributable cash flows discounted back to the present. But discounted cash flow, as we have argued in chapter 16, is by itself a critically flawed tool for making decisions of this sort. The values calculated to justify initiatives depend on projections, into the distant future, of growth rates, profit margins, costs of capital, and other crucial yet highly uncertain variables. Also, a typical discounted cash flow analysis rests on a number of critical assumptions about the nature and intensity of future competition that are rarely explicit and generally untested.

The strategic framework we have developed in this book, especially the view that the most important determinant of strategy is whether an incumbent firm benefits from competitive advantages, applies directly to issues of corporate development. In fact, the utility of this approach in clarifying decision making in this area is an important test of its worth. At a minimum, clarifying the competitive environment in which new initiatives will succeed or fail should provide an essential check on whether the conclusions of a discounted cash flow–based business case are reasonable.

MERGERS AND ACQUISITIONS

Decisions about mergers and acquisitions are essentially large-scale investment choices. They are based on an investment approach that has two main features. First, an acquisition is by definition a concentrated investment in a single enterprise or, in those cases where a conglomerate is being acquired, in a limited collection of enterprises. The firm making the acquisition has the option of making a different kind of investment, either directly or by distributing the money to its owners. It or its shareholders could purchase stocks in an economy-wide or even global portfolio of enterprises. Acquiring another company may help diversify the business of a previously highly focused firm, but it will add much less diversification than buying a broad-based portfolio of shares. Considered from this perspective, an acquisition or a merger, like all concentrated investment strategies, entails more risk than buying a portfolio of shares. There may be benefits to concentration that offset the additional risks involved. But unless these benefits can be identified with some precision, an acquisition policy is a priori an inferior choice for a firm with capital to invest or to return to its shareholders.

The second feature of mergers and acquisitions makes this investment approach even more difficult to explain. Acquisitions of publicly traded companies are invariably made at prices higher than the market price of the shares before the intent to acquire is made public. These premiums, which historically have averaged about 30 percent above the preannouncement price, may run as high as 70 or even 100 percent. Premiums for acquiring privately held companies may historically have been lower, but when acquisition markets heat up, investment bankers are able to shop a private company around or conduct bidding contests. Under these conditions, it is unlikely that the purchasing company is getting much of a bargain.

Taken together, these features produce a concentrated and therefore risky investment made at a premium to the market price. Adding in the hefty fees paid to the investment bankers who underwrite and advise on any deal increases the costs to the investors. Imagine being approached by a mutual fund salesman who is selling a fund that has limited diversification, sells for more than the net asset value of the shares it owns, and carries with it an exceptionally high commission.

Another reason that acquisitions have to overcome a heavy financing burden merely to come out even is the cyclical nature of the M&A business. When share prices are low, the acquisition market dries up; when prices rise, so does M&A activity. Instead of buying companies when they are on sale, acquirers tend to go shopping when the targets are expensive. It is as if our mutual fund announced in its prospectus that it would purchase shares only after they have gone up in price. Clearly, as an investment strategy, standard merger and acquisition practice requires a substantial additional rationale.

FINANCIAL AND STRATEGIC ACQUIRERS

It is common in merger and acquisition discussions to distinguish between acquirers that are simply making financial investment decisions and those that have a strategic purpose in mind (figure 17.1). While the differences are not altogether clear, the general idea seems to be that the strategic acquirer brings something to the deal that will enhance the underlying operations of either the target firm or the buyer itself. The financial buyer, by contrast, simply adds the acquired company to a portfolio of operations without changing the fundamental performance at either firm. Without such changes, a standard acquisition involves only a concentrated investment at above market prices with high transaction costs. It makes little or no business sense.

That leaves strategic acquisitions as the only kind that bear detailed consideration. In order for a merger or acquisition to be justified, the buyer has to contribute something to the combined enterprise. This contribution can be either of general value, like improved management or a tax advantage, or, more likely, something highly specific, such as

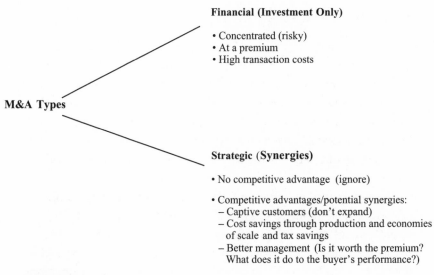

FIGURE 17.1

Types of mergers and acquisitions

special industry-related technology, joint economies of scale, or a marketing position within the industry. This kind of combination, by definition, produces "synergy," that happy situation in which the whole is greater than the sum of its parts.

Yet even in these presumably favorable circumstances, the history of strategic acquisitions has been painful for the shareholders of the acquiring company. Around the time of the acquisitions, the shares of the acquiring firm typically suffer a decline in price of roughly 4 percent, measured from twenty days before the deal is announced to the point at which it closes. The target companies, on the other hand, see their shares appreciate by more than 20 percent. The returns to shareholders of the acquiring company are dismal; the companies typically lose roughly 20 percent of their value over the next five years. Moreover, these figures may actually understate the negative effects of merger and acquisition transactions because many of the deals are done by serial acquirers, whose stocks may already be depressed in anticipation of more deals to come.

THE SEARCH FOR SYNERGY

It is not surprising that unrelated acquisitions, those of firms outside the acquirer's principal area of business, have shown especially poor results, since if any synergies do occur, they are bound to be insignificant. Most of these combinations are subsequently undone, one way or another. Companies that make many of these kinds of acquisitions end up with low stock prices, relative to their peers, and themselves become take-over targets for a buyer who intends to break them up and sell off the parts.

For all acquisitions, judged by accounting measures of performance, the postdeal operating results of the combined firms exhibit little or no improvement. An early study of the divisions of the target companies found that their average performance deteriorated after acquisition. Subsequent studies have identified some improvements in operating margins, but they tend to be in the range of 0.2–0.4 percent, not enough to cover the premiums paid to the targets.* At the plant level, the oper-ating costs of the target company plants are brought down, but this pos-itive development is offset by a coincident weakening in the operating performance of the acquiring company's plants. Given this history, checkered at best, it is important for evaluating potential acquisitions to identify those particular strategic factors that favor success.

Reviewing the diversification strategy of thirty-three large American companies in the period 1950–86, Michael Porter found that these firms had divested many more of their acquisitions than they retained. From the combinations that worked, he identified three traits as essential. First, the target company had to be in an "attractive" (profitable, fast-growing, etc.) industry. Second, there had to exist synergies between the operations of the acquirer and the target. Third, the acquisition pre-mium could be no more than these synergies were worth.

In practice, the requirements for a successful acquisition are actually more clear-cut than even this short list suggests. The last criterion is a matter of simple arithmetic. Obviously, if an acquirer pays too high a

---

*The scholarly literature is summarized in the article by Andrade, Mitchell, and Stafford cited in the notes.

premium, it is going to destroy rather than create value for its shareholders. The question is how to calculate the value of synergies that are likely to be realized in order to judge whether the premium is excessive. The first two criteria, on closer examination, are so intimately connected as to amount to almost the same thing.

Our contention in this book is that the definition of an "attractive" industry depends completely on one factor: the existence of incumbent competitive advantages or, using the alternative term, barriers to entry. Without these barriers, the process of entry by outsiders or expansion by incumbents will eliminate any returns above an industry's cost of capital. Firms with exceptional operating efficiency may produce extraordinary returns for a time, provided management stays focused and intact. But for an industry to be "attractive," so that even companies with merely good as opposed to stellar management can earn "attractive" returns, it needs to be protected by barriers to entry, with the incumbent firms enjoying competitive advantages.

COMPETITIVE ADVANTAGES AND SYNERGIES

The existence of synergies also depends on the presence of competitive advantages. The connection is clear. If the firm being acquired enjoys no competitive advantages, then the buying firm should be able to do on its own anything that might be done in combination after the acquisition. Even if the acquiring firm lacks the skills internally to perform these things, it can always find other firms willing and able to do for it whatever the acquired firm does. Given an active marketplace, these other companies will compete for the business of fulfilling these functions. Therefore, the acquired firm adds nothing of value to the combination, nothing that the acquirer cannot either do or hire someone to do. There are simply no synergies to be achieved when the acquiring firm can operate as well without the acquisition as with it.

Synergies moving in the other direction, from something the buyer contributes to the target, are equally unlikely. Because there are no competitive advantages in the target firm's market, none will be available to the two companies after the combination. Even if the buyer could transport some of its existing competitive advantages into the new market, it would do at least as well by selling them to any firm in this market as it would by restricting the benefits solely to the single acquisition target.

For example, if a distribution company had established a deep and efficient infrastructure within a given geographic region, so that it had some customer captivity and economies of scale, would it be better off buying one of its clients to lock in a distribution arrangement, or simply offering its services to the companies that might use them most profitably? The absence of competitive advantages in the target's market means that all the companies in that market are equally able to take advantage of anything the acquirer is providing. Therefore, without competitive advantages for the acquired firm, there will be no synergies from the combination. And, as a direct consequence, "attractive" markets, namely those in which competitive advantages exist, are also the only ones that may give rise to genuine synergies.

Many expected synergies, even some that seem obvious, never materialize. If the acquired firm now has a strong brand image, but no captive customers, it may appear that the acquiring company will be able to reap some benefits from this brand. By this logic, Chrysler should have benefited from the Mercedes-Benz image after it was acquired. But strong brands are not in and of themselves competitive advantages. In the luxury car market, Mercedes has a number of rivals; BMW, Jaguar, Acura, Lexus, and Infiniti all maintain prestigious brand identities. If the benefits of these brand images could be transferred without impairment to a company like Chrysler, then Chrysler should have been willing to pay for this benefit directly, through licenses, fees, or other kinds of arrangements. And the companies with the brands for hire would have been eager to do business. So if the benefits of the brand can be transferred, which is doubtful in most instances, there is nothing that restricts the synergies to an expensive merger or acquisition, nothing that can't be done more economically by a rental transaction.

Captive Customers

From the strategic perspective of this book, the first qualifying criterion to be applied to a merger and acquisition decision is whether the target firm enjoys any competitive advantages. Competitive disadvantages are obviously not worth acquiring. However, not all competitive advantages foster synergies. Customer captivity is not likely to travel well. Cola drinkers are among the most loyal customers around. But this habitual consumption does not make them any more likely to buy a particular brand of life insurance or even to favor a particular brand of salty snack or eat in a certain fast-food outlet. If Coca-Cola were to buy a cracker company, nothing about the combination would change a Coke drinker's habitual attachment to his or her existing cracker brand. Are Pepsi drinkers more loyal to Frito-Lay snacks than those who prefer Coke?

In financial services, the cost to a consumer of switching banks is not lessened when its existing insurance carrier is acquired by a rival bank. The separate customer captivities involved with the family's insurance and banking decisions generally stand distinct from one another. By their very nature, they are not undermined by a financial market transaction that combines an insurance company with a bank. More generally, the idea that particular financial service firms (e.g., stockbrokers) could extend their operations through acquisitions to become "financial supermarkets" has led to recurrent failures.

When AT&T acquired Teleport, a local telephone service provider with fiber-optic lines in a number of American cities, it expected customers to be attracted to a single integrated telephone company providing both local and long-distance services. Things didn't work out that way. AT&T did not win the local calling business of many of its existing long-distance customers, who stayed with their local providers. Despite CEO Michael Armstrong's claim of "powerful financial and strategic synergies for both companies," the number of AT&T customers who opted for integrated local–long-distance service was negligible. So both logic and experience indicate that competitive advantages arising from customer captivity do not travel in merger and acquisition packages. In spite of all the promise, it generally turns out that there are no significant synergies available from this competitive advantage.*

---

* Competitive advantages based on government licenses, regulations, or other interventions share with customer captivity the quality that they do not generally extend beyond their original scope when an acquisition takes place.

Cost Savings

After all the wishful thinking and deal-promoting propaganda have been cleared away, we are left with cost advantages—most frequently due to proprietary technology and economies of scale, fortified by some customer captivity—as the only potential sources of synergies in merger and acquisition transactions. With only cost advantages to consider, the task of evaluating potential synergies is considerably less complicated. When there are proprietary production technologies in either the target or the acquiring firm, they can reduce costs provided they can be successfully adopted in the other company. The combined companies may be able to realize joint economies of scale, mainly in the elimination of redundant fixed costs in distribution, marketing, research and development, and general overhead. The appropriate measure of the benefits of an acquisition is thus the size of the anticipated cost savings. Will they be large enough to offset the premium paid for the acquisition and therefore create some additional value for the acquirer?

If company executives and the bankers promoting merger and acquisition deals were forced to justify the proposed combinations using this test, it is likely many transactions would never see the light of day. (Admittedly, one should never underestimate the power of a compelling projection based on unwarranted hopes, a professional-looking spreadsheet, and an elegant PowerPoint presentation.)

AOL's acquisition of Time Warner, for which it paid a premium of roughly $50 billion, was justified by $600 million of anticipated annual cost savings. The cumulative value of these savings, appropriately discounted, was certainly less than $10 billion. AT&T bought cable properties where little or no cost savings were expected. It later sold them for about half of what it had paid. In late 1997, when Sealed Air Corporation acquired the Cryovac packaging division of W. R. Grace for a premium of $3 to $4 billion, it identified $100 million in annual cost savings it expected to realize. Discounted at 10 percent, these were cumulatively worth only $1 billion. The net result was a significant decline in Sealed Air's stock price. As a general rule, acquisitions at a premium to market prices need to be justified primarily with the costs savings that will ensue with the combination of the firms. Other vaunted synergies are considerably less likely to materialize.

Acquisitions of private companies should meet the same cost savings test as that applied to the purchase of public companies. Many of these are essentially "make versus buy" decisions, such as when major drug companies acquire drug development start-ups or when established record companies buy independent labels. The question is whether it is cheaper to obtain the products involved by internal development, licensing, or some other means short of an outright acquisition, which is generally an expensive way to go.

In some cases, it is clear that there is no alternative to acquisition, no other way to get hold of the desired product. But even in these instances, cost discipline should not be abandoned. By definition, the target company does enjoy a competitive advantage in these cases. Neither the acquiring company nor, presumably, anyone else can produce an equivalent to the desired product. The value of the target in this case consists of its value as a stand alone company, calculated by the customary methods (as discussed in chapter 16 on valuation), plus the value of the synergies. As usual, these synergies will be realized largely in cost savings, either from proprietary process technology or joint economies of scale. If, for example, the acquiring firm has an extensive distribution network through which to market and deliver the target's unique product, there are savings to be realized from economies of scale that would not be available to the target firm were it to do the distribution on its own or hire someone else to do it.*

Many mergers and acquisitions are also justified by the claim that the

---

* The diversification argument also promised cost savings, these from a reduction in taxes paid. A company with multiple lines of business should have lower fluctuations in operating income and thus can afford to carry more debt on the balance sheet. Debt is cheaper than equity because of the deductibility of interest payments. Also, when this capital is deployed within the company, rather than distributed to shareholders for their investments, it avoids the tax on either dividends or capital gains.

A separate diversification savings occurs when a company like Berkshire Hathaway acquires a privately held company in exchange for Berkshire stock. This enables the selling owners to buy into Berkshire's diversified portfolio of businesses without having to pay the capital gains they would owe if they sold their company for cash and reinvested the proceeds. Tax savings are thus an important justification in this case, which is probably highly uncommon.

superior management of the acquiring company will decisively improve the operations of the target company. This claim rests on two assumptions, both related to costs. The first is that payroll costs will be lowered simply by getting rid of the inferior managers of the target company. Either the managers from the acquiring company will take up these jobs without an increase in pay, or fewer and more capable people will be able to handle the tasks at a lower cost of employment.

The second assumption is that there will be additional cost reductions from improved operations in the target firm. Other kinds of improvement are less likely. Marketing expertise tends to be industry-specific. For the acquiring company to have the skills to improve marketing at the target, it is likely to be in the same or a closely related business. But if this were the case, why did it need to make the acquisition in the first place? It could have reproduced the target company's marketing efforts itself without the trouble of acquisition and reorganization. The benefits from better management will be largely confined to making the operations of the target firm better or eliminating some of them entirely. With fewer personal ties, the acquiring company may have an easier time in cutting back on employees. The payoff will be in cost reductions, which should be measurable.

An additional note of caution must be raised about the value of mergers and acquisitions that are to be justified by spreading "good management" onto the target company's operations. Sometimes improvements in productivity at the target company, though real enough, come at the expense of deterioration in productivity in the operations of the acquirer, eliminating any net gain. The attention of management, especially good management, is a scarce resource. It does not simply expand to cover all the operations for which it is needed. Deploying that resource to a target firm means diverting it from the acquirer's own operations. It is only the net improvement in overall performance that should be used to justify an acquisition. Also, the acquisition process itself, which adds nothing of value to the combined firm's operations, is an enormous devourer of management attention.

Some potential revenue gains may be expected from an intelligent acquisition. First, the increase in scale or efficiency that may come with the merger may make some marketing efforts profitable that previously were uneconomic. Still, these new efforts are unlikely to be of more than minor value. If they were significant, they would have already been undertaken, as they would have been profitable even without the benefits of economies of scale or increased efficiency. Therefore, the additional profit from these marginal efforts will be small even though the added revenue may be substantial. Second, if the merger eliminates a competitor, especially a troublesome, noncooperating competitor, it may improve industry price discipline. However, these are precisely the acquisitions most likely to be contested by the antitrust regulators. Also, it makes more sense for a potential acquirer to let some other industry player incur the expense of the takeover premium than to play hero itself. There is a strong incentive to be a "free rider" and watch from the sidelines.

THE M&A BOTTOM LINE

The strategic bottom line for mergers and acquisitions is that two fundamental requirements have to be met to warrant the effort and expense. First, there must be competitive advantages to produce the synergies that yield sustained benefits. Second, the synergies must consist largely of cost savings. Thus, for any additional value to be created by the combination, the takeover premium will have to be less than the clearly identified and realistic cost savings. There may be instances in which superior management will be able to improve the operations of the combined companies without benefit of a competitive advantage, but for reasons we have discussed, primarily limitations on the key resource of management attention, these instances will be infrequent. Finally, a rigorous justification of the takeover premium must set it against the benefits that a cooperative arrangement among independent companies might achieve without a merger or acquisition. If bargaining can produce most of the gains of direct combination, the premium paid must be minimal to be fully warranted.

When the acquisition is paid for in stock rather than cash, the calculations may need to be adjusted. In the AOL–Time Warner merger referred to earlier, AOL clearly overpaid, based on the size of potential cost savings compared with the premium over market price. But AOL used its own stock, which by almost any valuation measure was grossly inflated, for the purchase. Buying Time Warner with a debased currency made the deal a profitable one for AOL shareholders, although it took a while for that fact to become apparent. While it is generally better to be on the selling rather than the buying side in M&A transactions, when the acquirer pays with its own stock, using a currency whose future value it knows much more about than anyone else, then even the target must exercise care.

If a proposed transaction makes no business sense if done with cash, the only reason for doing it with stock is that the acquirer's shares are overvalued. The choice of stock or cash payment does not affect the underlying economics of the transaction. The acquiring company would never choose to use stock if its management felt that its stock was trading in the market at less than its true value. Historically, the stock market has treated acquisitions for stock more harshly than those done with cash, and the share price of the acquiring company has declined more severely upon the announcement of the deal.

VENTURE CAPITAL

Venture capital investing is a second area in which strategic considerations ought to play an important role. Like mergers and acquisitions, venture investments are strategic decisions. They involve large resource commitments, they have long-lived consequences, and they can shape the overall direction of a business. From the strategic perspective developed here, the outcomes of venture capital decisions depend critically on the actions of other potential entrants into the markets into which the ventures are being launched. Even new industries with enormous promise can be sinkholes for venture investments if there are no barriers to entry. The history of the disc data storage industry is a telling example of how enthusiastic venture investors can saturate an attractive market with new entrants, almost all of whom lose money.

According to conventional wisdom, success in venture capital investments depends upon two factors: the quality of the business plan and the capabilities of the venture team itself.* In practice, only the second of these considerations should count for much. By their very nature, venture capital investments take place in new or underdeveloped markets without entrenched, dominant competitors. Proprietary technologies, the venture investors hope, will be developed as the venture progresses. But when they start out, almost by definition, no firms have access to such technologies. Developing captive customers may be the goal of the venture, but at inception the customers in these nascent markets are up for grabs. Finally, though it may hope to grow rapidly and achieve economies of scale—hence the mantra "Get big fast"—no new venture begins life with that kind of advantage over its competitors. So, while a well-conceived venture business plan should look to the ultimate creation of competitive advantages, that vision is not itself a competitive advantage. Truly lucrative opportunities will attract other new ventures with a similar vision and a comparable plan. The larger the potential prize, in other words, the smaller will be the probability of winning the prize. There are many smart venture capitalists and no barriers to entry in generating business plans.

The quality of the venture plans is not totally irrelevant. Poor plans usually lead to poor returns. But plans that rely on general features, like identifying large markets and describing potential competitive advantages, are unlikely to pinpoint genuinely attractive opportunities.

The design of a successful venture business plan involves making delicate trade-offs between the size of the ultimate returns and the chance of realizing those returns. Crafting such plans requires a thorough knowledge of the industry and a dense network of industry contacts. But those are attributes of venture investors. Indeed, they are two of the principal resources that the venture sponsors, whether independent venture capital firms or corporate development departments, bring to a

---

*The return to the venture capitalists also depends on the deal made with the entrepreneurs. We will ignore that issue here, since we are focused on the success of the businesses receiving venture financing, not on the division of the spoils or the tactical effectiveness of the incentives for management built into the venture deal.

venture opportunity. There are no generally applicable characteristics of "good" business plans.* All good business plans are local.

An accomplished venture sponsor should also be able to assess the quality of a venture's management team. The sponsor should have a network of contacts that include skilled professionals who can be recruited to fill in gaps in the original team, potential customers who can help refine the venture's product offerings, and firms that can provide special facilities or other essentials that the venture needs to deliver its offerings. The sponsor should also be able to modify and refine the business plan to target those niches in which there is the greatest probability of success. The founders of Compaq originally approached Ben Rosen with a plan to develop and sell disk storage devices. He liked the venture team but not the proposal, and he redirected them toward the emerging PC business, where they could challenge IBM at the high end of this market.

Venture sponsors are ultimately in the knowledge business. They have to create and maintain information collection networks. They bring together knowledge of technologies, markets, people, and other essential resources and try to combine these ingredients to produce a well-functioning entrepreneurial organization. Like other industries in which there are no barriers to entry, success in venture capital ultimately depends on how efficiently the venture operation is run, which means how effectively venture sponsors remain focused within their core circles of competence. Ultimately, it is the people that matter, not the business plans in which they invest.

ECONOMIES OF SCOPE AND LEVERAGING EXISTING CAPABILITIES

Ventures that grow out of existing businesses usually differ in two ways from the stand-alone undertakings commonly funded by venture capitalists. First, extensions of current operations are more likely to address

---

* The eBay business plan may appear to be an exception to this rule. It clearly contemplated the development of significant economies of scale and the value that they would create for the company. However, the likely achievement of such economies of scale depended on the absence of competing ventures in this field. And this absence was due primarily to the revolutionary nature of the eBay concept. Unique insights of this sort are so rare that they cannot be expected to constitute the basis of many venture-development enterprises.

well-established markets than newly developing ones. Entering established markets is actually more difficult than moving into new ones. Barriers to entry are much more likely to exist in already functioning markets. If there are incumbent competitive advantages, they will work against the new venture. The best it can hope for is a level playing field. So although extending an existing operation may seem like an easier and more certain opportunity than beginning an enterprise from scratch, the nature of the market may actually weigh against it.

The second differentiating factor between extensions and stand-alone start-ups is that elements of the current operation—brand images, distribution systems, research and development programs, overhead support systems—can often be used to benefit the new venture. These are "economies of scope," and they may convey advantages on the new venture that competitors who operate solely in the target market do not enjoy.* If that is the case, it would seem obvious that the new venture will be profitable. Yet on closer examination, it turns out that sustained profitability depends on whether the venturing firm has a competitive advantage in its original market.

If there are no barriers to entry in that market, then the profits it enjoys from its expansion into a related area will draw competitors who can copy what it did—that is, who can operate in both the initial and adjacent markets and benefit from the same cost advantages that the original firm enjoys. At that point, the expansion strategy becomes solely a matter of efficient operations. The exceptional profits the original firm was earning from moving into the new market wither away, as is generally the case when there are no barriers to entry. The venture decision, then, rests on the status of competitive advantage. If one exists, then moving into a related market is a good idea. If one doesn't, success depends on operational efficiency and the competence of the people involved. Only when there are sustainable competitive advantages in the original market do economies of scope add something to the basic imperatives—chiefly, to operate efficiently—of a new venture.

---

*Economies of scope refer to potential efficiencies that may develop from extending the scope of marketing and distribution to include new types of products.

EXPLOITING BRANDS

One of the more obvious venture opportunities for extending an existing business is the use of an established brand to introduce products into a new market. The strategic principles are no different here than in most other new ventures. The payoff will likely depend on efficiency.

It is important to understand the sources of the value that a brand provides. Brands are not by themselves a type of competitive advantage, although some aspects of brand-related consumer behavior may lead to competitive advantages. To cite it one more time, Mercedes-Benz has not been able to leverage its first-class brand image into exceptional investment returns, which are an essential sign of competitive advantage. Brands are assets. Like other assets, they produce income, but they require both initial investments at the time of creation and continued spending to sustain their established status. In this regard, they are just like property, plant, and equipment—they need cash at the start to build or buy, and cash each year to ward off the withering effects of depreciation. Also, like a specialized piece of equipment, a brand is best used with the product for which it was developed. The value created by a brand is the difference between the costs of starting and maintaining it and the income the brand itself brings in, generally in the form of a higher margin that the branded product can command. In a market without competitive advantages, competition among brands will eliminate any return in excess of the investment required to develop and nourish the brand. In this regard, brand investments are no different from any other investments in competitive markets: they return the cost of capital and do not provide any net economic value to the firm.

All this would be more apparent were it not for the intangible nature of brand investments, which permits misconceptions to flourish. Most branded products fail to establish themselves in the marketplace. In figuring the average cost of creating a successful brand, these failed efforts have to be included in the calculation. The expected cost of creating a lucrative brand, which incorporates the probability of success (and failure), will be many times the actual investment made to get a specific successful brand off the ground. The future net income for which the brand is responsible has to be understood as a return on this expected cost, since no new brand is a certain winner. If, for instance, the chances of success are one in four for a new brand, then the return on investment is the present value of future net income divided by four times the actual investment made.

Since investments in failed brands conveniently disappear from view, it is natural to confuse overall returns on brand investments with the returns on only those brands that have succeeded. This is a major error, and in seriously overestimating the return on brand investments, it leads to the unwarranted conclusion that brand creation is a source of competitive advantage. Certainly there are brands that contribute to a company's competitive advantage—Coca-Cola, Marlboro, Gillette, Intel, and other famous names—but there are even more brands, widely known, instantly recognizable, even iconic, that labor on without producing any superior return for their corporate owners: Coors, Travelers, FedEx, AT&T, Xerox, Honda, Cheerios, McDonald's, and on and on.

Brands are associated with competitive advantages when they lead to customer captivity and, more powerfully, when that captivity is combined with economies of scale in the underlying production process. We need to distinguish between brand value, which is the premium that consumers will pay for a product with a particular brand, and economic value, which is additional return on investment that the brand helps generate. Coca-Cola is the world's most valuable brand not because it commands a remarkable price premium. It doesn't. No one is going to pay thousands of dollars to be identified as a Coke drinker, although they may pay that much to drive a Mercedes or wear Armani clothing. Brands of Scotch whisky, like Johnny Walker or Chivas Regal, have a much higher brand value than Coca-Cola, but also a much lower economic value.

Coca-Cola's brand is valuable for two reasons. First, there is a remarkable degree of habit formation associated with cola drinks as a category. We noted earlier that even regular beer drinkers are much less attached to their brand than their cola-drinking counterparts are. When they dine out, they often order a beer from the country whose cuisine they are enjoying, whereas cola drinkers stick with Coke or Pepsi, if it is available. The strength of attachment shows up in the higher market share stability in the cola market, another sign of customer captivity.

Compare that stability with the performance of brands in fashion-driven markets. Though brands are essential to operate in fashion markets, they are also victims of the desire for novelty that rules those markets. Fashion customers are by definition novelty seekers, and brands alone do not create habits or captivity. In the food business, habit and customer captivity vary directly with frequency of purchase. Food products purchased every day show greater market share stability than fast-food chains, which in turn have more stability than full-service restaurant chains. Brand images are important for all these food segments, but they only create a competitive advantage when frequent purchases establish habit strong enough to encourage customer captivity. Venture strategies to extend brands into new markets need to take this distinction into account.

The second reason that the Coca-Cola brand has great economic value is the existence of economies of scale. Coca-Cola enjoys them in its distribution function and, to a lesser extent, in its advertising. Fixed costs in both areas are large relative to variable costs, which means that for an entrant to be viable, it must capture a substantial part of the cola market. But the strength of customer captivity makes this task almost impossible. As Coca-Cola exploits its brands by selling its colas well in excess of costs, provided it can get Pepsi to go along, it does not have to worry about losing share to cola upstarts who try to win business with a low price strategy.

At the same time, many of the costs of creating a new brand are fixed by the size of the target market and do not increase with market share. The same distribution economies of scale that protect Coca-Cola's dominant market share apply as well to brand creation. Coca-Cola can spread the costs of new brand creation (in advertising, product development, promotion to the distribution channels) across many more potential customers than can its rivals, except Pepsi. Thanks to these economies, the company enjoys competitive advantages in creating and maintaining a new brand. Coca-Cola and other firms with strong franchises are much more likely to profit from brand extensions than companies in markets without barriers to entry. But because it has a powerful competitor, Coca-Cola will need to anticipate how Pepsi will respond.

By contrast, when Microsoft considers extending its brand by adding new applications to its Windows operating system, projected revenue gains need not be adjusted downward to account for competitive reactions. With fixed costs as the dominant component in Microsoft's franchise products, incremental profit margins on the added revenue are likely to be high and stable so long as Microsoft's competitive advantages remain intact. Successful product introductions actually strengthen Windows's competitive advantages. They raise the costs of switching to alternative operating systems, and they fill gaps in the application portfolio that might constitute entry points for potential competitors. An Internet browser application made Netscape a threat to the Windows empire until Microsoft incorporated that function into the operating system at no additional cost to consumers. Effective exploitation and protection of competitive advantages generally lead to aggressive brand extension strategies.*

Even for a firm with a competitive advantage, brand extensions into markets that lie outside the company's existing franchise will usually be less profitable. The competitive nature of the new market will cut into both revenue and profit margins. If there are any exceptional returns, they will come only to the extent that leveraging an existing brand image may lower the cost of entry. Anything more than that will be eliminated by competitors who are willing to pay the full price of entry. If this market is within reach of other companies that are also trying to extend their brands, then any excess returns will be reduced by these competitors. The value of these brand-extending opportunities can also be decreased by any impairment of the brand or cannibalization of demand in the established side of the business. Business plans that promise returns above these modest levels have probably ignored the impact of future entry and competition.

In sum, the value of migrating an established brand into another market, particularly a competitive market with no barriers to entry, is due entirely to the cost savings available from not having to build a

---

* From a cooperative perspective, it might be better for a company like Microsoft to adopt applications software offered by other providers into the Windows platform. This approach has the advantage of avoiding duplicative product development and promotion costs. The risks are that Microsoft's partners might ultimately turn on Microsoft, and these risks may well outweigh the benefits.

brand from scratch. These savings are part of the efficiency imperative that applies to all business functions necessary for a successful entry into a new market. For example, Microsoft's foray into the video game market with the Xbox requires a much higher level of cost management and focus than did the extension of its basic Windows franchise from the desktop onto servers or personal digital assistants.

· · ·

In each of the three areas of business development we have discussed— mergers and acquisitions, venture investing, and brand extensions— understanding the strategic context imposed by other economic agents is necessary for making informed decisions. Approaches that focus narrowly on financial details or marketing issues are essential for the effective implementation of a well-formulated plan, but without a grasp of the competitive environment, they will miss the forest for the trees. In the absence of competitive advantages and barriers to entry, new initiatives have only one strategic imperative: the efficient use of all the resources they require.

CHAPTER 18

The Level Playing Field

Flourishing in a Competitive Environment

MANAGEMENT MATTERS

A tenet of the prevailing wisdom in the literature on business strategy is that companies should operate only in markets in which they possess some sort of competitive advantage. This is not our position, even though we have dwelled at length on the significance of incumbent competitive advantages—on the need to identify them, understand their source, and to exploit those that a firm enjoys. The fact is that companies with sustainable competitive advantages are the exception, not the rule. Most firms in most markets do not benefit from competitive advantages, and when these advantages do not naturally exist, they are difficult to create. It is true that many firms may have the potential to enjoy competitive advantages in some markets. A company that chooses its niche market wisely, works assiduously to develop customer captivity, and organizes its operations to achieve economies of scale may be able to emerge from the pack and become the dominant firm in a market, now protected by barriers to entry.

Still, these triumphs are infrequent, no matter how brilliant the plan and flawless the execution. Instead of being protected by barriers to entry, most firms operate on a level playing field where they confront a large and frequently elastic set of competitors. Firms in this position (position 5 in figure 18.1) have a single strategic imperative: they need to

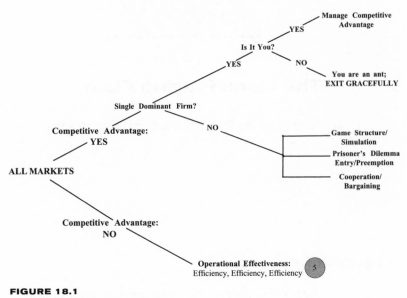

FIGURE 18.1
Where we are in the book

focus relentlessly on being as efficient and effective as possible in all of their business operations.

Efficiency clearly means controlling expenses up and down the line: raw material, labor, plant and equipment, utilities, even travel and entertainment. It also requires a productive return on the money spent. Output per hour of labor is the standard measure of productivity, but the concept also applies to the returns on marketing campaigns, research and development, technology and other capital expenditures, human resources, financial management, and all the other functions that make up a modern business. The rewards from superior management that stresses efficiency and productivity can be comparable to those arising from structural competitive advantages. Well-managed companies have been able to outperform their peers over long periods of time in industries without identifiable structural competitive advantages. Contrary to prevailing economic assumptions, all firms are not equally good at exploiting technologies or market opportunities. These potential differences in management effectiveness must be incorporated into any comprehensive treatment of strategy.

THE PRODUCTIVITY FRONTIER

High productivity is the source of our modern standards of living, both in material consumption available to us and in the quality of employment. Consider the differences between a life spent mining coal and one spent teaching, nursing, or doing virtually anything else. It is only from the growth of productivity that we get the economic dynamism that allows quality-of-life improvements. A historical perspective makes this conclusion inescapable. Compared with life four centuries ago, people of modest means in the developed world live longer, healthier, and materially more comfortable lives than did the elite in 1600.

The traditional discussion of productivity growth ascribes it to increases in potential output that arise from capital investment, a more educated workforce, and advances in technology. Policy prescriptions focus almost exclusively on reducing government debt to drive interest rates lower and stimulate private investment; spending money on education to raise the productive abilities of the workforce; and using either incentives or direct government expenditures in support of research and development.

There is an alternative perspective, one that has received far less attention. According to this view, most firms operate well within the "productivity frontier," which represents the limits of the possible given the availability of capital, the quality of the existing labor force, and the state of current technology. Higher productivity comes primarily not from extending the frontier but by better employing existing resources to close the gap between what is possible and what is actually achieved. The crucial factor, and thus the chief source of economic progress, is good management, especially management that pays close attention to efficiency. From this perspective, operating efficiency is at least as important as structural economic conditions in accounting for a firm's performance relative to its peers.* The evidence strongly favors this second view.

---

*Good management and the ensuing high levels of productivity may not always lead to high levels of profitability. In a market context, it is not absolute but relative productivity that matters for profitability. If all the firms in an industry are highly and equally productive, competition among them may lead to ordinary levels of profitability.

Evidence for the importance of management in achieving superior productivity shows up in many ways:

- Some companies do better.
- Things can change in a hurry.
- Manufacturing productivity has been transformed.
- Case studies tell the tale.

SOME COMPANIES DO BETTER

First, at the company level, there are large and persistent differences in performance across firms within any industry. Table 18.1 presents data on the cost of processing life insurance premiums for three mutual life companies from 1988 through 1991. The gap between Northwestern Mutual, the acknowledged industry leader in efficiency, and Connecticut Mutual, perhaps a laggard, was enormous. Even Phoenix Mutual, considered to be average for the industry, had costs two to three times as high as Northwestern Mutual's. And these distinctions persisted. In 2002, Northwestern Mutual's costs were still less than half those of Phoenix Mutual's.*

In the telephone long-distance market after deregulation, there were equally striking variations across companies. Long-distance costs are largely fixed. National providers must have national networks with similar software and control capabilities. The incremental capacity necessary

TABLE 18.1

How productivity varies in the life insurance industry (general expenses as a percentage of premiums)

	Connecticut Mutual	Phoenix Mutual	Northwestern Mutual
1988	20.9%	16.7%	6.8%
1989	19.8%	15.7%	6.9%
1990	20.2%	14.9%	7.4%
1991	20.9%	15.6%	6.3%

*Connecticut Mutual, perhaps deservedly, had been taken over by another company during the intervening years.

to handle additional traffic adds little to the cost of the basic infrastructure. Because billing and customer services are largely automated, they also are primarily fixed-cost items. The costs of advertising campaigns and a sales force ought not to differ significantly from one national carrier to another. Yet in spite of these similar requirements, in the early 1990s AT&T ran its long-distance network with around 120,000 employees. MCI managed the same tasks with fewer than 50,000. Sprint got by with an even smaller head count.

Similar differences of this magnitude—costs at the leader sometimes one-half or even one-third of those for the typical company—have been observed in many other industries and for very specific processes, like issuing bank cards.* These disparities are not transitory. Like the superior performance of Northwestern Mutual, they tend to persist for many years. Nor are they attributable to proprietary technology. These differences are as common among simple, low-capital-intensive, low-tech operations as they are among sophisticated, capital-intensive, high-tech firms.

In a particularly striking example, differences in performance of up to 40 percent existed for extended periods among the former Bell Telephone operating companies, both in terms of total cost per access line and with respect to more detailed performance areas like costs per customer service order processed (table 18.2). Yet these former siblings used the same basic equipment, the same support systems, and the same unionized labor operating under a common national contract. Some of these telcos improved productivity just as others saw it decline. Disparities in productivity across national economies mirror these intercompany differences and cannot be accounted for by divergences in either technology (which is globally available), capital investment, or labor force quality. The only plausible explanation of these divergences is difference in the quality and attention of management.

---

* A comprehensive study of comparative productivity in six thousand plants confirms this basic point, as does a range of other academic research cited by the study's authors (see Baily, Holten, anad Campbell in the references) and industry studies from the Sloan Foundation.

TABLE 18.2

Productivity differences among former Bell operating companies

Company	Cost per Access Line			Customer Service Cost per Access Line		
	1988	1991	Change	1988	1991	Change
New England Telephone	$482	$436	−9.5%	$41.70	$46.10	10.6%
New York Telephone	$531	$564	6.2%	$47.60	$49.30	3.6%
South Central Bell	$482	$430	−10.8%	$38.10	$40.40	6.0%
US West	$489	$401	−18.0%	$38.80	$32.40	−16.5%
Illinois Bell	$384	$384	0.0%	$36.00	$39.70	10.3%
Bell of Pennsylvania	$368	$388	5.4%	$29.60	$36.20	22.3%

THINGS CAN CHANGE IN A HURRY

A second piece of evidence that management matters is that patterns of change in performance are highly episodic. At the company level, costs in some years fall dramatically—up to 20 percent—and performance improves just as sharply. The motivating force is often competitive pressure. As we have seen, Compaq responded to its crisis in 1991 by tripling sales per employee over the next three years. In other years, performance can remain level or even deteriorate. Companies and industries regularly move from one pole to the other, from significant improvements to stasis to decline, without the impetus of new technology or changes in the availability of capital.

In contrast, changes in potential output almost certainly occur at a slow and measured pace, and almost by definition, move only in a single direction: upward. A company can change its workforce only gradually, and the pool from which that workforce is drawn changes even more slowly. Even high levels of new investment in any single year have only a relatively small impact on a company's overall capital stock. We also know that most kinds of technology diffuse slowly and steadily throughout both companies and industries.

The discrepancy between the brisk rate at which performance can vary and the much slower pace at which the factors that determine potential output—technology, capital investment, and quality of the labor force—

change suggests that management interventions, both positive and negative, are responsible for most of the improvements, and the declines.

MANUFACTURING PRODUCTIVITY
HAS BEEN TRANSFORMED

Third, the experience of productivity growth in manufacturing in the United States in the five years between 1980 and 1985 speaks strongly for the importance of management. From the end of WWII until 1970, manufacturing productivity in the United States grew at an annual rate of around 3 percent. But from 1970 to 1980, annual growth dropped to 0.7 percent. This performance was far behind that in most of the other advanced industrial countries. Japan, Germany, and Italy outpaced the United States. Canada and Britain did only slightly better.

As a result, the late 1970s and early 1980s were the years of America's "deindustrialization," when it appeared only a matter of time before all U.S. workers would be serving food to Japanese tourists, in buildings that Japanese investors had already purchased. Yet instead of continuing in this direction, between 1986 and 1991, productivity growth in U.S. manufacturing accelerated by about 2 percent per year, both absolutely and relative to most other major manufacturing countries. By the late 1990s, faster productivity growth in the United States had made it an unrivaled economic superpower.

This remarkable turnaround cannot be accounted for by the conventional economic sources of productivity growth. Government budget

TABLE 18.3

Manufacturing productivity relative to the United States, 1970–80 and 1985–91

	1970–80	1985–91
Japan	5.2 higher	2.3 higher
Germany	2.0 higher	−1.1 lower
Canada	0.2 higher	−2.6 lower
Italy	2.4 higher	0 even
United Kingdom	0.2 higher	1.1 higher

deficits and real (i.e., post-inflation) interest rates in the United States were far higher in the late 1980s than they had been in the late 1970s. The workforce did not benefit from any large influx of new workers substantially superior to existing employees. The educational performance of schools had improved only slightly, if at all, since the 1970s. Research and development expenditures had fallen, relative to those in the other industrialized countries, over the same period.

What had changed for the better was the attitude, training, and focus of American managers. Prior to 1980, management education in the United States had concentrated more on finance and marketing than on operations. But starting in the late 1970s, almost certainly induced by the intensity of overseas competition, that emphasis began to change. Techniques and goals like benchmarking, reengineering, quality circles and total quality management, just-in-time production systems, and six sigma standards helped to focus management attention on operational performance.

The improvement in manufacturing productivity has been sustained well past the point at which firms were threatened with extinction if they did not reform their operations. The rate of growth has accelerated without significant increases in the rate of capital investment, without measurable improvements in the quality of the labor force, and without a ballooning of spending on research and development. The one constant has been the revived emphasis on operational efficiency in management.

CASE STUDIES TELL THE TALE

The fourth and final kind of evidence on the importance of management comes from detailed case studies. These appear in a number of sources, but they convey a uniform message. Differences in productivity across firms and plants are surprisingly large and persistent, and these differences are due predominantly to differences in management performance. Three examples illustrate the general findings of these studies.

Case One: Connecticut Mutual

Just before Christmas 1990, a manager newly arrived from another company convened a task force whose goal was to increase productivity by 35 percent over the next two years in administrative support operations. She had had success at her previous positions in setting just such an arbitrary target and meeting it, and she intended to use the same tactic at Connecticut Mutual. The division involved had around 500 employees at the time the project began. The goal was to reduce that figure by around 175 full-time equivalent employees. In the first year, a labor force reduction of 20 percent was realized, against a target of 25 percent. By all measures, service quality improved and useful output increased, despite the drop in staffing. For the second year, the target was 15 percent of the remaining workforce; the actual result showed a 6 percent decline (table 18.4).

But the entire reduction was achieved during the first half of the year. At midyear, the company's chief executive announced his pending retirement, eighteen months hence. Both the manager of the project and the heads of the cooperating departments turned their attention to the succession process. Productivity improvements stopped for the remainder of the second year and all of the final year. The critical driving force in the improvement process was clearly management attention. When it focused elsewhere, the process ground to a halt.

The contributions of factors other than management attention to this performance improvement were limited. There was no upgrading of the labor force, no influx of new, highly trained workers. The technology used tended to be well-seasoned, usually five to seven years old.

TABLE 18.4

Head count changes at Connecticut Mutual (full-time equivalents)

	Planned Change	Actual Change	Change as a % of Total Workforce
1991	−125	−100	−20%
1992	−61	−28	−6%
1993	3	0	0%

TABLE 18.5

Expenses and savings at Connecticut Mutual ($ million)

	Capital Invested	Incremental Expense	Annual Savings	Net Cash Flow
1991	$3.6	$2.2	$1.7	–$4.1
1992	$0.7	$0.5	$3.7	$2.5
1993	$0.8	$0.5	$4.5	$3.2

Attempts to use cutting-edge technology were usually failures. Capital investments, both tangible and intangible, were essential. But as table 18.5 indicates, the returns on these investments were substantial.* These results are typical of performance improvement projects. When the projects involve a coordinated management effort, the returns range from 50 to even 100 percent or more. When the expenditures are less focused, the returns are smaller by an order of magnitude. The essential input is management.

Case Two: Bank Credit Card Operations

In this second example, management's attention was diverted not by a succession struggle but by more fundamental problems. The credit card operations of a major bank, widely regarded as the industry leader in efficiency, saw its administrative expenses rise sharply in all areas between 1992 and 1994 (table 18.6). In 1991, credit card loan losses had increased as a result of the 1990–91 recession. Initially, this familiar cyclical problem did not cause alarm. But when the level of losses persisted into 1993, after the end of the recession, all efforts were focused on fixing that problem. It was in the wake of this diversion of management's attention that productivity deteriorated. The loan losses represented a larger financial challenge, and stemming them was the correct priority. But the figures indicate how difficult it is to maintain a focus on efficiency while fighting fires elsewhere.

---

* The IRR (internal rate of return) on the investment comes to 80 percent annually on these assumptions: that no additional capital needs to be invested; that in 1994 and subsequent years, the annual savings rise to $4.8 million, since the improvements are in place for the entire year; and that the improvements last for at least ten years.

TABLE 18.6

Credit card operations: Efficiency and loan losses (1990 = 100)

	Administrative Expense	Net Credit Losses
1990	100	100
1991	106	150
1992	103	156
1993	123	127
1994	131	101

Case Three: Responding to a Strike

During a two-week strike in 1989, at a former Bell Telephone operating company, 52,000 workers, out of a total of 74,000 employees, walked off their jobs. It fell to the remaining 22,000 managers and other nonunion employees to keep the phone system running. In the first week of the strike, all but 1,000 of the managers filled in for the striking workers. But by the end of the second week, on-the-job learning had proceeded so rapidly that half of the managers could return to their regular work, leaving only 11,000 to do the jobs of the strikers. Essentially all the management work that had been done before the strike was then being performed. The only two tasks of the prestrike phone company that were not getting done were connecting new residential customers where the jobs involved rewiring of the network, and constructing new outside plant (lines, poles, junction boxes). Analysis of these tasks indicated that roughly 4,000 additional workers would have been required to get them done. It appears that in responding to a crisis, the company was able to perform all its prior tasks with 26,000 workers, about one-third of its prestrike labor force. The effort represented a tripling of productivity with no new capital or technology, but with a very intense application of management attention.

• • •

To summarize these studies and extend their implications, productivity improvement projects at the firm level have enormous returns on the capital necessary to fund them. These returns are so high that their attractiveness is unlikely to be affected by changes in the cost of capital of even 5 to 10 percentage points. Changes in a company's operating workforce associated with these successful projects were small to nonexistent. In most cases, it was the same workers who perform at high levels after these interventions who were performing at lower levels before they were introduced.

The head count, however, may have declined. The technologies employed tend to be seasoned, trailing edge rather than leading edge. Research suggests that attempting to take advantage of untried and innovative technologies often creates more problems than it solves. (For a number of companies, the true software "killer-app" has been a fully integrated, enterprise resource planning package; difficulties with implementing it effectively put some firms out of business.) The critical element in successful performance improvement is sustained, focused management attention.

MANAGEMENT AND COMPANY PERFORMANCE

The importance of focused attention emerges from other, broader analyses of good company management. In the study of companies making the transition from ordinary to outstanding performance described in Jim Collins's modern management classic *Good to Great*, almost all the firms that flourished began the change by adopting a simple and clear strategic focus. Kimberly-Clark sold its mill and concentrated on marketing paper products. Walgreen's and Kroger focused on simple, basic retail businesses in well-defined geographic markets. Wells Fargo concentrated on basic banking on the West Coast. Nucor focused on certain kinds of steel making and marketing. Abbott Laboratories dedicated itself to particular kinds of medical supplies. Gillette concentrated on razor technology and shaving products, Philip Morris on cigarettes, Circuit City on appliance retailing (although, to its detriment, it did not try to dominate any particular geographic region), and Fannie Mae on mortgages. Even Pitney Bowes, which expanded its attention beyond postage machines, was more focused than its potential rivals like Addressograph or Xerox.

The subsequent experience of some of these companies underscores the indispensable role of management attention. Where great companies' performances have deteriorated, there appears to be some important dissipation of management focus. Gillette moved into batteries; Circuit City tried to compete nationwide in an increasingly complex product arena. Walgreen's expanded nationally. Philip Morris has had to fight for its life in the courts, when it wasn't buying or selling food and beverage businesses.

Companies with outstanding performance have tended to be narrowly focused on particular industries or even subsegments of industries. The great exception to this rule is General Electric.* Yet even its history is not completely at variance with the overall pattern. Before Jack Welch became CEO in 1981, his predecessors had abandoned its strategic principle of being either the first or the second firm in every market in which it had a presence. Instead, GE had entered sectors like natural resources, where it could not hope to achieve that goal. At the time Welch took over, GE had returns on equity of 17–18 percent over the previous fifteen years. Without the entry into natural resources, made in the first half of the 1970s, its results would have been stronger.

Over the subsequent twenty-two years, with Welch in charge, return on equity rose to roughly 24 percent, while overall growth in earnings accelerated. This performance made GE the most valuable company in the world by the year 2000. It was not achieved by simplification of GE's segment focus. Although Welch did exit the natural resource business, much of its success was attributable to GE Capital Corporation, General Electric's profitable expansion into a broad range of financial services. The company also bought a television network (NBC) and developed a separate medical products group. Under Welch, it expanded from six segments, including a stand-alone international division, to eleven.

But Welch did reinstitute the policy of each GE business being either first or second in a market, or else getting out. At the same time, its decentralized segments were strongly refocused on operational efficiency and continuing cost reduction. Early in his tenure, Welch was awarded

---

* Berkshire Hathaway is a second prominent exception, but in its case there are unusual and perhaps nonreproducible circumstances. It is not an operating company, and the firms that CEO Warren Buffett has purchased outright conform to the rule of keeping a narrow focus, controlling costs, and tightly managing cash flow.

the nickname "Neutron Jack," acknowledging his forceful effort to reduce the workforce and cut costs (the "neutron" bomb is a nuclear device capable of killing people without damaging physical property). While GE entered a number of disparate businesses, its strategic principles were clear, unambiguous, and easy to apply. A simple strategic mandate allowed management at the operating level to concentrate on efficiency. The net result was outstanding business performance.

The important lesson to be drawn from all of this experience, as it relates to both productivity growth and overall business performance, is that effective strategy formulation is not the only source of superior returns. Without a doubt, strategy does matter. Pursuit of unrealistic strategic goals guarantees poor business outcomes. Warren Buffett has observed that when management with a good reputation meets an industry with a bad reputation, most often it is the reputation of the industry that survives. Ill-conceived initiatives that ignore the structure of competitive advantage and competitive interactions is a leading cause of business failure.

However, strategy is not the whole story. An obsession with strategy at the expense of the pursuit of operational excellence is equally damaging. There is simply too much evidence of variability among strategically identical firms, and of the speed with which performance can be improved without any changes in the larger economic environment, to discount the importance of management.

Strategy formulation should have three underlying goals. The first is to identify the competitive universe in which the company operates, and to locate its position regarding competitive advantages and barriers to entry. If the company does enjoy competitive advantages, the second goal is to recognize and manage effectively competitive interactions with other firms on whom the company's performance critically depends. The third goal, which applies to all companies whether or not they benefit from competitive advantages, is to develop a clear, simple, and accurate vision of where the company should be headed. This vision should allow management to focus the greater part of its attention on getting there. The approach to strategic analysis offered in this book has been designed to help managers accomplish these goals.

Methods for Measuring Return on Resources or Investments

In assessing a company's performance, there is a serious drawback in focusing on income, whether operating or net income, relative to sales. These measures are revealing when looking at a single company's performance over time, or comparing firms within one industry. But since industries differ in the amount of assets they need to generate a dollar of revenue, and companies differ on how they raise the capital to pay for the assets, margin comparisons that cross industry boundaries are apt to be misleading. So several additional methods have been used to make more sensible comparisons between firms in different industries and sharpen the test for the presence of barriers to entry.

One approach is return on assets (ROA), in which net income is divided by the total assets in the firm. A second is return on equity (ROE), which is net income divided by the book value of the equity on the balance sheet. This figure measures the returns to the owners of the business—how many dollars they receive for each dollar they invested. A third measure, and the one we normally prefer when all the data are available, is return on invested capital (ROIC), which counts the returns both to shareholders and to lenders. A company earning money can jack up its ROE by increasing leverage—raising debt and reducing the portion of assets funded by equity—without in any way improving its operations. More debt generally means more risk, but ROE by itself provides no information on debt levels. ROIC solves that problem by treating both debt and equity as invested capital.

There are a number of ways to calculate both the numerator (earnings) and the denominator (invested capital). For the numerator, we favor the same adjusted operating earnings figure that we use in calculating the margin on sales, and for the same reasons: no consideration of tax management skills, interest rates, or exceptional items. For the denominator, we take all the assets and then subtract the non-interest-bearing current liabilities. These include accounts payable, accrued expenses, taxes payable within the year, and a few miscellaneous items. They reflect the sources of funds a company gets just by being in business and on which it does not need to pay interest. We also subtract surplus cash, defined as all cash in excess of 1 percent of revenues, on the grounds that the surplus is not necessary for running the business and could be used to pay down debt or buy back equity. The result is the total of the necessary assets that have been funded by debt or equity. There are more sophisticated and intricate ways of figuring invested capital, but this approach is generally adequate and relatively easy to calculate.

> total assets
> *minus* non-interest-bearing current liabilities (NIBCLs)
> *minus* surplus cash (in excess of 1 percent of revenue)
> *equals* invested capital

NOTES

Many chapters draw heavily on business school cases for both narrative and quantitative information. All the relevant cases are cited at the beginning of the references for each chapter.

Unless otherwise noted, the figures that represent time series variables like operating income and return on invested capital are based on data from the companies' annual reports and 10K filings, as compiled and recorded in the Compustat database.

CHAPTER 1

4 Michael Porter, *Competitive Strategy: Techniques for Analyzing Industries and Competitors* (New York: Free Press, 1980).

CHAPTER 4

72 Hewlett-Packard printer share, Hewlett-Packard Web site (*www.hp.com*), citing IDC reports.
74 Apple's school share, *Education Week on the Web,* May 15, 2002. The diagram is reproduced with the permission of Harvard Business School Publishing.

CHAPTER 5

Wal-Mart

Harvard Business School, Case 9-387-018, Wal-Mart Stores' Discount Operations, 1986.
96 Target segment data from Target annual reports, 1994–2001.
Wal-Mart segment information, annual reports 1996–2002 and Form 10K filings.

Coors

Harvard Business School, Case 9-388-014, Adolph Coors in the Brewing Industry, 1987.

CHAPTER 6

Michael van Biema, Bruce Greenwald, and Charlotte Kaufman, "Corporate Rebirth: Compaq Computer," Columbia Business School Case.

CHAPTER 7

Philips

Harvard Business School, Case 9-792-035, Philips' Compact Disc Introduction (A).
138 Sony history is available on the company's Web site.

Cisco

147 and following: Paul Johnson, "Cisco and the Network Hardware Tornedo," in Geoffrey A. Moore, Paul Johnson, and Tom Kippola, *The Gorilla Game: Picking Winners in High Technology,* Revised Edition (New York: HarperBusiness, 1999); Paul Johnson, "An Open Letter to Warren Buffett Re: Cisco Systems," Robertson Stephens & Company Report, February 20, 1997; Paul Johnson, Research Reports on Cisco Systems, Inc., November 5, 2001, May 16, 2002, Robertson Stephens & Company.
149 Cisco annual reports, 1996–2003.
150 *Infrastructure,* "Router Market Stabilizes, Cisco Continues to Dominate," May 16, 2003.

CHAPTER 9

Harvard Business School Cases:
9-387-108, Coca-Cola Versus Pepsi-Cola (A), 1986
9-387-109, Coca-Cola Versus Pepsi-Cola (B)
9-387-110, Coca-Cola Versus Pepsi-Cola (C)
9-391-179, Coca-Cola Versus Pepsi-Cola and the Soft Drink Industry
9-794-055, Cola Wars Continue: Coke vs. Pepsi in the 1990s
9-799-117, A Hundred Years War: Coke vs. Pepsi, 1890s–1990s
193 Footnote, Warren Buffett in talk at Columbia Business School, May 9, 2002.
194 New Coke introduction, Jack Honomichl, "Missing Ingredients in 'New' Coke's Research," in Esther Thorson (Ed), *Advertising Age: The Principles of Advertising at Work* (Lincolnwood, IL: NTC Business Books, 1989).
198 Quotes from Goizueta and Ivester in Patricia Sellers, "How Coke Is Kicking Pepsi's Can," *Fortune,* 134:8 (October 28, 1996): 70–84.
198 Patricia Sellers, "Crunch Time for Coke," *Fortune,* 140:2 (July 19, 1999): 72–78.
199 The "rational player" phrase is from *Beverage World,* December 1999; see also the issue of January 15, 2000.

CHAPTER 10

Harvard Business School, Case 9-387-096, Fox Broadcasting Company, 1993.

CHAPTER 12

Harvard Business School, Case 9-390-025, The U.S. Airline Industry, 1978–1988, 1990.

238 Benjamin Graham, *The Intelligent Investor,* Fourth Revised Edition (New York: HarperBusiness, 1973), p. xiv.

239 Buffett quote, from a talk at the Kenan-Flager School of Business, University of North Carolina, on the PBS video *Warren Buffett Talks Business,* 1995.

248 Iverson quote, in *Forbes,* September 14, 1992.

251 pay cut to ward off Continental, in *USA Today,* September 22, 1994.

252 entrance of many new airlines, *Economist,* November 15, 2004.

253 Iverson quote, in *New York Times,* May 22, 1995.

Accumulated losses, from testimony of Danny Wright, President and COO of Kiwi International, before the House Committee on Transportation and Infrastructure, Federal Document Clearing House, March 22, 1995.

253 On Kiwi's demise, see also *Bergen Record,* June 18, 1996; *Aviation Daily,* October 16, 1996; *Aviation Week and Space Technology,* October 7, 1996.

CHAPTER 13

Harvard Business School, Case 376-266, Polaroid-Kodak, 1976; and Case 378-173, Polaroid-Kodak (B1), 1978.

256 Land quote, from *BusinessWeek,* March 2, 1981.

258 Land quote, from *Newsweek,* July 26, 1982.

266 Land quote, from *BusinessWeek,* March 2, 1981.

267 Polaroid's improving relationship with distributors, *BusinessWeek,* June 20, 1977.

268 instant cameras' share of the market, in *Forbes,* February 5, 1979.

269 decline in market share by 1981, *BusinessWeek,* March 2, 1981. On Kodak's losses, *Forbes,* November 15, 1984.

269 On the court case and decision, *New York Times,* September 14, 1985; *Los Angeles Times,* October 12, 1985. Layoffs by Kodak, *Chemical Week,* January 5, 1986.

270 almost $900 million in damages, United Press International, October 12, 1990.

271 "The day we deliver," in *BusinessWeek,* June 20, 1977.

271 Kodak in the copier business, *Forbes,* November 11, 1984, and *St. Petersburg Times,* March 18, 1999.

CHAPTER 15

Nintendo

Harvard Business School, Case N9-795-102, Power Play (A) Nintendo in 8-Bit Video Games, 1995.

302 virtuous circle, Adam M. Brandenburger and Barry J. Nalebuff, *Co-opetition* (New York: Currency Doubleday, 1996).

304 "Marketing Kombat," in *Advertising Age,* July 17, 1995.

Lead-Based Additives

Harvard Business School, Case 9-794-111, Marketing Practices in the Lead-Based Gasoline Additive Industry (A), 1995.
The EPA Web site, *www.EPA.gov*, History, Timeline, has the dates for EPA regulations.
Chemical Week, January 19, 1983.
312 "oligopoly," in *Chemical Week*, August 26, 1981.
313 Federal Trade Commission ruling, *Metals Week*, April 11, 1983.
313 Ethyl's additive as percentage of income, *Chemical Week*, April 14, 1982.
314 Ethyl's arrangment with Octel, *M2 Presswire*, December 12, 1997.
314 Great Lake's earnings by segment, *BusinessWeek*, May 15, 1995.
Ethyl segment information, Ethyl Form 10K, 1997 and 1998.
315 prior notification, *M2 Presswire*, April 1, 1998.
Octel annual reports, 2000–2002.

Sotheby's

316 introduction of buyer's premium and other background information, *Financial Times*, February 26, 2000.
317 sliding buyer's commission, *Independent*, February 27, 2000.
318 first meeting of Taubman and Tennant and other information from the trial, *New York Observer*, November 26, 2001.
318 Davidge's deal, *Financial Times*, January 29, 2000.
319 pressure on Brooks, *New York Times*, July 27, 2000.
319 settlement of $256 million, *New York Times*, September 23, 2000.
319 Tennant remained in Britain, *Daily News* (New York), December 6, 2001.
319 "They needed Mr. Davidge's notes," *New York Observer*, November 26, 2001.
319 shared some 90–95 percent, *Daily News* (New York), December 6, 2001.
321 increase in buyer's fees, *Wall Street Journal*, February 25, 2000.

CHAPTER 16

325 Figure 16.1 appeared originally in Bruce Greenwald, Judd Kahn, Paul Sonkin, and Michael van Biema, *Value Investing from Graham to Buffett and Beyond* (New York: John Wiley and Sons, 2001), which offers a fuller treatment of the value approach to investing.
340 footnote, Warren Buffett, "The Superinvestors of Graham-and-Doddsville," in Benjamin Graham, *The Intelligent Investor*, Fourth Revised Edition (New York: HarperBusiness, 1973). Buffett's essay was written in 1984.

CHAPTER 17

Michael E. Porter, "From Competitive Advantage to Corporate Strategy," *Harvard Business Review*, May–June, 1987.
346 footnote, Gregor Andrade, Mark Mitchell, and Erik Stafford, "New Evidence and Perspectives on Mergers," *Journal of Economic Perspectives*, 15:2, 2001.

349 AT&T acquiring Teleport, "AT&T Merges with Teleport," *Discount Long Distance Digest, January 19, 1998.*

CHAPTER 18

366 Table 18.1, Michael van Biema and Bruce Greenwald, "Managing Our Way to Higher Service-Sector Productivity," *Harvard Business Review,* 75:4, July–August, 1997.
Tables 18.2, 18.4, and 18.5 are drawn from the unpublished version of this paper, table 18.6 from the published version. Also A.M. Best Reports on insurance companies.

367 AT&T, MCI, and Sprint employee figures, the companies' annual reports 1992–94.

367 footnote, Martin Neil Baily, Charles Holten, David Campbell, "Productivity Dynamics in Manufacturing Plants," *Brookings Papers: Microeconomics,* 1992. This article is the source of table 18.3.

369 on the revival of U.S. manufacturing, Robert H. Hayes, Steven C. Wheelwright, and Kim B. Clark, *Dynamic Manufacturing: Creating the Learning Organization* (New York: Free Press, 1988).

374 Jim Collins, *Good to Great: Why Some Companies Make the Leap . . . and Others Don't* (New York: HarperCollins, 2001).

APPENDIX

378 G. Bennett Stewart's *The Quest for Value* (New York: HarperBusiness, 1991) has a detailed discussion of more precise ways of measuring ROIC by one of the originators of Economic Value Added analysis.

INDEX